GLOBALIZATION, TRADE, AND ECONOMIC DEVELOPMENT

GLOBALIZATION, TRADE, AND ECONOMIC DEVELOPMENT

THE CARIFORUM-EU ECONOMIC PARTNERSHIP AGREEMENT

RICHARD L. BERNAL

The University of the West Indies Press
Jamaica • Barbados • Trinidad and Tobago

The University of the West Indies Press
7A Gibraltar Hall Road, Mona
Kingston 7, Jamaica
www.uwipress.com

First published in English under the title *Globalization, Trade, and Economic Development: The CARIFORUM-EU Economic Partnership Agreement*, by R. Bernal, edition: 1

This edition has been reprinted and published under licence from Springer Nature America, Inc.

A catalogue record of this book is available from the National Library of Jamaica.

ISBN: 978-976-640-863-3 (paper)
978-976-640-864-0 (Kindle)
978-976-640-865-7 (ePub)

Cover design by Robert Harris

Printed in the United States of America

Contents

Illustrations

Figures

Tables

Preface

The signing of the CARIFORUM-European Union (EU) Economic Partnership Agreement (EPA) in June 2008 is the latest development in trade relations between the Caribbean and Europe, which dates back to the colonial era. The trade between Europe and its former colonies was governed by a series of Lomé Conventions commencing in 1975. These agreements were based on preferential access to the European market within which quota and price support arrangements were of particular importance to the vital exports of sugar, bananas, and rum. The preferential trade arrangements were supported by development assistance—the forerunner of what is now referred to as aid for trade.

For more than thirty years, I was an active lead participant in the negotiations of all the Lomé Conventions and the early stages of the EPA negotiations and the Cotonou Agreement. The responsibility of leading the negotiations for the more than seventy African, Pacific, and Caribbean group of countries (ACP) with the European Community and Spokesman of the ACP Ministerial Council on a number of occasions has provided me with an ideal perspective to introduce this book.

I also have the advantage of knowing the author since the late 1970s as he worked with the Government of Jamaica in a variety of capacities. As our ambassador to Washington and the OAS during my tenure as prime minister of Jamaica, his penchant and expertise in the field of international trade within a global market economy commanded my special admiration.

As the chairman of the CARICOM Prime Ministerial Committee on External Negotiations, I was instrumental in his assumption of the post of director general of the Caribbean Regional Negotiating Machinery (CRNM) and lead negotiator of the EPA. He brought to this task a combination of knowledge of international economics and development economics, and diplomatic skills in the complex trade negotiations, including the Doha Round.

International trade can promote or hinder the economic growth and structural transformation of small developing countries such as those in the Caribbean. For many years, these economies were dependent on the export of one or two commodities to the European market with development aid. In part, these arrangements contributed to middle income per capita levels.

With the advent of globalization, there has been a decline in Europe of a sense of contributing to a global environment that would facilitate over the medium term the economic development of countries made vulnerable by undiversified export structures, the legacy of colonialism, and constrained by poverty and small size. The withering of a concern of global development has much to do with the decline of Europe's ability to compete in global markets in the face of the rising international competitiveness of the rest of the role. Globalization exposed the EU to unprecedented competition and prompted the defensive response of relinquishing traditional preferential arrangements with the developing economies of the ACP in favor of the reciprocal trade, which resulted from the establishment of the World Trade Organization in 1994.

The advent of globalization and the enlargement of EU membership to encompass 26 nations have changed the ball game. Many of the new members make major financial demands on Community budgetary allocations for their own development and have no historical relationship or little interest with the Caribbean. This combination of external and internal pressures produces an approach to supporting economic development beyond the newly expanded boundaries of the EU, which was parsimonious in concept and actuality. This new attitude and concomitant approach was the basis of the Cotonou Agreement that set the stage for a transition to reciprocity. These contextual influences that had an impact on the EPA negotiations are discussed fully in the early part of the text.

One of the results of the Cotonou Agreement was to prevent the ACP from negotiating single group as they had done in previous negotiations with the EU. The EPA negotiations were, therefore, conducted as negotiations with six regions. I cannot conceal my severe disappointment at this outcome that deprived us of collective solidarity.

The erosion of effective negotiating forum of the ACP meant that the CARIFORUM countries (the Dominican Republic and the Caribbean Community) had to negotiate without the leverage that the ACP might have provided. In these circumstances, the government of CARIFORUM organized themselves to negotiate as a single group with one common position, no easy task given the diversity of interests, languages, and cooperation experience within the group. The CRNM provided technical work and coordinated the consultative process in support of a team of negotiators, superintended by ministerial and prime ministerial councils. The operation of the CRNM as a regional pool of trade expertise and its role in the negotiation and the institutional arrangements for political supervision is well chronicled and explained in the book. This is important because there are important lessons about how groups of developing countries can collaborate to increase their leverage in international trade negotiations.

The central issue of concern to the CARIFORUM countries in the negotiations with the EU was how to design an EPA that would promote their economic development, being aware that the EPA would be marked by a shift toward WTO-compatible reciprocity and the consequential reduction in preferential trade arrangements. Bernal's primary purpose is to answer this question.

The author having set the stage by reviewing and explaining the context in which the negotiations were conducted and the process of the negotiations goes on to explain that the agreement was based on the principle of special and differential treatment (SDT) for small developing economies within an agreement that had to be sufficiently WTO compatible while not going to the extreme of full reciprocity. SDT is extended in concessions across all subject areas of the EPA and asymmetrically phase implementations schedules in some cases as long as 25 years and conditional on aid for trade.

Bernal emphasizes that the EPA creates export opportunities that if utilized can promote the economic development of the small developing economies of CARIFORUM. He explains that if these opportunities are to come to fruition, then the Caribbean countries must undertake a process of increasing and maintaining the international competitiveness of their existing and new production of goods and services. He describes these national policy efforts as strategic global repositioning and argues that if pursued can mobilize the domestic and international resources to establish and operate productive capacity that is internationally competitive. He cautions that the potential economic benefits of the EPA can material only if the EPA is implemented quickly and comprehensively.

Bernal's work is an important contribution to the understanding of the components of the EPA, the negotiation process, and how the opportunities can be seized by the implementation of the EPA supported by appropriate national and regional policy actions. This publication will be of assistance to those countries in the process of implementing or negotiating an EPA. Beyond this, his work is a valuable contribution to countries seeking to participate in international trade in a way that can stimulate and sustain their economic growth and economic development.

Critical to seizing the opportunities of international trade is to shape the terms and conditions of involvement in trade through negotiation of trade agreements. The scholarly presentation demonstrates how through collective action and thorough technical preparation a group of small CARIFORUM states managed to conclude the EPA negotiations against the vastly more powerful EU. This offers important insights for small developing countries.

This timely book by Dr. Bernal will be useful to all those, be they scholars or policy makers, who are interested in issues of globalization, trade, and economic development. More specifically, it is an essential reading on how developing countries can shape the terms of trade agreements to create trade opportunities, which with appropriate national policies can promote their economic development.

Most Honorable P. J. Patterson, ON, PC, QC
Former Prime Minister of Jamaica

Acknowledgments

The CARIFORUM-EU Economic Partnership Agreement (EPA) is an important development because it is a WTO-compatible trade agreement between a group of developed countries, the European Union, and developing countries, CARIFORUM (15 small Caribbean countries) is based on special and differentiated treatment for the developing partners. At the time of its signing, it specified some subjects and provisions that were unprecedented in a trade agreement between developed countries and developing countries. Its objectives go beyond the expansion of trade to specifically target the promotion of sustainable economic development while supporting the progressive integration of the CARIFORUM countries into the world economy and economic cooperation among the CARIFORUM countries. It is, therefore, a model and a template for other such agreements in the future. In addition, the lessons to be drawn from the institutional arrangements for and conduct of the negotiations by CARIFORUM acting as a united group will be of interest to developing countries involved in international negotiations.

The political and economic context in which the negotiations were conducted reflected external circumstances of such policy changes in developed countries and developments in international trade policy including the erosion of preferential trade arrangements. This study locates the EPA in the context of globalization, paying special attention to the characteristics of the small developing economies of the CARIFORUM and how international trade impacts on the economic development. This book (1) is a review of the main features of the EPA; (2) is an explanation of how the EPA can promote economic development of the small developing economies of the Caribbean by providing export opportunities; and (3) points out the national and regional policy measures the CARIFORUM countries can pursue in order to produce internationally competitive goods and services to seize the opportunities inherent in the EPA. The conclusion of this study is that the CARIFORUM-EU EPA is an instrument that can be used by the CARIFORUM countries to promote their economic development.

This book draws on my 40 years of studying international economics and economic development, and in particular the relationship between international trade and development. Formulating policies that harness international trade and economic development was honed over many years of my involvement in international trade negotiations as a lead negotiator, including serving in the negotiations for the Free Trade Area of the Americas and for the Doha Development Agenda in the WTO. More specifically, my thinking evolved to a greater level of specificity during a four-year process of negotiations that led to an economic partnership agreement between the CARIFORUM countries and the European Union. During the negotiations, considerable time was spent explaining the goals of the CARIFORUM, how these would be achieved, and what the potential benefits could be. These explanations were in the context of reporting to governments, arguing the merits of our case in international fora, articulating positions to opposing negotiators, consulting the private sector and civil society, and in explaining to the media. Subsequent to the decision of the negotiations I had several opportunities to speak and write about the EPA and to address the frequently mooted question of how the EPA could contribute to the promotion of the economic development of the small developing economies of CARIFORUM.

Over the years, I have had the opportunity to interact with some of the world's leading trade specialists and negotiators and this has been a valuable learning experience. My thoughts were enhanced by interactions, collaborations, and debates with the like-minded and the critics, both of whom pushed me to clarify my positions, to constantly review them and improved the expositions of my proposals and actions. I benefitted from the wise counsel and experience of Sir Alister McIntyre who was my predecessor in the Caribbean Regional Negotiating Machinery (CRNM) and continued as the Distinguished Associate. My thinking was advanced by numerous discussions with the technical staff of the CRNM led by the late Henry Gill. The public debate about the EPA prompted me to explain many aspects of the EPA and the negotiations that I might not otherwise have committed to paper.

Some aspects of this project received their impetus and initial treatment in part from the 2008 Grace Kennedy Lecture on the Economic Partnership Agreement, which was the first attempt to develop some of the issues that would develop in greater depth and detail subsequently. It was the first building block in the process that culminated in this book. My article in the *Journal of Eastern Caribbean Studies* in 2008 was a preliminary overview of the "how and why" of the EPA negotiations. A chapter on sustainable implementation of the EPA in a 2011 book allowed me to review some aspects of what should happen after the agreement was signed. These initiatives were springboard for a much more extended and in-depth analysis, and along with these thoughts, several subjects that were not treated before became this book.

A trade negotiator must have, among other skills, a sound foundation in economics, experience in the practice of diplomacy, an aptitude for negotiations, and a capacity to lead teams. My competence in the discipline of economics benefitted from the foundation I gained from my teachers, in particular Professors Norman Girvan, George Beckford, Gita Sen, Anwar Shaikh, David Gordon, and Donald Harris. I have also had the benefit of interacting with C. Y. Thomas and Stuart Holland. The extent of my diplomatic skills owes much to imbibing by osmosis the consummate mastery of Prime Minister Michael Manley, conversations with Ambassador Don Mills, and a decade's experience as Jamaica's ambassador to the United States and the Organization of American States. Negotiating is as much art as science. The techniques and the methods of thorough preparation can be gleaned from any number of books. Beyond this there is the art that is innate and can be honed by experience. I make this observation without laying claim to having such a facility or expertise.

My commitment to creating an EPA that I am convinced can contribute to the promotion of economic development of CARIFORUM countries springs from a lifelong mission to assist in whatever way possible in the economic development of Jamaica, the Caribbean, and developing countries. This state of mind and sense of purpose is a natural outgrowth of coming of age during the transition period from colonialism to political independence in Jamaica. This orientation was nurtured while I was at the University of the West Indies in the halcyon days of the late 1960s. The privilege of a university education facilitated incumbent involvement in nation building. After all, the point of understanding the world is to change it for the better for the majority of people.

The EPA negotiations could not have been completed without the strategic political leadership and diplomatic involvement of P. J. Patterson, then prime minister of Jamaica and chairman of the CARICOM prime ministerial committee on external trade negotiations. Patterson's experience in the negotiation of Lome Conventions and his statesmanship were invaluable. Patterson demitted office before the EPA negotiations were signed and a crucial role was performed by Owen Arthur, then prime minister of Barbados, in ensuring cohesive coordination at the level of heads of government. Prime Minister Bruce Golding was thrust into the final torrid months of the negotiation and he responded astutely. Dame Billie Miller, the minister of foreign affairs and foreign trade of Barbados, was the minister charged with the political leadership of the CARICOM's external trade negotiations and the immediate political supervision of the EPA process, and she was invariably right in her guidance and suggestions to me.

I place on record my gratitude to the CARICOM heads of government for vesting me with their confidence my appointing me to lead the EPA negotiations. I greatly appreciate the fact that at every stage they gave me their full support and the latitude to make the decisive calls within the mandates stipulated by them. I am pleased that I was able to be of service, confident in the knowledge that service is its own reward.

None of this would have been possible without the love, understanding, and support of my wife Margaret. I was able to work with a peace of mind, which emanated from the enormous pride and joy of camaraderie I shared with my sons Brian and Darren. My determination to complete the years of reflection and research that have gone into this book was constantly energized by Nile and Elle. The audacity to dare to write a book was certainly born of the example of my father Franklin who published three books. Writing is, to an extent, the logical extension of avid reading my parents encouraged by indulging in the acquisition of any and all reading material in my formative years. That appetite for learning through reading has been a constant in my life. Acquisition of knowledge and the accumulation of information have been the ingredients for the process of finding my own answers. This process has also benefitted from a small coterie of friends and mentors who have consistently proffered encouragement. In the preparation of this book, Professor Vishnu Persaud supported the endeavor at every stage and had the onerous experience of reading parts of the manuscript.

Librarians, typists, and proofreaders too numerous to mention in the Caribbean, Europe, and the United States have helped by responding to my numerous requests. Kia Penso helped with editing and Sha-Shana Crichton gave valuable legal advice on intellectual property rights and copyright matters. I thank the editors and the production team of Palgrave Macmillan for their professionalism and diligence. I express my gratitude to all those who assisted in one way or the other but whom I have not explicitly mentioned.

The views expressed in this book are entirely mine and do not in any way reflect the views of the Inter-American Development Bank or any of the governments of the countries that are members of the bank.

I gratefully acknowledge the contribution of the late Dr. Joseph Powell in bringing the University of the West Indies Press edition of the book to fruition.

Introduction

The CARIFORUM-EU EPA is the first of its kind and, to date, is the only one of its kind. This alone would be sufficient to guarantee its uniqueness, but there are other distinctive features of this agreement that are noteworthy. The features that give importance to the EPA between the EU and the CARIFORUM[1] states include the following: (1) its scope is unprecedented in a trade agreement between developed countries and developing countries; (2) it is a trade agreement supported by development assistance, which differentiates it from other free trade agreements; (3) its objectives go beyond the expansion of trade to specifically target sustainable economic development, the progressive integration of the CARIFORUM countries into the world economy and the elimination of poverty; and (4) because of its unique combination of trade and development measures, it can become a model for agreements between the EU and other ACP regions and, indeed, between developed and developing countries.

The Caribbean is in a particularly difficult economic situation that requires urgent, creative, and decisive action. The challenging circumstances confronting the region emanate partly from the profound changes inherent in globalization and partly from the ossification of economic policy in CARICOM member states. As a result, many countries have been forced into reactive and ad hoc adjustment when they should have been proactively pursuing strategies of economic transformation, which anticipate and seize opportunities emerging in the global economy.

In June 2008, the EU and the CARIFORUM signed a trade agreement. This agreement, called an "EPA", is a World Trade Organization (WTO)-compatible trade agreement that is accompanied by the commitment on the part of the EU to provide development assistance in the form of trade-related adjustment, and to assist in the implementation of the agreement. The EPA liberalizes trade between the two entities with the objective of promoting the economic development of the CARIFORUM countries through the expansion of trade and investment. The agreement was negotiated over four years, a period marked by rapid and profound globalization.

The overarching objective of the CARIFORUM-EU EPA is the promotion of sustainable economic development. This is more than an agreement with a development dimension, because economic development is central to the EPA. All concerned with the EPA must disabuse themselves of the notion of an EPA, which contains a development dimension because such a characterization does not sufficiently recognize the centrality of economic development in the EPA. Instead it must be appreciated that development infuses all aspects of the EPA. The components of meaningful sustainable economic development are given clear expression in an overarching chapter on development in the EPA, which provides a holistic framework for the subject-specific measures in subsequent chapters.

The EPA contains measures intended to promote the economic development of CARIFORUM countries by liberalizing, over a 25-year period, trade in goods and services between the EU and CARIFORUM. The expanded access to the EU market will create opportunities for expansion and diversification of exports of goods and services from CARIFORUM. This, in turn, should stimulate increased domestic investment and prompt an inflow of foreign direct investment seeking to utilize CARIFORUM as a production platform for exports to the EU. The export opportunities will come to fruition to the extent that the EPA is complemented by appropriate national and regional economic policies in the CARIFORUM countries; the opportunities provided by the EPA will not automatically translate into growth and economic development unless there is a synergy between the agreement and development policies in CARIFORUM. Cognizant of this, the EPA makes ample provision for development policy space. This policy space needs to be utilized to translate many of the components of the EPA into active contributors to growth and development. The EU development assistance is intended to (1) provide funding and technical assistance to allow CARIFORUM governments to meet the financial cost and administrative requirements of implementing the EPA, and (2) support governments in carrying out development policies that they have formulated with a view for maximizing the potential benefits of the EPA. The EPA does not stipulate what specifically the development policy of any government should be, but it does presuppose a certain broad direction of development policy. This underlying development outlook was a compromise arrived at during the negotiation, as each party had its own strategy for development. The end result was a compromise, with much of the EU aspiration being shed, given the difficulty that the CARIFORUM had with several aspects that were either beyond the horizon or not realistic to contemplate in the near future because of current state of integration in the CARIFORUM area.

The objective of this book is to explain how the CARIFORUM-EU EPA can promote the economic development of the countries of CARIFORUM. It starts from recognition that in order to promote the economic development of CARIFORUM it was necessary to ensure that (1) the EPA included appropriate development-promoting measures incorporated into each and every subject area and all aspects of the EPA. (2) The EPA was based firmly on differential treatment in obligations and on asymmetry in implementation, to adequately address the differences in size and economic development between the EU and CARIFORUM. (3) The EPA is supported by aid for trade from the EU in the form of financial development assistance and technical assistance to aid the CARIFORUM countries with implementation and adjustment. The EPA negotiations took place in a context of globalization; the objectives of both the EU and the CARIFORUM were influenced by the state of globalization and the actual and anticipated trends of globalization. Chapter 1 outlines the main features of globalization and explains that globalization was the context in which the goals of the EU and the CARIFORUM with regard to the EPA were formulated. Chapter 2 reviews the process of negotiations that produced the EPA. A central role in the structure and process of the negotiations was performed by the arrangements for regional cooperation among CARIFORUM countries in the negotiations. The Caribbean Regional Negotiating Machinery (CRNM) was the institutional expression of cooperation among the CARIFORUM countries. Given its important and successful role, its operations are a model for how groups of small and/or developing countries can institutionalize regional cooperation in international trade negotiations. Chapter 3 is devoted to explaining its establishment and operations.

In order to comprehend the development requirements of the CARIFORUM countries, it is necessary to understand the circumstances and characteristics of CARIFORUM economies, and this is outlined in Chapter 4. Chapter 5 sets out the economic development objectives of CARIFORUM, which emanate from a combination of the characteristics of the economies of its member countries and the external economic environment shaped by globalization. Next, an overview of the measures in the EPA that can promote economic development of the CARIFORUM countries is provided in chapter 6. The economic opportunities provided by the EPA can only come to fruition if the EPA is fully implemented and measures are taken in the CARIFORUM countries to enable them to seize these opportunities and thereby realize the economic development that the region needs, wants, and aspires to attain. Chapter 7 sets out the institutional arrangements for governance of the EPA and the arrangements for revision of the agreement if such becomes necessary. The circumstances of both parties and the structure and character of the global economy in which they have to function will change over time; therefore, it will be necessary for the text of the EPA to be revised from time to time as appropriate and by mutual agreement. The extent to which there is a realization of the economic opportunities available through the EPA depends on the full and expeditious implementation of the agreement. This chapter also provides a brief overview of the current state of implementation. The EPA provides economic opportunities and some of the means to encourage taking advantage of the opportunities. These have to be complemented by national and regional policies in CARIFORUM to allow these economies the best prospect of seizing the opportunities. Chapter 8 provides an overview of the type of domestic development policy measures that will put CARIFORUM economies in a position to capitalize on the opportunities in the EPA and therefore enhance their economic development. A summary of the argument is set out in chapter 9.

Abbreviations and Acronyms

ACP	African, Caribbean, and Pacific states
ACS	Association of Caribbean States
CAIC	Caribbean Association for Industry and Commerce
CARICOM	Caribbean Community
CARIFORUM	Caribbean Forum
CBERA	Caribbean Basin Economic Recovery Act
CBI	Caribbean Basin Initiative
CDB	Caribbean Development Bank
CET	Common external tariff
CHA	Caribbean Hotel Association
CIDA	Canadian International Development Agency
COTED	Council of Ministers of Trade and Economic Development
CPDC	Caribbean Policy Development Centre
CRNM	Caribbean Regional Negotiating Machinery
CSME	Caribbean Single Market and Economy
DFID	Department for International Development
EC	European Commission
EPA	Economic Partnership Agreement
EU	European Union
FTAA	Free Trade Area of the Americas
GATS	General Agreement on Trade in Services
GATT	General Agreement on Tariffs and Trade
GDP	Gross Domestic Product
IDB	Inter-American Development Bank
ILO	International Labour Organization
IMF	International Monetary Fund
JAMPRO	Jamaica Promotions Corporation
NGOs	Nongovernmental Organizations
OECS	Organization of Eastern Caribbean States
PIOJ	Planning Institute of Jamaica
PSOJ	Private Sector Organization of Jamaica
SDE	Small Developing Economy
SDT	Special and Differential Treatment

STATIN	Statistical Institute of Jamaica
TBT	Technical barriers to trade
TCB	Trade Capacity Building
TTMA	Trinidad and Tobago Manufacturing Association
TWG	Technical Working Group
USAID	United States Agency for International Development
UWI	University of the West Indies
WTO	World Trade Organization

CHAPTER 1

Globalization and the Economic Partnership Agreement

Globalization is the context in which the Economic Partnership Agreement (EPA) was mooted and negotiated. The goal of having an EPA and the objectives pursued by both the European Union (EU) and the CARIFORUM were strongly influenced by the state of globalization and the actual and anticipated trends of globalization. Globalization involves the progressive reduction or elimination of national barriers to the international movement of goods, services, capital, and technology. Given that globalization is not a straightforward process but an uneven one, there has not been a complete standardization of the rules governing international transactions and flows. A basic set of principles guiding trade rules has been enshrined in the agreements that constitute the World Trade Organization (WTO), but coverage is not universal in either subject matter or country membership. It has proven difficult to extend the coverage and depth of WTO rules: there has been a pronounced proliferation of bilateral, regional, and plurilateral trade agreements. In a world where developed countries and gigantic multinational corporations (MNCs) can exercise disproportionate power to avoid, circumvent, ignore, and override multilateral rules and overwhelm the sovereignty of small, poor, and developing countries, trade agreements assume considerable importance for the weaker partner.

Rationale for Trade Agreements in Globalization

Given the extent of globalization it is not possible to avoid contact with and participation in the global economy. No consumer or producer in developed or developing countries, large or small, could operate if they were insulated from globalization. Life, as we know it, would be impossible without international trade. For example, without the foreign exchange earned from the export of goods and services, CARIFORUM countries could not import the oil necessary for electricity generation and modern transportation. Isolation is therefore not an option. Nor does free trade exist outside of economics textbooks; hence, neither autarky nor free trade is a realistic option. Globalization is a reality that poses both challenges and opportunities. It can generate growth and development, but it can also contribute to economic marginalization and poverty. The impact of globalization on countries depends on their own efforts and the terms and conditions that govern their participation in the global economy. One means of influencing the conditions of involvement in the global economy is the negotiation of trade agreements at the multilateral and regional levels.

The attempt to formulate rules to regulate the operation of an increasingly "globalized" world economy involves the negotiation of trade agreements at the multilateral level in the WTO and a plethora of regional and plurilateral agreements.[1] The coverage of trade agreements has expanded in recent years in an attempt to encompass as much as possible of international transactions in type and volume. Today the connotation of the word "trade" is no longer simply the international exchange of goods. Trade encompasses goods, services, and investment, as well as the policy measures that constitute the national environment in which trade is conducted, that is, competition policy, labor standards, and intellectual property rights.

Importance of Trade Agreements to Small Developing Economies

Trade agreements are important to small developing economies because of the following:

1. Small developing economies are highly open, which means that international trade is extremely important to their operation. Exports constitute a very large share of total production, and the import content of every good and service is substantial.
2. The objective of trade agreements is to increase economic growth by the expansion of trade and capital flows. The objective of negotiating trade agreements for developing countries such as those in the Caribbean is to promote economic development. The impact of international trade on growth depends in large part on the terms and conditions that govern the conduct of trade. The negotiation of trade agreements at the regional and multilateral levels can be an effective means of influencing the terms and conditions of participation in international trade.
3. Nearly all countries, developed and developing, are competing with each other to get the best access to the markets of as many countries as possible. If the CARIFORUM region does not conclude trade agreements, it will be at a disadvantage, and this disadvantage will increase as other countries sign trade agreements. Imports will cost more than they do now; exports will find it increasingly difficult to compete in global markets.
4. It has become increasingly difficult to persuade developed countries to grant preferential trade arrangements such as the former Lomé Conventions with Europe and the current Caribbean Basin Initiative (CBI) and CARIBCAN, with the United States and Canada, respectively. The developed countries that dominate international affairs are pushing for free trade agreements that

are based on reciprocity. This was, and continues to be, evident in positions advocated in the WTO and in other trade negotiations. CARIFORUM countries wanted the best possible access to the EU market for goods and services, and therefore sought to enshrine this requirement in a trade agreement.

Why an EPA with the EU

The decision to negotiate an EPA and to negotiate as six separate regions was entered into voluntarily by the governments of CARIFORUM when they signed the Cotonou Agreement with the EU in 2000. The reasons for agreeing to negotiations by regions rather than by theAfrican, Caribbean, and Pacific (ACP) Group as a whole are beyond the scope of this study but require a public explanation by those who advised CARIFORUM and by those who led those negotiations. Despite the change in the format of negotiations the CARIFORUM countries were interested in having an EPA with the EU because:

1. The preferential trade provisions of successive Lomé Conventions were replaced by the Cotonou Agreement, which provided a transitional arrangement in which the trade provisions would end on December 31, 2007. These trade provisions had to be replaced by a WTO-compatible trade agreement and this was to be the EPA.
2. A trade agreement with the EU was vital because it is a major economic bloc that has traditionally been a significant trade partner of CARIFORUM countries. The EU had been and was expected to continue to be a critically important export market for some of the most important exports such as sugar and bananas and source of essential imports. The EU also had the potential to be a major source of foreign investment and a continuing source of development assistance. Indeed, one of the attractive aspects of the EPA was the EU's pledge to furnish development aid to assist with the costs of adjustment and implementation.
3. CARIFORUM countries needed to avoid having less favorable market access than other developing countries from Africa and the Pacific that produce and export similar products such as sugar and bananas. The least developed countries of Africa already had duty-free, quota-free access and therefore would be in a more advantageous position if there were no EPA agreement between the CARIFORUM region and the EU.
4. The EPA was a priority because alternative agreements with other major trade partners were not an option at that time. (a) The United States did not have Trade Promotion Authority to negotiate trade agreements, and in any case, they have indicated unequivocally that any trade agreement would have to be a free trade agreement; the Dominican Republic-Central America-United States Free Trade Agreement (CAFTA) was the almost immutable template. (b) Negotiations with Canada were anticipated to have started in earnest early in 2008. (c) The negotiations in the WTO, designated the Doha Development Agenda, that were intended to address the issues of concern to the developing countries had been stalled for some time. The WTO negotiations had

degenerated into a political quagmire because of the failure of the developed countries to compromise on key issues, in particular, subsidies and domestic support for agriculture.

5. The political circumstances that allowed the preferential arrangements, which were the core of the Lomé Conventions and the Cotonou Agreement, had changed significantly, as was graphically illustrated by the erosion of the EU sugar and banana regimes at the behest of developing country members of the WTO. Therefore, concluding the EPA was fundamental to CARIFORUM interests for repositioning these economies in a new global context. In light of these considerations, CARIFORUM Member States, since the inception of the EPA negotiation process some five years ago, have been systematically engaged in a calculated exercise to capitalize on this opportunity to evolve a new trading relationship with Europe to promote the sustainable development of CARIFORUM, including the strengthening of regional integration.

How the EPA Differs from Past Agreements

The EPA differs from previous trade arrangement with the EU in the following aspects:

1. The EPA has to be WTO compatible, which means it must be in conformity with the rules of the WTO-governing free trade agreements. The EPA therefore had to meet two criteria: first, it must encompass "substantially all trade," and second, it must liberalize trade over "a reasonable length of time." There is no formally agreed definition of "substantially all trade" in the WTO, but by precedent and general acceptance a figure of 90 percent of both the volume of trade and the number of tariff lines has emerged. The EU, we are told by Curran, Nilsson, and Brew, "aims for at least a 90 percent threshold when negotiating its FTAs."[2] This was accomplished by the EU providing duty-free, quota-free access to their market, thereby allowing CARIFORUM to liberalize less than 90 percent and attaining an overall 90 percent level for the EPA. A reasonable length of time referred to in paragraph (c) of Article XXIV "should exceed 10 years only in exceptional cases."[3] Specifically this means moving toward reciprocity over a period of 10 years. The negotiators for CARIFORUM succeeded in preserving preferences as long as possible and carefully calibrating the tariff liberalization to the capacity to adjust. The adjustment will be as long as 25 years in some instances and will involve a set of moratoriums.
2. The EPA introduces a new model of development promoting trade based on special and differential treatment for CARIFORUM, the developing country partner, but no one-way preferential treatment, that is, no measure of reciprocity for the EU, the developed country partner. The model inherent in the former trade arrangements was one-way preferential market access for CARICOM in the form of guaranteed quotas and prices above those prevailing in the world market. There is differential treatment for the less-developed partner, namely, CARIFORUM. Differential treatment is

expressed in (a) asymmetrical timeframes for liberalization, for example, the EU will provide duty-free, quota-free market access immediately as the EPA comes into effect. CARIFORUM will phase its import liberalization over periods extending as long as 25 years. (b) The obligations assumed by the EU and CARIFORUM differ in several subject areas in a manner designed to favor the developing country partner. Asymmetries are not intended to be utilized for the deferment of adjustment but to allow adequate adjustment time and policy space to facilitate the enhancement of international competitiveness and the diversification of exports.

3. The EPA is WTO plus in some respects as both sides agreed on some areas where it was desirable to be ahead of the WTO agreements and left many issues to be examined if and when there was some advance in the WTO. An EPA that only liberalized trade in goods and that did not go beyond the WTO in areas such as services would have been of limited value to the CARIFORUM countries, which in most cases depend very heavily on services. The CARIFORUM countries were not unaware or taken by surprise nor were they underprepared when they engaged on issues in the EPA negotiations, which were not yet resolved in the WTO. The CARIFORUM governments and their negotiators were technically well prepared and knew exactly how far they would go and what they were not prepared to negotiate. In many instances, the CARIFORUM position stopped well short of those the Dominican Republic had agreed to in the Dominican Republic-Central American-United States Free Trade Agreement. Nearly all the CARIFORUM negotiators and many officials of governments and Caribbean Regional Negotiating Machinery (CRNM) technicians had worked on these subject areas in the Free Trade Area of the Americas (FTAA) and WTO.
4. The EPA, unlike the Lomé Conventions, does not guarantee quotas and prices. It like any agreement that liberalizes trade, creates opportunities, and these can only be brought to fruition by investment. The sources of investment induced by the trade agreement will be both foreign and domestic private investment. These investment flows will be more productive if accompanied by adequate and appropriate public sector investment. In recognition of the complementary role of public sector resources, the EPA will be accompanied by development assistance from the EU. Trade agreements are not usually linked to development support, although the coexistence of "trade and aid" has been a tradition in the EU and the ACP countries.

Context of Globalization

The multidimensional process of globalization is rapidly transforming in profound ways all aspects of national and global activities and interactions. The pace, character, and extent of the economic, social, and political dimensions of globalization may vary across sectors and local circumstances, but its economic thrust is on the erosion or elimination of national barriers to the international flow of goods, services, capital, finance, and information. The persistence and intensification of globalization is evident in the fact that since 1950 the rate of growth of world trade has consistently exceeded the rate of growth of world output. During the period 1950–2007, world trade in real terms grew at an average rate of 6.2 percent per annum, while world gross domestic product (GDP) grew by an average of 3.8 percent per annum.[4] Even during the period 2005–2011, when there was a global economic recession, world exports grew at 3.5 percent compared to 2.0 percent for world GDP.[5] The ratio of world trade in goods and services to output now stands at 22 percent, having increased from 7 percent in 1950.[6] In the past 30 years, flows of foreign direct investment have grown at rates in excess of those at which international trade and world output have expanded.[7]

1. Reducing National Barriers to International Transactions

In economic terms, globalization has involved the systematic elimination or persistent reduction of national barriers to international transactions involving goods, services, technology, knowledge, and capital. It is this phenomenon that led Thomas Friedman to proclaim, perhaps prematurely, that "the world is flat."[8] This is clearly evident in the reduction of tariffs on international trade. Successive rounds of multilateral trade negotiations, conducted under the auspices of the General Agreement on Tariffs and Trade (GATT), have reduced tariffs and other national barriers to international trade. The multilateral rules were codified with the establishment of the WTO in 1994. The reduction of national barriers to international trade has also taken place through the conclusion of regional trade agreements (RTAs). There are 363 RTAs in force, of which there are 25 customs unions, 111 integration agreements, 212 free trade agreements, and 15 partial scope agreements.[9] National markets are increasingly coalescing into global markets because their operations are subsumed and increasingly dominated by trans-border flows. Every business, whether producing for the national or the world market, must become globally competitive, either to be able to export or to withstand competition from imports. The competition is no longer local, it is global, in fact, and knows no boundaries.[10] For example, in the United States, the country with the largest domestic market, over 70 percent US domestic production is now exposed to international competition compared to only 4 percent in the 1960s.[11]

2. Increased International Competition

As national barriers to international transactions are reduced or overcome, the global marketplace is characterized by an inexorable increase in the extent and intensity of international competition. Coping with exposure to more international competition has posed severe challenges to all countries, but more to developing countries and in particular to the least developed. Competition in global markets has intensified among firms and countries as the world economy becomes more integrated. The implication of global competition is that even goods and services that are produced and exchanged within the national markets have to meet standards of quality and costs of production that are available globally. The fusion of computer technology with telecommunications makes it possible for firms to relocate an ever-widening range of operations and functions to wherever cost-competitive labor, assets, and infrastructure are available. These technological developments have transformed organizational structures, the nature of work, and the character of products, production techniques, and international marketing. Indeed, the "death of distance" has revolutionized the way people live and work[12] as speed and availability of information have grown exponentially in an "age of globally networked intelligence."[13]

3. Exponential Rate of Change

Technology has always been an influential factor in economic growth, but it has become even more important as a driver of growth and has become more skill intensive and more quickly available across the world. Globalization is characterized by the rapidity of change and speed with which business is conducted both nationally and internationally. Indeed, the only certainty is that there will be change. Change on a global scale is the mode of existence of globalization. With modern communications, billions of dollars can be moved across the globe in seconds. Marx characterized this when he wrote: "Constant revolutionizing of production, uninterrupted disturbance of all social conditions, everlasting uncertainty and agitation distinguishes the bourgeois epoch from all earlier ones. All fixed, fast-frozen relations, with their train of ancient and venerable prejudices and opinions, are swept away, all new formed ones become antiquated before they can ossify. All that is solid melts away into air; all that is holy is profane."[14] Schumpeter describes this incessant change and constant innovation as "creative destruction."[15]

There has been rapid technological change, and profound new technological innovations affect the production possibilities of all countries and, perhaps even more, the options open to small developing countries. The implications in some circumstances are negative as they portend changes that may be difficult for the nanofirms[16] of small developing economies. In other instances, new technology has opened up opportunities previously prohibited by the inability to attain economies of scale. The increasing globalization of economic transactions and activities has been facilitated and in some instances impelled by the rapid development of new technologies of communications, informatics, and manufacturing. The new developments in information processing and telecommunications propel globalization by reducing the costs resulting from distance, the importance of location, and the advantages of large size.[17] The expansion in the use of electronic technology has altered, fundamentally, the conduct of financial services, telecommunications, entertainment, and various other services, and is projected to grow exponentially.[18] New technologies have considerably reduced transaction time and in some instances eliminated the constraints of geography and distance, thereby creating 24-hour trading. These trends are compounded by the reduction in time between conceptualization and production. In this environment, the "mindset must be speed."[19]

4. Growth of Services

In 2011, the exports of commercial services by WTO members totaled just over $4 trillion.[20] Services are the fastest growing component of the world economy, growing at 8 percent per annum during 1990–1995, 5 percent in 1995–2000, 11 percent in 2000–2005, and 8 percent in 2005–2010, while world merchandise trade has grown by 3.7 percent annually and GDP increase by 2.3 percent.[21] Services exports of developing countries have been growing more rapidly than the export of manufactured goods.[22] The trend of the share of services in total trade to increase was evident from the 1990s and similarly service industries accounted for 50–60 percent of total foreign direct investment flows.[23] Even then services account for 65 percent of GDP in high-income countries and between 38 percent of GDP in low-income countries.[24] In the United States, services generate 72 percent of GDP, 30 percent of US exports,[25] and 75 percent of total employment.[26] In Great Britain and Switzerland, exports of services exceed the export of goods. Services account for 50 percent of the foreign direct investment of developing countries.[27] Services constitute the most important sector in several small developing economies, for example, the Bahamas and the Cayman Islands (tourism/financial services) and Barbados and Antigua (tourism).

5. Financialization

The world economy has in recent years experienced a process best described as "financialization," that is, growth in the importance of financial flows, financial markets, financial motives, and financial institutions. Finance has become disconnected from trade and investment on a global scale. Money has been increasingly free to move across national borders, and the volume and value of financial transactions have increased exponentially so that it is now beyond the control of national monetary authorities. Electronic communications have accelerated the speed with which financial flows can take place, but the process of the internationalization of finance had been emerging since the early 1990s, when Wriston was speaking with prescience about "the twilight of sovereignty."[28] A significant share of financial flows was short term and speculative, prompting Susan Strange in 1997 to coin the term "casino capitalism."[29] About this time, there was a concerted push involving the advocacy of the International Monetary Fund to free capital from national controls. Dani Rodrik explains that "the quest reflected a remarkable new consensus among officialdom in the advanced countries. Clearly, the case for removing government controls on international financial markets had become widely accepted."[30] The enthusiasm was undeterred by the Asian financial crisis and was not tempered until the global financial crisis of 2008. Unregulated trans-border financial flows were a major factor in the global financial crisis sparked by the subprime housing finance debacle in the United States. Avinash Persaud observes that even in this milieu of meltdown "the IMF and World Bank tended to downplay the external conduit of instability. Attempts to restrict through capital controls and exchange rate arrangements were at best frowned upon. At worst, those who promoted such efforts were dismissed as relics of a past era."[31] So interlinked and open are global financial markets that the subprime mortgage in the US metastasized into a global pandemic.[32]

6. Enlargement of Economic Entities

As globalization proceeds, economic units are becoming larger, as is evident from the enlargement of MNCs, and the integration of national economies to form regional economic or trade blocs.[33] These blocs are a prominent feature of the world economy, both in terms of the share of the world trade they encompass and the number of countries that participate in them. It is estimated that they are responsible for one-half to two-thirds of world trade.[34] Among the larger trade blocs are the EU, The North America Free Trade Area (Canada, the United States of America, and Mexico), and the Mercosur (Argentina, Bolivia, Brazil, Paraguay, Uruguay, and Venezuela). In the corporate realm, MNCs now account for about a third of world output and a significant share of world trade. They also account for half of world trade in goods[35] and 80 percent of the world's land cultivated for export crops.[36] Their dominance is also evident in the value of foreign assets they control, the volume of foreign sales, and size of foreign employment.[37] The trend toward enlargement of corporate entities and the dominance of the MNC is likely to continue. Emerging in the late 1990s and continuing, although unevenly, the composition of direct foreign investment has shown an increase in mergers and acquisition of existing assets and entities compared to "greenfield" investments.[38] Cross-border mergers and acquisitions account for between 76 percent[39] and 83 percent[40] of world foreign direct investment, and in the EU, mergers and acquisitions account for over 75 percent of foreign investment flows.[41] In the last decade, the value of mergers and acquisitions has fluctuated, but in 2011 it amounted to $526 billion.[42]

7. Diminished Autonomy of National Policy

The process of globalization involves the coalescing of national markets into global markets. This is evident in the transformation of the global financial architecture from one constituted by nation-states with some international links, to a predominantly global system in which some residual local differences in markets, institutions, and regulations persisting as vestiges of a bygone era.[43] The capability of governments to manage their economies is increasingly constrained by multilateral organizations, MNCs, and transactional financial institutions[44] that increasingly wield economic and political influence, which is global in scope. The policy autonomy of the nation state is also weakened by the transnational production processes and value chains,[45] which transcend the reach of the nation state. A quarter of world trade is intrafirm transactions, that is, taking place within MNCs[46] and consequently this substantial portion of world trade and capital movements is beyond the control of governments and insulated from global and national market forces.

8. Global Connectedness

Rapid and continuous innovation in the technologies for handling and communicating information has transformed social, economic, and political life in every part of the planet. The instant global availability of information via satellite, computers, and telecommunications technology has irrevocably changed all aspects of human life. Gleick describes this reality as the acceleration of just about everything.[47] Technological developments in telecommunications, computerization, and informatics have eliminated the barriers of distance and time, resulting in the reconstitution of the world into a single social and psychological space. In this milieu, there is a greater willingness to live and work all over the world, a growing acceptance of cultural and ethnic diversity, and an increasing openness to products and services regardless of origin. Developments in information and communication technologies (ICTs) have been an integral and influential part of the current wave of globalization that has encompassed, challenged, and transformed the world economy. It has established unprecedented levels of economic connectivity and made global economic life more inclusive; it has sped up and reduced the cost of international economic transactions. The availability of ICTs has confirmed the global market as the dominant economic environment for both tradable and nontradable goods and services. Producers, consumers, and policy makers respond to the dominant reality of the global market and the concomitant intensified international competition. In this milieu, the type and amount of information and the speed with which it can be accessed, transmitted, and employed in economic decision making determine gains and losses and separate the winners and the losers in the global economy. So pervasive is the availability of ICTs across the globe that nobody and nowhere is beyond what Castells calls the information-driven networked society.[48]

Globalization and Changes in EU Trade Policy

A proper understanding of the EPA must be firmly located in an understanding of the reality of globalization and the changes in the external economic environment in which the CARIFORUM countries, especially those of CARICOM, have operated. Concerns about globalization and the emergence of advanced developing countries prompt changes in EU trade and aid policy toward the developing countries. The EU was very concerned about its ability to be internationally competitive. A European Commission document titled "Global Europe: Competing in the World" explains the prevailing state of mind: "More countries than ever before are seizing the opportunities of globalisation. In the second half of the twentieth century, the United States, Europe and Japan drove the global economy. Today they are being joined by increasingly open and expanding economies, in particular China and India, but also Brazil, Russia and others. China is already the third largest exporter and likely to become the second largest national economy a few years from now. Within the same timeframe, India may become the sixth largest... The nature of global trade is changing as a result... Trade policy and our whole approach to international competitiveness need to adapt."

The ideological and political milieu in which the negotiations leading to the Cotonou Agreement were conducted was one in which there had been a decisive shift in perspective on the world economy and on relations between the developed and developing countries. Neoliberalism had become the dominant paradigm, and, concomitantly, a shift was seen from compensatory and interventionist policies toward developing countries to a reliance on the forces of the global market. These changes were reflected in a new approach by the EU to the developing world, and were the basis for a new policy toward supporting development in the ACP. There has been a pronounced decline in empathy in the developed countries for the plight of developing countries, coinciding with the rise to prominence of economic neoliberalism. The decline in empathy has manifested itself in the dismantling of preferential trade arrangements, the reduction of development assistance in real terms, and the forced graduation of middle-income developing countries from eligibility for concessional lending, grants, and certain trade concessions, such as the Generalized System of Preferences. Barbados and Antigua and Barbuda, for example, have been graduated from certain facilities.

The formation, deepening, and expansion of the EU brought changes in its policy toward developing countries, and this caused a major change in how it would deal with its longstanding association with the ACP group of countries. The change in the EU's approach to relations with developing countries was reducing aid both in development assistance and in preferential trade with the ACP. This was the effect of several factors coinciding and interacting, including (1) the deepening of its internal integration process, which served to strengthen the conviction in regionalism as a framework for promoting economic and political development; (2) the expansion of membership to include many countries that had no tradition of a relationship with the former colonies of some western European powers. Indeed, the EU regarded development assistance to the ACP countries has been reducing development funding for their own economies; (3) there was a decline in empathy for developing countries in the advanced countries. There may also have been a feeling of debt fatigue because the EU had been providing aid to the ACP for almost half a century; and (4) the rise to prominence of the free-market paradigm in the economics profession, which came to prominence during the administrations of Margaret Thatcher in Britain and Ronald Reagan in the United States.

The new approach to the relationship with the ACP involved a shift from in trade policy of permanent unilateral preferential trade arrangements toward reciprocity. Reciprocity not meaning total reciprocity but enough to be approved as a free trade agreement by the WTO. This change in approach mirrored a global movement toward a prescription of free trade policies for developing countries and former Communist countries as the most efficacious strategy to attain rapid growth and stimulate market-driven economic development. This approach was being vigorously propagated by the multilateral financial institutions such as the World Bank and the WTO. The view was also prevalent among the technocrats and bureaucrats of the European Commission in a more fundamentalist form than among the political leadership, even those of a conservative bent. The Social Democrats, Liberals, and Socialists in national legislatures and the European Parliament, while very sympathetic to the developing world, were never able to seriously modify this approach, although there were some very able advocates, notably Glenys Kinnock. The EU was convinced that regionalism could not be effective on an ACP-wide basis and eventually prevailed on the ACP to be categorized into six regions. This strategy was also motivated by the desire to dismember the ACP as a negotiating group, although this was never explicitly articulated in any document or official speech.

The ACP countries were extremely disturbed by the new approach and stridently denounced the EU's proposed actions. Prime Minister P. J. Patterson, writing to the president of the EC on behalf of CARICOM in April 1998, stated bluntly that the region was "alarmed at the nature of these (EU) proposals" because of the "high degree of intrusiveness into ACP policy." He remonstrated with the EU stating that, "We have repeatedly reaffirmed our determination to maintain ACP solidarity and the integrity of the ACP as a negotiating partner. This should be the fundamental basis for the future negotiations; but it will be jeopardized from the outset were we to agree to negotiating structures the EU is now contemplating." He expressed his consternation that, "the European Union should have nothing to gain by seeking to fragment relationships between the ACP countries that have been nurtured into maturity over 25 years of Lomé experience—at least if it is serious about furthering the development of ACP countries."[49] The complete letter is reproduced in appendix I.

1. Dismantling Preference Trade Arrangements

Developing countries by the 1980s had achieved a set of rules and provisions within the multilateral trading system that afforded them special treatment. These provisions included (a) preferential access to developed-country markets under the generalized system of preferences (GSP), (b) asymmetric phasing of trade liberalization, (c) support for their exports through subsidies, although they remained open to the risk of countervailing duties, (d) protection of infant industry on balance of payments grounds, (e) commodity stabilization schemes, for example, STABEX, and (f) the right to give preferential treatment to other developing countries. However, Michalopoulus points out that "just as developing countries appeared to have successfully secured a set of trading rules that would be beneficial to their development, the intellectual underpinnings of these rules started to be extensively questioned."[50]

Developed countries have shifted away from the belief that special and differential treatment can boost economic growth and development in poor countries. They strongly advocate reciprocity as the most fecund foundation for development, conveniently overlooking their own long experience of economic gestation and maturation through the employment of developmental protectionism.[51] The argument that increasingly prevails is "Why should the consumers of any country pay a higher price for a product than that available from the least expensive source?" Increasingly the answer is that there is no rationale for paying higher prices. This sentiment is growing in strength in both developed and developing countries. Consumers in the EU see no justification for preferences as development assistance, except to the least developed countries.

The erosion of trade preferences has occurred and is likely to continue to occur through (1) the dismantling of preferential trade arrangements whose compatibility with the core principles of the WTO have been challenged through the dispute settlement process and (2) trade liberalization through negotiations at the bilateral and multilateral levels. Critics start from the assumption that most-favored-nation (MFN) liberalization is a public good for the global community and hence preferences are not desirable. They have alluded to the potential negative effects of trade preferences, which they argue include inefficient resource allocation and a disincentive to striving for and attaining internationally competitive exports.[52] Preferences have propped up some inefficient export sectors and thereby deprived other more competitive industries of resources, infrastructure, and the attention of governments.[53] Page and Hewitt have suggested that some industries would collapse without preferential access to markets in developed countries.[54] It has been argued that preferences discourage trade liberalization and even participation in negotiations aimed at trade liberalization.[55] Ozden and Reinhardt claim that countries removed from the GSP pursue more liberal trade policies than those that continue to be eligible.[56]

2. Reduced Development Assistance

Beyond humanitarian motivations, the rationale for providing foreign aid has always been the belief that it can promote economic development in poor countries by bridging the resource and foreign-exchange gaps,[57]which seem to be inherent in these countries. There have always been some who questioned the efficacy of aid and therefore challenged the wisdom of these resource transfers. The contentious discussion about foreign aid started in the 1950s and has ebbed and surged ever since. There has been a resurgence of the debate about the efficacy of aid and the abuse of aid to pervert policy in the recipient country. The current debate is a repeat of the early debate of the late 1950s and1960s when the question of the efficacy and desirability of foreign aid was first mooted. One virulent critic of aid, Milton Friedman, argued that aid was ineffective at best and harmful to development at worst.[58] Foreign aid, it was said, was an instrument of foreign policy of developed countries,[59] and this invariably implied that the development objectives were diluted. Foreign aid was so much a "tool of foreign policy of the more advanced industrialized nations during the Cold War" that one commentator suggests that the words foreign aid should be replaced by the term "foreign state investment."[60]

Some still felt that the foreign policy motivations for foreign aid were not detrimental to its beneficial effects.[61] Indeed, Little has ventured that, "It may be good policy on occasion to prop up a regime with aid even if the regime is not very interested in sound economic development."[62] Others saw the political motivations as rooted in the capitalist system on a world scale and therefore as a pernicious instrument of imperialism.[63] In reality, the motives for foreign aid were and continue to be a complex amalgam of motives reflecting different objectives of different parts of the donor government.[64]

The faith in the procreative power of development aid persisted in spite of criticisms and has been the conventional wisdom since World War II. The conviction that aid can spur economic development was the rationale for the creation of the World Bank and the subsequent establishment of regional development banks, such as the Inter-American Development Bank. With the Marshall Plan[65] as emblematic of what could be accomplished by foreign aid, the question shifted to making sure that there was sufficient foreign aid to boost economic development in poor countries. Every major international report of development, starting with the Pearson Report, has called for the developed countries to meet the commitment to devote 0.7 percent of their GDP to the provision of development aid to developing countries. The Human Development Report of 2005 states, "In the 36 years since the Pearson Report there has been no shortage of commitments to the 0.7 percent target. But rich countries have habitually failed to back promises with actions" and aid "flows were at an all-time low in 1997 when the figure was 0.22 percent and it was not until 2002 that aid levels surpassed the 1990 level." [66]

Small states as defined by the World Bank and the Commonwealth Secretariat suffered steep declines in aid flows in the period immediately before the commencement of negotiations for the EPA. Aid flows to small states declined from just over $2.4 billion in 1993 to below $1.8 billion in 2001 and aid flows to the Caribbean dropped in both absolute value and aid per capita between 1996–1997 and 2001–2002.[67]

The paltry effort to attain internationally agreed aid targets was a result of a combination of economic, political, and ideological factors. Among the causes was the resurgence in the doubt about aid as a means of promoting growth and development. The fact that the international accepted target of 0.7 percent of GDP has never been met leaves open the question whether the persistent poverty of developing countries is not a reflection of inadequate aid rather than that aid itself is ineffective. The inadequacy of the amount of aid was one of the factors that prompted attention to the issue of how to make aid more effective. This concern spawned an unending discussion and voluminous literature on ways to make aid more effective.[68] Several reports have been commissioned by international organizations to improve the efficacy of development aid. A recent example is the "The Paris Declaration on Aid Effectiveness" in March 2005, which enumerates 50 commitments to improve quality of aid and 12 indices for monitoring progress.

The voluminous literature on aid effectiveness has not assuaged skeptics who point to numerous examples of waste, corruption, and inefficiency. By the 1990s, the themes of virulent critics of the 1950s and 1960s, such as Bauer,[69] were being echoed by Easterly.[70] Moyo, an African author, attracted much notoriety when she proclaimed in 2009: "Aid has not lived up to expectations. It remains the heart of the development agenda, despite the fact that there are very compelling reasons to show that it perpetuates the cycle of poverty and derails sustainable growth."[71] Some empirical studies are more sanguine, limiting their conclusions to development aid having no significant impact on economic growth in the recipient countries.[72] An IMF working paper by Minoiu and Reddy, in which they distinguish between developmental aid and nondevelopmental aid, concluded that developmental aid has a positive, large, and robust effect on growth, while nondevelopmental aid is mostly growth-neutral and on occasions is negatively associated with economic growth.[73] Different types of development aid have different implications; for example, Headey found that multilateral aid was more effective than bilateral aid, which was largely motivated by geo-political considerations.[74]

The really important question is: under what conditions will aid contribute positively to economic development? The answer is that aid works if it is administered in the context of appropriate policy measures. Burnside and Dollar found that aid is effective when there is a policy environment that promotes growth, but the availability of aid does not prompt the adoption of "good" policies.[75] Some seek to be more specific in the identification of the type of policy that is appropriate. Mosley suggests that the effectiveness of aid, like economic growth, was associated with outward-oriented policies.[76] Other determinants of the effectiveness of aid include project implementation capacity, quality of human resources, and infrastructure.

3. Trade not Aid

While many in the CARICOM region regard foreign aid as an essential ingredient for economic growth, there has been a debate over the impact of aid. Over the past 50 years, there has been no resolution between the opposing positions that (1) aid has a positive relationship with growth[77] and (2 aid does not necessarily benefit the recipient countries and in many instances has a negative effect. It has been suggested that aid can undermine institutional quality and encourage rent-seeking and corruption.[78] Some studies find either positive or negative effects of aid on growth[79] and some have proffered the sage advice that "aid has a positive impact on growth in developing countries with good fiscal, monetary, and trade policies but has little effect in the presence of poor policies."[80] There is a "slightly positive correlation between net financial flows and economic growth" in the Caribbean[81]; therefore, it is reasonable to assume that development assistance can have a positive impact on growth. The strength of the correlation varies among countries in the region, no doubt reflecting the fact that domestic policy and governance influence the efficiency with which aid is translated into growth.[82] However, perhaps more importantly, foreign aid can be habit forming and there are many in the Caribbean that had become addicted. Fiscal systems in some countries have come to depend heavily on development aid to finance a significant proportion of the capital budget. Zartman suggests that in Africa aid dependency has metastasized to being "aid driven" and that "the experience of Lomé and other negotiations shows that African states' most powerful bargaining tool is an appeal to the sense of 'richesse oblige' of the Europeans."[83]

The primary purpose of the EPA is not the provision of development aid. It is a trade agreement complemented by development assistance aimed at helping countries to implement the EPA. The EPA is everything but alms, that is, it encompasses a wide range of subjects but is not an instrument for meeting every conceivable project related to any aspect of development. In an expansive interpretation of the EPA, everything, regardless of how tangential, is affected by and affects everything. This is patently untenable. The development assistance that accompanies the EPA is not meant to substitute for the existing aid that the EU has committed to provide for the region. It relates specifically to the adjustment in policy instruments and institutional arrangements that emanate from the implementation of the EPA.

CARIFORUM Position

The CARICOM countries within CARIFORUM held very different views about future trade arrangements with the EU. Essentially, these countries held the view that the EU should continue to provide as far as possible preferential trade arrangements to the ACP supported by development aid. This was a perspective not born of ideology but arose from the dependence of commodity exporters who depended on the Sugar and Banana Protocols for a market and for a price above their cost of production and above the world market price. This was of vital importance to the banana exporting countries of St. Vincent, St. Lucia, and Dominica that were heavily dependent on those exports. The view was held that the EU should provide aid to CARICOM because of the difficulties faced by small developing countries and as a form of reparations for European colonialism.

1. Retention of Preferential Trade Arrangements

Sir Shridath Ramphal speaking on behalf of the Caribbean as far back as 1973 made it clear that "As regards trading arrangements with the Community, we do not consider it to be appropriate that the negotiations should proceed on the concept of a free trade relationship; and we reject entirely the notion that of duty-free entry into to the Community for the main products of developing states with whom the arrangements are concluded should be the reciprocation of trade benefits."[84] The elimination of preferences would have severely affected preference-dependent economies.[85] The magnitude of the losses to the Caribbean would be very substantial in sugar; the Caribbean beneficiaries received a price based on prices to domestic producers. The EU intervention price was more than three times the world market price and the US producer's price was twice the world market price.[86] The countries of the eastern Caribbean were only able to export bananas to the United Kingdom because of preferential arrangements. Yields in bananas were 11 tons per hectare and 4 tons per worker compared to that of 32 and 26 in Central America.[87] If there was a removal of preferential arrangements, Belize, Guyana, Mauritius, St. Kitts and Nevis, and St. Lucia would suffer export declines ranging from 7.8 percent to 11.5 percent of exports.[88] In the case of the small developing economies of the Caribbean, almost one half of US imports from the region received preferential treatment in 2003 and over 75 percent of EU imports during 1995–1999 were covered by preferences under the Lomé Convention and Cotonou Agreement.[89]

Liberalization of international trade escalated steadily during the 1990s eroding preferential trade regimes. In a 1999 Commonwealth Secretariat report on ACP-EU relations after Lomé IV, Stevens, McQueen, and Kennan warned that "the whole edifice built up over the years by the EU is subsiding gently as its foundations are weakened by liberalization."[90] The postcolonial trade arrangements are at an end, globalization is a reality, and the vast majority of EU member states feel no need to provide one-way preferential trade arrangements or development aid to a group of middle-income developing countries. These EU countries have no colonial history to live down, and they believe that if they provide aid it should target extreme poverty in Africa and Asia.

Even if the EU wanted to keep in place nonreciprocal preferential trade arrangements for the ACP countries, it would have to contend with the current disposition in the WTO, which is resolutely opposed to such arrangements. Moreover, the prevailing state of mind is to dismantle nonreciprocal preferential trade arrangements. This conviction is no longer confined to the increasingly unsympathetic developed countries but is rampant among developing countries where it is spawned by desperation, evangelical free trade beliefs, or churlishness. It was developing countries that forced the scaling-down and/or elimination of the EU special regimes for the importation of bananas and sugar. The charge was led by the Latin American countries, aided and abetted by the United States in the case of bananas[91] and by an advanced developing country, Brazil, despite expressions of solidarity with Caribbean countries. There were undoubtedly some in the EU who were pleased to see the withering away of a system in which they had no vested interests or lingering responsibilities.

2. Retention of Development Aid

"Aid should be thought of as a hand up, not a hand out," Human Development Report 2005.

The EU has been providing development aid in the form of financial (86–90 percent as grants[92]) to the ACP countries through the European Development Fund (EDF) since 1959. The EDF has operated 10 cycles of five years. The EU has increased the amount of aid in each cycle. The fourth EDF provided E3.4 billion and this was increased to E15.2 billion in the ninth EDF, a real increase of 16 percent.[93]

The Lomé Conventions were regarded by most persons in the CARIFORUM countries as an aid mechanism consisting of two complementary components, first, preferential trade arrangements involving (1) preferential market access and (2) price above world market prices for sugar and bananas, and second, development aid. The EPA template as agreed to by the EU and the ACP countries committed to replace the Lomé Convention with a WTO-compatible agreement, which meant reciprocity to be defined in the subsequent negotiations. There was a view in the CARICOM part of CARFORUM that the form and amount of development aid would continue. Indeed, there were strong advocacy of the view that CARIFORUM was entitled to aid because of the small size and as a form of reparations for the exploitation by European colonialism. There are some persons who feel that transfers are owed, if not on grounds of small size, then as payment for colonialism. The claim has been made in the following way: "the fortunes of Europe's rich were made on the plantations and other resources of Caribbean states. Those states owe a duty of development to the Caribbean that was not fulfilled by preferential access to their markets for the narrow range of products such as sugar and bananas upon which they made the Caribbean dependent."[94]

Being a small developing country does not entitle the governments in these countries to development assistance in the form of grants. In the CARICOM region, there are many who regard aid as a right in perpetuity. This entitlement is seen as reparations for colonial exploitation, and there is much that is valid and just about this proposition. This conviction is pandemic among politicians, government employees, and the NGO community, and is even prevalent in academia. Ironically, even the private sector has a view that they are in a small economy that "needs" development assistance. The attitude goes beyond the self-interested recognition that foreign aid contributes to the government's capacity to support their activities with physical infrastructure and services. It takes the form of a mixture of a sense of entitlement and a perceived need among some in the political leadership and among the senior civil servants. The governments of the CARIFORM region are habituated to drawing up the capital expenditure of their budgets based on the amount of project financing they anticipate from external aid agencies and loans from multilateral financial institutions. Thinking in this regard is hermetically sealed, with rare exceptions. Former Prime Minister Bruce Golding of Jamaica repudiated this attitude and called on the region to "purge this mendicancy."[95] His comments drew opprobrium, especially among those who saw the EPA primarily as a vehicle for foreign aid from the EU. They felt that the EU was depriving the member states of the region of preferential trade arrangements, and that therefore the EU should have increased aid as just compensation for what they regarded as a breach of a solemn commitment to maintain preferential trade arrangements for sugar and banana imports from the Caribbean.

There is a real need for resources to fund some of the costs of adjustment—indeed as much of this cost as possible, hence there is a valid case for EU development assistance—but no entitlement. Happily the EPA will be accompanied by EU development assistance and technical assistance. Trade agreements are not usually accompanied by development assistance, even in the case of agreements between developed and developing countries. It is a tribute to CARIFORUM diplomacy and negotiations that development aid has been extracted from the EU given the disappearance of the last residues of colonial guilt in European political and policy circles. The justification is increasingly difficult to sustain for many middle-income countries that have achieved high per capita incomes and impressive growth rates despite their small size and vulnerability. Nevertheless, the EU remains one of the largest sources of development assistance to the region.

3. Apprehension over Trade Liberalization

There was concern in the CARIFORUM countries about the impact of trade liberalization and some felt it would have a negative effect on the small developing economies that comprised the group. There is nothing inherently harmful about trade liberalization; on the contrary, trade liberalization can be growth promoting. Trade liberalization, when properly sequenced and appropriately calibrated to allow adequate time for firms to carry out adjustments, can promote economic growth. The EPA provides for tariff liberalization to be implemented over extended periods depending on the product. For some products, the period provided is up to 25 years, an unprecedented concession in any trade agreement and a first for the EPA. A debate about the EPA emerged in the CARICOM countries in which the view was expressed that trade liberalization could be harmful to small, open developing countries. The view was an amalgam of different perspectives including apprehension about globalization and some who were in denial about the erosion of preferential trade arrangements. At times the EPA was portrayed as full blown free trade.

In a world economy experiencing rapid and profound globalization, a certain amount of trade liberalization is unavoidable; hence, there was little point in trying to avoid liberalization or trying to postpone any liberalization indefinitely. Trade liberalization, when properly designed and implemented in a manner that adequately takes account of structural and institutional characteristics, can boost economic growth and promote economic development. The literature on the relationship between trade liberalization and economic growth reveals that liberalization does not guarantee that growth will occur.[96] Trade liberalization can promote growth if it is formulated and executed in a way that is appropriate designed for a specific economy and does not function in isolation from complementary supporting domestic economic measures. Trade liberalization can best come to fruition if it is complemented by suitable macroeconomic policies. The policy package will be unique to each particular economy. While there are certain broad policies that are essential to any growth/development promoting policy framework, the mix has to be specifically calibrated to the peculiar circumstances of each economy.

Trade liberalization can be beneficial to the economic growth of CARIFORUM countries, but they have to put themselves in a position to seize the opportunities created by the trade liberalization. The economies of developing countries can benefit, and has benefited, from trade agreements with industrial countries and fast-growing trading partners.[97] If trade agreements are properly designed, as in the case of the EPA, developing economies can plug into the dynamic of the global economy and this impetus can boost their economic growth. World trade has grown five times in real terms between 1980 and the onset of the global economic crisis of 2008, and its share of world GDP has risen from 36 percent to 55 percent during this period.[98] For trade liberalization to promote the economic development of the CARIFORUM states, it must be complemented by (a1) speeding up the flagging and frequently postponed process of establishing the CARICOM Single Market and Economy (CSME), (b2) completing the CARICOM-Dominican Republic Free Trade Agreement, and (c3) appropriate national development policies, including fiscal reform. Fiscal reform will be necessary to prevent the revenue loss from reducing or eliminating tariffs by shifting the derivation of revenue to other forms of taxation, for example, sales tax. There does not have to be any loss of revenue because it is possible to extract the same amount of tax revenue from the economy by using alternative forms of taxation.

4. Complexity of the Negotiations

The CARIFORUM countries were concerned about the complexity of the negotiation of an EPA because of the scope of its subject matter, inclusion of new issues, and the technical complexity of some of the issues. A negotiation such as that warranted by the EPA was unprecedented for the CARICOM countries and less so for the Dominican Republic, which had been exposed to some of the issues in the negotiations for the CAFTA. The character of the engagement was also going to be different because it was no longer a matter of extracting benefits from the EU but of a negotiation in which there was to be an exchange of concessions. Ravenhill captures the difference in character of the ACP's position as confined to being "demandeurs" concentrating in justifying preferences and relying on ways to "embarrass the EU into maintaining or extending the relationship."[99] The diplomacy of the ACP countries was not that of negotiations among contending parties in which both sides had something that the other wanted, but eliciting support for the maintenance of its preferential arrangements with the EU. This required vigorous effort because EU trade policy progressively reduced the value of ACP market access by lowering its MFN tariffs, concluding preferential agreements with non-ACP countries, and by extending its GSP system. The most notorious example was the bilateral deal between the EU and the United States on tariffs on distilled spirits, made in the margins of the WTO ministerial in Singapore in 1996. This deal could have nullified the protocol on rum without subsequent remedial action.

The ACP countries were critically dependent on preferential trade arrangements, especially the commodity protocols and the development aid from the EU. Conversely the value of trade with the ACP countries was not particularly significant to the EU. Indeed, the commodities imported from the ACP producers could have been sourced from less expensive suppliers. Bananas and sugar are vivid examples of products where imports from the ACP cost far more than they do on the prevailing world market. The EU regime was a nontransparent development aid mechanism through which individual farmers earned a bounty paid by the unwitting consumers across Europe. The system of preferential trade also reflected entrenched corporate interest, shielding the European market from US MNCs such as Chiquita and Dole.

The negotiations that took place between April 2004 and December 2007 were, therefore, the most difficult in the history of the relationship between the EU and the Caribbean. The process was one of discussion, compromise, and cooperation between two parties tenaciously and creatively seeking by every means to satisfy their respective interests. It therefore differed from the engagements of the past in which the Caribbean negotiated primarily for sugar, bananas, and development aid. The scope of the EPA was far wider and therefore placed unprecedented demands on negotiators and technical support staff. The EPA negotiations were a break with tradition because they were not arguing for a case for aid and preferential quotas and prices. This was not the diplomacy of mendicancy but hard bargaining by CARIFORUM negotiators to extract every gain from a group of more powerful countries. While the EU had little real need for CARIFORUM products and markets, especially the minute CARICOM market, their negotiators were resolute in the pursuit of shedding the preferential arrangements of the past in the shortest possible time. The complex amalgam of motivations included foreign policy concerns to undergird economic development for political stability, although these never trumped corporate interests. The negotiations involved give and take on both sides, with neither party getting everything that it aimed for or wished for. This is the nature of negotiations. The CARIFORUM countries did not, in the words of President John F. Kennedy, negotiate from fear, nor did they fear to negotiate.

The external economic environment in which the developing countries have operated has changed adversely and significantly, reflecting both trends in globalization and changes in the policy of developed countries toward developing countries. The future is not what it was[100] because in the past the CARICOM countries had nonreciprocal preferential trade arrangements, and because development assistance was still viewed in the developed countries as an essential ingredient in the development process. The negotiations were now occurring in a milieu in which many of the arrangements under which international trade was conducted by CARIFORUM were threatened by changes that were regarded as adverse and disruptive. The future appeared to require changes about which the small developing economies, particularly the smallest, were apprehensive. The attitudes to realities facing the CARIFORUM and the need to change so as to thrive in the contemporary global economic environment ranged from frank acceptance to outright denial. A psychology of doubt prevailed in some quarters, which was reflected in demands for protectionism, permanent nonreciprocity, and development assistance. Brewster and Thomas speak of "the claustrophobia of size"[101] that is rooted both in history and in contemporary reality. Fortunately the Principal Negotiator, the EPA College of Negotiators, and the CRNM approached the negotiations with confidence in the region's ability to compete with the EU and indeed, by extension, with the global economy.

5. Changing the Trade-development Model

Inherent in the Lomé Convention was a trade-led development model based on special and differential treatment in the form of preferential access to the EU market. In the case of bananas and sugar, preferential arrangements took the form of a quota system and special price mechanisms for sugar. Special and differential treatment in the form of nonreciprocal preferences has been subjected to severe and sustained attack aimed at discrediting it as a mechanism of development assistance. The result of the withering intellectual and political assault has been the growing and increasingly resolute resistance among the WTO membership to permitting the continuation of preferential trade arrangements. It is a serious error and has engineered the erosion of these schemes. Preferential trade arrangements are a better type of aid mechanism than transfers of funds to government-sector projects because the beneficiaries are individual farmers or firms that earned through production rather than getting a handout. These arrangements were comfortably accommodated by the affluent consumers in the developed countries who neither noticed nor cared very much about the price of bananas. Aid in the traditional forms, and the "aid-for-trade" initiatives, are not a substitute for the aid through nonreciprocal preferential trade arrangements, because their impact on the receiving economies is very different.

The EPA, while not being a fully reciprocal trade agreement, shifted away from preferential arrangements. The trade-led model underlying the EPA is market driven, unlike the previously available arrangements, which centered on the management of the market through quotas and price support arrangements. The EPA provides the duty- and quota-free access to the EU market of 450 million. To date, this is preferential access, is shared with the least developed countries, that trade under the EU's "everything but arms" initiative, and with ACP countries that have signed interim agreements and EPAs. The extent to which CARIFORUM countries will gain from this market access will depend on the international competitiveness of its products vis-à-vis the ACP producers and, to a lesser extent, vis-à-vis the rest of the world.

Overview

Autarky is not a viable option, especially for small countries; therefore, exposure and involvement with globalization are unavoidable. The issue for each country is how to mediate the encounter in a manner that can benefit its economic growth and promote its economic development. Globalization poses both challenges and opportunities for all countries, large and small, developed and developing. To seize the opportunities, they have to be proactive and strategic in their international economic policy. Specifically, countries can use international trade agreements to influence the terms of integration into the global economy at the multilateral level through the WTO, or, at the regional or bilateral level, through trade agreements. The degree to which countries are successful in concluding the type of trade agreements they want depends on a raft of economic, political, and institutional factors.

The EU, like many other developed countries, found that they were facing increased international competition as globalization proceeded, and wanted to use their international trade policy to address this issue. There was a growing concern over several developing countries variously described as the Asian tigers, the newly industrialized countries, and emerging markets, and, in particular, over China. Part of the shift in EU thinking was to change the terms of their engagement with developing countries, including the ACP countries. The EU decided to convert extant preferential trade arrangements into WTO-compatible reciprocity. The EU also had an interest in preserving access to export markets in developing countries and, conveniently, in maintaining access to those markets in the ACP with which it had a long association. The enlargement of the EU coincided with the pronounced decline in empathy for developing countries in the developed countries and, consequently, with a shift in thinking away from preferential trade and aid to "every man for itself" in the global marketplace. The conventional wisdom on international trade had by the 1990s come to gravitate around the notion of free trade and there was a hardening of attitudes against special and differential treatment for developing countries. In this political atmosphere, it would have been increasingly difficult for the EU to get the membership of the WTO to grant waivers of the kind that would have been required by the continuation of the Lomé Conventions. As Ravenhill points out, "The EU's lack of interest in expending further political capital to secure a continuing WTO waiver for its trade relations with ACP was symptomatic of the low priority that the relationship held for Brussels by the mid-1990s."[102] What is clear is that trade with the ACP was not a priority interest to the EU. More specifically, the CARIFORUM markets, with the exception of the Dominican Republic, are so small that increasing their market share was not a major motivator for the EU. At the commencement of the negotiations, the total CARIFORUM market was 25 million and total GDP was approximately $70 billion, less than a third of Ireland's GDP.[103]

The CARICOM countries, more so than the larger Dominican Republic, were aware that the reduction or loss of preferences would have an adverse impact, particularly in the smallest countries; they made the fundamental error, along with the ACP, of agreeing in the Cotonou Agreement to EPAs based on reciprocity that was compatible with the standard set by the WTO. The ACP may have felt that the key commodity protocols for sugar and bananas were sacrosanct. It was pressure from the United States and some developing countries in the WTO that compelled the EU to eventually relinquish these protocols, although there were some in the EU who wanted to dismantle the protocols. It may also have been a factor that not signing the Cotonou Agreement may have influenced the EU's disposition toward development aid.

Appendix I

April 6, 1998

Dear President,

I am writing to you in my capacity as Chairman of the Caribbean Ministerial Sub-Committee on External Negotiations and I am doing so to all ACP Heads of Government.

This Sub-Committee of Heads of Caribbean Governments owes its origin and derives its authority from a decision that we need to keep a close focus on a wide range of external economic negotiations, prominently among them, of course, Lomé and the WTO. Since then we have created dedicated Regional Negotiating machinery with a Chief Negotiator to steer us through these uncertain times. In the last few weeks, my committee met in Barbados and all Caribbean Heads of Government get immediately after Grenada.

A principal focus of our discussion in both places was the "draft directives" which the European Commission had sent early in February to the European Council of Ministers and member states—in effect proposing the EU's negotiating mandate for the post-Lomé arrangements. We were quite frankly alarmed at the nature of these proposals and it was agreed that we should do a number of things, including my writing to you as I am now doing.

Your advisors will have alerted you already to the nature of these directives and the very serious implications that they carry for the ACP countries. The nature of the directives obliges us all to take a serious view of this development. Two implications stand out above the others.

The first relates to the fundamental change from the Lomé system by which the EU seeks to relegate trade issues to post-2000 negotiations and to the limit the negotiations beginning in September 1998 to an overall framework agreement which is frankly a political document. This structure of the negotiations is even more unacceptable when what seems to be contemplated by the overall agreement is a political regime which a high degree of intrusiveness into ACP policy frameworks in the social and political spheres.

Human rights, democracy, the rule of law and good governance (all values which have been part of our political ethos even before some EU member states) are to be part of a system of virtual EU certification of ACP states: not dialogue, but diction. We are convinced that the present agreement which now exists between 15 European and 71 ACP countries is worthy of a more enlightened succession in the mutual interest of all countries.

The second matter is the clear intention of the draft directives to split the ACP into three (3) or even six (6), parts, for the trade negotiations which would begin in 2000. This is not the "regionalization" of which the ACP speaks. Indeed, it is precisely the opposite. We have repeatedly reaffirmed our determination to maintain ACP solidarity and the integrity of the ACP as a negotiating partner. This should be the fundamental basis for the future negotiations; but it will be jeopardized from the outset were we to agree to negotiating structures the EU is now contemplating. Indeed now the European Union should have nothing to gain by seeking to fragment relationships between ACP countries that have been nurtured into maturity over 25 years of Lomé experiences—at least if it is serious about furthering the development of ACP countries and assisting out integration into the world economy.

The combination of these two strategies of negotiating a framework agreement with the ACP followed by three (3) or six (6) separate regional or sub-regional trade negotiations becomes the more sinister by the fact that the framework agreement contemplated is designed to secure ACP agreement in advance for unspecified trade arrangements to be negotiated subsequently, leaving the ACP at that stage with the extremely limited options and making us hostage to EU manipulation in fractured negotiations.

We came to the conclusion in Grenada that there is a clear need for us to counter this strategy and to do so with urgency. Two dates highlight our need for action. The first is the ACP/EU Ministerial meeting in Barbados on May 5–8, 1998. The second is the expectation that the EU's draft directives could be approved by European member states by the end of June 1998—after which time, unless the ACP have developed an alternative strategy and counter proposals, the EU's directives will become, effectively, the agenda on which we are negotiating in September.

We do have the old preparatory process for Lomé negotiations involving a number of Committee of Ambassadors in Brussels; but we believe that the essentially diplomatic process is not adequate to the needs of the evolving situation and entirely new Lomé.

It requires direct political involvement and direction it must now be supplemented by a much more activist process building on the Libreville Declaration—not its emasculation as envisaged by the directives. It is to this end that I am seeking your co-operation.

Briefly, I am proposing that we establish immediately an ACP Strategic Group drawn from the ACP's regions, bringing together our best people under political superintendence. To be more specific, I envisage the establishment of a Group of 18 with a membership of 3 from each of the four regions of Africa, 3 from the pacific and 3 from the Caribbean- each led by a Minister (or head of government) with two high-level technical persons. I believe that only such actions can redress strategic imbalance produced by directives and so in time to allow the ACP to prepare itself for more meaningful negotiations in September.

My proposal is for us to try to agree to this arrangement by "round robin" and if so to select our teams in time for the first meeting of the Group of 18 to be held in Barbados. The group would decide on its future method of work with meetings perhaps convened and serviced in Africa and the Pacific. We feel strongly in the Caribbean that we must reject this EU attempting to trap the ACP into unsuitable dangerous negotiating structures, and that to do so we must develop and present professionally sound and well thought out alternatives. We are convinced that such a process requires political direction now. Caribbean countries will continue our preparations in response to the developments as I know you will be doing yourself in your region, but we will all be stronger f we work together and we certainly do not want to proceed in a separate way. It was

ACP solidarity that won us Lomé. It is only ACP solidarity that can save what is best and improve what is not.

Jamaica is a member of the ACP Ministerial Bureau which will be meeting specially in Brussels in April. I hope that the Bureau can agree formally on this there.

I would welcome your early and favourable response and trust your positive support could also be conveyed to your regional or sub-regional representative on the Bureau. Please accept my best wishes and warm regards.

Yours sincerely,
P. J. Patterson
Prime Minister of Jamaica

CHAPTER 2

Structure and Process of Negotiations

> All too often yesterday's innovation becomes today's orthodoxy and tomorrow's anachronism
>
> —P. J. Patterson, July 24, 1978[1]

This chapter discusses the structure and process of the negotiations between the EU and CARIFORUM. The broad goals, guiding principles, and overall schedule were established by the Cotonou Agreement, which was negotiated and agreed to by the EU and all the countries that constitute the ACP Group. The Cotonou Agreement is an international agreement between the members of the EU (15 at the time) and the 79 member states of the ACP Group. It encompasses trade, development assistance, and political relations. The ACP consists of 48 African countries, 15 Caribbean, and 14 Pacific as well as Cuba and East Timor, both of which are not signatories of the agreement. Although operating informally since 1963, it formally constituted only in 1975 when the Georgetown Agreement was signed.

Given the overarching character of the Cotonou Agreement, this chapter begins with an overview of the pertinent provisions of the Cotonou Agreement, which are in Part 3, Title II, Articles 34 to 37 of Chapter 1. This chapter deals with the objectives and principles of economic cooperation and trade. Such an analysis must be preceded by an over view of the Lomé Conventions that were the forerunners of the Cotonou Agreement.

The Lomé Conventions

The Cotonou Agreement was preceded by four Lomé Conventions based on preferential trade and development assistance. There was dissatisfaction with the results—for example, during Lomé I (1) the ACP's share of the European Economic Community (EEC) market declined, doing worse than other developing countries, (2) ACP exports to the EEC declined as a percentage of the ACP's total exports, and (3) ACP exports to the EEC experienced limited diversification.[2] While the

EU felt that Lomé I was successful, the ACP did not. P. J. Patterson of Jamaica speaking as ACP spokesman stated, "To the ACP therefore, the Lomé always represented no more than a step, albeit a significant one, towards their goal. It is not its final achievement."[3] Hewitt and Stevens concluded that Lomé II was a little more of the same in trade and a lot less of the same in development aid.[4] Sutton dismissed Lomé as moving "from neo-colonialism to neo-colonialism" because "for the Commonwealth Caribbean, Lomé appears more to preserve the past within a new set of arrangements than to prefigure the future."[5]

The EU-ACP relationship has been appositely described by Ravenhill as "asymmetrical interdependence."[6] Ravenhill described the ACP position in the negotiations with the EEC as "collective clientelism."[7] The attitude of the EEC "negotiating style" during the negotiations of Lomé II has been described by Hewitt and Stevens as "a blunt take-it-or leave-it approach which made few attempts to slip a velvet glove over the iron hand."[8] However, the Commonwealth Caribbean proved to be effective negotiators because, despite being composed of some independent countries and some colonies of Britain, they decided as early as 1970 to negotiate as a single unit.[9] A common negotiating brief was approved by the Commonwealth Caribbean Heads of Governments in November 1972. Among the goals were the preservation of the sugar quota and the provision of aid. It also established the format of negotiation the tenets of which continued into the format for the negotiations for the EPA. It mandated negotiation as a group while developing the closest cooperation with the African countries. Intense diplomatic activity in Europe and invitations to visit the Caribbean were conducted to increase the awareness of the special problems of the region.[10] This initiative was the prelude to pleading the case for special and differential treatment.

The Commonwealth Caribbean pooled its technical expertise and shared its output freely with the African countries. Sutton records that when Commonwealth Secretary-General Shridath "Ramphal rose to present the Commonwealth Caribbean's view at the opening of formal negotiations for the new convention in July 1973 he had behind him a considerable array of technical talent and political experience on which to draw."[11] It has been suggested that it was as a result of the outreach and cooperation initiated by the Caribbean toward the African countries that the nascent notion of the ACP emerged.[12] The Commonwealth Caribbean approached the negotiations for a Lomé convention with confidence. Sir Shridath recalls, "in the seventies, there was still a sense of possibility; in our capitals the political issue was the choice of policy options. In the region we talked of ideological pluralism; and in relations beyond the region we had a sense of negotiating potential" and "it was our unity in CARIFTA that led to the ACP and the eventual Lomé Convention. Regional unity in CARIFTA allowed us to forge a clear strategy for negotiating a sui generis with Europe, and it was in furtherance of that strategy that we were play so leading a role in creating the ACP. We had to begin by helping to secure a closing of ranks in Africa itself between its French-speaking and English-speaking countries."[13]

Development aid from the EEC and later the EU had the advantages of being multiyear in duration, negotiated with the beneficiaries rather than imposed, administered in collaboration with the ACP and consisting of a high portion of grants. However, the experience has been one of a process of disbursement, which has been extremely bureaucratic. The result is that a sizeable amount of undisbursed resources remains at the end of the scheduled programme. "In fact," Grilli states, "stability and predictability of EC aid applied more to commitments than to actual disbursements."[14] The perennial position of the EU has been that disbursements are hindered by the absorptive capacity of the ACP countries, but even when the EU is willing to pay for technical expertise to design projects, the EU tender process can be very prolonged. In some cases, by the time a suitable specialist is identified and contracted, deadlines for submission of project proposals have expired.

For many in the ACP countries, the Lomé Conventions were synonymous with preferential arrangements for commodities and aid with little or no attention to the opportunities for nontraditional export products and foreign investment. This deeply engaged attitude carried over into the Cotonou Agreement and the EPA negotiations. This attitude of entitlement and the habituation to aid go back to the colonial era and have survived intact. The beneficiaries of colonial aid in the form of grants were never satisfied and felt that the United Kingdom was too parsimonious. The view that colonial aid was grossly inadequate prompted Eric Williams to opine: "Development is absolutely unthinkable in such terms, and migration is inevitable. . . The only answer is economic aid for development."[15]

The Cotonou Agreement

The Europeans started thinking about changing the Lomé Convention arrangements from as early as the mid-1990s. The new thinking in Europe was cogently set out in a 1996 Green Paper[16] in which the message was expressed by one EU Commission official as "the status quo would not do, change was needed."[17] In long-term strategic thinking, the EU was far ahead of the ACP by articulating its own form of the future partnership, while the ACP concentrated its efforts on critiquing the EU position. The ACP's intention was to block any change to the Lomé Convention approach and therefore the group did not prepare its own comprehensive strategy. The stance of the ACP centered on resistance to proposals perceived to be not in their interest was an understandable and necessary initial reaction of the ACP. It should have developed a position paper as an alternative to the EU vision, which demarcated the intellectual terrain in which to conduct a dialogue. In many instances, the ACP was resisting or opposing on an issue-by-issue basis without adequately posing these in a clearly thought out and cogent espoused holistic template. Indeed, some of the leading negotiators of this period were later to criticize the CARIFORUM-EU EPA for not gaining or, more correctly, regaining objectives that they had failed to secure or had given up and signed away in the Cotonou Agreement. The most notable example was nonreciprocity as the basis for future trade agreements. The mindset of opposition was such that insufficient attention was given to the contemplation of possible changes, for example, the protocols governing bananas and sugar. The admission that the protocols were not immutable was regarded by some as a heresy to the ACP position. Furthermore, such a prospect was regarded in some quarters as a sign of weaknesses and disloyalty.

Ambassador Edwin Laurent, the ambassador of the Eastern Caribbean States to the EU Commission, reflecting on the negotiation process leading to the Cotonou

Agreement, comments, "Linked to the potential legal vulnerability of the Protocols exposed by the banana challenge is the perception that they have ceased to be sacrosanct. It is no longer politically incorrect to challenge provisions of the ACP-EC Agreement. Although the Commission conducted a spirited defense before the Panel, the EU clearly lost the will to continue to defend the contentious provisions of Protocol V. When the first opportunity arose to dispense with its obligations, the EU sought in the negotiations for the 2000 Partnership Agreement with the ACP (Cotonou) to exclude all market access commitments from the Banana Protocol."[18]

The Cotonou Agreement was of fundamental importance to the negotiations for EPAs with the six ACP regions because it established the goals, principles, and ambit of the EPAs. The Cotonou Agreement conceded certain possibilities even before the negotiations began and, consequently, some aspects of the development dimension that governments asked their negotiators to secure in an EPA were already conceded by the same governments in the negotiations of the Cotonou agreement. It was therefore not possible in the EPA negotiations to recapture the concessions enshrined in the Cotonou Agreement. One of the most outstanding examples was the demand for nonreciprocity made by numerous political leaders, officials, and other persons outside the negotiation process. The public in general failed to grasp the fact that the ACP countries had signed an international agreement with the EU, which committed them to produce an EPA that was based on reciprocity and conforming to WTO compatibility. There was also "willful ignorance" on the part of some who should have understood and who persisted in calling on the EPA negotiating team to get that which had been given up in the Cotonou Agreement and to the absence of which the ACP governments were legally bound.

Sir Shridath Ramphal, the chief negotiator for CARIFORUM in the negotiations for the Cotonou Agreement and head of the CRNM, assessed the Cotonou Agreement as "not the best that can be envisaged but overall it represents a considerable advance on the arrangements contemplated by the EU at the start of the negotiations."[19] Apart from the fact that no negotiator gets everything they want in the final agreement, the comment reveals that the ACP had to resist ideas proffered by the EU as the basis for an agreement. The reality was that the ACP came to the process of negotiations for an agreement to supersede the extant Lomé Agreement without a common position and indeed, in many respects, without clear goals. The EU seized the opportunity to fill the vacuum with its perspective on what an agreement should constitute. Embedded within the vision set out in the European Commission's Green Paper on EU-ACP Relations circa November 1996 was a development strategy expressed mostly implicitly but in some instances explicitly. The ACP countries were caught off guard and unprepared, and therefore, from the start the group was in the position of reacting to the template that had been carefully thought through and articulated by the European Commission. These circumstances are indicative of how much better prepared the EU was at the commencement of the negotiations and of the lack of comity, coherence, and cooperation within the ACP Group.

The ACP group was subject to both centrifugal and centripetal forces. Although it was never overtly stated, the EU had long wanted to shed the tiresome links to a bloc of seventy-odd developing countries and this desire was compounded by an abiding faith and fundamentalism about regionalism as a mechanism for political and economic development. While there is much merit in regional economic cooperation and integration as a framework for enhancing and facilitating economic development, it cannot be introduced from outside. The EU, with little political sensitivity, and apparently having learnt nothing from the imperialist division of Africa[20] in the late nineteenth and early twentieth centuries, arbitrarily delineated regions on the basis of their physical contiguity.[21] So strong was the European conviction of the validity and efficacy of regionalism[22] that it induced a sort of myopia about the profound divisions among the regions of the ACP. Regionalism for the Europeans was a "deus ex machina" for the development problems of the ACP countries. The regions were artificial, with significant economic, political, and ethnic differences[23] and a glaring absence of existing functioning institutional structure for integration. The CARIFORUM group was the least encumbered with divisive factors because it was essentially a task of bridging the bifurcation between the Dominican Republic, on the one hand, and CARICOM encompassing the rest of the countries in the "region," on the other.

Any chance of maintaining unity in the ACP Group was shattered when the ACP agreed to negotiate as six regions with some elements common to all the regional EPAs. Even the subjects for all ACP deliberations engendered only perfunctory cooperation. The problems of cooperation and coordination of the ACP Group had become progressively severe because of growing differences in size and level of development. The interests of the least developed countries (LDCs) that were beneficiaries of the "Everything but Arms" (EBA) initiative of the EU were different from those of other developing countries outside the ambit of the EBA. The wide gap in costs of production between different producers in banana and sugar meant that changes to the respective protocols had different implications for Africa and for the Caribbean. The Caribbean's strong desire for the inclusion of services in the EPA was not shared by the African countries. There were also different dispositions on whether and to what extent "new generation" or "Singapore issues" should be incorporated into an EPA. These issues included investment, government procurement, competition policy, trade facilitation, labor, and environment.

Tradition and a narrow range of interests around which there was commonality were not sufficient to create an adequate bonding. This tension has plagued the ACP from its inception, and differences among the group were evident during the negotiation of first Lomé Convention[24] and have continued. Divergences are to be expected in such a large group but persisted in spite of the establishment and operation of an ACP secretariat charged with co-coordinating positions and purveying common technical advice. Ravenhill's comment regarding the experience of Lomé I is just as accurate now as it was then.[25] "With a staff of only a dozen experts, the Secretariat was overwhelmed by the mountain of material that emerged during the negotiations. As a consequence it was not able to undertake the detailed work necessary to give statistical and technical support for the ACP case. Although a number of reports had been commissioned from outside experts, in some instances financed by the Commonwealth Secretariat, these were hastily drawn up and, rather than providing the required technical advice in areas such as the rules of origin or the processing of ACP raw materials, called instead, in the time-honored academic manner, for further studies. There was an almost total dependence on the EEC for statistical data... While members of the ACP Group have been quick to criticize it for its failure to provide necessary background papers, they have not given it a sufficient budget to enable it to play an effective role in the relationship. Inadequate resources have confined the Secretariat to a role that is largely reactive to European Proposals, and have prevented it from seizing the initiative."[26]

Among the concerns shared by all ACP countries was the desire for the largest possible amount of development aid, maintaining agricultural preferences for as long as possible, specifically the commodity protocols and the resistance to importing the political dimension (human rights, democratic principles, and the rule of law) into an EPA. The political dimension was regarded as particularly pernicious because it was felt that this was too intrusive and could further impair the already fragile sovereignty of the ACP countries. Article 8 of the revised Cotonou is strengthened by Annex VII, which stipulated the modalities for "formal, structured dialogue" involving joint drawing up of benchmarks based on international standards.[27]

Byron explains that within the ACP Group, there are marked differences in history, geography, and levels of development, with consequent high potential for divisions. Cohesion has to be constantly reconstituted by dint of internal bargaining, trade-offs, and coalition formation. Unified positions can be so vague as to be meaningless. Solidarity often rests on maintaining very traditional positions at the expense of proactivism and innovative approaches. The search for compromise has often prevented the ACP from narrowing down their desired objectives to fewer priorities that might produce more effective negotiation outcomes.[28]

While the ACP group suffered from some ambiguities and even contradictions among its ranks, it has been suggested that the EU intended to dismember the ACP as a coherent political entity. A former ambassador of Trinidad and Tobago has surmised that EU policy was intended to "de-ACP" the Caribbean and the Pacific.[29] Ambassador Cumberbatch bemoaned the decline: "dialogue between ACP and EU leaders, a constant in previous years, is becoming less and less frequent. Regular and personal contacts and discussions between ACP and EU Heads of State and Governments and at the Ministerial level about ACP matters contributed significantly to the closeness of the relationship and the success of the co-operation. In meetings of the ACP-EU Council, EU Ministers rarely turn up. This is due partly to their lack of interest in ACP matters and partly to the sterility of the agendas and procedures where important political issues do not feature. It is not that European leaders are not interested in Africa. Their attendance at AU, Asian and Latin American Summits attest to their interest."[30]

Even if the ACP group had been able to maintain tight cohesion, exercising influence on the EU had been made more difficult by the enlargement of the EU. The new EU member states had no historic association with the ACP group; nor did they have any guilt born of having imposed colonial rule. There was far less empathy, a lack of familiarity, and unwillingness to see any justification for a special relationship expressed via preferential treatment or substantial aid.

Concomitantly, the ACP countries individually and collectively failed to adjust their diplomatic demarche to take account of the new members.[31] The ACP continued to concentrate on, and rely on, relations with their traditional allies who had diminished weight in the enlarged EU membership. In part the inadequacy of the thrust and ambit on the diplomatic front was due to the paucity of human and financial resources; but this does not diminish the myopia of the political leadership. The sheer failure to recognize this shortcoming is an enigma, but elements of an explanation would include lack of vision, complacency, insufficient confidence to engage the unfamiliar, and a certain amount of dismissal of the importance of the new members of the expanded EU.

Objectives and Principles of the Cotonou Agreement

The objectives of trade and economic cooperation as stated in the Cotonou Agreement are as follows:

1. Promoting sustainable development and contributing to poverty eradication in the ACP countries by fostering the smooth and gradual integration of the ACP states into the world economy, while giving due regard for their political choices and development priorities.
2. Enabling the ACP states to play a full part in international trade. "In this context, particular regard shall be had to the need for the ACP States to participate actively in multilateral trade negotiations. Given the current level of development of the ACP countries, economic and trade co-operation shall be directed at enabling the ACP States to manage the challenges of globalization and to adapt progressively to new conditions of international trade thereby facilitating their transition to the liberalized global economy."
3. Improving the trading capacity of ACP countries by enhancing capacity for production, to attract investment and to handle all issues related to trade.
4. Full conformity with the provisions of the WTO, including special and differential treatment, taking account of "the Parties' mutual interests" and their respective levels of development.

The broad goals of sustainable development and poverty eradication are laudable goals that gave assurance to the ACP countries that promoting development would not be an empty phrase. References to these goals portend the negotiation of a particular type of development measure. The ACP accepted these goals but harbored residual doubts about Europeans trying to use the text: "integration into the world economy" and "full" participation in international trade. They resolved to temper the integration with "gradual" pacing—more accurately described as very extended. The question of how full the participation would be constrained ACP arguments about their relative and low level of development. The EU retort would be provision for technical assistance, and development assistance to building capacity for trade and alleviation of supply-side constraints. The EU intended to base the justification for the shift away from preferential trade arrangements on their limited and declining conformity with some of the core principles of the WTO. The ACP was resolved to resist this by relying on the principle of special and differential treatment, which they correctly regard as a core tenet of equal standing with that of MFN and non-discrimination. The thinking prevailing among the CARIFORUM states was in accord with the views of the rest of the ACP group.

Principles undergirding the manner in which the common goals would be given expression in a new WTO compatible trade agreement were set out in Article 35. These principles were as follows:

1. The new pact would be a partnership more specifically "a true, strengthened and strategic partnership" building on "the strengths and achievements of the previous ACP-EC Conventions." Particular regard would be given to trade development measures to enhance competitiveness by addressing supply and demand side constraints.
2. Build on regional integration initiatives of ACP States.
3. "Economic and trade co-operation shall take account of the different needs and levels of development of the ACP countries and regions. In this context, the Parties reaffirm their attachment to ensuring special and differential treatment for all ACP countries and to maintaining special treatment for ACP LDCs and to taking due account of the vulnerability of small, landlocked and island countries."

The EU officialdom and political leadership are imbued with a deeply rooted fundamentalism about regional integration as a mechanism and framework for economic development. This is a philosophy raised to the level of theological certainty reinforced by the experience of the last half century. However, regionalism existed in only one of the six artificially designed regional groupings: that group was CARIFORUM, which encompassed CARICOM (an existing regional integration group) and the Dominican Republic, which had a trade agreement with CARICOM. The other five groupings were nothing more than imagined communities that the Europeans were arrogant enough to assume they could forge into functioning entities. The regional groupings in formal existence at the time are listed in table 2.1. The failure of the EPA negotiations to force even consistent regional cooperation bedeviled and contributed to failure to complete EPA negotiations except with CARIFORUM. Nevertheless, the Europeans held the conviction that regional integration was a key instrument for the integration of ACP countries into the world economy.

The ACP, for reasons yet to be explained, agreed to six regional groups that were based on crude geographic proximity and therefore as arbitrary as the European imperialist partition of Africa in the late nineteenth and early tweintieth centuries. The six regional groups defined for the purpose of negotiating EPAs with the EU bore little relationship to existing formal groupings in the ACP, as listed in tables 2.1 and 2.2. Perhaps, their having secured robust language on "ensuring" special and differential treatment and a clear acknowledgement of the vulnerability of small island states and least-developed countries, the ACP felt that these gains would assuage their concerns about European development paradigms.

Table 2.1 Regional groups of the ACP

Caribbean Community (CARICOM)	Antigua and Barbuda, Bahamas, Barbados, Belize, Dominica, Grenada, Guyana, Haiti, Jamaica, St. Kitts and Nevis, St. Lucia, St. Vincent and the Grenadines, Suriname, Trinidad, and Tobago
East African Community (EAC)	Kenya, Tanzania, and Uganda
Melanesian Spearhead Group (MSG)	Papua-New Guinea, Fiji, and Solomon Islands Vanuatu
South African Customs Union (SACU)	Botswana, Lesotho, Namibia, South Africa, and Swaziland
Southern African Development Community (SADC)	Angola, Congo, Lesotho, Malawi, Mozambique, Tanzania, and Zambia
Union Douanière et Economique de l'Afrique Centrale-Communauté Economique et Monétaire de l'Afrique Centrale (UDEAC-CEMAC)	Cameroon, Congo, Central African Republic, Chad, Gabon, and Guinea Equatorial
Union Economique et Monétaire Ouest Africaine (UEMOA)	Benin, Burkina Faso, Côte d'Ivoire, Guinea Bissau, Mali, Niger, Senegal, and Togo
Countries not participating in formal regional associations	Burundi, Cape Verde, Comoros, Cook Islands, Djibouti, Dominican Republic, Eritrea, Ethiopia, Gambia, Ghana, Guinea, Kiribati, Liberia, Madagascar, Marshall Islands, Liberia, Madagascar, Marshall Islands, Mauritania, Micronesia, Nauru, Nigeria, Niue Palau, Rwanda, Samoa, São Tomé e Príncipe, Palau, Rwanda, Samoa, São Tomé e Príncipe, Seychelles, Sierra Leone, Somalia, Sudan, Tonga, Tuvalu, and Zimbabwe

Table 2.2 Regional groupings for negotiating with the EU

West Africa CEDEAO + Mauritania	*Central AfricaCEMAC + STP*	*Eastern Southern AfricaESA*	*Southern Africa "SADC group"*	*Caribbean*	*Pacific*	*East African Community EAC*
Benin	Cameroon	Comoros	Angola	Antigua, Barb	Cook Is.	Burundi
Burkina Faso	Centr. Africa	Djibouti	Botswana	Bahamas	Fed. Micron.	Kenya
Cape Verde	Chad	Eritrea	Lesotho	Barbados	Fiji	Rwanda
Gambia	Congo (Brazzaville)	Ethiopia	Mozambique	Belize	Kiribati	Uganda
Ghana	Congo (Dem. Rep.- Kinshasa)	Malawi	Namibia	Dominica	Marshall Is.	Tanzania
Guinea	Equat. Guinea	Mauritius	Swaziland	Dominican Rep.	Nauru	
Guinea Biss.	Gabon	Madagascar	South Africa	Grenada	Niue	
Ivory Coast	S. Tome, Princ	Seychelles		Guyana	Palau	
Liberia		Sudan		Haiti	Papua N. G.	
Mali		Zambia		Jamaica	Samoa	
Mauritania		Zimbabwe		St Lucia	Solomon Is.	
Niger				St Vincent	Tonga	
Nigeria				St. Ch. & Nevis	Tuvalu	
Senegal				Surinam	Vanuatu	
Sierra Leone				Trinidad and Tobago		

The modalities were outlined in Article 36. These were as follows:

1. The conclusion of a new WTO-compatible trading agreement that progressively removed barriers to trade.
2. The new trading arrangements should be introduced gradually and recognize the need for a preparatory period.
3. During the transition to the new trading arrangements, the nonreciprocal trade preferences applied under the Fourth ACP-EC Convention would be maintained during the preparatory period for all ACP countries.
4. Recognizing the importance of the commodity protocols, there would be a review of them in the context of the new trading arrangements, in particular, as regard their compatibility with WTO rules, with the objective of safeguarding the benefits derived.

Article 37.1 is worth quoting in its entirety because it demonstrates that the EU and ACP voluntarily agreed to a schedule for the completion of the negotiations. "Economic partnership agreements shall be negotiated during the preparatory period which shall end by 31 December, 2007 at the latest. Formal negotiations of the new trading arrangements shall start in September, 2002 and the new trading arrangements shall enter into force by 1 January 2008, unless earlier dates are agreed between the Parties."

A period of five years appeared reasonable to both parties; however, it proved a difficult challenge for the ACP countries. This was anticipated in the provision made for ACP groups that could not complete the negotiations in the mutually stipulated timeframe. There were some in the ACP countries who felt that this was not really a hard and fast date and that it could be rolled back. Others thought that not meeting the deadline was an astute strategy because the EU would not adhere to the withdrawal of extant arrangements. This it was felt would be a tactic that would extend the duration of prevailing arrangements including the commodity protocols for sugar and bananas.

The preparatory period would also be used for capacity building in the public and private sectors of ACP countries, including measures to enhance competitiveness, for strengthening of regional organizations and for support to regional trade integration initiatives, where appropriate, with assistance to budgetary adjustment and fiscal reform, as well as for infrastructure upgrading and development, and for investment promotion.

Negotiations of the EPAs would be undertaken with ACP countries that considered themselves in a position to do so, at the level they considered appropriate and taking into account regional integration processes within the respective ACP regions.

In 2004, after consultations, the European Community would assess the situation of the non-LDC, and if they were not in a position to enter into EPAs, it would "examine all alternative possibilities, in order to provide these countries with a new framework for trade which is equivalent to their existing situation and in conformity with WTO rules."

Negotiations for EPAs began at approximately the same date, although it was obvious that the levels of development, the extent of preparedness for negotiations, and the capacity to execute the negotiations varied considerably among the six ACP groups. It was never certain that all the groups would complete the negotiations nor that the LDCs would be able to adhere to the commitments in a comprehensive EPA. There were, therefore, provisions anticipating that the LDCs would have to have a less onerous agreement. The EU committed to examine all alternative possibilities and devise an arrangement that would be the equivalent of the existing situation. What exactly that would come to mean was open to widely different interpretations including that the LDCs could simply retain existing market access for goods and make no concessions to EU imports into their markets.

"On the Community side trade liberalization shall build on the acquis and shall aim at improving current market access for the ACP countries through, inter alia, a review of the rules of origin. Negotiations shall take account of the level of development and the socio-economic impact of trade measures on ACP countries, and their capacity to adapt and adjust their economies to the liberalization process. Negotiations will therefore be as flexible as possible in establishing the duration of a sufficient transitional period, the final product coverage, taking into account sensitive sectors, and the degree of asymmetry in terms of timetable for tariff dismantlement, while remaining in conformity with WTO rules then prevailing."

For those groups contemplating an EPA, it is of paramount importance that as far as possible they ensure that the EU lives up to the provision committing the EU to an agreement in which trade liberalization is built on the acquis and aim to improve the access of the ACP groups to the EU markets. Taking account of the circumstances of the ACP countries, the EPAs should "be as flexible as possible" within the prevailing WTO rules as regard product coverage, liberalization timetables, and the duration of transitional periods. The CARIFORUM never tired of reminding the EU negotiators and political leadership of this "binding commitment." What specificity it would be given was a matter for hard fought negotiations. The EU, in spite of this lofty commitment, pressed as hard as possible for their objectives even when they were felt by the ACP to constitute a high price.

Formulation and Execution of Negotiating Positions

The approach to the negotiations by the CARICOM countries build to the tradition of a joint team of negotiators, unity around a common negotiating brief, and the pooling of technical expertise. This tradition dates back to the negotiation for the first Lomé Convention in the early 1970s, and this format has been deployed ever since in a wide array of negotiations and diplomatic engagements. The antecedents of joint negotiation go back to joint negotiations with the British colonial authorities over sugar quotas and preferential prices. The habit of collaboration and the utility of cooperation were strengthened by the West Indies Federation, although it lasted only for a brief interlude. The acceptability and practice of a team was symbolized by the West Indies cricket team and the culture of joint undertakings reinforced by institutions of functional cooperation such as the University of the West Indies and the Caribbean Development Bank.

Tradition of Joint Negotiations

The CARICOM member states have had a long tradition of joint negotiations dating back into the colonial era and predating the formation of CARICOM. As colonies of Britain collectively referred to as the West Indies, these countries were administered by Britain as a region or collective. The leadership in these colonies met with the British Colonial Office on several occasions to discuss and amend the terms and conditions covering the export to Britain of certain commodities, the most important of which related to sugar and bananas. This type of joint negotiation of external trade arrangements goes back as far as the 1920s. The practice of negotiating as a group became more formalized with the short-lived West Indies Federation during the period 1957–1962 and the establishment of the Caribbean Free Trade Association (CARIFTA) in May 1968, the forerunner of the Caribbean Community (CARICOM) that was established in 1973.

The practice developed further when the region was involved in the negotiations of the Lomé Conventions. The CARIFTA Council in 1972 made the decision that the member states would negotiate with the EEC as a group, and so, at the opening conference in Brussels in July 1973, the region announced that it would sit together as a group under the nomenclature of the "Caribbean Countries" and would speak with one voice.[32] The Revised Treaty of Chaguaramas (1983) in Article 6 (g) and (h) establishes as objectives "the achievement of a greater measure of economic leverage and effectiveness" in external relations and "enhanced coordination of Member States' foreign and (foreign) economic policies."[33]

The institutional arrangements for the conduct of the region's international trade negotiations were led at the political level by a committee of three or four ministers. Their advocacy was supported by technical work undertaken by the staff of the CARICOM Secretariat. The technical preparations were supplemented by research by scholars from the University of the West Indies, either undertaken on their own initiative or contracted by national governments or regional organizations.

In 1996 the CARICOM countries found themselves confronting the unprecedented situation of simultaneous involvement in negotiations for the WTO, the FTAA, originally scheduled to be completed by 2005, and the successor agreement for the Lomé Convention IV, which was due to expire by the end of 2000.[34] The international political environment in which these trade negotiations were slated to take place was becoming more demanding of political and diplomatic intervention after events such as the signing of the North American Free Trade Area (NAFTA) in 1991, the formation of the European Single Market in 1992, and the establishment of the WTO in 1994. The ambit and technical subject matter before the WTO had increased very substantially, eventually forming the Doha Development Agenda. The scope of subjects in the discussions for the FTAA and with the Europeans had expanded to encompass topics and issues with which CARICOM previously had to grapple, for example, government procurement and financial services. It was against this background that in 1997 the CARICOM Heads of government decided to establish the CRNM.

The Experience of Joint Negotiations

CARIFORUM benefitted from CARICOM's experience of working together in earlier external trade negotiations. The CRNM charged with the technical preparations for the negotiations had gained from the experience of joint negotiations. First, the Chief Negotiator/Principal Negotiator Richard Bernal who was also head of the

CRNM was someone with considerable experience in international negotiations on behalf of the CARICOM countries. Several of the technical staff also had exposure to international trade negotiations and, therefore, where necessary, could be and were deployed as negotiators at the technical level. Second, the preparedness of CARICOM governments benefitted considerably from their participation in the negotiation for the FTAA. The FTAA experience exposed the region to a range of issues not previously encountered, and the technical work and involvement in discussions provided a foundation on which more detailed and precise positions could be formulated. The FTAA negotiations, although these did not come to a successful conclusion, were a useful learning experience for CARICOM and for many who served in the CRNM.

The CARIFORUM region, despite its size and financial constraints, deployed a world-class team of negotiators utilizing the technical advice of the CRNM (discussed in chapter 3) and directed by mandates stipulated by the Heads of Government and supervised by trade ministers. The negotiating positions were formulated through a transparent and intensive consultative process involving technical working groups (TWGs) with participation from governments of member states, regional institutions, the private sector, academia, and civil society. The process also drew on specialized expertise from international institutions such as the WTO, Inter-American Development Bank (IADB), and the World Bank.

The CARIFORUM Heads of Governments were at the apex of the structure of negotiations and they provided mandates to the trade ministers who, in turn, provided political guidance and oversight of the negotiations. The actual technical negotiations were undertaken by a team of trade experts drawn on the basis of merit from all member states and from diverse professional backgrounds. They were superintended and guided by a Principal Negotiator working in close collaboration with the minister designated with responsibility for EPA negotiations, and they, in turn, had reference to the prime minister in charge of external negotiations.

It is not practical or advisable for every recalibration in negotiations to be shared with all the stakeholders. Stakeholders have to make their inputs to their governments and to the CRNM and trust the officials, technocrats, and negotiators to execute to the best of their ability the task of representing their interests. Some governments allowed private sector participation in their delegations, which were headed by government personnel. The negotiators and ministers were responsible and dedicated public servants and must be credited with capacity to make a sound judgment about what could be made public and when and what had to be kept confidential.

After four years of negotiations and nine months of review by the governments, the CARIFORUM countries (except Haiti and Guyana) signed the CARIFORUM-EU EPA on October 15, 2008 in Bridgetown, Barbados. A week later, Guyana signed the EPA in the privacy of its embassy in Brussels. This was the culmination of an enigmatic campaign, which failed to reopen the negotiations. Haiti, because of persistent political difficulties, was unable to resolve issues relating to services and investment in time to sign.

Schedule of Negotiations

Commentary in the media at the time gave the misleading impression that CARIFORUM countries were being forced by the EU to conclude an EPA by the end of 2007. It implied that this put the Region's negotiators at a disadvantage and suggested that a more prudent course of action would have been to extend the duration of the negotiations. Its most extreme exposition took the form of the sound bite: "no agreement is better than a bad agreement." This was simply incorrect and was a disservice to the negotiating structure, the apex of which was CARIFORUM Heads of Government. The mandate to the negotiators as repeatedly reiterated by the ministers and heads was to finish the negotiations on the schedule mutually designed and agreed to by the CARIFORUM and the EU. The rationale for these instructions was that the Region would be worse off without an EPA in place on January 1, 2008, and completion at a later date would put the region in a disadvantageous position.

The Cotonou Agreement signed in 2000 after the expiration of Lomé IV provided a framework of political and economic partnership between the ACP countries and Europe was designed to provide the foundation on which to construct a WTO-compatible trade agreement, namely, the EPA. The EPA negotiations presented an opportunity to craft a trade arrangement with an important historical trading partner complemented and supported by development cooperation to assist in meeting the costs of adjustment, implementation, and international competitiveness.

Rationale for Completing Negotiations on Schedule

The negotiations of an EPA with the EU were according to the terms of the Cotonou Agreement and the Plan and Schedule adopted by CARIFORUM, due to be completed in time for the entry into force of the Agreement on January 1, 2008. The reasons for trying to complete the negotiations by December 31, 2007 were as follows:

1. The GATT Article 1 waiver, which allows for the grant of nonreciprocal preference by the EU to the ACP Group, was due to expire on December 31, 2007.
2. If an EPA was not in place by January 1, 2008, CARIFORUM countries would have had to conduct trade on the basis of the EU's GSP regime, which is less advantageous because its product coverage does not include several important CARIFORUM exports and several of these would have incurred tariffs. Completing the negotiations on schedule allowed the Region to avoid operating under the GSP scheme.
3. The possibility of extending the duration of the negotiations had been suggested; however, the WTO waiver, which permitted access to the preferential provisions of the Cotonou, was to expire on December 31, 2007. At the end of 2007, it would not have been possible to activate a temporary extension of a WTO waiver for a trade regime that had ceased to exist. To extend market access to the trade provisions of the Cotonou Agreement, the ACP and the EU would have had to agree to the establishment of a new Protocol to resuscitate the trade regime before a new waiver could be sought. Reaching such an agreement would take some time to achieve and it would be difficult to secure passage except on the basis of reciprocity.
4. Even if all this was implemented, successfully attaining the waiver would be improbable in an international political environment, where other countries,

including non-ACP developing countries continually seek to "level" the playing field by dismantling preferential trade arrangements. Mobilizing adequate international support for another waiver was highly unlikely.

5. The EU had indicated that countries could sign a less than full EPA and complete the negotiations on a more extended schedule after January 1, 2008. However, this option was only available to those regions, which had concluded an agreement on market access for goods (industrial and agriculture). Ironically the market access negotiations have been the most difficult to complete. In the case of the CARIFORUM-EU negotiations, the other subject areas were largely settled before some of the more contentious aspects of market access. Therefore, these options did not provide a feasible alternative to completing the negotiations on schedule.

CARIFORUM'S Unique Situation

While all ACP States share certain commonalities, the consequences of not having an EPA in place by the end of 2007 were not the same for all ACP States. Failure to establish an EPA would inevitably have led to the implementation of the EU GSP in 2008. In the absence of an EPA, African States, most of which are classified as LDCs, would continue to benefit from nonreciprocal preferential access for goods to the European market under the EU GSP system. From the African perspective, while this level of access may not be considered ideal, it could be regarded as satisfactory until an EPA is established. In marked contrast, it is well documented that CARIFORUM States with the exception of Haiti, which are not classified as LDCs, face no such acceptable alternative under the GSP system. Therefore, for CARIFORUM in particular, the necessity of meeting the deadline for the completion of the EPA was voluntary and pragmatic and was a response to pressure from the EU.

Where there was an advantage to be gained, CARIFORUM negotiators at the technical and political levels have collaborated with the ACP group of countries. During the course of the negotiations, there were several meetings of ACP ministers and EU-ACP ministerial meetings. On these occasions, there were formal and informal exchanges at both bilateral and multilateral levels. Exchanges also took place outside of the formal settings, but unfortunately a cohesive collaborative process did not develop sufficiently among the Brussels-based diplomatic missions. The CRNM shared information and technical work (but not negotiating positions or strategies) with technicians in the ACP countries. This experience revealed areas of common interests and areas of divergences, and no amount of diplomacy or romantic allusions to the past could alter the fact that there were substantive differences rooted in different objective realities. The technical contribution was minimal and that which was provided to the ACP countries was weak and generally only became available at or just before meetings. Technical research on issues and aspects of the EPA negotiations was provided to the ACP governments and to the public by institutions such as the Commonwealth Secretariat and the European Centre for Development Policy Management.

Dangers of Delaying Completion of EPA Negotiations

Delaying the completion of the negotiations could have exposed the CARIFORUM countries to the following risks.

1. The expiry of the waiver would leave the ACP preferential access arrangements unprotected in the WTO and vulnerable to challenge. Such an eventuality would mean that the Region's key commodity exports to the EU, namely, sugar, bananas, and rice could suffer even greater damage than has already been the case. It would be almost impossible for the EU to accommodate the Cotonou-type preferences under its GSP for the simple reason that, under the WTO rules that make the GSP possible, all developing countries must, by and large, be treated equally.
2. The EU's GSP would have two effects on the exports of the CARIFORUM countries: (1) a range of products that could be exported by the ACP under the Cotonou arrangements at various levels of tariff preference were excluded altogether. These included sugar, bananas, beef/veal, products, citrus, brown rice, aluminum oxide (alumina) and aluminum. (2) Other products would have attracted a tariff where ACP exports enter duty free, including fish, crustaceans, and mollusks; ornamentals, vegetables, various tropical fruits (including mangoes, guavas, and avocadoes), palm oil, various cocoa products including chocolates, tobacco products, plywood and similar materials, a range of garments, and electronic parts for TVs, cameras; and so on.
3. The impact of an expiry of the Cotonou waiver had to be taken seriously. It was not cpmparable to the expiry of the CBI waiver, the absence of which has not (yet) resulted in any adverse consequences. The thinking at the time was based on the view that the CBI arrangements had not been the target of legal challenges, as was the case with the EU banana regime and, to some extent, sugar. There was a conviction in both the EU and CARIFORUM camps that the Latin American banana exporting countries could be expected to challenge the entire set of ACP arrangements when the waiver expired. This would be harmful to the EU and CARIFORUM countries. There was a calculation that if there was a slippage of a few months in concluding the EPA, this might not materially affect the dynamics of the situation. If, however, the delay were to stretch beyond a short period, then the probability of a challenge would have increased.
4. Experience at the WTO Ministerial meeting in Doha shows that requests for waivers are likely to be attained only by concessions made to other WTO members. In the case of the Cotonou waiver, the EU was forced to give Thailand and the Philippines an additional quota and a 50 percent reduction in the MFN duty of loin tuna. In addition, the EU had to give commitments on the further liberalization of its banana regime in a way that committed it to returning to dispute settlement in the event that a regime satisfactory to the MFN countries was not put in place by 2006. If another waiver were to be requested, it was not clear what conditionalities would have been attached during the WTO deliberations and how adversely these could impact on

CARIFORUM. Other countries, it was felt, would use the occasion to secure agreement on issues of importance to them but unrelated to the waiver. The Latin American banana-exporting countries would certainly have leveraged the situation to try to lower tariffs on their bananas entering the EU. In addition to the banana-producing countries of Latin America, some delegations felt that seven years was sufficiently long to conclude the EPA negotiations; a request for a new waiver would, according to Bassilekin, "give rise to requests for concessions that would be costly both for the EU and the ACP States, and the main products at the centre of the discussions would be, in addition to bananas, tuna, beef, sugar, textile and many others."[35]

5. It has been suggested that none of the adverse consequences that would have befallen CARIFORUM would have actually materialized if all the ACP regions decided to delay the completion of the negotiations beyond December 31, 2007. This specious argument was based on the premise that there was a sufficiently strong commonality of interests that the ACP group would operate in concert as in the so-called halcyon days of the Lomé negotiations. This was not so because of the different circumstances of CARIFORUM and the other ACP regions. Although other ACP regions lagged far behind in the EPA negotiations, their objective circumstances differed markedly from those of CARIFORUM, in particular, because the other regions consisted mostly of LDCs, they already had the duty-/quota-free provisions of the EU's EBA. The EBA provisions had security of tenure because they were not subject to the requirement of a WTO waiver. Going beyond the delay would have seriously injured CARIFORUM countries while having no adverse consequences for the vast majority of the other ACP states.

Being the First Region to Complete an EPA

It was no secret that most other ACP regions were much further behind in their negotiations than CARIFORUM and were not likely to complete the EPA negotiations by the stipulated deadline. The question had been posed: What advantage would CARIFORUM gain by maintaining the political commitment to complete the negotiations within the agreed schedule? Some had even suggested that finishing before the other ACP regions would be disadvantageous because the EU could subsequently offer greater concessions to other regions. This was not a real danger because the MFN clause in the EPA binds the EU to provide to CARIFORUM any better terms subsequently included in EPAs with other ACP countries.

The objective circumstances of the other ACP regions differ significantly from those of the Caribbean. The major difference lies in the fact that while CARIFORUM is composed essentially of non-LDCs (Haiti being the only exception), most of the other regions are dominated by LDCs. In their relations with the EU, LDCs have the advantage of being beneficiaries of the EBA initiative by which the EU offers them full duty- and quota-free access on a nonreciprocal basis. This arrangement is not subject to a waiver since it is covered by the WTO's "Enabling Clause," the very provision that houses the GSP, and which allows for further discrimination in favor of LDCs.

The EC was clearly very interested in concluding an agreement, which could then be used as a model for other regions. The successful conclusion of at least one of the EPAs within the stipulated timeframe was regarded as of immense benefit to the EU's public profile. The EU had not recorded any success in trade negotiation at either the multilateral or bilateral level, and this was one of its strong motivations for investing so much political capital in the EPA process. The Caribbean, rather than being in a position of weakness, as some commentators have opined, was in a position to capitalize on the anxiety of the EU to attain certain gains and concessions.

Indeed, CARIFORUM extracted some significant concessions and also forced the EU to back down from some of its earlier positions. For example, the region has been able to extract from the EU a commitment to a timeframe for tariff liberalization of 25 years, a concession unprecedented in any trade agreement. The EU has been forced to agree to the inclusion of specific provisions on development support in the text of the agreement. The EU had to relinquish its initial insistence that CARIFORUM should form a customs union, and had to concede that the Caribbean wwould not make commitments in the area of tax governance.

The Caribbean region can rightly claim that, in its dealings on the international stage, it has adhered to its stated commitment to engage and bargain in good faith. The value of this should not be underestimated because relations with the EU are not confined to trade and development cooperation but embrace a raft of economic, political, and security issues. The historical friendship and contemporary links with individual EU member states have continued to prove valuable in advancing the region's interests in the international arena.

CARIFORUM, due to the seriousness of application that it displayed in the negotiations and its demonstrated commitment to making every effort to adhere to agreed deadlines, enhanced its profile as a serious partner. The sense of purpose evinced by both parties created an atmosphere conducive to constructive dialogue and to hard bargaining. While such a rapport was at times lacking at the political level, the principal negotiators worked assiduously to establish and maintain a process of interaction, which facilitated continuous communications. This created a culture of trust and openness, which set the tone for the conduct of the technical negotiators. This mode of engagement, together with the quality of the technical preparation (which continuously surprised the EU negotiators), contributed to the timely execution of the negotiations. Indeed, there was no weaker party, as in many respects the EPA was shaped by CARIFORUM in ways not anticipated or readily accepted by the EU. Among these are the overarching emphasis on development that framed the entire EPA and the reference to innovation rather than the more limited construct of intellectual property rights.

Institutional Arrangements for the Negotiations

The governments of CARIFORUM region faced with the unprecedented complexity and magnitude of the EPA negotiations and given the necessity for common positions decided that it should pool its technical resources and regularize its cooperation and coordination. The pooling and cooperation were the only way that these small governments with limited technical capacity and financial constraints could have deployed a competent team of negotiators armed with adequate technical advice. The central institution was the CRNM. The CRNM, directed by mandates stipulated by the Heads of Government and supervised by trade ministers, provided the technical work to inform the decisions of the CARIFORUM governments and the Principal Negotiator. Several of the subject negotiators were drawn from the ranks of the staff of the CRNM. The CRNM, in conjunction with the CARICOM Secretariat, organized a consultative process involving TWGs with participation from governments of member states, regional institutions, the private sector, academia, and civil society. The process also drew on specialized expertise from international institutions such as the WTO, IDB, the World Bank, and the Commonwealth Secretariat.

The institutional arrangements employed for the conduct of the EPA negotiations are illustrated in figures 2.1 and 2.2. The Heads provided overall political direction and they provided mandates to the trade ministers who provided political guidance and oversight of the negotiations. The actual technical negotiations were undertaken by a team of trade experts drawn on the basis of merit from all member states and all sectors of society. They were superintended and guided by a principal negotiator Richard Bernal[36] working in close collaboration with the Dame Billie Miller of Barbados,[37] the minister designated with responsibility for EPA negotiations, and they in turn had reference to the prime minister in charge of external negotiations. The immediate political supervision of the negotiations was carried out by CARIFORUM Council of Trade Ministers, which consists of CARICOM Council of Trade and Economic Development (COTED) and the ministerial representative of the Dominican Republic. The actual technical negotiations were conducted by the EPA College of Negotiators.

The technical work to inform the discussions of negotiating positions was prepared by the technical staff of the CRNM, and supplemented where deemed necessary with papers and studies by experts from academia and international organizations within and beyond the Caribbean. These technical inputs formed the basis for discussion in the TWGs. At least 29 meetings of TWGs were convened since the official launch of the EPA negotiations in 2004. Topics included market access issues in goods, agriculture, services and investment, legal and institutional issues, and trade-related issues, which included competition policy and government procurement. Participating in the TWGs were technical experts from the CRNM, officials from regional organizations, for example, CARICOM Secretariat, OECS Secretariat, and senior government officials.

The combined inputs of the participating stakeholder groups obtained from the national consultations and from the TWGs went into formulating the overall strategy, which was implemented by the EPA College of Negotiators and CRNM technical negotiating staff. In the EPA negotiations, the College was composed of lead and alternate lead negotiators for each of the negotiating issues. The College consisted of the best technical expertise available to the region and its composition had to be approved by the CARIFORUM Council of Ministers. The negotiators were recommended by the Dean of the College after consultations and careful review based on skill and experience. Regional balance and conflicts of interest were also taken into account, but governments did not have the right to nominate whomever they wished nor was size of country a consideration. Some individuals who were not selected resorted to every means possible to achieve inclusion by demanding quotas for certain types of countries, complaining about some negotiators, proposing new negotiating groups that they would lead, and obstructing the work of all levels of the negotiating structure—most particularly by withholding their participation in a regional consensus on some spurious grounds.

The primary objective of the EPA College of Negotiators was to devise a negotiating strategy and to ensure coherence among the Region's positions as the negotiations progressed. The College's harmonized strategy recommendations were referred

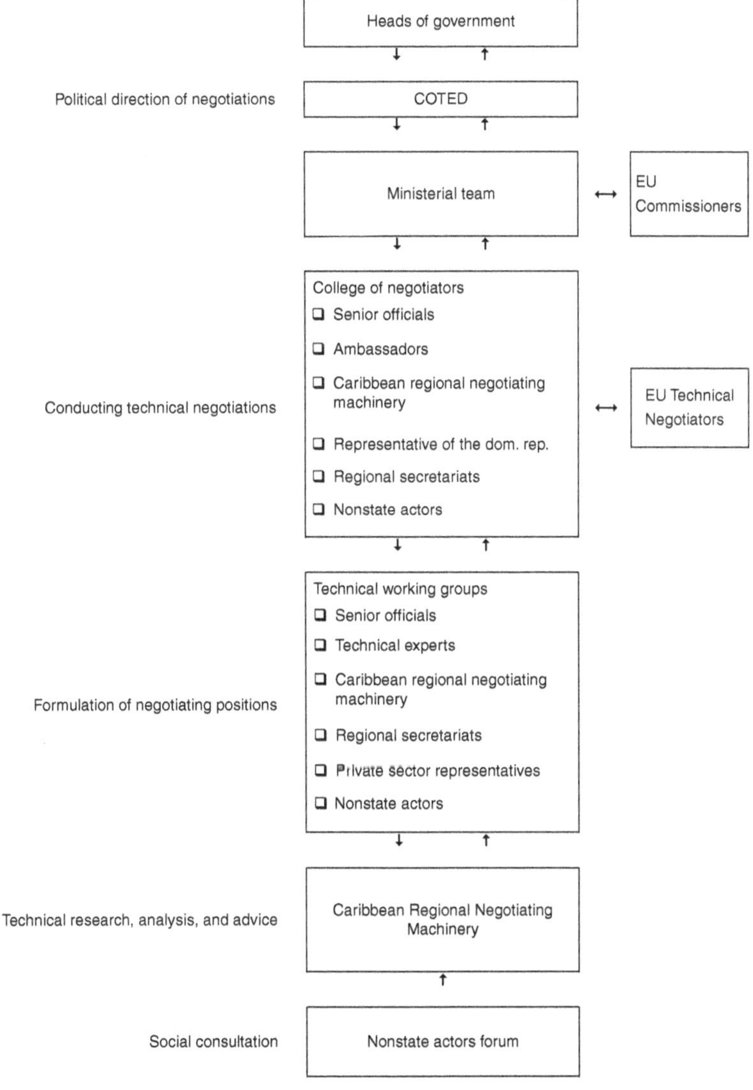

Figure 2.1 Levels of coordination/negotiation.

Components	Task	Responsibility	Location
Political	Overall direction negotiating mandates negotiating strategies	Council on Trade on Economic Development (COTED) Ministerial Spokesperson	Europe and the Caribbean
Diplomatic	Expand and enhance diplomatic relations in support of all component	Ambassadors	Europe
Technical	Negotiate detailed technical trade issues	College of Negotiators ❑ Senior officials ❑ CRNM ❑ CARICOM ❑ Other regional secretariats ❑ Ambassadors private sector rep. ❑ Nonstate actors	Mainly in the Caribbean. The majority of the negotiating rounds will be held in the Caribbean in order to facilitate the Region's optimal participation while reducing travel and other associated costs.
	Identification of EPA development support measures	Regional preparatory taskforce ❑ National authorizing officers ❑ RNM ❑ CARICOM sec. ❑ Caribbean Development Bank	Europe and the Caribbean

Figure 2.2 Tasks, responsibilities, and location of EPA negotiations.

to COTED, as well as to the CARIFORUM Council of Ministers for review and consideration. At this level of the process, these institutions determined the negotiating mandate with the authority of CARIFORUM Heads of Government. The approval of strategy and final positions, therefore, lay firmly within the ambit of the Region's elected representatives.

This process of review ensured, among other things, that the negotiating positions took account of the interests of all member states, including the Dominican Republic, and that the positions were not at variance with the agenda of the CARICOM integration process as outlined in the Revised Treaty of Chaguaramas. To this end, a number of Special COTED meetings on External Trade Negotiations and CARIFORUM Ministerial meetings were convened. Those meetings continuously considered and refined the region's positions as the EPA negotiations evolved.

To complement the consultative process that took place at these levels, a parallel process of consultations was also facilitated and coordinated by the CRNM. It must be recognized that firms, not countries, conduct international trade. This recognition was the rationale for a concerted effort to provide timely information to the region's business sectors and to learn through dialogue the objectives of exporters and importers. The engagement with the business sector took place through training sessions, in-person presentations, specially prepared written briefings, and by eliciting submissions. Some sectors were well organized, in particular rum, sugar, and bananas, all of which had been involved in international trade for decades, and were steeped in the art of lobbying governments and regional organizations. In some instances, with my permission, their representatives attended some of the negotiating sessions. Some sectors became organized during the course of the negotiations, notably the poultry sector, which identified and provided a technician to the negotiating sessions to watch their interests. Most businesses opted to keep their governments informed and relied on their spokespersons to articulate their concerns as part of the national platform.

The Private Sector Outreach Programme of the CRNM, which started in 2005, with the appointment of a Private Sector Liaison officer provided the business sector with a systematic opportunity to participate in a comprehensive series of training and consultation sessions. The building of knowledge capacity was further aided by effective use of weekly regional radio broadcasts of "*Caribbean Trade Beat*," which sustained the sensitization of the sector as well as the general public. Special non-technical briefs were prepared and distributed by e-mail to close to 1000 recipients and were posted on the CRNM website. This was complemented by the preparation of assessments of key regional industry sectors such as the Telecommunications, Agro-Food Distribution, and Cultural sectors.

Awareness building also involved two-day trade policy training seminars, "Trade Negotiations Boot Camps," which were conducted in several countries. I as director general (DG) of the CRNM and the technical staff spoke at countless "town hall meetings," business conferences, and meetings of business associations. These encounters were an invaluable mechanism for garnering the view of business persons. Private-sector-related activities were held in every country participating in the EPA negotiations.

Workshops for the regional media were also mounted to immerse journalists in trade issues with the goal of improving the extent and quality of coverage of trade in the various branches of the media. Given its immediacy, the EPA was given particular attention in all of these outreach and training activities. The result was more and better material, particularly the business sections of newspapers.

The prioritization of capacity building in the business sector did not prevent the engagement with regional nonstate actors (NSAs) from taking place. The initiative for dialogue originated from both civil society and from the CRNM. This interaction with the NSA community helped secure views that were considered in formulating the trade negotiating agenda. In the course of the negotiations, the CRNM met with the leadership of the trade unions and, given the importance of labor, also addressed meetings of ministers of labor. Nongovernmental organizations, general and those with specific concerns, for example, environment, were consulted, even when they opposed the very notion of an EPA. There was interaction initiated by the CRNM with sector interest groups such as culture and entertainment. Some institutions that had concerns submitted their own policy paper, notably the University of the West Indies on the trade in higher education services.

Through the consultation process, the ensuing dialogue and exchange of positions through proposals and research papers would have engendered continuous consensus building. When these opportunities for dialogue and exchange were effectively utilized by stakeholders from member states, the private sector, and the wider NSA community, the resulting feedback was invaluable to the successful coordination and formulation of the regional negotiating positions. In the consideration of stakeholder inputs, a weighing and balancing unfolded in the determination of which inputs would be given priority in the final formulation of the negotiating strategy. The outcome of such weighing and balancing would have been facilitated by the negotiators but would have been determined through consensus of the participating stakeholders themselves and, ultimately, by the Heads of Government of CARIFORUM.

Consultation and Participation of Civil Society

It is not practical, nor advisable, for every recalibration in negotiations to be shared with all the stakeholders. Stakeholders had to make their inputs to their governments and to the CRNM and trust the officials, technocrats, and negotiators to execute the task of representing their interests. The negotiators and ministers are responsible and dedicated public servants and must be credited with the requisite capacity to make a sound judgment about what can be made public and when and what has to remain confidential.

Consultation with the diverse stakeholders of civil society in the 15 CARIFORUM countries, which vary in language and are spread across vast distances, was challenging. Fortunately from the inception of the EPA negotiations, member states recognized the importance of broad participation and inclusion of civil society, particularly from the business sector. The heads of CARIFORUM agreed on a negotiating structure, which provided ample opportunity for the CRNM and the Region's negotiators to benefit from the dialogue with governments and stakeholders. The objective was to ensure that, as far as possible, negotiating positions adopted would reflect the combined interests of stakeholders across the Region (figure 2.3).

A wide range of actors participated in this process and included Government representatives, private sector agents, and NSAs. Participation was facilitated at two levels: (1) the national level and (2) the regional level. Each government established some institutional apparatus that allowed for consultation with the public. The efficacy of this process varied from country to country, but the effectiveness of the consultation mechanism, although far from perfect or comprehensive, belied the region's resource and financial constraints.

At the regional level, under my leadership the CRNM set out to encourage the widest possible participation because its DG was convinced that (1) it could enrich the negotiating positions with knowledge of sector and products that only the producers themselves would know, (2) it allowed the CRNM to hear directly without the filter of governments, the goals, and concerns of civil society, (3) it provided

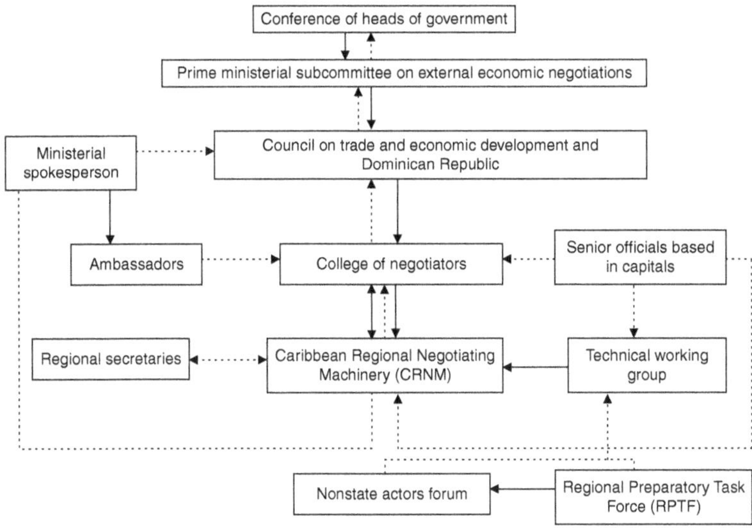

Figure 2.3 Policymaking and reporting structure.

ownership of the process, which was the inalienable right of those on whose behalf we were working, and (4) the open participation and provision of information created the transparency, which has given the EPA the legitimacy, which is a prerequisite for acceptance and implementation. Much to the chagrin of those who vigorously advised against this, the DG and staff of the CRNM provided access to those who expressed opposition to trade liberalization because the CRNM wanted to, as far as possible, hear all opinions, even those that were nothing more than destructive criticism.

Principal Negotiator for CARIFORUM and the team of negotiators that he led and directed did not in any circumstances sacrifice the quality of the EPA to meet any given schedule. The position of CARIFORUM, mandated by the heads of Government, and adhered to faithfully, was that if the negotiating team could not complete a satisfactory EPA in time for it to come into operation by January 1, 2008, the negotiations would continue for as long as it took or until instructed by the Heads of Government of CARIFORUM to cease negotiating. In straightforward terms, no agreement was better than a bad agreement.

The political leadership of the region could not afford to delude itself or succumb to those who refused to face reality. Some of civil society organizations were misled by a barrage of inaccurate information by a few who were in a persistent state of denial about the long-term continuation of preferential trade arrangements and the existence of an open spigot of development assistance if only the negotiators would press the EU. There was also the perplexing willingness of the media to transmit the comments of persons with no practical experience in international trade negotiations. Typical of the hysteria was the bemoaning of the magnitude of the displacement of tax revenue when this impact was minimized by the design of the EPA less than 1 percent of total tax revenue in the first ten years, in the case of Jamaica.

The CARIFORUM region did not have the luxury of complacency about the pace of change and the character of adjustment, which is necessary to cope with rapid and far-reaching change, and more importantly to thrive in the current and future global economic environment. Caribbean economies have demonstrated that they can produce goods and services that are internationally competitive; their future economic development requires that they seek every opportunity to do so. The CARIFORUM-EU EPA will provide improved access to the EU market and, therefore, create opportunities for expanded and diversified exports. The EPA can be a vehicle for accelerating the process of economic development and establishment of a seamless regional economic space. The extent to which this is achieved depends on the efforts of CARIFORUM countries.

There were elements in the political and official levels of government in the CARICOM region that were convinced that their economies could not compete internationally. They take for granted that they can and will produce world-class performers and indeed world champions in every field of sport and the creative arts but doubt that our entrepreneurs and workers can be internationally competitive. The evidence is that the region has produced world champions, and that record of accomplishment should strengthen the belief that CARICOM producers can and will meet global standards. The EPA negotiations demonstrate that the region has the capacity to mediate the encounter with globalization and can influence the terms of its integration into the global economy.

Political Leadership

The political leadership of CARIFORUM was fully aware of the goals of an EPA and they were briefed on a regular basis by the CRNM at meetings at the level of heads of government and minister. They provided mandates and monitored the progress and conduct of the EPA negotiations. They interacted with their counterparts, particularly at the ministerial level, on an agreed schedule and, when necessary, on the advice of the principal negotiator for CARIFORUM. The ministers also used opportunities that were not, strictly speaking, EPA related, to further the interests of the region, for example, at WTO meetings and during bilateral foreign policy engagements. The key role at the ministerial level was performed by the minister in charge of supervising the EPA negotiations who, conveniently, was also the minister with responsibility for co-coordinating all trade matters. This role fell to the minister of foreign affairs and foreign trade of Barbados, Dame Billie Miller.

At the level of prime ministers, oversight was provided by the prime minister of Jamaica because Jamaica was designated to take charge of all external trade negotiations operating as chair of the prime ministerial subcommittee on external negotiations. CARIFORUM was fortunate to have the vastly experienced P. J. Patterson for most of the duration of the EPA negotiations. He had achieved renown as an adroit negotiator during the various Lomé Convention negotiations. In the crucial final six months, the region was most ably served by Prime Minister Golding of Jamaica and by Prime Minister Owen Arthur of Barbados. They provided intellectual leadership at the level of heads of government while executing the roles of chair of CARICOM heads of government and prime minister in charge of superintending the completion of the CSME. As principal negotiator for CARIFORUM, I had access at all times to Arthur, Golding, and Miller and the two prime ministers were indispensable, particularly during the last scheduled day of negotiations. Their ability to make courageous decisions and consolidate political agreement allowed me to fully exercise my initiative, discretion, and judgment within the mandate given to me by the heads of government. They intervened when requested, for example, a letter from Prime Minister Golding to EU Vice President Barbaroso was instrumental in increasing the number of service sector, which the EU was willing to open to CARIFORUM. Some prime ministers had issues of particular interest to their country or subregion and were allowed to lead on those issues on behalf of the whole region. Prime Minister Ralph Gonsalves of St. Vincent and the Grenadines fought unrelentingly for bananas and many heads of government crusaded for more development assistance especially to facilitate adjustment in the sugar and banana industries.

The understanding of the importance of the EPA, the potential benefits, and the resolute commitment to completing the negotiations was vital to the process. This is not to say that there were not differences among the political leadership of the region and variation of judgment, but these are the foibles of any international negotiation involving a group of countries. Prime Minister Arthur acknowledged the end of nonreciprocal trade preferences and the need to expand the sector coverage of an EPA to encompass the services sectors. He stated, "we could not help but be aware that the days when Europe could confer on Caribbean societies special trade benefits that it was not prepared to grant to other developing countries, without making any benefits consistent with international trade law, were over . . . the old order which focused our relationship with Europe on trade in goods only, and the grant of aid, bore no sensible relation to the requirements of modernizing and transforming societies." He recognized that the impetus for growth would come from "the expansion of service sectors, especially, and other areas of activity which are internationally competitive, without benefiting from preferential trade arrangements."[38]

Arthur understood that the EPA addresses the development requirements of the CARIFORUM region when he acknowledged that "especially trade in services and related disciplines, the EPA recommends itself as a more meaningful tool for development than Lomé-type arrangements" and that "the services component of the EPA has been conceived to give the Caribbean a special window of opportunity in a sphere where it is immediately competitive."[39]

There was a view among some officials of CARICOM governments that the "value" of the EPA should be measured primarily in terms of the amount of aid granted by the EU. However, Golding stated categorically to the first CARICOM heads of government meeting after the conclusion of the EPA negotiations: "A trade agreement must be assessed on the basis of what it provides and the rights it conveys. It cannot be measured in terms of what development assistance it contains."[40] He also dismissed the dangerous speculation that CARIFORUM could have opted for a waiver and prolonged the trade provisions of the Cotonou Agreement: "we couldn't have applied for a waiver because we would have had no *locus standi* under WTO rules. It is the preference-granting party and not the preference-receiving party that has the option of making an application for a waiver. Based on clear signs that were given, the European Commission had no intention of going back to the WTO and even if they did, the chances of succeeding perhaps would have been as good as a snowball has of remaining a snowball in hell."[41]

Information Dissemination

To ensure informed feedback and contributions from the business sector and civil society, governments and the CRNM provided information to the public. Each government had its own arrangements and methodology for sharing information with the public. The execution was uneven across the region, so the CRNM sought to provide uniform information to all the countries in the CARIFORUM region.

The CRNM formulated and executed a public information campaign that was designed to inform stakeholders and the public in general about external trade negotiations with an emphasis on the negotiation of the CARIFORUM-EU EPA. This outreach programme was aimed at generating informed inputs and feedback from stakeholders. Even with the activities of the CRNM and those of governments, there was some misunderstanding and misconception among some stakeholders.[42] Clearing up misconceptions was intended to build support for the negotiations and indeed to give the public ownership and participation in the negotiations. The public information programme involved the use of all forms of media and a variety of forms of dissemination to try to reach as many people as possible.

To undertake the function of the provision of public information, an officer was devoted full time, supported by a consultant, and with some of the specialized expertise contracted for specific tasks, for example, in the production of the radio programme. This combination of skills was made necessary by the need for a technical officer to translate complex technical concepts and jargon into layman's language, while at the same time furnishing summaries to a more technically capable audience across the globe. The outreach was conducted through the following means.

CRNM Website

The CRNM operated a website, www.crnm.org, covering trade issues and the negotiating arenas in which the CARIFORUM member states were engaged. It provided news, reports, speeches, and links to other sources of information as well as outlines of each of the negotiations and activities in which the CRNM was active. The CRNM website received a total of 2,669,961 hits for the period April 1, 2007 to March 31, 2008 or an average of 222,497 hits per month. The number of persons and institutions that used the CRNM website increased steadily during the course of the EPA negotiations. This increased usage reflects several factors such as increased awareness of the website, improvements to the website with respect to user friendliness and content, and undoubtedly the increased interest in the EPA negotiations. The number of hits jumped to 2,669,961 from a total of 2,290,596 hits, with a monthly average of 190,883 hits for the period April 1, 2005 to March 31, 2006. This represented an increase of 379,365 or 15 percent. The website was a source of information to those outside the region, many of whom were following the negotiations because 65–70 percent of the visits to the CRNM website originated from outside the Caribbean region through a heavy reliance on search engines.[43]

The CRNM also operated a secure website (the Virtual Secretariat (VS)) for authorized persons, namely, officials of governments and regional institutions as well as negotiators and CRNM staff. The use of the VS escalated in direct correlation with the intensification of the negotiations and as the negotiations approached the scheduled completion. The VS was the main medium used for sharing information during the EPA negotiations including RNM briefs, working documents, reports, and inputs from governments. Since its inception in March 2004, usage increased from 43,179 hits during the period March to December 2004 to 259,675 during January to December 2007.[44]

RNM Update

The CRNM produced and distributed by e-mail a bimonthly bulletin to 6,000 individuals and institutions all over the world. The Update carried material of a more technical nature as well as briefings and information, which was too much for the media or which the media chose not to use. The readership of the Update was also made aware of new material available on the CRNM website and other pertinent internet sites providing information on international trade issues. The number of hits on the website reached a peak of 10,000 per month during the final months of the EPA negotiations.

Written Communications

The CRNM used written communications as the primary communications tool. The information was disseminated to our stakeholders, including the regional press, via e-mail and the CRNM website. The publications included ten technical briefs produced by technical staff and a four-part series titled "EPA Fact vs. Fiction" produced by the Trade Information officer and technical staff. The private sector liaison officer generated over 20 two-page to three-page notes specifically for the private sector on trade topics including aspects of the EPA negotiations. In June 2008, the CRNM compiled a short publication titled "The EPA at a Glance." A newspaper supplement on the EPA produced in collaboration with the EU Delegation to Barbados and the Eastern Caribbean was published in the *Nation Newspaper of Barbados*. Unfortunately, the supplement was not available throughout the region because funding constraints prevented wider regional dissemination of the newspaper supplement.

Radio and Television

In order to reach the largest possible audience and the largest number of stakeholders, the CRNM used radio and television to the greatest extent possible. Despite the constraint of limited financial resources, the CRNM produced and broadcasted a 13-episode regional radio programme series titled "Caribbean TradeBeat Extra" in August–September 2008. The programme was broadcast across 11 member States and was accessible through CRNM's website http://www.crnm.org/private_sector.htm and was available by podcast at http://caribbeantradebeat.mypodcast.com/. In addition, the official EPA signing ceremony was televised via regional public broadcast through the CMC television network in late October 2008.

Media Interviews of Senior Technical Staff

The CRNM's Director-General and senior technical staff conducted interviews in person and over telephone on radio and television. These interviews were disseminated via the OAS Radio network, which included coverage in Trinidad and Tobago and Barbados. Interviews were also broadcast on extra-regional media such as the BBC Caribbean Service. The DG was also interviewed by the *Courier*, the *Magazine of Africa–Caribbean–Pacific and European Union Cooperation and Relations* and other periodicals. Members of the technical staff of the CRNM were interviewed on the weekly radio broadcasts of "Caribbean Trade Beat."

Public Meetings and Seminars

The CRNM initiated or responded to countless meetings, conferences, and seminars with all types of stakeholders. When invited, CRNM used the opportunity to sensitize and explain all aspects of the EPA negotiations. The DG and technical staff met with political leaders, government officials, business associations, trade unions, NGOs, and educational institutions of all levels. The CRNM and national governments held meetings with stakeholders of every kind from musicians to engineers, importers and exporters, and foreign and local entities. The CRNM conducted this process of concerted engagement in all the countries of CARIFORUM and as participated in public activities in the EU with European stakeholders. The interaction with European stakeholders was calculated to build support for the EPA and to mobilize a vocal European constituency for the goals and negotiating positions of CARIFORUM.

Workshops for Journalists

It was vital to educate the members of the Fourth Estate about the process and state of the EPA negotiations. A series of workshops was undertaken to promote and improve the accuracy and quality of reporting and commentary on issues related to the EPA. Three workshops were held involving 25–30 selected journalists both during the negotiations and at the conclusion of the negotiations.

Private Sector Participation

The DG of the CRNM mounted a wide-ranging and vigorous campaign to ensure the maximum involvement and participation by the private sector. The DG made it a priority of the mode of operation of the CRNM. It is firms, and not countries, that conduct trade; therefore, it is of paramount importance to garner and incorporate the views of the businesses involved in international trade and those who could be affected by the exposure to imports consequent on the liberalization of import regimes in the CARIFORUM region. With the aid of funding from USAID, a private sector liaison officer was appointed, dedicated full time to servicing the private sector. A comprehensive and unprecedented campaign was mounted involving a section of the CRNM website devoted to the private sector featuring short briefing papers prepared especially for the business person. I also created a private sector advisory council under the chairmanship of Mr. Jimmy Moss-Solomon, a businessman well known throughout the Caribbean, who was on sabbatical from Grace Kennedy for a year and was able to devote considerable time to mobilizing the private sector. He traveled extensively and attended meetings of every kind as a member of the CRNM team and was therefore able to provide a private sector input. He was allowed to speak independently at meetings and to network the private sector with the advantage that the sector would be hearing from one of their own. He was ably assisted by the members of the private sector advisory council, which consisted of members from all parts of the region and from a cross section of sectors and industries.

Despite strenuous efforts by the CRNM, the participation of the private sector was uneven, varying among countries and sectors. All governments attempted to establish and operate some form of institutional arrangement to garner the views of their business communities and to hear their views. The responses varied widely from one government to another depending on the "strength" of the private sector, the level of awareness, the extent to which they perceived the EPA to have an impact on their livelihood, and the tradition and national culture of public sector–private sector dialogue. Where the practice of dialogue had not already existed, the EPA negotiations alone could not create such interaction, although it did prompt some specific arrangements, for example, in Belize and the Bahamas.

The industries that have traditionally been involved in international negotiations were well organized and had CEOs and managers who had the first-hand experience and knowledge of international trade negotiations. These sectors were in a position to supply technical briefs and technical experts to attend meetings and would fund their attendance at meetings in any location whether in the Caribbean or Europe. In the case of sugar, bananas, and rum, they had representatives located in Europe, for example, in London. Some of these representatives were employees and others were consultants and advisors. The representatives of these sectors participated as resource persons in the actual negotiations and conducted a parallel private sector diplomacy, which effectively complemented the formal intergovernmental negotiations. They interacted with their corporate partners to put pressure on various governments in the EU. They lobbied governments in the EU countries, both in the executive and parliamentary arms of government. They worked in close collaboration with the Principal Negotiator on overall strategy and tactics and worked closely with the technical staff of the CRNM and with the subject negotiators, particularly those in agriculture. The rum industry, acting through the West Indies Rum and Spirits Association (WIRSPA) and led by the very experienced Patrick Mayers, was a model of what private sector participation should be. They watched the calendar of negotiating meetings and a couple days before each meeting they would furnish the CRNM with an updated brief.

Preparedness and awareness varied considerably and some sectors never paid sufficient attention to make their views heard. Some came to a realization, in many instances, at the instigation of the CRNM and became organized early enough to have an impact on the negotiations, notably the citrus industry. The poultry industry, once organized across the CARICOM region, provided their technical expert to attend meetings both in the Caribbean and worldwide including WTO meetings. The tourism sector having been alerted by the CRNM designated an officer in the Caribbean Tourism Organization to monitor the negotiations, and their executives were readily available for consultation. In general, the large associations, specifically those from the larger countries, were better able to participate since they had the resources to attend meetings and to host seminars and conferences. The Private Sector Organization of Jamaica had a trade committee, which followed the negotiations. One of the alternate services negotiators was a member of staff of the Trinidad and Tobago Manufactures Association.

Appendix I

Feature address delivered by the
Hon. Christopher Sinckler, minister of
foreign affairs, foreign trade, and
international business on the occasion
of the signing of the economic
partnership agreement between the
European Union and CARIFORUM
October 15, 2008

Master of Ceremonies,
President of the Council of the European Union
Vice-President of the European Commission,
Fellow Ministers,
Secretary General of CARIFORUM,
Other specially invited guests,
Members of the Press,
Ladies and Gentlemen

Allow me to join my colleague, Minister of State Hon. Donville Inniss in welcoming you all to Barbados on this very important and auspicious occasion as we the member countries of the CARIFORUM and the European Union affix our signatures to the Economic Partnership Agreement negotiated between us over the past four years. Barbados is honoured to have been invited by its peers to be the host country for this historic event.

I especially want to extend a warm Caribbean welcome to all our visiting ACP and European colleagues and friends. Though your stay might be short, and your appointed task here even shorter, Barbadians would not at all object if you find time to enjoy the many delights of our beautiful island—that is at least for sure the ones for which some monetary contribution is required.

It would be remiss of me if I were to let this occasion pass without recognizing the leadership role played by two of the stalwarts of the negotiations that led us to this occasion, even as they now take decidedly different paths in their personal and professional lives.

I speak in the first instance of role played by Rt. Hon. Peter Mandelson, former EU Trade Commissioner, whom we learned, quite unexpectedly has returned to his native land to perform the function of Minister in Her Majesty's Royal Government at Westminster.

His leadership on the EU side and generally in the entire negotiations process was as critical as it was at times controversial. But, in all things never failing to recognize, I am told, the grave importance of concluding an agreement that made sense for both sides.

In common parlance it is now fashionable when bidding a colleague adieu, as they take on some new and challenging task, to invite them to "go break a leg". Unfortunately, knowing just how tough Mr. Mandelson can be, rendering such an investiture might not be the best in these circumstances. However I am sure you would all join with me in wishing him every success in his new role.

Equally, I wish to take this opportunity also to pay tribute to my predecessor in this Ministerial portfolio, Dame Billie Miller, the former Senior Minister and CARIFORUM Ministerial Coordinator for the EPA negotiations. Her contribution to this entire exercise cannot and should not be forgotten. It was in a few short words—sterling and outstanding. Indeed her wisdom, foresight, forthrightness, and utter dedication to the task entrusted to her by our Heads of Government and her colleague trade ministers played no small role in steering the region and its negotiators through arguably its most challenging set of negotiations to date.

What we sign here today is as much due to Dame Billie's work as it is to anyone else's involved in this process and I feel compelled to pause as I invite you to acknowledge her contribution this morning.

More than nine months ago, right here in Barbados, regional governments along with their EU counterparts laid ensconced in the early hours of the morning, in a cold and presumably uncomfortable room faced with a major decision. It was a decision which, though conditioned and shaped by several external factors, including a now infamous WTO deadline, all of those present knew would have potentially life altering implications for all the countries of this small region of ours.

After close to four years of intense negotiations, heated arguments, studies on top of studies, impact assessments, text and redrafted text and countless hours of study and meetings—a decision was called upon to be made.

In the end, given all the arguments, CARIFORUM, ably led by the Caribbean Regional Negotiating Machinery (CRNM), and as mandated by regional Heads of Government initialled the final negotiating text.

By taking such a decision our governments were doing basically two things. First they were pulling the curtain, or so they thought, on the most intense phase of the process leading to production of a new guiding framework for economic relations between the Caribbean and Europe.

Secondly in doing so they were, according to all analyses, ushering in a fundamental break with the past and entry into a new world of economic, political and social existence for the Caribbean region and its people.

The major question then, as it is now, and will always be going forward, is whether our region, whether we as a people could afford the luxury procrastination even in the face of fundamental global change.

Perhaps we don't believe it, even though we say often enough, and surely witness it every day with the naked eye. But it cannot escape us, either as nations or as individuals that this world economy in which we are made to exist has radically changed and will continue to do so whether we like it or not.

For me the scholastic observation of former World Bank Chief Economist and now Noble Laureate in Economics, Joseph Stiglitz, that the fundamental problem facing developing countries in dealing with globalization and economic liberalization is that "they do not set the policy agenda ... and because of this will always be at a disadvantage in engaging radical change." This is the critical point of intercession for our region in answering the question—do we engage or not engage.

Knowing our limitations as small and vulnerable states with weak and underdeveloped economic sectors, with limited productive capacity but intrinsically hemmed to a volatile global economy, we understand that we are fundamentally disadvantaged in the process. It is an inescapable truism.

But is also true that those systemic and characteristic features of regional economies will not go away anytime soon and rather could potentially get worse if as small economies we do not intercede at the most critical junctures to at least participate in helping to shape the very instruments that will affect every facet of our lives.

Now, we may not have set the agenda which established the requirements for this type agreement to be negotiated. Indeed we certainly did not set the excruciating and some would even say unreasonable timelines that governed the work of the negotiators. But at least unlike what has transpired in many different forums in which agendas are set and prescriptions imposed on us without our input, this process afforded us the opportunity to influence in some significant way the destiny of our future relations with Europe and perhaps even the rest of the world.

And it is against that backdrop that regional governments established clear guidelines as to the overall mandate which they gave to the region's negotiators.

The core principles of that mandates were:

1. That in agreeing to liberalize "substantially all trade" that our most sensitive sectors would have to be shielded entirely from exposure to liberalization. It is now indisputable that the final agreement has seen to that.
2. That any liberalization of tariffs/duties would have to reflect the ultimate sensitivities of regional economies to the need for revenue to be raised and so would have to be implemented in a manner least likely to cause major financial dislocation. I believe that the final agreement provides for that.
3. That given differences in levels of development between the region and Europe that the level of commitments on both sides would have to reflect a high level of asymmetry consistent with the best practices of unequal treatment for unequal partners. I believe that the agreement provides significantly for this.

4. That given the very sacred and surely fragile nature of our own CSME process, that any EPA would seek to enhance rather than destroy the regional integration process. I am yet to be convinced despite commentary to the contrary that anything in this EPA will so impinge on our own process as to render it useless.
   Conversely it may even act to accelerate the pace at which we integrate.
5. That regardless of whatever we negotiated with the EU the provisions agreed by us in defence of our CARICOM LDCs as provided for in the ART. 164 of the Revised Treaty must be explicitly recognized and incorporated into the EPA. Surely in this agreement such provision has indeed been made.
6. That where it was clear that CARICOM had not advanced its own integration in respect of disciplines such as government procurement that any EPA would not commit us beyond the level at which we had already reached. In this EPA clearly this too has been achieved.
7. That as consideration for our efforts at liberalization with Europe and mindful of the cost associated with the liberalization itself that an appropriate infusion of development priorities and actions would characterize the agreement not only in one section but through the entire agreement. A careful read of the EPA will show that this too has been achieved in keeping with and at times surpassing the best practices of development infused trade relations.
8. That the cost of liberalization, adjustment, and the implantation of the agreement itself had to be supported in large measure by the provision of financial assistance sufficient to allow our region to make the transition from basic commodity preferential dependence, to fully capacitated open trading partner. Clearly we have made a significant start in this regard but surely our EU colleagues would agree that we are not quite there yet. I will speak more specially to this point in a moment.

But from a fundamental platform of eight core objectives within the general mandate given to our negotiators as the benchmarks against which success or failure in these negotiations would be measured, it would not be a stretch of the truth for me, or anyone else to conclude that we have not done our best in the circumstances.

We knew it was going to tough; we knew that serious sacrifices and compromises would have to be made, and likewise we knew that it would, in the end, usher in a completely new era of economic and trade relations with Europe in which this region would finally have to face the realities of a changed, changing and ultimately more unfriendly global economy.

Our signature of this agreement today in my view represents a fundamental signal to the rest of the world that Caribbean countries are maturely and decidedly breaking with a long loved past that in fact has now past.

Of course there are those among us who prefer like Lot's wife to look back at a life which we must have enjoyed and longed for to continue. We can have no quarrels with that.

But surely they understand that we must move on. Clearly they are those who, like Charles Dickens' Oliver Twist, will always say we have not got enough keep on negotiating until you get all you want. But surely they too understand that this is impractical and realities of the agenda set for us do not allow us that luxury so we must move on.

And then they are those like the inimitable character in V. S Naipaul's classic Miguel Street who sawed and hammered and nailed day in and day out hoping to produce the perfect piece of furniture only for it to be discovered by his neighbours that such a piece will never be delivered. Surely they too must understand that no negotiated agreement is perfect and can produce perfect results.

What we can do however is to set realistic objectives and target our energies to achieving substantially the essence, spirit and letter of those goals. That as a region we have been able to do, so this in large measure is something to be satisfied with and not degraded.

So with this act today we embrace an uncertain future. And now our attention and energies must be focused not on what could have been but what has to be moving forward.

This is a highly complex and comprehensive agreement and the effort needed to implement it will be at times more onerous that that spent negotiating it.

Our task now is to set in motion a CARIFORUM wide process at both regional and national levels to create effective mechanisms and structures to allow each and every country in this region to take advantage of the opportunities which this EPA presents.

In Barbados, the Cabinet has agreed to the establishment of an EPA Coordination and Implementation Unit charged with the responsibility of studying the entire agreement and devising strategies and programmes to enhance the capacity of our ministries to implement and the private sector to engage and exploit this agreement.

I am confident several of our regional colleagues are doing likewise.

Equally, at the regional level, I am advised that the CARIFORUM Secretariat has already devised a comprehensive, though only preliminary, road map for implementation of the EPA for regional governments.

I expect that at the earliest opportunity CARIFORUM Ministers of Trade will sit down to refine and agree on that road map and the mechanisms needed to successfully implement it. The time is short and the stakes way too high for procrastination or prevarication.

Finally, a short word to our colleagues from the EU. As the first region to have negotiated and signed a comprehensive EPA, CARIFORUM has demonstrated a level of seriousness of purpose that many thought was beyond us. We understand fully the positive and yes the negative implications likely to arise from the implementation of this agreement. But we equally know and understand the levels of commitments which Europe has made in an effort to assist this region in implementing this agreement must now come to fruition.

In this regard, I wish to remind our EU partners of their commitment to providing development support to buttress regional integration, facilitate the implementation of EPA commitments, and improve supply capacity and competitiveness in accordance with priorities identified by CARIFORUM across the broad spectrum of negotiating subjects. The EPA text (Article 7.4), underlines the obligation of both CARIFORUM and the European Commission to take all measures necessary to ensure the effective mobilization, disbursement and utilization of the resources which facilitate development co-operation.

Although mindful that the development dimension of the EPA is not limited to the direct transfer of resources, I must emphasise that the timely delivery of necessary financial support will be vital if the EPA is to achieve the objectives which both sides set out in their negotiating mandates.

We equally expect the Commission and EU Member States to become more proactive in helping the region to put in place the necessary institutions and processes to enable our exporters to become more competitive in the delivery of both goods and services.

Colleagues, ladies and gentlemen—We see the EPA as a package, incorporating Development Co-operation, Trade in Goods, Trade in Services, and Trade Related Issues. In our view, the effective execution of the first of these elements is a prerequisite for the success of the other three.

The EU Aid for Trade (AfT) facility represents an important source of additional funding for the implementation of the CARIFORUM EPA. The EU AfT commitment envisages increasing trade-related development support to €2 billion per year by 2010 with half of these AfT resources being earmarked for EPA implementation in ACP regions. The CARIFORUM EPA text includes a declaration that the region will benefit from an equitable share of the one (1) billion Euros, which represents the commitments of EU Member States (not including the Commission) for EPA implementation.

But I hasten to add that to date the modalities governing access to the AID FOR TRADE resources of EU Member States have not yet been properly elaborated although these were to have been in place since the end of last year and, secondly, questions have been raised about the actual amount of net additional AID FOR TRADE resources, which will be available. I am optimistic these concerns will be immediately addressed.

Failure to satisfactorily do so or to meet those commitments to their fullest extent will not only compromise the implementation of this agreement but permanently damage our futuristic relations.

In concluding, allow me to express our appreciation to the valuable and valued work of our negotiators and all others involved in this process from its beginnings and at various points along the way.

As I reflected in the beginning of this presentation, today signals the start of a new era in our relations with the EU and even with the rest of the world. So as we proceed to affix our signatures, let us in this region together reflect on the poignant words of Baroness Young who in a lecture to the UWI in 1996 was moved comment:

"It follows that whatever happens after the year 2000 will have to be negotiated against a background of a changed world in which many EU member states question every aspect of the EU development policy, let alone ask why there should be a special relationship with a limited groups of nations. The message is clear: the scenario will be bleak for any ACP nation unable to adapt to this new reality. The issues are no longer about morality. This conclusion is now almost certainly the defining truth about future ACP/EU relationships."

Ladies and gentlemen welcome to the future. I thank you

Appendix II

Presentation by
Prime Minister Bruce Golding m.p.
on the European Partnership Agreement
at the 19th Inter-sessional Meeting
Nassau, Bahamas
March 7–8, 2008

You will recall that at the outset of the meeting, I expressed some concerns that the agenda was overloaded and that one consequence of that was likely to be our inability to allocate the appropriate time and attention to issues that were both important and urgent. I can think of no item on the agenda that is more urgent, more important, particularly because it involves more contentious issues than the question of our external trade negotiations and more particularly the EPA arrangements that we have entered upon.

Members are already aware that on the 16th of December, CARIFORUM States and the European Union reached an agreement on a new economic partnership. This was done merely 15 days before the deadline that was set for the conclusion of an agreement.

The negotiation, the conclusion of an agreement and the deadline, were mandated by the Cotonou Agreement and the terms of the waiver which was granted by the WTO in November 2001. Let me try to set this agreement in some context. The Cotonou Agreement signed in March of 2000 assimilated the preferential arrangements which we enjoyed under Lomé. It however required that these arrangements which were inconsistent with WTO rules and therefore required a waiver; it required that these arrangements be replaced by an Economic Partnership Agreement and the deadline for completing that was set for the 31st December 2007.

There have been as we all know some very trenchant criticisms of the agreement. Some of them coming from Caribbean personalities, very distinguished, and whose concerns must not be dismissed. What have been these criticisms?

One was that we approached the negotiations with undue and even reckless haste to sign. I challenge that. We knew from 2000—seven years and nine months before the deadline—we knew that this was the timetable that was set. The clock had started to tick and we should have heard the ticking of that clock. The negotiations began in April of 2004. Could we have started the negotiations earlier? Should we have started those negotiations earlier? I think so. In hindsight I believe that we should have proceeded more diligently in order to avoid finding ourselves in a crunch time position approaching the end of the negotiating period. In hindsight too, I don't think that we were sufficiently seized—certainly many of the critical stakeholders in this effort—I don't think that we were sufficiently seized of the implications of any new agreement with Europe and therefore, had we been more sensitized to this new adventure, perhaps we would have been better prepared for the negotiations themselves.

Some critics have argued that we did not have to sign and on that score I agree with them. We did not have to sign because there are choices. We could have made one of two choices. We could have eschewed any agreement if we felt that the agreement was not in the best interest of the Caribbean, of the region. We could have opted to enter upon trade with Europe determined by WTO rules which would have involved regional exports to Europe being subject to the general system of preferences. That was a choice. We could have looked that choice straight in the eye and determined whether or not, all things considered, that was a better arrangement for us.

Some critics say well, we could have applied for another waiver. Well, the truth is we couldn't have applied for a waiver because we would have had no *locus standi* under WTO rules it is the preference granting party and not the preference receiving party that has the option of making an application for a waiver. Based on clear signs that were given, the European Commission had no intention of going back to the WTO and even if they did, the chances of succeeding perhaps would have been as good as a snowball has of remaining a snowball in hell.

A third criticism is that we could have resigned ourselves going on the GSP arrangement but continue negotiations towards concluding a more appropriate agreement. My view and I offer this just as my own view, is that such an approach would have offered us—would have put us in a position to secure no better terms. I don't think that it would have given us any greater leverage. Indeed, it is possible that the disposition of the European Commission to continuing those negotiations would not have been as favourable as they would have been.

Two other points I want to mention very quickly in terms of recognizing some of the concerns that have been expressed. One is the argument that we have allowed access to our market in return for a continuation of access to the European market when we know that we have capacity limitations and will not be able to exploit the opportunities that access to the European market gives. My response to that Mr. Chairman is well whose responsibility is that? If we have a capacity problem whose job is it now to address that problem and to get that problem right? And more than that, forget about Europe. If we are going to stand up to competition which we have to face—not just in external markets but on our own supermarket shelves—then we are going to have to address our capacity deficiencies whether we enter into an agreement with Europe or not. If we are to survive, if we are to offer our people the opportunity for development and growth, we are going to have to address that capacity issue.

The other point finally before I move on, is an argument that the development chapter—the development component of the agreement—is weak. That is an issue I think we could probably debate for the next ten years. I do feel—again I am expressing a view which I hold very strongly—that in these negotiations, reserving our right not to enter upon an agreement—Europe has no obligations to offer us any development assistance in the same way we are not obliged to allow them duty-free quota-free access to our market. These are choices that we have. These are choices that Europe has. And therefore we can discuss the strength of the development component but simply to say that this is not a contingent liability in a trade negotiation. A trade agreement must be assessed on the basis of what it provides and the rights it conveys. It cannot be measured in terms of what development assistance it contains.

What is it that we have agreed to Mr. Chairman? In terms of goods, immediate duty-free quota-free access for all CARIFORUM exports to the EU with the exception of rice and sugar. Rice will enjoy duty-free quota-free access commencing in 2010 with increase quotas for duty-free quotas for 2008/2009. In so far as rice is concerned, the distinction that has been preserved between whole-grain and broken rice is to be eliminated. As far as sugar is concerned, it will enjoy duty-free quota-free access commencing in October of next year with increased tariff rate quotas of 60,000 tones—30,000 for CARICOM and 30,000 for the Dominican Republic—between now and then, and inter-regional reallocation of quotas in the event of delivery shortfall.

In terms of goods again, duty-free quota-free access of EU exports to CARIFORUM states but limited as follows. Four hundred and ninety-three items, amounting to 13 percent of CARIFORUM imports from the EU, will be permanently protected from tariff liberalization. These include fresh fruits and vegetables, dairy and cheese products, processed agricultural products, chemicals, furniture and industrial products. One of the points I think we need to note is that 75 percent of the agricultural imports which come in now from Europe will continue to be protected by tariff and have no sunset clause. Those will be protected in perpetuity. Secondly, I think we must note that the EU is required to eliminate export subsidies on all the agricultural products which we liberalize. That's the other 25 percent.

What are the tariff related commitments that CARIFORUM has made? It is important to appreciate where we are starting from. Our starting point is that up to the 31st of December without any EPA, 51 percent of the imports from Europe already attracted zero duty. 51 per cent! The ending point which is where EPA is intending to take us, will still leave us with 13 percent of imports from Europe being protected from liberalization. So that what is to be liberalized over the next 25 years is 36 percent—that's 51 percent plus the 13 that will not be liberalized, meaning no change to the status quo. The status quo change will affect 36 percent of our tariffs. In that, we have sought to phase the liberalization to give us space to make the adjustments that we will be required to make.

Immediately—in terms of additional liberalization—immediately upon coming into force of the agreement, we would liberalize 1.8 percent of imports which are regarded as nuisance tariff because they don't really impact upon our domestic economy. In the first five years another 3.2 replace; In the next five year another 8.3 replace; In the next five years which would take us up to the fifteen year basket, 21.7 replace, which amounts to 60 percent of the new tariff liberalization that has to be done. So, 60 percent of what we have to liberalize beyond what was liberalized from the very beginning, 60 percent of that is in the 15 year basket. In the 20 year basket we will liberalize another 1.9 percent and finally in the 25 year basket the final 2.3 percent which would bring us up to 87 percent liberalization—actually 86.9 replace.

So, there is no liberalization apart from the 1.8 percent of nuisance tariff. There is no liberalization for the first three years. Tariffs on revenue sensitive items such as gasoline, motor vehicles, motor vehicle parts, are to be phased out in years eight to ten and in so far as other duties and charges are concerned another major negotiating issue. Current ODCs are to be maintained for the first 7 years and then phased out in years eight to ten.

Finally on goods Mr. Chairman, during the first 3 years the EU is to exclude CARIFORUM exports from application of multilateral safeguard measures and employ constructive measures before imposing anti-dumping and countervailing duties. In regard to services, the EU will immediately liberalize 94 percent of the W120 list of sectors. The Dom. Rep. has committed to liberalizing 90replace, CARICOM MDC to liberalize 75 replace, CARICOM LDC to liberalize 65 replace. The Bahamas and Haiti are to submit their liberalization schedules within six months.

The EU is to grant access to CARIFORUM professionals in 29 sectors for Caribbean contractual service suppliers subject to them having secured contracts and limited to up to ninety days aggregated in any calendar year. This includes importantly entertainers for which a stout battle had to be fought and we have got acceptance of that to all EU countries with the exception of Belgium and Italy. The EU will also grant access to CARIFORUM professionals in eleven sectors for temporary entry. This has to do with CARIFORUM independent professionals or self-employed persons.

In the area of investment, reciprocal market access will be provided in most areas of agriculture and forestry, manufacturing, mining and service sectors. CARIFORUM has reserved protection for public services, utilities and other sensitive sectors. CARIFORUM will retain special protection for small and medium enterprises in specific sectors and special rules governing investment in tourism, e-commerce, courier services, telecommunications, financial services and maritime transport will apply.

A sticking point in the negotiations had to do with MSN treatment. The EU, the EC argued and insisted that the obligation should exist that would require us to extend to each other, us to them and them to us, similar treatment to that entered into by either party with a developing country that commands 1 percent or more of world's merchandise exports or, in the case of a bloc of developing countries 11/2 replace. This of course was in reaction to the fact that we do have some developing countries like China and Brazil that are major exporters and it was in a sense to square bracket them and to indicate that if we entered into trade agreements with them which were better that were contained in EPA, that those arrangements would also have to be extended to them. In so far as regional preferences are concerned the EU insisted that any concessions granted by CARIFORUM to the EU in goods and services must automatically be extended from one CARIFORUM state to another. We found it difficult to oppose that because that is certainly consistent with the principles of the CSME and indeed the principles of CARICOM. It does not preclude CARIFORUM states from granting to each other, terms that are more favourable than those granted to the EU.

The question of removing tariffs from EU imports circulating within CARIFORUM was another issue on which we were not able to reach agreement and therefore what we agreed to do was to use our best endeavours. We took that position because we do not yet have a CSME free circulation regime and we did not wish to compromise any decisions that we may make in the future in that regard.

No commitments were given relating to government procurement since we did not want to compromise the design and implementation of CSME government procurement regimes which remain a work-in-progress and which we anticipate will go far beyond anything that we might have to assume under the EPA arrangement.

Regarding the development chapter Mr. Chairman, while the EPA does not provide an indication of the levels of assistance that would be available to facilitate implementation, the commitments undertaken by CARIFORUM are in many instances conditioned upon delivery of such assistance. There are five sources of EU funding that are available to support the implementation of EPA. They are the national indicative programmes, the CARIFORUM regional indicative programme, the all ACP facility, the general budget of the EC and the aid for trade programme. CRIP constitutes a…the tenth CRIP amounts to €132 Million with the CARIFROUM Ministers having decided in October of last year to allocate 30 percent of CRIP to EPA implementation. That will be complemented by reserving all of the incentive tranche of the 33 Million, to EPA implementation.

The question of the…of the all ACP facility of €2.7 Billion which is also inserted in the ten EDF is a matter of concern because we did not—and it is an area of disappointment I found—we were not able to secure any commitments regarding the allocation from that fund to CARIFORUM. This is an all ACP facility and the further concern we have is that the disposition of the European Commission could well result in a bias being shown towards African countries because of their own stage of development and would work to our disadvantage. The modalities governing access to this facility are still being worked out and it is something that we need to pursue aggressively. But we need to put ourselves in a position where we can tap into this source which means that the projects that would qualify for assistance under that funding head are things that we have to pursue as a matter of urgency.

The status Mr. Chairman of—lets looks at a couple of issues—I will try to be as brief as I can. Among the things arising out of this experience has been the need for us to do an evaluation of the negotiating process that was used, the structures that were employed, the results that have been obtained and whether or not that represents the way forward in terms of future negotiations and what arrangements we need to put in place regarding implementation. This brings me to what is emerging as perhaps the most contentious issue and that has to do with the role of the CRNM.

The CRNM was established in 1996 by the Heads of Government acting in their wisdom. Questions have been raised about the status of the CRNM. As you know COTED commissioned a consultant evaluation of the process and among the issues that they raised was the legal status, whether it was a legal entity because it is not a Treaty-based defined entity. It was set up and it operated under the political direction of the Heads and was subject to supervision by the Prime Ministerial Sub-committee on External Trade Negotiation. It is an issue that has to be addressed and it may well be that the Heads may decide that this is an issue that is better addressed in caucus. But let me raise some general issues here. It needs to be addressed because there are inherent conflicts between the mandate of the CRNM and established Treaty-defined Community organs, COTED being one. In the case of COTED, COTED has special delegated authority to deal with things like tariffs that impact significantly on any trade agreement.

The complaint has been made and the independent consultants have pointed to what appeared to be a disconnect at times between the CRNM working in collaboration with the Heads of Government and COTED which complains that it was many instances left out of the loop. The observation was made in the discussion with the independent consultant that the level of supervision of the Prime Ministerial Sub-committee was less than what was required. Concerns have been raised for example about the funding of the CRNM and whether or not the sources of funds could have given the appearance if not the actuality of a compromising loyalty. Concern was expressed as well that the negotiating brief that was provided to the CRNM even though clearly defined, as the negotiations progressed and as they got into dealing with tight sticking point issues, that the negotiating briefs offered, fell into some level of ambiguity.

It is something that has to be addressed. I think it is a well known secret that there has been tension between the CRNM and the secretariat. I don't think that we can afford to enter upon any further negotiations until we confront that issue head on. It is something that I would suggest Mr. Chairman that perhaps the Heads in caucus need to focus on. Do we revisit that decisions that was made in 1996 to determine the value of that approach and to seek to resolve the matter dispassionately, devoid of emotion, respecting the Treaty and the institutions that are created thereby, but at the same time allowing for pragmatism and recognizing that one of the challenges that we have faced in the past has been how to execute decisions of the Community and to do so expeditiously and in a timely manner.

When you are entering upon trade negotiations you cannot afford to have ambivalence. Most importantly, you cannot effectively anchor those negotiations if there is uncertainty in the minds of the negotiators when they go to the negotiating table. So it is an issue that I believe has to be addressed.

In so far as the consultants reports were concerned which was engaged by COTED, they made a number of recommendations which the Heads will have to address. One is that the negotiating machinery must be Treaty-based with shared responsibility between the negotiating machinery, secretariat, COTED and other designated organs of the Community. It went further to suggest that the secretariat needs to be restructured to better manage the economic co-operation functions of the region and that these functions would have to include the implementation of trade agreements and they are suggesting that that should be assigned—should be placed under the directions of a single directorate headed by a Deputy Secretary General.

They went further to propose that the CRNM should be integrated into the restructured secretariat. They urged that we accelerate preparation for the implementation of EPA. They urge that we fast track the CSME implementation—let me just spend just a short moment on this.

The observation was made and I think that it has merit—that, CSME is in danger of being smothered under EPA because of how EPA was structured. EPA was not a negotiation between Europe and CARICOM. For the purpose of the negotiations the Dom. Rep. was included in the bargaining unit and therefore at the negotiating table it was not possible to give preeminence to a CARICOM position because our negotiating stance had to accommodate the interest of Dom. Rep. And the observation was made that one of the negative effects of this is that our own internal need to deepen our integration process to expand the reach of the CSME and to in fact carry out parts of the mandate that was given for the establishment and development of the CSME suffered, because we were now in this wider theatre of negotiations.

They also suggests in the consultants recommendations that greater care be taken to synchronize national and regional development objectives into future negotiations—the criticism having been made that a number of member states were not able, perhaps because of limitations in capacity or for other reasons, were not able to have their own national development strategies placed in the basket of issues that were going to be pursued in the negotiations.

Just two final points before I wrap up.

In terms of implementation we are at a stage now where we have some challenges. We have some important—some imperatives that we have to respond to. There are certain obligations under the EPA which require immediate action such as for example establishing the CARIFORUM/EC council, establishing the CARIFORUM/EC committee on trade and development, the CARIFORUM/EC parliamentary committee, the CARIFORUM/EC consultative committee. We on our side are required to establish national coordinators in each member state, as well as a regional CARIFORUM coordinator to help to manage the process of implementation. It was to that end that I took the liberty of asking the secretary general to prepare a road map for implementation, setting out the various obligations that have to be met, the legislative action that have to be taken, the administrative structures that have to be put in place. I thought it was necessary to do that—this was not a decision making enterprise or endeavour—it was simply asking the secretary general to prepare for our consideration and to assist us in making the appropriate decision—a schedule of the things that have to be done in order to give life to the agreement that we have signed. I do want to commend the secretary general because having reviewed that document myself I think it is a well prepared document that can assist us both collectively as actions that have to be taken by individual governments in order to actualize the provisions of the agreement.

We face challenges Mr. Chairman, let's be very clear. One of the things that have been said for example is that in terms of duty-free quota-free access we had that before so we have gained nothing more. My response to that is that we were about to lose it and therefore it is a question of retaining what we have enjoyed for a long time and were on the verge of losing. But duty-free quota-free access is not going to be of any value to us unless we can penetrate those markets. That is an area that I feel that we ought to turn our attention to in a very aggressive way. I believe that there are tremendous opportunities not only for local producers to seek to identify those areas of this vast market of 450 million people with an average per capita income of some US$17,000.00—not only do I believe that with the appropriate institutional arrangements and support, we have producers who can get in there. We may be able to find just a niche because I don't believe that we will ever be mass producers in that European market but, a niche of the right size in that market can put thousands of our people to work. It is a question of identifying those niches and seeing to what extent we can get ourselves up to the level of efficiency and productive competence to be able to penetrate those.

I think also that something that we have not seen enough of—and the blame perhaps has to be shared by both government and the private sector—but I have not seen enough efforts being made for private sector companies in the region to recognize that while they may be huge giants in their own territories, in terms of the world stage they are merely specks that can hardly be seen. One of the decisions that we are going to have to make within this region is whether we want to be whales in a swimming pool or we are prepared to be minnows in an ocean with the expectation that in that ocean there may be sufficient nutrients to enable us to grow. It is not so much a decisions it's a process. I have been surprised and impatient that somehow we don't seem to be moving in that direction. We perhaps need to look from the point of view of government and the institutional arrangements. Are we doing enough to facilitate, to induce, to encourage and we have to enter into dialogue with the private sector to find out now why is it that you seem intent on continuing to compete among yourself, sharing this limited economic space that we have in the region and in the process, instead of creating wealth, very often all of these good efforts are simply redistributing the poverty that we have so much of and which we want to get rid of. It is an issue that I really feel that we as a community need to address and to address in a serious way.

There is a third window of opportunity that if we handle it strategically, I believe can reap rich dividends. And that is to say to the foreign investment community that look, you want to get into Europe? Here is a place to set sail from. A big part of the success of Ireland was, when Ireland in joining the EU was able to join under preferential arrangements in terms of taxes, in terms of a whole host of concessions, they went out to the world and said now look, if you guys want to get into Europe the gateway to Europe—preferred gateway is Ireland. Because, if you come to Ireland and you set up your businesses in Ireland—lower taxes, lower this, lower that—and that was so much a part of what we now know as Irish miracle.

But I don't think it is something that is going to come about by our standing at the waving galleries of our airports and looking at the aircrafts coming in to see which foreign investors are deplaning. I do believe that we have to deliberately, in an organized structure strategic way, we need to go into the international capital market—the investor community—to go and promote and to sell the advantages that EPA offers and to see to what extent we can attract that kind of capital and that kind of investment into Jamaica.

Mr. Chairman if I have said I was going to close early and I didn't I apologize. One final point. One final, final point!

This is not the first, this is not the first trade agreement we have entered into. If we do a clinical examination of the previous ones, our benefits have fallen far short of the promise that they offered. Was that because the agreements were bad? Or was it because our own response to the opportunities there was lethargic? I mean, you look at CBI for example, it certainly has not provided us with the benefits that we had anticipated. You look at CARIBCAN you can say the same thing. So, we have a questionable tradition of having agreements but somehow not being able to absorb the benefits that the agreements offer. We need to look very clinically at ourselves to find out why we didn't. We have a number of other negotiations that are scheduled. There is disagreement as to the speed with which we should enter upon those agreements.

The independent consultants have in fact proposed that in fact we should list them in some order of priority. They have proposed Canada first, Dom. Rep. second, USA third, Costa Rica fourth, Central America fifth. As far as the Jamaican delegation is concerned we have slightly different views in terms of the order of priority. Those are matters that we need to discuss and to determine. We know of the initiative being taken by Congressman Rangel which Prime Minister Spencer brought us up to date on. We are called upon to have a presence in several theatres at the same time. It is going to put strain on our negotiating capacity. I think that we have built up considerable capacity coming out of EPA and whatever may the criticisms we make of the CRNM I do feel that the CRNM is an institution of which we can be proud and I think that they have performed. As to how they ought to be configured within the CARICOM structure is something I believe the Heads will have to examine.

My colleague is saying I am so ethnocentric that I spoke of about attracting investors to Jamaica. I didn't mean to offend but I hope that Jamaica gets some of it. So, we need to examine that because Canada is anxious to start and I am concerned as to whether or not it is in our interest to set our own timetable because we have to determine whether or not that agreement is in our interest. If it is not in our interest then we can hold back. If it is in our interest, then I don't think that we should put them on indefinite hold.

There is the US situation which is tied up with Congressman Rangel's initiatives and there are of course other negotiating commitments that we have closer within the region. We need to take decisions on those, but before we embark on that we have to reconcile and clarify the ambiguities and uncertainties regarding our negotiating machinery.

I thank you Mr. Chairman.

CHAPTER 3

Negotiation by CARIFORUM Regional Cooperation

The CARIFORUM was the first group of ACP countries to complete negotiations for an EPA with the EU and the only group to accomplish this task. There are many reasons that explain this achievement, among the most important of which was the successful cooperation among the small developing countries of CARIFORUM. Central to the cooperation among CARIFORUM states in the negotiations was the operation of the CRNM, a model of cooperation among developing countries that warrant analysis by practitioners of trade policy and trade negotiations. The lessons learnt from the role and operation of the CRNM during the conduct of CARIFORUM's negotiations for an EPA with the EU can be valuable to other developing countries.

Context

Origins

The idea of international and regional cooperation and integration dates back to the nineteenth century and attempts to achieve them date back nearly as far. In the Caribbean, the formal process of integration had its beginnings in the failed attempt at political federation. The West Indies Federation was established in 1958 and lasted until 1962. In 1968, the goal of Caribbean integration received new impetus with the formation of the CARIFTA. In 1970, the Caribbean Development Bank was established. In 1973, the CARICOM were established by the Treaty of Chaguaramas, and the CARICOM Secretariat was also created within that year. By the Treaty of Basseterre in 1981, the Organization of Eastern Caribbean States (OECS) was formed as a subregional entity. The decision was taken in 1989 to deepen economic integration by the establishment of the CSME.

The formal process of integration was predated by several informal arrangements and the practice among the Commonwealth Caribbean territories of cooperating as a group, which resulted in common practices, culture, and traditions as an accepted part of Caribbean affairs. The impetus within the region for collaboration and cooperation was reinforced by the British and US governments' habit of dealing with the territories of the region as a group. The common laws, institutions, and language established by the British over 300 years of colonial rule meant that there was a commonality that made it easier to cooperate and to feel a spirit of community. Intergovernmental and private regional institutions aimed at facilitating cooperation in a wide range of fields preceded the formal institutions of integration. Notable examples are the West Indies Cricket Team, dating back to the 1930s, and the University of the West Indies, which was established in 1948.

Objectives

The objectives of CARICOM are set out in Article 4 of the Revised Treaty of Chaguaramas and are based on the following three pillars:

1. economic integration through a common market and common trade policies;
2. functional cooperation (pooling of resources and sharing of services in the area of human and social development); and
3. coordination of foreign policies (presenting a united front in its relations with countries outside the grouping).

In 1989, CARICOM commenced the process aimed at establishing the CSME. The objective was to go beyond facilitating the liberalization of intraregional trade for the creation of a single economic space regional trade, production, and investment. Twenty years after the commencement of the CSME process, virtually all intraregional trade is unimpeded by barriers,[1] but the other aspects of the CSME are not yet a reality. There is still a plethora of restrictions on capital mobility, movement of labor, provision of services, and the rights of establishment of enterprises.[2] The "implementation deficit" in attaining free movement of goods, services, persons, and capital is estimated at 50 percent,[3] and much is still to be done to achieve a harmonization of laws. The current target date for completion of the CSME is 2015.

The objectives of the CSME are as follows:

1. to strengthen, coordinate, and regulate economic and trade relations among member states and to stimulate their harmonious and balanced development;
2. to promote continued expansion and integration of economic activities and to share equitably the benefits arising from such activities, paying particular attention to the need to provide special opportunities for the less developed countries (LDCs); and
3. to work toward achieving a greater measure of economic independence and effectiveness of member states in their dealings with other states and groups of states.

During the mid-1990s, the CARICOM member states became simultaneously engaged in negotiations in the WTO, the FTAA, an EPA with the EU, and exploring bilateral trade agreements with a view to efficiently and effectively servicing these three negotiating arenas. CARICOM established the CRNM in 1997, with the motive of increasing the bargaining power of the small states of the Caribbean in international fora and external negotiations such as those related to trade. Article 6 (g) of the Revised Treaty of Chaguaramas, which establishes the CSME, states that one of the key objectives of the Community is "the achievement of a greater measure of economic leverage and effectiveness of Member states in dealing with third States, groups of states and entities of any description."[4]

Membership

The member states of CARICOM are Antigua and Barbuda, the Bahamas, Barbados, Belize, Dominica, Grenada, Guyana, Haiti, Jamaica, St. Kitts and Nevis, St. Lucia, St. Vincent and the Grenadines, Suriname, and Trinidad and Tobago. The CSME includes all the countries of CARICOM, except the Bahamas.

Characteristics

The member states differ in size, per capita income, and language as reflected in table 3.1.

Rationale for Regional Cooperation

The rationale for regional cooperation among small developing countries to negotiate external trade agreements and in the WTO is as follows.

Table 3.1 CARICOM economic indicators

Country	*Population thousands*	*Land area (km²)*	*GDP, current prices, billions US dollars*		*Per capita GDP US dollars*
			2008	*2009 (e)*	
Antigua and Barbuda	84	442	1.3	1.3	84
The Bahamas	337	38,608	7.5	7.3	337
Barbados	276	431	3.7	3.8	276
Belize	320	22,966	1.4	1.4	320
Dominica	72	750	0.4	0.4	72
Grenada	106	345	0.6	0.7	106
Guyana	764	216,970	1.1	1.2	764
Haiti	8,786	27,750	7	7	8,786
Jamaica	2,699	10,991	14.4	12.8	2,699
Montserrat	5	103	0.05 –2007		5
St. Kitts and Nevis	53	269	0.6	0.6	53
St. Lucia	170	616	1	1	170
St. Vincent & Grens.	107	389	0.6	0.6	107
Suriname	533	163,820	3	3.3	533
Trinidad and Tobago	1,305	5,182	24.8	25	1,305

Source: IMF-WEO and CARICOM Secretariat.

Enhancement of Negotiating Leverage

Small countries exercise limited influence in trade negotiations because their small national markets and insignificant share of world trade provides little or no leverage in bargaining. One of the principal benefits of regional cooperation among small developing countries in trade negotiations is enhancing the leverage that comes from operating as a coherent group instead of as individual states. By operating as a group, small developing countries can reduce the asymmetries encountered in bilateral negotiations with larger, more powerful countries or groups of countries. The group approach is also helpful in multilateral trade negotiations. The decision-making process in the WTO, while formally by consensus, is in reality dominated by a small number of developed countries.[5] Consensus does not mean unanimity but usually means that (1) no country present in the meeting strongly objects to the proposed decision and (2) one or a few member states cannot block decisions "unless it happened to one of the major trading nations."[6] This decision-making rule gives small developing countries operating as cohesive groups the ability to exert greater influence than they would individually.

Through collective advocacy and negotiating as a cohesive group, CARICOM was able to initiate and exercise leadership on the issue of "small economies" in the FTAA process and on "small vulnerable developing countries" in the WTO. In both instances, it was successful in having language included in the draft text of the FTAA and the Ministerial Declaration of the WTO ministerial meeting in Hong Kong in December 2005. By operating as a group, CARICOM has also become a more attractive strategic ally for other countries or groups of countries.

More Effective Participation

Often small developing countries find the costs of participating in the negotiation and adjudication of rules in the multilateral trading system (MTS) very costly. Indeed, many governments in small countries—especially those that are developing or least developed—regard the cost of full and sustained participation as prohibitive. By pooling their human and financial resources and cooperating, CARICOM countries have become more effective participants in the multilateral trading system. Their presence has become more consistent and effective through sharing representational duties and preparatory technical work.

The member states of CARICOM, like other small developing countries, need to pool their human resources in order to engage effectively with larger countries, especially developed countries whose capacities for trade negotiations are far larger. To illustrate, the trade section of the ministry of foreign affairs and foreign trade ministry of Trinidad and Tobago has a staff of 12, while in Dominica and St. Kitts and Nevis the entire trade and foreign affairs ministry employs four officials. Because they have to handle all trade matters, they are "generalists" who find it difficult and at times impossible to respond on specific technical issues such as rules of origin for the EPA.

By way of comparison, the Office of the US Trade Representative has a technical staff of around 120. Canada's Department for Foreign Affairs and International Trade has some 100 professionals working on the negotiation and implementation of the country's trade agreements. The European Commission's Directorate for Trade, which conducts EU trade policy under the direction of EU Trade Commissioner, has more than 300 full-time technical staff.[7]

Meeting the Cost of Representation

One of the most important limitations on the effective participation of developing countries in international trade negotiations is the very serious constraints on their capacity of small developing countries to send representatives to meetings. Individual small developing countries like those in CARICOM are unable to adequately carry out their representational duties because of their small institutional capacity, limited human resources, and financial constraints, for example, their attendance at the WTO. Many small developing countries and LDCs do not have representation based in Geneva; consequently, attendance is periodically by way of their representatives from diplomatic missions in Brussels, Bonn, Paris, and London. This was the situation faced by the countries of CARICOM, of which only three have ambassadorial-level representation at the WTO, namely Barbados, Jamaica, and Trinidad and Tobago. The other countries have accredited their ambassadors in London, Brussels, and in the case of Antigua and Barbuda, their ambassador to the United Nations in New York. The smallest countries in the region that have established the OECS have combined to have joint representation by a technical mission funded by the Commonwealth Secretariat and international donors[8] in an arrangement similar to the establishment of the Pacific Island Forum[9] mission to the WTO in March 2004 with five years of funding from the EU.[10]

Even where there is representation, the average small developing country has 1.2 persons attempting to cover the myriad of issues in the various bodies of the WTO.[11] It is impossible to cover the approximately 1,200 meetings per year.[12] In some weeks, there are as many as 50 meetings scheduled by the WTO, not including numerous informal consultations. The one-person missions make it impractical for small country representatives to serve as chairs of bodies and committees of the WTO, which further diminishes the influence of small developing countries. In these circumstances, the CRNM established a two-person technical mission housed in one of the member state embassies. The team functioned as (1) a conduit of information between the CRNM and the member states at the WTO. It sent to the CRNM head offices reports on the discussions in Geneva and briefed member states on the technical advice from the CRNM. (2) The CRNM representative attended meetings, provided on-the-spot technical advice and (3) assisted in forging consensus proposals and common negotiating positions among the representatives of member states.

Regional cooperation is a way of overcoming the inadequacy of participation, which derived from insufficient human and financial resources to enable member states to attend all pertinent meetings. By sharing the representational duties and common representation, the cost to each country was reduced.

Enhancing Technical and Institutional Capacity

The small and very limited institutional capacity of small developing economies severely constrains their ability to conduct technical work, formulate negotiating positions, and increase and maintain an expanded institutional capacity for trade policy formulation and strategies for negotiation. In some small states, the ministry responsible for trade or the department for international trade in a ministry responsible for several subjects is as small as three officials. Apart from inadequately staffed trade ministries, some "small island developing states" also suffer from inadequate computer and communications equipment, lack of resources to conduct systematic outreach to stakeholders, constrained information gathering and dissemination, and insufficient access to training and research.

Regional cooperation is a solution to limited institutional capacity providing for more collaboration, and the sharing and rationalization of resource use among small developing economies. One approach that can facilitate better participation is for groups of countries to combine their human and financial resources. This cooperation can take a variety of forms, ranging from collaboration for common positions to joint statements. All too infrequently small developing countries form common entities to undertake technical work, formulate shared positions, coordinate negotiating strategies, and execute joint representation. Collaborative institutions and joint representation are made easier if the countries are in close physical proximity, for example, Central America, or are in a regional integration scheme such as CARICOM.

Improving the Prospects for Strategic Alliances

When they operate as a coherent group, small developing economies become more attractive partners for strategic negotiation alliances. Both groups of countries and individual countries are more willing to seek and maintain alliances with groups of small countries than with individual small states. In fact, small developing cannot get meetings with powerful, influential, or developed countries unless they form a group. At a WTO ministerial, the United States or the EU will not meet an individual CARICOM country but will meet the group or a spokesperson for the group.

Caribbean Regional Negotiating Machinery

The CRNM was established in 1997 by the CARICOM Governments to be the principal regional intergovernmental organization mediating the Caribbean's encounter with the multilateral trading system. The CRNM was charged with the responsibility for coordinating and spearheading a cohesive, coherent, and comprehensive international trade policy, both strategically as well as on technical issues under negotiation. The specific mandate of the CRNM was to develop and maintain an effective framework for the coordination and management of the Caribbean's external trade negotiating resources and expertise. The CRNM was designed to help Member States maximize the benefits of participating in global trade negotiations.

Membership

The Member States of the CRNM included the following countries: Antigua and Barbuda, the Bahamas, Barbados, Belize, Cuba, Dominica, the Dominican Republic,

Grenada, Guyana, Haiti, Jamaica, St. Kitts and Nevis, St. Lucia, St. Vincent and the Grenadines, Suriname, and Trinidad and Tobago. The CRNM serviced the CARIFORUM group of countries, which is CARICOM plus the Dominican Republic and CARICOM is the countries in the CSME plus the Bahamas.

Objectives

The small developing economies of the Caribbean Community when faced with the unprecedented task of simultaneous negotiations in the WTO and with the EU as well as several bilateral initiatives decided to establish a single regional organization to assist the member states in their external trade negotiations. The purpose of the CRNM is to assist member states in maximizing the benefits of participation in global trade negotiations by

1. providing sound technical advice;
2. Facilitating the generation of national and regional positions;
3. Coordinating the formulation of a cohesive negotiating strategy; and
4. leading negotiations where appropriate.

Functions

To attain its mandated objectives, the CRNM carried out the following functions:

1. Consultations and formulation of regional negotiating positions: Ensuring maximum effectiveness to be obtained from presence at negotiating arenas by facilitating the involvement of national and regional resource groups/individuals in the development of strategies through the use of information technology, convening of TWGs, and preparation of technical papers.
2. Representation in negotiating forums to ensure that the region is present at the negotiating table so that its interests are reflected in the content of agreements.
3. Building of regional negotiating capacity to ensure technical capacity, and trade negotiation skills are developed and sustained in the region.
4. Research and studies to enable provision of appropriate advice on strategies to negotiating teams by identifying and addressing knowledge gaps and needs through technical research and analysis.
5. Strengthening technical and professional capacity of the both CRNM and member states to effectively support the negotiating teams by identifying needs and mobilizing human and financial resources to achieve the region's goals.

Negotiating Theatres

The CRNM was simultaneously involved on behalf of its member states in a several negotiating arenas. The agenda of trade negotiation was the most formidable undertaken by the region up to that time, in both scope and complexity. The negotiating theatres in which the CRNM was involved were as follows:

1. the WTO
2. the EPA with the EU
3. the FTAA, and
4. bilateral negotiations mainly with Canada.

Governance

The governance structure established by the CARICOM heads of governments called for reporting to the COTED, which provided CRNM with guidance and its negotiating mandate. The DG and the CRNM were also required to report directly the Caribbean heads of government through the Prime Ministerial Committee on External Negotiations. Financial oversight of the CRNM was carried out by a Finance Committee, which comprised representatives of some member states, a representative of the CARICOM Secretariat, and the CRNM DG and director of finance and administration.

Organization Chart

The CRNM was headquartered in Jamaica, whose prime minister holds prime ministerial responsibility within CARICOM for external negotiations. Barbados housed the CRNM's suboffice, and the CRNM also maintained presence in the OECS in St. Lucia, as well as in the Co-operative Republic of Guyana, the Republic of Trinidad and Tobago, Brussels, and Geneva.

The CRNM management team was composed of a director-general, who as head had overall responsibility and a senior directorwith responsibility for the technical work of the organization. A Director, Technical Co-operation, Partnerships and Information,, had responsibility for relations with international development partners (IDPs) and the overall management of grant agreements. A Director, Finance and Administration is responsible for budget finance and administration matters. The staff consisted entirely of citizens of the CARIFORUM countries who were experts in the various issues, which were the subject of the negotiations.

The CRNM deployed representatives in Brussels, Geneva, Georgetown, and Port-of-Spain and provided technical support staff to some member states and subregional organizations, including the Secretariat of the OECS. The Geneva-based team of two technicians provided day-to-day support to the CARIFORUM permanent missions including attending meetings with the resident CARIFORUM Permanent Representatives and preparing technical reports.

Funding

The costs of the activities carried out by the CRNM were beyond the limited financial resources of its member states. Therefore, more than half of its budget has traditionally been sourced as grants from bilateral and multilateral development partners. Grant funding has been used to support technical work, as well as the retention of expertise in required areas, studies, and call-down expertise. During the negotiations with the EU, resources from various European agencies and institutions were indispensable to meeting the cost of conducting over 30 TWGs over a three-year period. Some of the resources also enabled officials of the smallest countries to attend meetings.

The following is an indicative list of regional partners and international development partners that have provided support to CRNM, either through grant funding, grant assistance, or call-down expertise:

Asia, Caribbean, and Pacific (ACP) Secretariat
Canada—Canadian International Development Agency (CIDA)
Caribbean Community (CARICOM) Secretariat
Caribbean Development Bank (CDB)
Commonwealth Secretariat (COMSEC)
European Union (EU)
Federal Republic of Germany—Deutsche Gesellschaft für Technische Zusammenarbeit (GTZ)
Food and Agriculture Organization (FAO)
Inter-American Development Bank (IDB)
Inter-American Institute for Cooperation on Agriculture (IICA)
International Lawyers and Economists Against Poverty (ILEAP)
International Trade Centre (ITC)
Organization of American States (OAS)
Organization of Eastern Caribbean States (OECS)
United Kingdom of Great Britain and Northern Ireland—Department for International Development and Co-operation (Caribbean) (DFIDC)
United States of America—Agency for International Development (USAID)
University of the West Indies (UWI)
United Nations Conference on Trade and Development (UNCTAD)
United Nations Economic Commission for Latin America and the Caribbean (UN-ECLAC)
World Bank World Intellectual Property Organization (WIPO)
World Trade Organization (WTO)

Operation

The CARIFORUM region, despite its size and financial constraints, deployed a world-class team of negotiators utilizing the technical advice of the CRNM directed by mandates stipulated by the heads of government and supervised by trade ministers. The negotiating positions were formulated by and through transparent and intensive consultative processes involving TWGs with participation from member states, regional institutions, the private sector, academics, technical experts, and civil society. CARIFORUM Heads of Governments were at the apex of the structure of negotiation, which involved a combination of political, diplomatic, and technical levels. This is illustrated in figure 3.1.

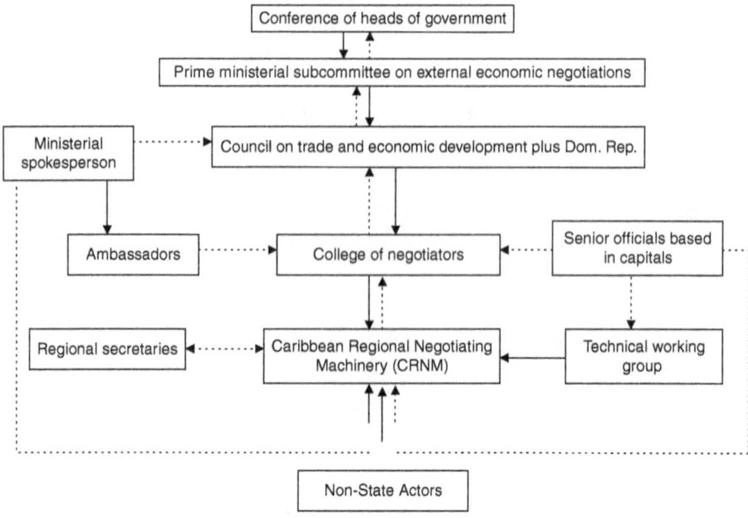

Figure 3.1 Policymaking and reporting structure of the CRNM.

The actual technical negotiations were undertaken by a team of trade experts drawn on merit from member states and all sectors of society. They were guided by a principal negotiator working in close collaboration with the minister designated with responsibility for the negotiations, and they in turn had access to the prime minister charged with the responsibility for external negotiations. The immediate political supervision of the negotiations was carried out by the CARIFORUM Council of Trade Ministers, which consisted of CARICOM's COTED and the ministerial representative of the Dominican Republic. The actual technical negotiations were conducted by a College of Negotiators.

The technical work to inform the discussions of negotiating positions was prepared by the technical staff of the CRNM, and supplemented where deemed necessary through papers and studies prepared by experts from academia and international organizations from within and beyond the Caribbean. These technical inputs formed the basis for discussion within the TWGs. Participation in the TWGs also included technical experts from the CRNM, officials from regional organizations such as the CARICOM Secretariat, OECS Secretariat, as well as senior government officials (figure 3.2).

The combined inputs of the participating stakeholder groups obtained from the national consultations and from the TWGs were fed into formulating the overall strategy, which was implemented by a College of Negotiators that included CRNM technical staff. The College was composed of Lead and Alternate Lead negotiators for each of the negotiating issues, and consisted of the best technical expertise available to the region. Its composition had to be approved by the CARIFORUM Council of Ministers. The negotiators were recommended by the dean of the College after consultations and careful review of their skill and experience. Regional balance and conflicts of interests were also taken into account. Governments also did not have the right to nominate whomever they wished, nor was size of country a consideration.

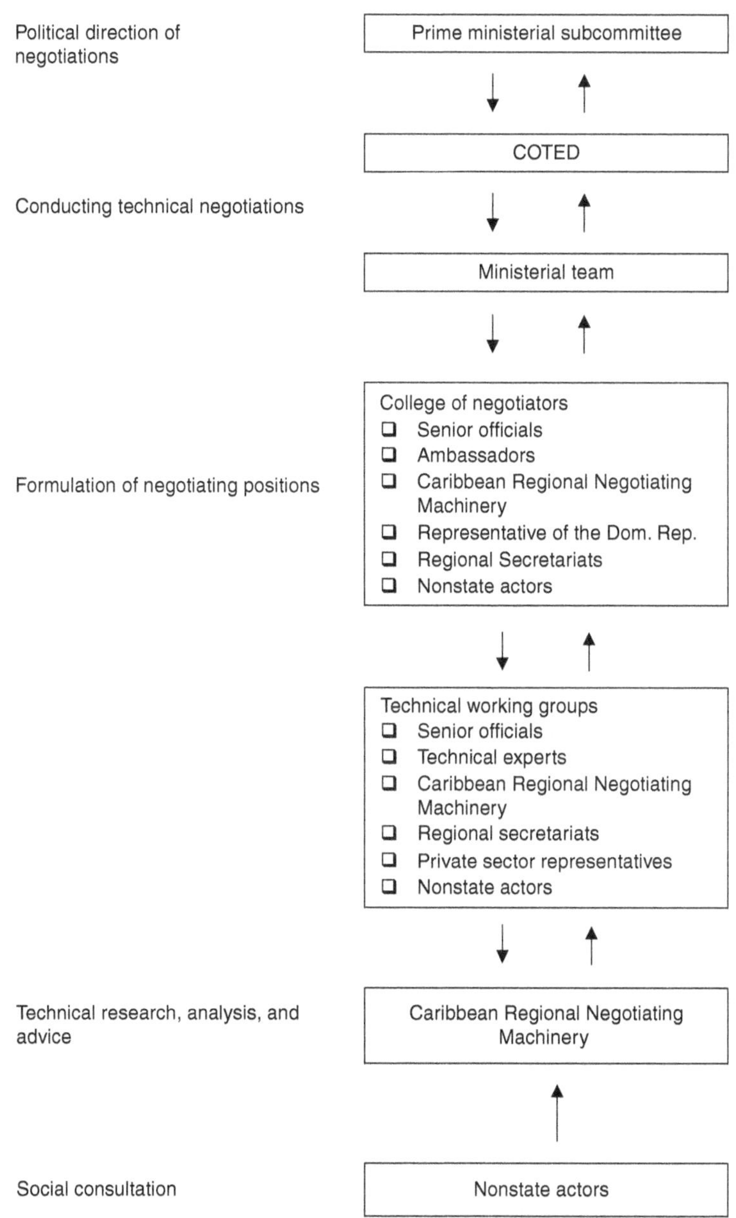

Figure 3.2 Role of CRNM in negotiations.

The primary objective of the College of Negotiators was to devise a negotiating strategy and to ensure the coherence of the region's positions as the negotiations progressed. The College's harmonized strategy recommendations were referred to the COTED and the CARIFORUM Council of Ministers for review and consideration. These institutions determined the negotiating mandate with the authority of

CARIFORUM Heads of Government. The approval of strategy and final positions, therefore, lay firmly within the ambit of the Region's elected representatives.

This process of review ensured, among other things, that the negotiating positions took account of the interests of all member states, including the Dominican Republic, and that the positions were not at variance with the agenda of the CARICOM integration process as outlined in the Revised Treaty of Chaguaramas. To this end, a number of Special COTEDs on External Trade Negotiations and CARIFORUM ministerial meetings were convened. Those meetings repeatedly considered and refined the region's positions as the negotiations evolved.

Outreach to Stakeholders

To complement the consultative processes, a parallel process of in-country and regional consultations was also facilitated and coordinated by the CRNM.

1. A concerted effort to provide timely information to the region's business sectors and to ascertain through dialogue, the objectives of exporters and importers. The engagement with the business sector took place through training sessions, in-person presentations, specially prepared written briefings, and by eliciting submissions. The Private Sector Outreach Programme of the CRNM provided the business sector with a systematic opportunity to participate in a comprehensive series of training workshops and consultation sessions. The building of knowledge capacity was further aided by weekly regional radio broadcasts of "*Caribbean Trade Beat*." Special nontechnical briefs were also prepared and distributed by e-mail to close to 1,000 recipients and were posted on the CRNM website.
2. Workshops for the regional media were held to sensitize journalists on various trade issues, with the goal of improving the extent and quality of coverage of trade in the various branches of the media.
3. Extensive consultation also took place with civil society, NGOs, trade unions, and other NSAs. The initiative for dialogue originated from both civil society and from the CRNM, and helped secure views that were considered in the formulation of the trade negotiating agenda.

Output

The CRNM between 1997 and 2009 successfully fulfilled its functions and delivered significant results, including the CARIFORUM-EU EPA, the most comprehensive Caribbean trade agreement ever negotiated. The CRNM performed a vital role in all of the region's external trade negotiations. These were as follows:

1. Cotonou Agreement
2. CARICOM-Cuba Trade and Economic Co-operation Agreement
3. CARICOM-DR Free Trade Agreement
4. FTAA
5. CARIFORUM-EU EPA

6. WTO-Doha Development Agenda
7. CARICOM-Canada Trade Agreement
8. CARICOM-US Trade and Investment Council
9. Initial exchanges with MERCOSUR on possible negotiations for an FTA
10. Possible CARICOM-Costa Rica Agreement

The CRNM carried a variety of activities in trade negotiations and these varied depending on the negotiations and the mandates given to it by the political leadership. Among the activities were the following:

1. technical work on all subjects relevant to its negotiation mandate, including negotiations anticipated by the region;
2. technical coordination among the states it services;
3. consultations with nationally and regionally organized sector and industry groups, as well as a wide range of nongovernmental entities;
4. tabling negotiating proposals for approval at various decision-making levels, and ensuring coherence across the various negotiating arenas;
5. coordinating those negotiations under its mandate through the College of Negotiators, as well as leading them at the Principal Negotiators' level;
6. collaborating with the CARICOM and OECS Secretariats in a broad range of areas, including in those negotiations that CRNM has not been specifically mandated to lead;
7. interacting with ambassadors and other representatives of Caribbean states in capitals where negotiations take place;
8. training national officials and potential negotiators;
9. providing technical assistance to Caribbean states, the private sector and other relevant bodies, as well as to requesting ACP states;
10. communication and information dissemination;
11. building relationships and confidence with the donor community to secure funding;
12. performing representation functions in various regional and extra-regional forums;
13. providing technical support to, and accompanying ministerial spokespersons on, various missions (e.g., EPA lobbying in European capitals, WTO Mini-Ministerial meetings outside of Geneva);
14. interacting with representatives of various regions (e.g., African and Pacific groups) and countries;
15. collaborating with a range of international institutions for information and technical exchange; and
16. providing negotiators from lead negotiator to technical negotiators in specific subjects.

Lessons Learned

The experience of the CRNM demonstrates that regional institutions can be effective and that they can make a meaningful contribution to the realization of the goals of regionalism by the successful conduct of external trade negotiations. It is useful to other developing countries that might need to collaborate in external trade negotiations to extract the lessons of the experience of the CRNM. It could be invaluable in time and money not to have to learn the hard way. The lessons learnt from the experience of the CRNM are the following:

Consensus-building Is Critical

The member states of CARICOM differ in size, economic structure, rates of economic growth,[13] level of development, economic policy, and institutional capacity. GDP ranges from US$460 per capita in Haiti to US$16,691 per capita in the Bahamas; the population of St. Kitts and Nevis is 42,000, and that of Haiti is 8.1 million.[14] These kinds of differences complicate the operation of regional institutions such as the CRNM because they make the formulation of common positions in external trade negotiations more difficult. These differences are rooted in differences in national interests that arise from different real economic interests, divergent economic policies, and goals. Misplaced nationalism, economic xenophobia about ownership, and the assumption that locally owned firms have a higher propensity to reinvest their profits in their domicile have stymied the free movement of capital and labor, thereby depriving firms of means of improving their efficiency.

At the operational level of interaction, the negotiators and technicians have devoted the necessary time to develop trust, explain issues, and canvass the thinking of ministers of government, government officials, the business sector, civil society organizations, and interested parties of all sorts. This can be time consuming, especially if travel is involved, but is absolutely essential. Trust, information sharing, and good communications depend on "face time" and personal relations.

Concerted Political Will

There must be the necessary political will among the governments if regional institutions are to be created, empowered, and properly governed. In the absence of concerted, resolute, and united political will, regional institutions will be undermined because they will not receive the promised financial contributions, their decisions will be ignored, and their authority will be compromised. A united expression of political will is most likely to exist where there is a common vision, where there are drivers external to the political arena and where there is a shared sense of urgencies. The existence of these commonalities overrides the inevitable differences of goals, processes, and timing. There is also the intangible of leadership, which if it exists in quality and vigor is invaluable, but its occurrence is purely fortuitous.

Delegation of Authority to Regional Trade Body

The extent to which member states are willing to yield national sovereignty to gain enhanced collective regional sovereignty has a major effect on the operations of regional institutions. A critical weakness in CARICOM has been the lack of legal enforcement effectiveness of decisions and lack of implementation capacity. The current institutional arrangements vest the locus of decision making in the governments of the individual nation-states. This constitutes intergovernmental cooperation in which there is very limited transfer of sovereignty to supranational regional institutions and bodies. Implementation is at the discretion of governments and the record demonstrates that it has been very difficult to accomplish the actions required to achieve implementation. The existing arrangements and practices do not encourage the member states to yield sovereignty, which is in contrast to the EU where the institutional arrangements provide for supranational decision making and legislative authority.

The "paradox of sovereignty" is that a greater degree of effective sovereignty is attainable by each member country only through surrender to the regional collectivity of some of its formal national sovereignty. Belatedly the inadequacies of the current institutional arrangements have been recognized by the CARICOM Heads of Government and it is proposed that decisions on a new structure will be made in the immediate future based on the recommendations of the Prime Ministerial Expert Group on Regional Governance.

Efficiency of Regional Governance

The costs of political governance of regional processes, operating regional institutions, and implementing decisions to give effect to regional goals can be considerable for small or poor developing states. This constraint is compounded when there has been a proliferation of regional institutions. The human and financial costs of regional decision-making processes and the operations of a plethora of regional institutions can place a considerable strain on member states, especially the smallest ones. Financing the operational costs will depend on both the resources of member states and development assistance from extra-regional sources.

Public Awareness and Support

Regional institutions will find it easier to operate when there is strong public support and this is only possible if the public understands the goals and operations of the regional institution. There is a widespread lack of awareness or inadequate knowledge of regional institutions and policies. In many instances, regional institutions and national governments have to mount extensive and intensive public education campaigns. There is a considerable lack of public awareness about the CSME among, for example, 65 percent of Jamaicans have never heard of the CSME.[15] Many in the business sector, who will be most directly and immediately affected, do not evince the type of resolute commitment to the CSME that might energize the process of implementation. A survey of CEOs of Caribbean companies revealed that only one in ten CEOs expected increased global competitiveness to be one of the benefits forthcoming from the completion of the CSME.[16] This is disturbing because one of the objectives of the CSME is to improve competitiveness to the point where Caribbean firms can survive and thrive in the global marketplace. The prime minister of St. Lucia, Dr. Kenny Anthony, has bemoaned the need to "shorten the distance between the hallowed halls of regionalism and the fallow footprints of popular aspiration."[17]

Nonpolitical Drivers

Regional trade negotiating institutions are likely to operate more effectively if they are driven by factors additional to the vision of governments. These include (1) deadlines established and agreed to, for example, the EPA, (2) a genuine sense that external trade can promote development, (3) corporate integration demanding deeper market integration, and (4) intraregional trade liberalization.

In many instances of successful external trade negotiations, the driving force, after the initial conception by governments, has been the business sector. In Western Europe, the impetus to deepen the integration process through the creation of a common market and on toward an economic union, including a common currency, emanated from the desire of firms for a larger market and the free movement of factors of production. Similar impulses lay behind the establishment of the NAFTA and the MERCOSUR. In the EU and NAFTA, it was changes in business organization, the expanded size of firms, and the pursuit of economies of scale and scope that propelled governments to strive to create, as quickly as possible, a single economic space.

In the case of CARICOM, it was governments that envisioned the regional market and have endeavored to deepen regional integration in the hope of spurring a transformation of the size, structure, and operations of locally owned firms. In the CARICOM integration process, corporate integration through strategic alliances, mergers, and takeovers is a recent and nascent development.[18]

Avoiding Parallel Bureaucracies

The existence of parallel bureaucracies in which the respective roles are not clearly demarcated leads to duplication and inertia. This issue relates to (1) the roles of separate regional institutions and (2) between national and regional institutions. The role and authority of the regional institutions must to be clear and unambiguous and even then there can be resistance at the national levels. The extent to which the duplication of institutions at the national and regional levels can be avoided will reduce the costs of the operations of a regional institution charged with executing external trade negotiations. In CARIFORUM, external trade policy was the responsibility of national ministries of trade and the CRNM. These collaborated with the CARICOM Secretariat and the OECS Secretariat to ensure coherence and consistency with the regional and sub-regional integration processes. Coordination of regional institutions is complicated by the work of specialized regional organization. These sector- or interest-specific regional organizations e.g. the Caribbean Tourism organization, can enrich the preparation of negotiating positions and provide valuable advice to negotiators, but it is essential to avoid duplication of work and to make a concerted effort to ensure harmonization of positions.

Sound Financial Basis for Regional Institutions

Regional institutions must be placed on a secure financial basis if they are to operate effectively. The CRNM was never on a secure financial foundation and was continually having to mobilize funds from outside the member states of CARIFORUM. External funding accounted for more than half of the CRNM's budget and the reporting obligations were onerous even, when they were coordinated reporting formats for donors. Specialized staff had to be employed to service relations with international donors and international organizations. It is ideal for the regional external trade negotiating body to be funded entirely by the member states. If this is difficult for groups of developing countries to accomplish, then resort should be made to multilateral donors that are not directly involved with negotiations. The CRNM was able to draw on resources from the Inter-American Development Bank and the Commonwealth Secretariat.

CRNM as a Model

Developing countries do not have the luxury of complacency about the pace of change in international trade matters and the negotiations which are necessary to cope with the challenges of the subject matter and more importantly, have their interests adequately realized. Small developing economies have demonstrated that they can produce goods and services that are internationally competitive, but this is a necessary but not sufficient condition. They require good and secure access to external markets so as to increase and diversify their exports. International trade agreements can be vehicles for accelerating the process of economic development but only if they provide suitable terms. This in turn depends on the quality of the negotiations conducted on their behalf.

Why does the region take for granted that it can and will produce world-class performers and indeed world champions in sports and the creative arts but doubt that our entrepreneurs and workers could be internationally competitive? The evidence is that we have, and that should strengthen the conviction that we can, and will meet these standards. The EPA negotiations demonstrate that the region has the capacity to mediate the engagement with globalization and can influence the terms of its integration into the global economy.

The unique experience of the CRNM demonstrates that small developing countries, indeed, developing countries can benefit from combining their human, political and financial resources to negotiate complex and comprehensive international trade agreements. The success of the small developing countries of CARIFORUM acting through the CRNM in negotiating the EPA is tangible demonstration of the benefits of regional cooperation among countries in negotiating external trade agreements. Developing countries, especially small ones, can learn from the experience gained by the CRNM. They may wish to emulate the CRNM model redacting it to their unique circumstances and needs.

In all of this a critical determinant is the intangible of leadership at the political, technical and administrative levels. While the leadership at the political level is what emerges from the electoral process their efficacy can be improved by advice from the technical and negotiation levels. The caliber of the ministers directly responsible for international trade is a crucial factor in determining the success of external trade negotiations. Fortunately for CARIFORUM the cadres of trade ministers were able and hard working.

CHAPTER 4

Characteristics of CARIFORUM Economies

This chapter describes the structural and institutional characteristics of CARIFORUM economies. The dominant feature is their small size relative to the majority of countries in the world. Small developing economies have certain characteristics,[1] such as a high degree of openness, limited diversity in economic activity, export concentration on one to three products, significant dependency on trade taxes, and small size of firms. Some developing countries and least developed countries, in general, may exhibit some of the characteristics listed as defining small developing economies. This has led some to argue that many of the problems attributed to small developing economies are not unique to them or can be addressed by appropriate policy measures and therefore smallness does not differentiate economies.[2] However, careful analysis reveals that the characteristics, which small developing economies share with other types of developing countries, differ by degree between the different types of developing countries. What sets small developing economies apart and defines them as a distinct genre of developing country is the combination of characteristics and the degree or extent to which these characteristics predominate.

Small Size

The countries that comprise CARIFORUM are small developing countries as illustrated by their populations, GDP, and land area (table 4.1).

Acute Vulnerability

The high degree of openness and the concentration in a few export products, particularly some primary products and agricultural commodities whose prices and demand are subject to fluctuations in world markets, make small developing economies vulnerable to external economic events. Substantial dependence on external

Table 4.1 Size of CARIFORUM economies

Country	*Population (2009 estimate)*	*GDP 2006 estimate (current US$ in millions)*	*Land area (km^2)*
Antigua and Barbuda*	85,632	1,610	442
Bahamas	309,156	8,413	13,943
Barbados	284,589	5,214	430
Belize**	307,889	2,820	22,966
Dominica	72,660	691.2	751
Dominican Republic**	9,650,054	77,430	48,310
Grenada	90,739	1,120	344
Guyana**	772,298	3,010	214,969
Haiti **	9,035,536	11,590	27,750
Jamaica**	2,825,928	20,880	10,991
St. Kitts and Nevis	40,131	735.6	261
St. Lucia	160,267	1,732	539
St. Vincent and the Grenadines	104,574	984.9	389
Trinidad and Tobago**	1,229,953	24,190	5,130

*GDP 2007 estimate.

**GDP 2008 estimate.

Source: CIA World Fact book.

sources of economic growth makes small developing countries acutely vulnerable to exogenous shocks. The exposure of small developing economies to real shocks is much greater than in larger economies, which are usually more diversified in structure and exports. Gonzales regards vulnerability as such a critical aspect that he speaks of small vulnerable transitional developing states as a distinct category of economy.[3]

Economic vulnerability can be a feature of an economy of any size and level of development, but it is compounded by small size, a high degree of openness, narrow export concentration, susceptibility to natural disasters, remoteness, and insularity. Small developing economies have structural features that make them more vulnerable to external shocks.[4] Indeed, acute vulnerability is a feature that is unique to small developing economies differentiating them from other types of economies that may share characteristics such as openness, weak adjustment capacity, and limited institutional capacity.

The characteristic of small developing economies that most differentiates them from other developing countries is acute vulnerability. This condition arises from a high degree of openness compounded by a high degree of export concentration and export market concentration. Export concentration is not unique to small developing economies; it is a feature of several developing countries and is particularly common among the least developed countries. However, concentration on a few exports, concomitant with small size of productive units and a disarticulated adjustment capacity, gives export concentration an importance in small developing economies beyond that in other developing countries.

High Degree of Openness

External transactions are large in relation to total economic activity, as indicated by the high ratio of trade to GDP. There is heavy reliance on external trade because of a narrow range of resources and the inability to support certain types of production, given the small scale of the domestic market. Economic openness is measured by imports and exports of goods and services as a percentage of GDP. The trade to GDP for the Caribbean countries is averaged 111 percent during 1995–2005.[5] A high degree of openness is not peculiar to small developing economies, as the growth of interdependence and the increase of international transactions relative to national production have resulted in all economies showing increased levels of openness. Small economies exhibited a much higher degree of openness than large economies. The median trade (exports and imports of goods and services)/GDP ratio during 1986–2005 was 114.4 for small states and 64.6 for large states.[6] Many developed countries exhibit a high degree of openness; however, the implications are very different for small developing countries. A high level of openness coexists in most small developing economies with extreme export concentration and internationally uncompetitive production, resulting in acute vulnerability. In contrast, a high degree of openness in developed economies is indicative of their integration in the global economy and their ability to compete in global markets.

Export Concentration

The limited range of economic activity in small developing economies is reflected in concentration on one to three exports (table 4.2), accompanied, in the majority of cases, by a relatively high reliance on primary commodities and low-skilled labor-intensive manufactured goods. In extreme cases, one export, often a primary product or tourism, accounts for nearly all of exports. Empirical analyses have detected a positive and statistically significant relationship between export concentration and export instability[7] and through its effects on terms-of-trade volatility has a major effect on income volatility.[8] The terms-of-trade volatility is 30 percent higher for small developing economies than that for other developing countries.[9]

Export Market Concentration

In many small developing economies, export concentration is accompanied by export market concentration, and this is manifested as a dependence on one or two export markets. For example, Britain was the sole market for the bananas exported from Dominica, St. Lucia and St. Vincent, and the Grenadines. The case of Dominica was one of extreme dependence because bananas at times accounted for 91 percent of agricultural exports and 68 percent of total exports.[10] The Agricultural Census prompted the observation that "practically everyone in Dominica and St. Lucia who owned even the smallest plot of land, provided it was not in an area too dry for

Table 4.2 Export concentration

2009	*Main export as % total exports*	*Two main exports as % total exports*	*Three main exports as % total exports*
Antigua and Barbuda*	57.6	64.4	68.6
Bahamas	21	40.1	58.4
Barbados	12.8	24.6	35.6
Belize**	40.1	59.6	71.7
Dominica**	33.1	53.1	61.1
Dominican Republic	13	19.4	25.5
Grenada**	24.9	34.9	44.5
Guyana	23.5	45.8	61.9
Haiti*	55.5	61.4	67.1
Jamaica	28.1	44.4	57.3
Montserrat	34.2	47.7	59.8
St Kitts and Nevis**	42.1	67.6	74.4
St. Lucia**	19	32.3	40.5
St. Vincent and the Grenadines	17.3	33.1	43.7
Suriname**	82.3	93.1	94.3
Trinidad and Tobago	42	63.7	67.4

Source: Inter-American Development Bank.

bananas, participated in the industry."[11] Even where a country's exports were more diversified, individual export products relied on one or two markets; for example, sugar exports from CARICOM countries went to Britain and the United States. In 2000, Jamaica exported 162,000 tons of sugar, 150,000 tons to the EU and 12,000 tons to the United States.[12] The diversification of exports that occurred with the emergence of tourism, financial services, and manufacturing has reduced export market concentration. However, there are instances in the export of services where there is concentration, for example, 79 percent of tourist arrivals in the Bahamas emanate from the United States.[13]

Export Marketing Monopoly

The effect of export market concentration is particularly detrimental to economic development if the export marketing is controlled by a single MNC.[14] Corporate monopolies in export commodity marketing develop for a variety of corporate motives such as exclusion of competing firms and ensuring secure supplies. The single-company arrangement also occurs because of factors directly related to the small size of the supplying country, such as very small export volume, for example, the export of bananas[15] and sugar from the Caribbean. Even where an export is handled by several MNCs, the transactions constitute intrafirm trade[16] and not the arms-length international trade of economics textbooks. For a long time, the world bauxite trade was conducted on the basis of intrafirm transfers,[17] and there was no genuine world market in operation.

Exports of bananas from Dominica, Grenada, St. Lucia and St. Vincent, and the Grenadines were handled exclusively by Geest[18] and sold only in Britain. Geest Plc is a leading producer and distributor of fresh chilled foods to the United Kingdom, Benelux, and French markets. It started banana import operations in the mid-1950s, drawing its supplies from the Windward Islands (St. Lucia, St. Vincent and the Grenadines, Grenada, and Dominica). It had an agreement giving it exclusive right to purchasing, shipping, and marketing all the bananas that these islands could produce.[19] By the 1960s, Geest had successfully captured 50 percent of the UK banana market. In 1996, Geest sold its banana operations to a joint venture formed between Fyffes and a company established by the Windward Islands.

Acuteness

The extent of vulnerability of an economy can be measured by a "vulnerability index," for example, the index constructed by Atkins, Mazzi, and Easter[20] incorporates economic exposure, susceptibility to environmental events, and remoteness and insularity. Gonzales uses income volatility, growth resilience, and preference dependence.[21] Becker synthesizes arable land area, population, and isolation based on distance to the nearest continent.[22] Different vulnerability indices have been formulated, differing in which variables are included and the methodology of weighting. Despite differences, all vulnerability indices reveal a relationship between vulnerability and size: the smallest countries are the most vulnerable. Atkins et al. found that 28 of the 30 most vulnerable were small developing economies.[23] A Commonwealth Secretariat/World Bank study has shown that of 111 developing countries, 26 of the 28 most vulnerable were small countries and that the least vulnerable economies were all large countries.[24] All economies exhibit openness to external economic developments, but for large economies this exposure does not amount to vulnerability: Argentina, Brazil, Canada, and the United States have vulnerability indices of 0.2 or less, while the 10 smallest countries range from 0.59 to 0.84.[25]

Growth Volatility

There is no direct correlation between size and economic growth[26] and level of development. Small size however is an additional constraint on economic growth as small size reduces growth in Caribbean economies by 0.3 percent per annum and in combination with island reduces growth by a further 2.8 percent.[27] Many countries, small in terms of standard indicators such as population, land area, and GDP, are ranked favorably according to levels of GDP per capita and the UN's Human Development Index. Small developing economies such as those of CARIFORUM have traditionally experienced pronounced volatility in economic growth, which arises directly from their structural characteristics, in particular, their acute vulnerability to external and exogenous developments. Volatility is costly because of its adverse impact on financial intermediation, exchange rates, inflation, income distribution, resource allocation, productivity, and investment.[28] Income volatility has a strong negative effect on economic growth in developing countries[29] and adversely affects investment.[30] A high degree of trade openness in an economy raises exposure to turbulence emanating from world markets.[31] It does not, however, mean that more open economies are necessarily more volatile,[32] especially if these economies are diversified.[33]

Small developing economies experience higher levels of volatility than other economies,[34] indicating that small size is directly related to volatility. Empirical studies have documented greater volatility of output[35] and real per capita income[36] in small economies. Income volatility is directly and inversely related to size; hence, income volatility increases inversely with the size of the economy.[37] The World Bank and Commonwealth Secretariat estimate that "the standard deviation of annual real per capita growth is about 25 percent higher."[38] Small developing economies experience difficulty in sustaining economic growth and they may, as Looney argues, be incapable of sustaining economic growth.[39] During the period 1980–1998, only 24 of 53 small island countries achieved growth and the "average per capita growth rate was negative."[40]

Volatility of growth and income occurs in small developing countries because of the following:

1. Income volatility is affected by the frequent external shocks to which these economies are prone because of what Becker refers to as the "multiple vulnerabilities." He explains, "While it might be feasible to routinely overcome one or even two types of exposure, once countries are disadvantaged by several such factors, it becomes less likely that they can overcome all of them all the time and escape the adverse consequences of their vulnerabilities."[41]
2. The volatility of income and output in small developing economies is directly related to their export concentration and import dependence. Terms-of-trade volatility is 30 percent higher in small developing economies than in other developing countries; in addition, foreign aid that flows to many small states is highly volatile.[42] Jansen's econometric analysis reveals that "export concentration has a positive and significant effect on terms of trade volatility. This effect increased if exports are concentrated in commodities, including oil, that are characterized by high price volatility. In other words the more concentrated the exports, the more volatile a country's terms of trade."[43] Terms of trade volatility, in turn, affect income volatility as shown in the work of Raddatz.[44]
3. Volatility is a feature of developing countries, which export primary products, particularly agricultural commodities and minerals and experience fluctuations in capital flows. Developing countries have acute vulnerability to fluctuations in capital flows, which are especially severe when export earnings depend on products that are prone to instability such as primary products[45] or goods whose market access depends on voluntary preferential arrangements in developed countries. This instability is heightened when exports depend on a few external markets, because exports are exposed to fluctuations in

demand and price, and changes in market access policy in importing countries. It has been suggested that many small economies can reduce export instability by shifting to services, particularly tourism and financial services; however, the change in export composition toward the service industry has not always been accompanied by reduced instability in export earnings.[46]

4. One of the peculiarities of small developing countries, particularly small islands, is the prevalence of natural disasters and susceptibility of their fragile ecologies to the environmental damage from natural disasters. Sosa and Cashin in a study of the islands of the eastern Caribbean (part of CARIFORUM) found that external shocks, including external demand, oil prices, climatic shocks, and interest rate changes were a critical cause of macroeconomic fluctuations, accounting for more than 50 percent of output fluctuations and that of these exogenous shocks "climatic shocks represent a dominant factor driving output fluctuations."[47] Natural disasters have been a recurring factor in the volatility of small developing economies, particularly small islands. The impact of a natural disaster on a small economy and its financial sector can be far more devastating than it is on a large economy, where the damage is relatively localized. For example,, the damage caused by hurricane gilbert in St. Lucia in1988 was the equivalent of 365 percent of GDP and hurricane Ivan in Grenada in 2004 was 203 percent of GDP (Heger et al. 2008).

The Caribbean experiences a high frequency of natural disasters because it is susceptible to hurricanes, earthquakes, and volcanic eruptions (table 4.3). Jamaica has experienced 19 natural disasters in the 30 years from 1970 to 1999 (table 4.4).

Table 4.3 Natural disasters in the Caribbean—1970–1999

Country	*Number of occurrences*	*Total fatalities*	*Economic losses (1998 $m)*	*Economic losses as % of GDP (1995)*
Antigua	7	7	105.7	18.1
Bahamas	4	5	290.4	9.5
Barbados	5	3	148.4	6.3
Belize	6	5	33.8	5.4
Dominica	7	43	133.4	55
Grenada	4	0	30.1	9.5
Guyana	5	0	29.8	4.6
Jamaica	19	271	1,988.10	29.3
Montserrat	5	43	323.7	899
St. Kitts	7	6	312.5	116.5
St. Lucia	8	54	1,554.60	272.3
St. Vincent	9	5	47	16.5
Trinidad and Tobago	8	9	16.7	0.3

Source: Inter-American Development Bank report "Natural Disasters in Latin America and the Caribbean: An Overview of Risks," October 2000.

Table 4.4 Services contribution to GDP and exports in CARIFORUM

Countries	*Services as percent of GDP 2005*	*Share of total exports (replace) 2006*	
		Goods	*Services*
Antigua and Barbuda	89.0	13.4	86.6
Bahamas, The	57.2	22.1	77.9
Barbados	70.2	20.6	79.4
Belize	40.5	54.6	45.4
Dominica	45.1	33.4	66.6
Grenada	41.2	22.0	78.0
Guyana	43.9	80.1	19.9
Haiti	13.7	70.8	29.2
Jamaica	41.7	44.6	55.4
St. Kitts and Nevis	55.9	29.7	70.3
St. Lucia	65.9	16.8	83.2
St. Vincent and Grenadines	63.1	21.5	78.5
Suriname	31.3	83.4	16.6
Trinidad and Tobago	9.5	91.5	8.5
Dominican Republic	18.2	60.4	39.6
CARICOM (Average)	47.7	43.2	56.8
OECS (Average)	60.0	22.8	77.2
CARIFORUM (CARICOM + DR)	45.8	44.3	55.7

Source: Caribbean: Accelerating Trade Integration (World Bank, 2009), 72.

The smallest countries of CARIFORUM, that is, Antigua and Barbuda, Dominica, Grenada, St. Kitts and Nevis, St. Lucia and St. Vincent, and the Grenadines are among the ten most disaster prone in the world, which means that "they are more than 12 times as exposed as the average country."[48] In addition to the frequency of natural disasters, the intensity of their impact is magnified by the spatial concentration of habitation and economic activity. This is a particularly pronounced feature of small islands where nearly all economic activity is located on the coast.[49] Natural disasters are followed by declines in GDP, exports, and government revenue and increases in debt, imports, and unemployment. The damage can reach catastrophic dimensions such as the damage wrought when Hurricane David hit Dominica in 1979. It killed 42 persons, damaged 95 percent of the buildings (destroying 12 percent), and wiped out the entire banana crop. In the wake of the hurricane, the GDP collapsed by 17 percent, prompting one in four persons to temporarily leave the island.[50]

Imperfect Markets

The small size of markets in small developing economies results in market structures characterized by substantial imperfections. These imperfections derive from

the limited number of participants and in many cases they are monopolies and oligopolies.[51] Even where there are large numbers of producers or traders, one or a few firms effectively dominate the operation of markets in the financial and the real sector. Market imperfections, of one kind or another, are to be found in economies of all types, but in small developing economies these imperfections are particularly perverse. For example, apart from the capacity to manipulate prices and supply that all monopolies enjoy, monopolies in small developing economies are especially inefficient because the market is so small that they also suffer from the lack of economies of scale and benefit from protection from imports.
The particular imperfections of small markets have several implications for resource use allocation and mobilization, including the following:

1. A firm's competitiveness depends on its capacity to continually innovate in production techniques and products. The national market conditions in which the company operates are a significant variable in its drive to develop its competitive advantages. The lack of market-driven competition leads to higher costs, as firms are not driven by the dynamics of competition to optimize efficiency and introduce new technology and improved production systems.
2. Financial markets in small developing economies are "shallow,"[52] having financial sectors with few banks, smaller institutions, a narrow range of services, smaller turnover of foreign exchange, absence of economies of scale, and fewer international correspondent banking connections. The median number of banks for smaller economies is six, and the three largest banks account for about three-fourths of total bank assets.[53] Small developing economies have underdeveloped equity markets; some do not have stock exchanges, and those that do have relatively few listings and few brokers. Empirical work by Hervé Ferhani, Mark Stone, Anna Nordstrom, and Seiichi Shimizu reveal that 25 percent of smaller economies have secondary government securities markets developed enough to involve foreign institutions. Only 40 percent of smaller economies have a stock exchange, and "trading in many of them is so low that their economic impact is minimal."[54] The absence or narrowness of equity markets constrains the financing options available to businesses; hence, the heavy reliance on bank financing in these economies. Financial intermediation delivers fewer services at higher cost, and limits the possibilities for portfolio diversification and risk transfer; this drives up the cost of all economic activity. The small total market and limited number of institutions is often too small to afford specialized regulatory institutions and fiduciary oversight systems.
3. Efficiency is suboptimal because small developing economies cannot provide opportunities for specialization. In these circumstances, highly skilled personnel function as generalists reducing their productivity and this inherent trend is compounded by the migration of a significant portion of university-trained persons seeking jobs suited to their type and level of training. In some situation, a highly specialized person, for example, a neurosurgeon may not be able to find sufficient work in an economy of 100,000. Small developing economies such as Haiti, Jamaica, and Trinidad and Tobago have more than

60 percent of their highly skilled population living abroad and the figure reaches 83 percent in the case of Guyana. The comparable data for large developing economies show Brazil, China, India, Indonesia, and Thailand at less than 3.2 percent.[55]

Nanofirms

It is firms, not countries, that conduct international trade. Firms in small developing economies are small by global standards, although they may be very large by local standards. Firms from small developing economies are small by global standards, that is, by comparison with firms in large economies and with MNCs. The differences in size are so enormous and these firms are so minute that their reality cannot be adequately captured by the nomenclature of small firms in the accepted connotation but are best described as "nanofirms."[56] The concept of nanofirms draws the distinction between a small firm in a small developing economy and other firms because (1) they are much smaller than the conventional definition of a small firm; (2) they are small in comparison to the firms in large economies; (3) a small firm in a large economy, even a large developing economy can grow by realizing economies of scale not available in the domestic markets of small developing economies; (4) a small firm in a developed economy has the benefit and possibility of networks, clusters, and strategic alliances with other firms, small and large; (5) small firms in a developed economy have the advantage of modern infrastructure and a public sector that can assist them. Indeed, most developed countries have special programmes to nurture and support small firms and help them enter international markets;[57] and (6) many of these firms are family-owned firms and suffer from some of the suboptimal characteristics of this type of firm.[58]

The difference in the size of total sales of the largest national firms is a good indicator of enormous gap between firms competing in the global marketplace. A comparison of the top 20 firms in CARICOM, Canada, Europe, and the United States for 2003 reveals the gigantic difference in size. The largest CARICOM firm, Grace Kennedy of Jamaica, had revenue of $412 million compared to George Weston of Canada with $22 billion, BP Oil and Gas in Europe with $174 billion, and Wal-Mart Stores in the United States with $244 billion. Grace Kennedy's revenue was 0.17 percent of Wal-Mart's revenue and 0.2 percent of BP's. In other words, Wal-Mart is 592 times larger than Grace Kennedy and BP is 422 times larger. The total assets of the largest national CARICOM firm, the National Commercial Bank of Jamaica (NCB) in 2003, were $2,431 billion, which is 4.4 percent of the assets of Petrobas of Brazil, and 0.002 percent of the $1,097,190 million of assets of Citibank of the United States, Allianz Worldwide of Germany with assets amounting to $796,262 million is 328 times larger than NCB of Jamaica; Citibank is 451 times larger. The largest employers in the CARICOM region are Neal & Massey of Trinidad and Tobago with a staff of 6,000 and Lascelles Demercado of Jamaica with 6,800—compared with 484,000 employees of ING of the Netherlands and General Motors and Wal-Mart of the United States with over 600,000 employees.[59] Sales and employment of some MNCs are larger than the GDP and population of many small developing economies.

Firms in small developing economies are constrained by a business environment that is less conducive to attaining international competitiveness than that in large developing countries or developed countries. In these environments, economies of scale cannot be realized without involvement in export activity and firms can benefit from modern infrastructure, large markets, and enterprise clusters. Small firms even in developed countries find it more difficult than large firms to overcome the difficulties of breaking into export markets[60] and undertaking foreign investment. The result is that less than 0.2 percent of small firms have multinational operations.[61] Despite these difficulties, some firms in small developing economies have attained international competitiveness,[62] established worldwide brands, and become multinational enterprises. It is however extremely difficult for most firms in small developing economies to be viable. Most services firms in the Caribbean that are not engaged in tourism or financial services have less than 20 employees and an annual turnover of less than $500,000.[63] The consequences of being very small include the following:

1. The small scale of operation of firms mean that they cannot benefit from lower prices by purchasing inputs, including imports, in bulk. These constraints prevent the attainment of economies of scale for a wide range of products and their reliance on imports contributes to high unit costs of production, especially in manufacturing.[64] Small market size also tends to cause high costs because there is often a lack of competition, and in many instances, the markets are oligopolistic or controlled by monopolies. Higher cost of local services is also due to the relative inefficiency of small governments, for example, an importer in a small island developing state needs seven days to clear goods compared to global best practices of 2–3 days.[65] In addition to the difficulties related to local supplies, small developing economies are heavily dependent on imports. For example, in the Caribbean, production sometimes has to be halted while an essential part for machinery is purchased in the United States and flown out from Miami.
2. Firms in small economies, especially small developing economies,[66] are at a major disadvantage compared to large firms in the global context. These small firms cannot attain either internal economies of scale[67] (where unit cost is influenced by the size of the firm) or external economies of scale (where unit cost depends on the size of the industry, but not necessarily on the size of any one firm). Firms in small, developing countries such as those in CARICOM have severe difficulties in attaining "economies of scope," that is, economies obtained when a firm uses its existing resources, skills, and technologies to create new products and/or services for export. Exposure to global competition requires small firms to invest heavily just to survive in their national market, and more so in order to export. Larger firms are better able to generate new products and sources from existing organizations and networks. A small economy, and by extension small industries (including export sectors), is unlikely to foster the competitive dynamic necessary for firms in small economies to achieve competitive advantage. Competitive advantage in the sense in which Porter[68] uses the term is more likely to occur

when the economy is a developed one and is large enough to sustain "clusters" of firms connected through vertical and horizontal relationships and where there are networks[69] of related and supporting industries. A firm working with world-class local suppliers can benefit from cross-fertilization opportunities and overcome information asymmetries. Related industries can also be an important source of innovations and provide strategic alliances and joint ventures.The disabilities constraining small firms increase the smaller the developing economy in which they operate. Firms in microdeveloping economies face even higher costs than other small developing economies[70] and find it more difficult to consistently supply local and export markets, even when there is a clear comparative advantage. Local farmers in small developing countries are unable to consistently supply to hotels and therefore the hotels opt to import foodstuffs because the supply is reliable. The unreliability of quantity and quality of supply is not surprising given the minute size of most farms. Small-scale farms in the Caribbean are typically less than 5 acres (2 hectares) and just under 90 percent of the small-scale farmers operating on less than 10 hectares of land are small farmers and occupy 55.20 percent of the land area.[71]

3. Small developing economies pay higher prices for imports because of the small size of purchases and higher transportation costs. This type of economy is an aggregation of firms, which are small in the world market, and therefore "price-takers," that is, exercising no influence on world market prices for goods, services, and assets. Inputs, including imports, cost firms in small economies more compared to large firms, thereby making firms in small economies relatively less efficient. These firms buy in smaller amounts and cannot negotiate price concessions that larger firms can extract from suppliers. Small developing economies pay higher transportation costs[72] because of the relatively small volume of cargo, small cargo units, and the need for bulk breaking. Small economies pay an average of 10 percent of the value of merchandise exports as freight costs, compared to a 4.5 percent worldwide average and 8.3 percent for developing countries.[73] Small developing economies spend more on freight costs as a percentage of imports than do large countries. The world average is roughly 5.25 percent, whereas the small developing economies of the Caribbean pay between 9 and 13 percent.[74]
4. Small firms face prices for public services that are high by global standards because the public sectors in small developing economies are so small that they cannot attain economies of scale. An important aspect of this relatively high cost of government services is that some essential services are provided by government-owned public utilities, for example, water, electricity, and telephone. These public utilities are not only small, but they are monopolies and not as efficiency driven as a large privately owned company. The small scale of certain activities and/or the existence of many suppliers that are too small to be viable have induced governments in small developing economies to assume roles that in larger economies are carried out by private enterprise. This explains in large part why the size of government is larger in small countries than in large countries. Alesina and Spolaore even venture to suggest

that there is an inverse relationship between country size and size of government.[75] Data for the microstates of the Pacific show that government spending as a share of GDP is higher than in other small developing economies.[76] On the basis of data for 42 small states, Cas and Ota find that on an average small states have larger governments and higher public debt.[77] The public sector and government expenditure in small developing economies accounts for a larger share of GDP[78] than they do in larger countries. This is a reflection of the indivisibility of public administration structures, the lack of economies of scale in the provision of public goods, and the execution of certain roles and functions, which every country, no matter how small, has to carry out, for example, head of a state, a parliament, a police force, and so on. The growth of the public sector has also been due in part to attempts to compensate for the absence of the private sector in certain economic activities, and for the inability of firms in small developing economies to financing for large infrastructure projects either in the narrow local capital market or in international financial markets.

A small government suffers similar disabilities to those of a small firm without the freedom of private enterprise to find solutions. This puts the nanofirms in its economy at a major disadvantage because these governments have neither the adequacy of resources nor the complement of specialized human resources to provide a full range of services at internationally competitive rates. Deryck Brown concludes that institutional capacity in the small states of the Commonwealth Caribbean is weak and this constrains efforts to promote economic development.[79] It requires 65 days to start a business in small island economies compared to 33 days in the rest of the world.[80]

5. Firms in small developing economies, to the extent that they have to purchase inputs produced locally, will have higher production costs. This is because they are buying goods and services produced by other local entities, both private and public, which are high-cost producers because of lack of scale. In many instances, imports are not an alternative, for example, where electricity is generated by a monopoly, which exists because the market is too small to support more than one producer or to allow efficient production. The cost of government services and public goods is more expensive because of lack of scale and lack of specialization causes higher per-unit costs. For example, a ministry of government with two or three officers cannot provide specialized technical responses since of necessity they must be "generalists." Governments in small developing economies are not able to support local firms with research, infrastructure, and financing. The public sector cannot help nanofirms to overcome their inability to undertake research and development and product enhancement, which are key factors in the innovativeness of large firms.[81]
6. The small size of the market and the prevalence of small firms make it difficult for small economies to attract private foreign investment and joint venture partnerships even when the policy regime and economic fundamentals are better than competing locations. This makes it difficult for firms to enlarge their operations to achieve economies of scale and access the latest

technology. The result is enterprises at a level in both the public sector and the private sector, which is suboptimal in efficiency.

7. Small firms in small developing economies find it more difficult to start to export and to survive against larger firms and MNCs. Small firms are at a disadvantage in the global marketplace because they cannot realize economies of scale, are not attractive business partners, and cannot spend significant funds on marketing, research, and development. Firms enter markets where the resource requirements for entry can be met by their capital and capabilities,[82] with the result that small firms will be largely confined to export niches in large external markets. Small firms and farms find it more difficult than larger entities to meet the cost of compliance with international standards; in developing countries, enterprise size is the key variable in the ability of to comply with sanitary and phytosanitary measures in developed country markets.[83] The key to whether small firms in small developing economies will succeed in breaking into or expanding their presence in export markets is to develop appropriate policy to support their efforts, and that, in turn, must be firmly based on an in-depth understanding of exporting in small and microenterprises.[84]
8. Inconsistency of product supply and quality: Small firms and farms are unable to sustain a consistent supply in volume and quality in both the local and export markets and this causes their elimination from the market even where they are competitive in price and on most occasions acceptable in quality. For example, the tourism sector often imports food products that are produced locally because supply and quality are not consistent.[85]

Importance of Services

Services have become the most important type of economic activity in the CARIFORUM economies, where tourism[86] and financial services dominate in many of the economies. Tourism accounts for an average of 45 percent of GDP reaching a high of 89 percent in Antigua and Barbuda. The sector contributes 44 percent of total earnings from the export of goods and services and more than 75 percent in Antigua and Barbuda, the Bahamas, Barbados, Grenada, St. Lucia and St. Vincent, and the Grenadines. The contribution to GDP and total exports is listed in table 4.4. In most countries in the region, tourism dominates the export of services as listed in table 4.5.

Foreign Capital Is Important in Gross Investment

Small developing economies exhibit a high reliance on foreign capital inflows in the form of private foreign direct investment (FDI) and development aid. The average of the ratio of the volume of capital flows to GDP is larger in small developing economies than in other developing countries and the ratio of foreign aid to GDP is about 20 percent, which is double than that of other developing countries.[87] Official development assistance is almost 15 percent of gross national income (GNI) far exceeding than that in other developing countries where the comparative figure is

Table 4.5 Tourism contribution to CARICOM countries

Country	*Estimate of the percentage generated by the travel and tourism industry (both directly and indirectly) in 2007*	*Tourism services exports as a percentage of GDP in 2005*	*Tourism exports annual average growth rate (percent) 2000–2005*
Antigua and Barbuda	75.8	38.5	2.9
Bahamas, The	53.6	34.6	3.6
Barbados	43.4	29.0	4.4
Belize	26.0	18.4	13.0
Dominica	25.0	23.1	2.9
Grenada	35.2	14.0	-5.0
Guyana	9.5	4.3	-14.1
Haiti	7.5	2.0	-9.1
Jamaica	31.1	16.4	3.0
St. Kitts and Nevis	33.4	25.2	13.5
St. Lucia	46.0	40.5	4.9
St. Vincent and Grenadines	32.3	24.4	5.0
Trinidad and Tobago	17.2	3.0	16.3

Source: World Trade and Tourism Council. "Caribbean Travel and Tourism Navigating the Path Ahead," 2007. IMF, *Balance of Payment Statistics Database*, February 2008 Edition. IMF, *World Economic Outlook Database*, October 2007.

1 percent. FDI per capita in the small states averaged US$220 during 2000–2004 compared with an average of about US$34 for all developing countries. In 2004, Caribbean small states average FDI per capita of $399 compared to $40 for all developing countries.[88] Small developing economies are at a disadvantage in attaching FDI compared to larger developing countries. This is in part due to the perception that smaller countries are riskier investment environments. Even when they have sound economic policies and the macroeconomic fundamentals are good, small developing countries are rated 29 percent more risky.[89]

Conventional development economics has always argued that it is desirable for developing countries to have a net capital inflow, as this raises the level of gross investment. Small developing economies tend to experience high levels of foreign capital inflows compared to developing countries. This is partly explained by the fact that small developing economies have received a higher level of aid/GDP and aid on a per capita basis than larger developing countries.[90] In 2011, direct foreign investment accounted for 23 percent of capital formation in small island developing states.[91]

Reliance on Trade Taxes

There is a high dependence on trade taxes as a percent of government revenue in small developing economies. Import duties as a percentage of total tax revenue was

7–10 percent in Barbados, Jamaica, and Trinidad and Tobago; 34 percent in Belize; 43–48 percent in St. Kitts, St. Lucia, and St. Vincent and the Grenadines; and 52 percent in the Bahamas.[92] The importance of trade taxes as a source of fiscal revenue accounts for the resolute and persistent resistance of governments in small countries to contemplate tariff reductions. This, rather than protection of local industry, has delayed or blocked trade liberalization in small developing economies. Ironically, more costly imports due to high tariffs result in high input costs, which reduce the international competitiveness of exports of goods and services.

Constrained Adjustment Capacity

The high import content of production and consumption and the rigidity inherent in the undiversified economic structure of small developing economies severely hampers resource allocation, which makes the adjustment process more difficult and slower than in larger economies. In many situations, adjustment requires resource creation as well as resource allocation. The undiversified economic structure of small developing economies causes the adjustment process to be more difficult, larger relative to GDP, and of necessity slower than in larger countries.[93] There is a high degree of openness in small developing economies, one consequence of which is that movements in the price of imports dominate the overall domestic price level. The prices of nontraded goods also tend to adjust rapidly through the impact of foreign prices on wages and other costs. Exchange rate changes do not have the desired effect on the balance of payments because of low import and export price elasticities.

Stabilization policy must be designed specifically for small, developing countries, taking cognizance of the structure of markets and the nature of their operations. The uncompetitive nature of these markets, particularly where monopolies and oligopolies exist, and the limited number and type of institutions make resource utilization and allocation more problematic than in large developed economies. These types of market situations are characterized by rigidities, which make the adjustment process more time consuming, and which diminish the efficacy of conventional policy measures such as open market operations and recalibration of economy-wide prices such as the exchange rate. Furthermore, structural adjustment, like stabilization, is a more difficult process in small, developing economies because the inherent rigidities in the structure and operation of markets complicate the process of resource reallocation. The nature of these small markets also restricts the ability of private-sector entities and the government to mobilize additional resources, either within these economies or from external sources.

Small, developing economies have structural features that need to be changed (where feasible), if these economies are to cope with the rapid and profound changes associated with globalization. Adjustment will not suffice to enable these economies to successfully manage the changes in the global economy since adjustment implies marginal and incremental modification to an economic structure that is fundamentally sound and conducive to sustainable economic growth. Economic transformation goes beyond the resource utilization, reallocation, and mobilization intrinsic in stabilization and structural adjustment to incorporate resource creation over the medium to long term. Transformation in the current and future global economy will entail the ability of small developing economies to facilitate the rapid and frictionless international mobility of goods, services, finance, capital, and technology, which is the essence of a seamless global economy.

Limited Institutional Capacity

Small developing economies have very limited institutional capacity, and this has a number of implications that increase the cost of goods and services provided by the state, which in turn increase the cost of production in the private sector. In many instances, the government cannot sustain specialized services, with the result that these are either not available or have to be imported. Even where the state has the capacity to supply certain goods and services, these tend to be of high cost because of the absence of economies of scale and the indivisibility of certain public service functions. In some of the smallest countries, the ministry responsible for international trade is three persons as in the case of St. Kitts and Nevis. When Jamaica negotiated its bilateral intellectual property rights agreement with the United States, the Jamaican team was led by a very able lawyer who specialized in international law and the US delegation was led by a person who was a specialist in negotiating bilateral intellectual property right (IPR) agreements.

CHAPTER 5

CARIFORUM's Development Objectives

The economic development objectives of EPA are as follows.

Sustainable Economic Development

Sustainable economic development must involve two interrelated dimensions: (1) the quantitative dimension, that is, economic growth involving increased output, exports, employment, and investment resulting in an improved standard of living of the majority of the population, and (2) the qualitative dimension that must involve (a) the transformation of structures and institutions and (b) the diversification of production for both domestic use and export to reduce vulnerability to external shocks and create a platform for sustainability of the growth process. The goal of increased growth would benefit from increased production, exports, investment, and employment—which would be prompted by improved access to the high income EU market. The qualitative changes would enhance the dynamic of growth and reduce the volatility in economic growth. Export diversification will reduce the dependence on a few exports, thereby reducing the vulnerability of the economies in terms of trade shocks, which have been so integral to the volatility of economic growth in smaller economies.[1] The more diversified a country's exports the less the volatility that can emanate from a high degree of openness.[2]

The desire to achieve sustainable economic development gained urgency because of the anemic economic growth of many CARIFORUM economies in the years immediately before the commencement of the EPA negotiations. The Caribbean economies have not grown at rates acceptable to the governments and people of the region. The rate of growth of GDP during the period 1990–2005 was 2.8 percent, which was lower than that of developing countries and small states. In addition, "average growth has slowed in each decade since the 1970s, the gap between rich and poor states in the region continues to widen, and total factor productivity appears to have stagnated."[3] The Caribbean has experienced a sharp slowdown in economic growth since the onset of the global economic crisis and has been particularly affected by the recession in the United States and turmoil in world financial markets. The recent slowdown in the world economy, emanating from the US economy, makes it imperative that CARICOM countries seek new sources of growth, particularly those not dependent on the US economy and for export diversification. The slowdown has affected remittances to the Caribbean, where they are the equivalent of 23 percent of GDP in Haiti and 25.6 percent of GDP in Guyana.[4]

For exports to the EU and, by extension, to the global market to be increased, several things have to occur that serve to increase the production of exports and to make goods and services internationally competitive: (1) increased output from existing productive capacity, (2) increased exports from the installation of new productive capacity, (3) diversification by the creation of new exports, which requires new productive capacity and/or the reallocation of existing productive capacity (somewhat easier in services than in goods), (4) investment, local or foreign or both. Goods and services only become exports when they are internationally competitive in price and quality. International competitiveness requires (5) appropriate national development policies that encompass a raft of measures (discussed in chapter 9), (6) increased levels of private and public investment and (7) regional integration to create an enlarged and seamless economic CARIFORUM space generating numerous potential benefits including the attainment of economies of scale and reallocation of resources on a regional scale. (8) The small developing economies of CARIFORUM need to avoid being immediately exposed to full free trade, but should not indefinitely postpone further integration into the world economy. These economies needed adequate adjustment and asymmetrically phased implementation.

Expansion and Diversification of Exports

Increased Export Earnings

Increasing export earnings can be generated by increasing the volume and/or prices of exports of goods and services. Increased foreign exchange earnings can be derived from the expansion of already established exports such as rum and the emergence of new exports, particularly in services. The steady growth of services exports other than tourism is indicative both of a comparative advantage and an improving capacity. The prospects for industrial exports and food processing are brightest in the energy-based industries of Trinidad and Tobago. Economic activities where economies of scale are not a determinant will also thrive based on the quality of human resources. It is noteworthy that the inability to attain economies of scale has not prohibited the export of some manufactured goods, for example, electronics in St. Kitts and Nevis and windows in Antigua.

It is inevitable that the composition of exports will change over time in response to changes in external demand, competition in the world market, and internal supply conditions. There are few permanent economic activities and even these experience changes in character, and hence some traditional exports will wane even with the EPA in place. At the same time, new export opportunities emerge continually as products, tastes, and technologies are constantly changing. Some traditional industries have become uncompetitive, given less expensive producers elsewhere in the world. There has been a relative decline in industry and even deindustrialization, notably apparel in Jamaica and sugar in Barbados, St. Kitts and Nevis, and Trinidad and Tobago. Bananas could not be insulated from WTO panel rulings[5] with serious adverse implications in St. Lucia, St. Vincent, and the Grenadines and Dominica. The share of industry in the CARICOM's GDP has declined from 38 percent in the 1960s to 25 percent in the 1990s,[6] while the share of services has expanded steadily. There is scope to continue the growth of the financial services industry and internet gaming. There is a continuing role for sugar and bananas in those countries that can produce competitively.

Export Diversification

The economies of CARIFORUM exhibit a very high concentration of exports of both merchandise and services, where it is typical for one or two exports to dominate. In addition, many of these exports, for example, sugar, have not been internationally competitive for decades but survived because of preferential trade arrangements. Other export sectors lost their comparative advantage over time, but resources have not been reallocated, for example, bananas. The EPA will require export restructuring because so many traditional exports will have less protection and preference, and there will be improved market access creating new export possibilities. Export diversification—resource reallocation from uncompetitive exports to other activities—has been frustrated by (1) the perception of lack of alternatives, (2) policy inertia in shifting support and incentives to other sectors with better prospects, for example, tourism, (3) preferential trade arrangements, and (4) failure to create an economic environment that is encouraging and facilitating of new ventures, for example, university education.

Governments cannot pick winners: for example, nobody predicted the entry and expansion of foreign universities in tiny island states such as Grenada and St. Kitts and Nevis, demonstrating that remoteness is not always a disadvantage. The small, narrow markets of most of the CARIFORUM economies have not always provided a dynamic environment for new ventures; nor has development planning compensated for the deficiencies of the market, because in many instances it floundered for lack of implementation. It is not the task of the EPA to remedy this failure of development policy, but if poor policy continues CARIFORUM economies will not realize the full potential of the EPA. Export diversification requires the market and policy in tandem to identify new export possibilities and to reallocate resources to and create resources for these new export activities.

Merchandise exports as a share of total exports have declined over the last 20 years and now account for just over 40 percent.[7] Merchandise exports are concentrated in primary products and natural, resource-based manufactures accounting for 37.4 percent and 34.9 percent, respectively. In contrast, high-technology manufactures comprised only 1.4 percent of total merchandise exports.[8] Not surprisingly, the Caribbean's share has declined since 1980 from 0.5 percent to just approximately 0.15 percent.

Services account for over 60 percent of the region's GDP. Payne and Sutton point out that the "Caribbean is the most tourism-intensive region in the world, with tourism accounting for 18 percent of total GDP and 34 percent of total employment."[9]

Existing exports such as tourism will have to be diversified and new exports developed, for example, health care,[10] health tourism, and wellness. The export of university-level education can expand considerably and so can entertainment and culture. It is possible with the right policy mix to create bioindustries.[11]

Export concentration has been detrimental to the economic growth of developing countries.[12] The appearance of new exports will facilitate the diversification of exports, which will serve to stabilize overall export earnings,[13] strengthen economic growth, and reduce its volatility. Export diversification is particularly stimulating to growth if it involves a shift from primary products to manufactured goods or goods with higher value added and better demand and price prospects. This was the gravamen of the arguments proffered by Prebisch, Singer, and Chenery.[14]

Increasing Investment

In order to increase and diversify exports, CARIFRUM economies will have to increase existing productive capacity, install new productive capacity, and improve international competitiveness of goods and services both for export and to withstand increased competition from imports. Small developing economies exhibit a high dependence on inflows of foreign capital including development aid, commercial loans (to both the private and public sectors), and private FDI. The EPA was seen as a vehicle for stimulating an increased volume of foreign capital inflows by creating export opportunities, establishing new productivity capacity, generating new economic activities, and improving productivity. The objective was to craft provisions that would stimulate capital inflows while protecting the policy space of the CARIFORUM governments.

Improving International Competitiveness

The international competitiveness of CARICOM economies needs to be improved if they are to thrive in a globalized world economy. Table 5.1 reveals that Barbados leads the region in competitiveness ranking 50th of the total of 130, countries while at the other end of the table Guyana is at 126. Jamaica is at 78 and Trinidad and Tobago at 84. Unfortunately, the index does not capture the data for countries designated by CARICOM as less-developed countries. In subindex A that covers basic requirements, Barbados is the strongest performer particularly with regard to health and primary education, in respect of which Barbados was placed 9th out of 130 countries. In this same area, the remaining countries lag very far behind with Trinidad and Tobago coming in the second position and Suriname in the third, with 62nd and 68th position, respectively. In subindex B, efficiency enhancers, all countries are hampered by small market size, with Jamaica standing out in goods market efficiency, ranking 57th out of 130 countries. Subindex C, which relates to innovation and business sophistication, shows Barbados as the best overall performer in 57th position. Jamaica is second best, followed by Trinidad and Tobago and Guyana and Suriname at 113th and 115th, respectively.

Market access is a necessary but not sufficient condition for increased exports and economic growth. The sufficient condition is the ability to produce goods and

Table 5.1 Global competitiveness index 2007–2008

Subindices	*Barbados*	*Guyana*	*Jamaica*	*Suriname*	*Trinidad and Tobago*
Rank (out of 131 countries)	50	126	78	113	84
Basic Requirements					
1. Institutions	25	121	87	98	92
2. Infrastructure	29	106	63	102	69
3. Macroeconomic stability	105	130	120	74	16
4. Health and primary education	9	81	72	68	62
Total	36	125	86	92	57
Efficiency Enhancers					
5. Higher education and training	32	97	71	100	70
6. Goods market efficiency	70	103	57	127	75
7. Labor market efficiency	38	109	53	101	62
8. Financial market sophistication	41	100	49	102	45
9. Technological readiness	34	102	43	118	66
10. Market size	125	126	113	128	102
Total	59	119	69	126	74
Innovation and sophistication factors					
11. Business sophistication	66	98	69	116	77
12. Innovation	56	122	59	115	82
Total	57	113	62	115	79

Source: The Global Competitiveness Report 2007–2008 (Oxford University Press, 2007).

services that are internationally competitive in price and quality. This is not a new issue,[15] but it is one that is yet to be adequately addressed but becomes urgent with the advent of the EPA. CARICOM firms will be progressively exposed to competition with European firms as the import liberalization is implemented in years 4 to 25 of the EPA. As listed in table 5.2, 21 European countries are ranked higher than Barbados, which is the most competitive CARICOM country. Barbados is ranked 50th of 131 countries and Jamaica is next at 78th. Of the EU countries, nine are among the 20 most competitive in the world. The implication of these differences in competitiveness is the urgent need for firms in CARICOM countries to increase the international competitiveness of their goods and services. The increased exposure of CARICOM firms to competition with European firms, which will take effect after year three of the implementation of the EPA, comes at a time when according to the World Bank "the Caribbean has seen a reduction in its competitiveness over the last decade. Shares in world markets have fallen, trade has fallen as a share of GDP, and the current account has deteriorated."[16] During the period 1985–2000, CARICOM's market share in goods entering the EU market declined steadily.[17]

Improving international competitiveness requires improved productivity through increased investment, enhanced education, and the introduction of new technology,

Table 5.2 Global competitiveness index 2007–2008 of the EU and the CARIFORUM states

Country/economy	*Rank (out of 131 countries)*		*Score (out of a total of 7)*
	EU	*CARIFORUM*	
Denmark	3		5.62
Sweden	4		5.55
Germany	5		5.51
Finland	6		5.49
United Kingdom	9		5.41
Netherlands	10		5.40
Austria	15		5.23
France	18		5.18
Belgium	20		5.10
Ireland	22		5.03
Luxembourg	25		4.88
Estonia	27		4.74
Spain	29		4.66
Czech Republic	33		4.58
Lithuania	38		4.49
Slovenia	39		4.48
Portugal	40		4.48
Slovak Republic	41		4.45
Latvia	45		4.41
Italy	46		4.36
Hungary	47		4.35
Barbados		50	4.32
Poland	51		4.28
Cyprus	55		4.23
Malta	56		4.21
Greece	65		4.08
Romania	74		3.97
Jamaica		78	3.95
Bulgaria	79		3.93
Trinidad and Tobago		84	3.88
Dominican Republic		96	3.65
Suriname		113	3.40
Guyana		126	3.25

Source: The Global Competitiveness Report 2007–2008 (Oxford University Press, 2007).

among other things. To achieve this impact, the EPA would have to include addressing investment, intellectual property rights, and trade facilitation. The EPA was not only necessary to respond to economic relations with the EU but is necessary to survive and thrive in the global economy of today and tomorrow. In preparing for the challenges presented by the EPA, the CARIFORUM countries will be preparing for global competition.

Strengthen Regional Integration

Both the EU and CARIFORUM believe in the regional economic integration paradigm as an indispensable framework for promoting economic development. The then prime minister of Barbados, Owen Arthur, expressed the thinking of the region when he stated, "CARICOM must not only hasten to complete the integration process for internal reasons, but also as the best platform from which the Region can plug into the global economy so as to derive maximum benefits for the peoples of the Caribbean."[18] Article 1 of the Cotonou Agreement enshrined the strengthening of regional integration in the ACP regions, and Article 29 indicates some of the areas among which are enhancing intraregional trade liberalization and the encouragement of intraregional investment. Regional economic integration was important to promote internationally competitive production of goods and services. Article 78 of the Revised Treaty of Chaguaramas, which deals with the objectives of trade policy, states in paragraph (b): "the active promotion of export of internationally competitive goods and services."[19] Integration would contribute to international competitiveness by enlarging the market and allowing the attainment of economies of scale and scope, the allocation of resources on a regional scale, enlarging the amount and range of raw materials, and allowing nanofirms to enlarge across the regional market and improve the efficiency of production by competition in the regional market.

The EU has practiced an increasingly deep integration process for more than half a century, while CARICOM has had an integration process since the late 1960s and is committed to deepening this toward a single market and economy. The Dominican Republic has not been a formal participant in a regional economic or political group but sees the advantages of involvement in a Caribbean economic space. The membership in CARIFORUM has led it to moot the possibility of becoming a member of CARICOM. CARIFORUM was primarily committed to maintaining the integrity of the extant concept of regional integration and retaining full control of the pace of attaining the long term vision of an integrated region. The EPA was, from the CARIFORUM perspective, to complement the existing regional integration process but not to uncomfortably accelerate the pace or overall design. The EU were surprised that CARIFORUM did not want to speed up the integration process, while CARICOM stoutly and with justification made it clear that they were in the best position to judge what was feasible.

The question has been raised as to whether full implications of the EPA for CSME were taken into account during the EPA negotiations.[20] It is highly unlikely that the hundreds of technicians, officials, and politicians who were involved over the four years of negotiation and review of the EPA overlooked some implication.

The EPA was the outcome of a comprehensive consultative and inclusive process, and all negotiating sessions and preparatory meetings were conducted with the active participation of the senior officers and technical staff of the CARICOM Secretariat, including the CSME Unit and the presence of officials from the governments of CARIFORUM. The CRNM worked in close coordination and collaboration with the CARICOM Secretariat on a daily basis and with these branches of the institutional arrangements of CARICOM/CARIFORUM. Any suggestion that the CRNM, CARICOM Secretariat, and the governments of CARIFORUM were somehow hermetically sealed entities is completely inaccurate. During the negotiation of the EPA, the governments and the public in the CARICOM region were made aware of the implications of the negotiations and the completed EPA for regional economic integration.[21] The state of the CSME and its prospects for implementation were an integral part of the foundation of the CARIFORUM positions in the EPA negotiations.

The CARIFORUM negotiators were able to ensure that the EPA would not disrupt the CSME and the process of its completion. The state of the CSME was the main reason for not going further in several subject areas of the EPA, for example, (1) the competition obligations do not go beyond the CSME treaty obligations and support the CSME Competition Framework and (2) there is no market access obligations in the government procurement provisions, which were guided by the CARICOM government procurement policy document and ensured the benefits of transparency to the CARIFORUM region, including increased public confidence and strengthening the democratic framework of governance. The limits placed on several issues were based on a conservative projection of where the CSME could reasonably be expected to be. In any case, the reasons that account for the state of the CSME[22] are not likely to be aggravated by the implementation of the EPA.

Extended and Asymmetrically Phased Adjustment and Implementation

The CARICOM countries were aware as the EPA negotiations approached that they were facing a profoundly and rapidly changing global economy and that structural adjustment and economic transformation were imperative. A report by an expert group titled "Improving Competitiveness for Caribbean Development," published just before the commencement of the EPA negotiations, emphasized the urgent need for adjustment. The report alerted the region to the fact that "the stage is set for radically different trade arrangements" and that whatever form these take "they will necessarily entail reciprocity, non-discrimination, and the implementation of the commitment already given to the progressive removal of barriers between the parties."[23]

To capitalize on the export opportunities provided by the EPA, the small developing economies of CARIFORUM will need adequate time for adjustment. Adequate time has to be provided to allow local firms to become more internationally competitive, in terms of exporting and withstanding increased exposure to imports. This is so because the characteristics of small developing economies limit their capacity to adjust, necessitating extended periods of adjustment. The length and phasing of the adjustment period has to be carefully calibrated to ensure that it is neither too short nor too long. Too long an adjustment period is harmful because it induces complacency in both government and the private sector. Complacency is the antithesis of strategic proactive adjustment and tends to lead to the postponement of adjustment until near the end of the schedule of implementation. If the adjustment period is too short, it can be devastating if the local firms and farms are prematurely exposed to a higher level of international competition. With this firmly in mind, a complementary negotiation objective of CARIFORUM was to incorporate in the EPA adjustment periods that were (1) extended, (2) asymmetrical, and (3) capable of recalibration through safeguards.

The pace of import liberalization required extended adjustment periods and flexibility for recalibration of liberalization schedules. One of the issues that had to be addressed was the dependence on taxes on international trade. Governments have traditionally relied heavily on tax revenue from tariffs and customs duties as is the case in CARICOM, particularly in the smallest countries. Imports from the EU account for 15 percent of total imports; therefore, there will not be a loss of revenue because the revenue foregone from lower tariffs can be garnered from other forms of taxation. The import liberalization will be phased in periods of up to 25 years, which is more than enough time to devise and implement fiscal reform.

Local firms will have a chance to gradually upgrade their international competitiveness and should make sure to utilize the three-year moratorium on import liberalization to invest in new machinery, adopt the latest technology, identify export niche markets, formalize strategic corporate alliances, and improve the productivity of management and labor. Strategic corporate alliances are an important means for small firms to enter export activity.[24] The first step in the creation of an export-oriented policy is a change of mindset[25] and local firms must accept and respond proactively to changes in global economic reality. They have to respond not only to the EPA but also to competition from the United States, China, Brazil, and India, indeed to the world economy. All countries and the firms that operate therein are in a fierce unavoidable competition for capital, customers, technology, and skilled human resources. This global rivalry does not permit anyone the luxury of adjusting at their own pace and not adjusting is simply out of the question, especially for small developing economies and nanofirms.

Maintaining Policy Space

The governments of CARIFORUM were fully aware that further integration of their highly open economies exposes them to greater risk of the impact on external economic events. They also were fully cognizant that a trade agreement could impinge on their development policy space, and were determined to retain as much development policy space as possible, both at the national and regional levels. Small developing economies are concerned about policy freedom, which is already constrained by their small size and acute economic vulnerability.

Minimizing the Impact on Fiscal Revenue

Given the importance of revenue from tariffs and customs duties in some countries particularly the smallest economies, there was a need to design an EPA that would have minimal impact on these sources of fiscal revenue. The objective was to keep to a minimum the number of items to be liberalized and the remove tariffs from revenue sensitive items over a period that was sufficiently long to allow the governments to put in place substitute sources of revenue such as income tax or sales tax.

Goals and Characteristics of CARIFORUM Economies

The overall goal of the CARIFORUM countries on entering the negotiations for the EPA was to put their economies on a path of sustainable economic development. This meant steady economic growth and trying to make their economies less vulnerable. More specifically, the attainment of sustainable economic development required increasing and diversifying exports, and that, in turn, required improved international competitiveness. To achieve continuous improvements, it would be necessary to expand productive capacity, with implications for increased investment in the form of local and foreign investment. It also implied the strengthening of regional integration with the benefits that it could accord such as economies of scale. All of this plus the limited institutional capacity would require adjustment over a sufficient time and a manageable pace of implementation to allow these economies to adjust; in particular, adequate time would be needed for the nanofirms to redimension so as to attain international competitiveness. Understanding that committing to a legally binding international trade agreement involves some limitations on policy, the CARIFORUM wanted to retain as much policy space as possible.

CHAPTER 6

How the EPA Promotes Economic Development

Discussions of the effect of international trade on development date back to the mercantilist's writings of the seventeenth century,[1] which focused on the effects of a surplus (deficit) in the trade account.[2] Later, Adam Smith's advocacy of free trade was aimed at facilitating the maximum accumulation of capital,[3] but the first cogent theory of international trade was produced by Ricardo[4] in 1817. During the 1950s and 1960s, the virtues of international trade for economic development were extolled by Viner,[5] Harberler,[6] and Craincross,[7] but elicited vigorous criticism from several perspectives. It was claimed that the history of the now developed countries was a vindication of free trade policies with the experience of Britain,[8] Italy,[9] and the United States[10] in the nineteenth century cited as evidence. The experience of developing countries contrasted with the predictions, prompting different explanations. Nurske[11] pointed to the lagging demand for primary products and the enclave nature of export industries was also put forward.[12] By far the most telling comments highlighted the deteriorating terms of trade between manufactured goods and primary products. Prebisch[13] and Singer[14] identified the problem of developing country trade as inherent in the structure of the world capitalist system, the international division of labor, and the deformed economic structure of developing countries. The developed/industrialized countries, which form the core, export manufactured goods, while the developing countries export primary products from the periphery. The core derives a disproportionate share of the gains from international trade because of differences in the income and price elasticities of demand for primary products and manufactured goods and differences in technology, industrial organization, and the operation of labour markets, which are a part of the structure of the core-periphery system. Lewis[15] argued that in a dual-sector economy with labour surplus, low productivity in the subsistence sector is the critical factor whatever the demand conditions. Myrdal[16] also focuses on low productivity, which is caused by the structure of underdeveloped countries that generate a predominance of "backward effects" (growth retarding) over "spread effects" (growth stimulating).

The disadvantaged position of developing countries gained credence because the majority of empirical studies provided support in the form of evidence of the long-term deterioration in the terms of trade of primary products, which were the export mainstay of the developing countries. There has been deterioration in the relative real prices of nonoil commodities throughout the twentieth century.[17]

Trade and Economic Development

The relationship between international trade and economic development has not enjoyed consensus among economists. Indeed, there is a range of widely divergent views on the trade-development nexus. There are three basic models:

1. Free trade promotes economic growth and stimulates economic development in developing countries. The Neoclassical theory of international trade is the basis for the advocacy of free trade and the claim that trade ensures that all participating countries derive benefit. Every country has a comparative advantage in some good or service, and trade on this basis will generate growth and maximize consumer welfare.[18] International trade on the basis of comparative advantage as determined by their different factor endowments[19] is supposed to be best for individual countries and the world economy as a whole. The paradigm is referred to by its proponents as "the pure theory of international trade"[20] and is to be found in standard economic textbooks. The policy prescription is free trade: it is the intellectual foundation of the WTO and is espoused by the developed countries, although in their formative years they vigorously practiced more interventionist trade policy. In this conception, the mission of the WTO is to establish a MTS of free trade and the advice to developing countries is to integrate as quickly and completely as possible. Diaz-Alejandro refers to "the ultra-pro-trade arbiter dicta of the professional mainstream," which "leaps with remarkable ease from the sensible proposition that some trade can potentially make everyone better off, as compared with no trade, to the conviction that more trade is always likely to do just that."[21]

The deficiencies of the neo-classical paradigm inevitably prompted attempts to incorporate a greater measure of realism. These deficiencies include the incorporation of imperfect competition and increasing economies of scale,[22] but these developments only cast further doubt on neo-classical trade theory without resolving the dispute over trade and growth. Ocampo's survey of the literature concludes that new trade theories do not justify protectionism or laissez-faire industrial policy; nor do they substantiate an automatic connection between liberalization and productivity. Indeed, "they indicate that trade liberalization should be coupled with an active industrial policy, particularly in sectors subject to significant economies of scale."[23]

On the basis of the neoclassical theory of international trade, it is asserted that trade liberalization can and does increase economic growth. This is a proposition often advocated by developed countries, for example, an OECD publication states, "Exposure to international trade is a powerful stimulus to efficiency. Efficiency in turn, contributes to economic growth and rising incomes. The report goes on to claim that in "the last decade countries that have been more open have achieved double the annual average growth than others."[24] This assertion is supported by reference to empirical studies, which purport to show an association between policies of openness such as trade liberalization and higher rates of economic growth.[25] One of the policy implications of this approach that trade liberalization should be comprehensive and implemented expediously and converselyinadequate or delayed trade liberalization reduces the growth of developing countries. In keeping with this view, governments in many developing countries are said to misguidedly avail themselves of certain types of special and differential treatment, which retard the realization of their growth potential.

The empirical studies that support the liberalization-cum-growth theory exhibit serious weaknesses such as specification problems and endogeneity, making it very difficult to separate what can be attributed solely to trade liberalization. Billmeier and Nannicini concluded that neither cross-country statistical analyses nor the case study approach are definitive so that the "relationship between trade openness and economic liberalization on the one hand, and income or growth on the other, is one of the main conundrums in the economics profession."[26] A comprehensive survey of the literature concludes that there is little definitive evidence that open trade policies, which lower tariffs and nontariff barriers to trade, are significantly associated with economic growth.[27] The literature has to be read carefully to derive the lessons. Some studies stress the point that trade liberalization that was strong and sustained and accompanied by appropriate macroeconomic policy was associated with increased exports and growth.[28] Other studies claim only that those countries that have grown rapidly have implemented economic policy that included trade opening.[29] The real issue is the quality of domestic macroeconomic policy as shown by the fact that developing countries with sound policies achieve efficiency, international competitiveness, and growth, and are able to take advantage of open trade regimes. Rodrik has suggested that macroeconomic stability, human resources, investment, and good governance should be the focus of developing countries seeking enhanced economic growth.[30] Even the Asian Tigers[31] or newly industrialized countries, which are often cited as examples of the success of outward-oriented policies, on closer examination reveal that their strategies involved selective import liberalization over an extended period.[32] The causality is not that the economy is opened and then economic growth follows. There is no automaticity in this sequence and this is evident in the numerous instances of developing countries that have liberalized their trade regimes with disastrous consequences. There is a growing recognition that the growth-enhancing effect of trade may depend on structural characteristics and the quality and productivity of factors such as human capital and the quality of existing institutions. Trade-induced economic growth is best realized by the simultaneous pursuit of complementary institutional reform and supportive policy action.[33]

If trade liberalization is the best way to stimulate the expansion of trade and promote growth, any policy that deviates from this will produce second-best results and is therefore harmful. Reference is made to the fact that the majority of developing countries have not achieved the kinds of growth rates warranted for economic development and poverty reduction despite the existence of extensive special and differential treatment. More specifically, preferential market access has not prompted export expansion and thereby not promoted economic growth. Nor have infant industries graduated into competitive export industries, despite extended periods of protection from the full brunt of competition from imports. Indeed, it is the competition from imports, which will either eliminate industries that are not viable or force them to become sufficiently efficient to survive. The conclusion of this line of reasoning is the abolition of provisions that are intended to nurture infant industries. This amounts to what Chang calls "kicking away the ladder," which was a key element in the development of the now developed countries.[34]

Recent developments in trade theory, which incorporate imperfect competition and increasing economies of scale,[35] cast further doubt on neoclassical trade theory but do not resolve the dispute over trade and growth. Ocampo's survey of the literature concludes that new trade theories do not justify protectionism or laissez-faire industrial policy, nor do they substantiate an automatic connection between liberalization and productivity. Indeed, "they indicate that trade liberalization should be coupled with an active industrial policy, particularly in sectors subject to significant economies of scale."[36]

Economic growth in small developing economies requires access to external markets, but while this is a necessary condition, it is not a sufficient condition. If access to external markets is to promote growth and development, it must be accompanied by domestic policy that facilitates internationally competitive production of goods and services. The EPA does provide improved market access, but it is not a panacea that will guarantee economic development and structural transformation. Economic development will require the harmonization and complementarity of the internal economic policy and external frameworks such as the EPA.

2. Trade as a cause of underdevelopment with the policy prescription of withdrawal or minimization of involvement in the world economy while attempting to create a more just international economic order. This is the analysis and policy of the structuralist, dependency, plantation, and neo-Marxist schools of thought. These approaches share the overarching analytic framework of a world capitalist economy in which differences in levels of development and power produce development and underdevelopment and pointed to the deteriorating terms of trade between manufactured goods and primary products. Prebisch[37] and Singer[38] identified the problem of developing country trade as inherent in the structure of the world capitalist system, the international division of labour, and the deformed economic structure of developing countries. The developed/industrialized countries that form the core export manufactured goods and the developing countries export primary products from the periphery. The core derives a disproportionate share of the gains from international trade. The core-periphery model is framework employed by dependency economists, for example, Furtado,[39] Cardoso,[40] Sunkel,[41] and neo-Marxists, for example, Amin[42] and Emmanuel[43]. Plantation School economists, for example, Beckford,[44] and some dependency proponents, for example, Girvan,[45] identify the MNC as the institutional mechanism responsible for depriving developing countries of fair returns.

In recent years, there has some softening of the extreme positions of the trade and development debate. Costoya, Utting, and Carrion[46] observed this trend, opining that the debate has been "recast." The traditional antinomy—free trade versus protectionism, the market versus the state—has clearly waned in mainstream policy circles. Some who trace their intellectual heritage to Prebisch and Gunder Frank have accepted the basic liberal principle of outward-looking growth, while others who trace their lineage to Friedman have come to accept that markets are not perfect but suffer from multiple distortions.

3. Special and differential trade for developing countries. The assumptions of the neoclassical approach are very restrictive and bear little relationship to reality. The policy prescriptions have elicited skepticism and prompted alternative views about the role of trade in economic development, employing models that more accurately reflect the reality of developing countries. The divergence between reality and the assumptions underpinning this theory of international trade has forced even the most avid proponents of free trade, such as Bhagwati, to concede that "if markets do not work well, or are absent or incomplete, then...free trade cannot then be asserted to be the best policy."[47] The approach that concludes that international trade in a capitalist world economy is a cause of underdevelopment advocates autarky. This is not possible; hence, the policy must be (1) to minimize the engagement in trade with more developed countries, that is, the core of the capitalist world economy, (2) south–south trade between developing countries, and (3) to the extent possible the cultivation and expansion of trade with socialist countries. This last aspect of trade policy has diminished in importance with the implosion of the Soviet Union and the gradual but systematic shift in China toward a mixed economy best described as "Market Leninism." Pragmatic thinking has pointed to trade policy to promote growth of developing countries being based on countervailing measures to attenuate the differences in size and level of development between the developed and developing countries. These measures have come to be known by the nomenclature of special and differential treatment.

There has been a protracted and unresolved debate about the efficacy of SDT—in particular, preferential arrangements provided to developing countries by developed countries. It has frequently been said that SDT in the form of nonreciprocity has produced perverse trade policy choices in developing countries. Specifically it has encouraged them to be protectionist, delaying trade liberalization[48] as long as they can get away with it. This is the natural course of action because there is no obligation to reciprocate, prompting some to speak of the "perversity of preferences"[49] of schemes such as the GSP. The existence of SDT is purported to "discourage effective efforts to integrate into the world economy" and "merely exacerbate the difficulties of pursuing satisfactory policies" and "should be phased out as soon as possible."[50] This kind of attribution is too superficial because it overlooks the motivations for deferring trade liberalization, which are present in every country whether or not it enjoys SDT. The common motivations emanate from the desire to preserve market position by minimizing competition from imports and to garner economic rents and higher profits.

What has not been definitively established in the debate on the efficacy of SDT is how each measure of SDT is directly related to a specific aspect of developing countries. This is partly due to the wide range of countries covered by the existing outmoded nomenclature of "developing country" and "least-developed country." It is extremely difficult to identify a typical developing country or a feature that is common to all developing countries to the same extent. Not all developing countries exhibit all the features and problems ascribed to the category.

While there is substance to the statement that developing countries have not grown as expected or desired despite SDT, it is also grossly inaccurate because it is based on an incomplete analysis of the international trade environment in which developing countries have operated. The evaluation of the performance of the trade of developing countries must include (1) the harmful policies of developed countries starting with the $311 billion of subsidies lavished on agriculture in the OECD countries in 2001, an amount that exceeds the GDP of sub-Saharan Africa and is six times total foreign aid.[51] Tariff peaks stymie developing country exports, for example, 60 percent of imports from developing countries entering Canada, the EU, Japan, and the United States were subject to tariff peaks.[52] There is also tariff escalation, nontariffs barriers, quotas, sanitary, and phyto-sanitary measures, and a host of other protectionist policies and trade-distorting practices such as dumping. Ironically what these policies amount to is SDT granted unilaterally to themselves by the developed countries. (2) It is very problematic to assess the efficacy of SDT for developing countries because most of the measures are best endeavored commitments couched in hortatory language, not specific and definitely not enforceable. Even more disappointing is the new trend for developed countries to offer technical assistance as the answer to demands for SDT. It is a gesture that developing countries cannot refuse, but in reality is more of a placebo than a lasting solution.

It is ironic that the developed countries that never tire of exhorting developing countries to relinquish "special and differential treatment" for reciprocal trade have quietly continued to deploy an array of protectionist barriers especially against imports from developing countries. In addition, the extensive system of subsidies, domestic support, and export subsidies in the agriculture sector of developed countries, most notably in the United States, the EU, and Japan is tantamount to unilaterally appointed SDT. The double standard goes even further when the governments in the developed countries maintain special programmes for vulnerable producers in their national markets. They operate programmes for small- and medium-sized firms, family-owned farms, and disadvantaged regions. These involve finance at below-market rates, technical assistance, and reserving a part of the market in government procurement. The practice of SDT at home does not diminish the virulence of their opposition to SDT for developing countries in the MTS.

Developing countries can benefit from international trade if they are accorded SDT. The case for SDT is even more compelling for small developing economies. Until the establishment of the WTO in 1994, developed countries of Europe provided preferential market access to the developing countries of the ACP group. The Lomé Convention provided one-way preferential market access to the ACP countries. There was a shift in this disposition of developed countries toward preferential trade, which was epitomized by the rules of the WTO. The change in attitude was evident in the EU as well as an awareness that it was going to be increasingly difficult to get approval of preferential trade agreements in the WTO. Future preferential trade agreements would have to meet the requirements of the WTO such as liberalization of substantially all trade. The signing of the Cotonou agreement by the ACP countries was a binding acceptance that the EPA would be based on SDT but not on the type of the Lomé Conventions, that is, one-way nonreciprocal preferential trade. This approach is adequate to facilitate economic development in

CARIFORUM countries. The fact is that many of the most successful export sectors emerged and expanded without preferential market access, for example, tourism entertainment, meanwhile many of the major industries that have had decades of preferential export arrangements are in decline and are uncompetitive.

The EPA eschews the notion that trade causes underdevelopment and with justification is skeptical of the heralded promises of free trade and, hence, is based on SDT. However, the EPA is not based on the extreme form of SDT, which is nonreciprocal preferential treatment. The key to achieving economic development through expanding international trade is producing goods and services that are internationally competitive in price and quality. The critical role of export competitiveness as the means of trade-led development applies to all countries, small and large, developed or developing. In fact, it is vital for the small, developing economies even if they have to rely on only a few exports and niche markets.

Special and Differential Treatment

The Cotonou Agreement states that the EPAs negotiated between the EU and the ACP will be based on SDT. Article 35.3 states that "economic and trade co-operation shall take account of the different needs and levels of development of the ACP countries and regions. In this context, the Parties reaffirm their attachment to ensuring special and differential treatment for all ACP countries and to maintaining special treatment for ACP LDCs and to taking due account of the vulnerability of small, landlocked and island countries."[53]

The EPA seeks to promote economic development through the expansion of trade based on SDT for the CARIFORUM countries. SDT can be expressed in a variety of forms.[54] The Lomé Conventions and the trade provisions of the Cotonou Agreement were based on one-way preferential market access/arrangements. The SDT on which the EPA is based and which infuses the agreement is a different form of SDT than the one-way preferential treatment in the trade provisions of the Cotonou Agreement. SDT is given justifiable expression in the EPA by (1) differences in obligations, (2) asymmetrically phased implementation schedules, (3) development aid to assist in defraying the cost of implementation, and (4) attaining some commitments are conditional on technical assistance.

The principle of SDT as expressed in the EPA obtains not only between the EU and CARIFORUM but is also applied among CARIFORUM countries. For example, the more developed countries will commence the application of regional preference after one year, whereas for the less developed countries it starts after two years. A similarly bifurcated schedule is stipulated for transparency in public procurement with MDCs having two years to implement while the LDCs are allowed five years. The LDCs are accorded an exemption from the provisions on intellectual property, except for the implementation of the TRIPS Agreement. They also have until January 1, 2021 to implement the standards and enforcement provisions on intellectual property.

The SDT in the EPA must be concatenated with appropriate domestic and regional policies. The experience of developing countries with SDT and trade liberalization indicates that the benefits are not automatic but can be realized when coupled with appropriate domestic policies; what is appropriate is unique to each country. There are some commonalities which emerge from the experience of the developing countries. These include macroeconomic stability, human resources, investment, and good governance should be the focus of developing countries seeking enhanced economic growth.[55] Apart from policies that enhance the general economic environment, the development policy space in a proactive and interventionist manner. Trade liberalization will also entail a certain amount of institutional change in both the public and private sectors.[56] The real issue is the quality of domestic policy, as shown by the fact that developing countries with sound policies achieve efficiency, international competitiveness, and growth, and are able to take advantage of open trade regimes.

Domestic policy and, where appropriate, regional policy have a role to play in the realization of economic gain from trade liberalization. The process of achieving this must involve structural transformation, which goes beyond structural adjustment to involve strategic global repositioning. A prerequisite is sound macroeconomic management embedded in a stable network of institutions, thereby providing a predictable economic environment. This must be complemented by a modernization of the business environment synchronized with the dynamic trends and sectors in the world economy, which can help unleash innovation and entrepreneurship. An integral aspect of this is strengthening markets at the national and regional level to intensify the dynamic stimulus of increased competition. The focus must be on the enhancement of the international competitiveness of goods and services for both export and domestic consumption. This involves attaining greater efficiency by increasing productivity of labour, capital, and management in both the private and public sectors.

It is firms not countries that compete; therefore, it is essential to facilitate the redimensioning of corporate entities by a framework of appropriate fiscal policies and regulation conducive to mergers, joint ventures, and strategic corporate alliances. Growing domestic and foreign investment if possible at an exponential rate is imperative. While foreign investment brings access to new technology, this needs to be accompanied by improving local capacity to generate and assimilate new technology. The application of technology can benefit from creating the knowledge space by expanding research, education, and on-the-job training. The growth of export earnings will entail expansion of existing exports as well as diversification and rebalancing exports to introduce new exports and right-size traditional industries—in particular sugar and bananas. To ensure that competitive goods and services become exports requires effective, creative marketing strategies, including branding.[57]

Economic Partnership Agreement

Globalization involves the reduction and/or elimination of national barriers to the global movement of goods, services, technology, and capital. No one, consumer or producer, in developed or developing countries, large or small, can be insulated from globalization. It is not possible to avoid contact and participation in the global economy. Small developing countries have limited influence in global markets and on the policies of powerful developed countries. Trade agreements are an attempt to impose rules over international economic transactions, and for small developing countries, they can be an effective means for the exercise of some countervailing impact on more powerful countries and corporate actors. Trade agreements involve liberalization, which does not automatically generate growth but can do so if properly designed and accompanied by appropriate national and regional economic policies. The objective of negotiating trade agreements for developing countries, such as those in the Caribbean, is to promote economic development. For developing countries, trade agreements mediate the encounter with globalization and offset the power of developed countries by codifying the rules of engagement for international trade. The objective of negotiating an EPA with the EU is to increase economic growth by the expansion of trade and capital flows.

The remaining preferential treatment embodied in the trade component of the Cotonou Agreement was scheduled to end on December 31, 2007, when the WTO waiver permitting these provisions expired. The alternative to the conclusion of an EPA was either the EU GSP system—which would result in incurring additional onerous tariffs that could price the exports of the region out of the EU market—or an Interim Agreement that was confined to trade in goods depriving the region of gains in services and investment. Given these alternatives, the CARIFORUM countries decided to opt for an EPA, thereby avoiding losses and gaining the improved opportunities to export goods and services to the large lucrative EU market.

The overarching objective of the CARIFORUM-EC EPA is the promotion of sustainable economic development. In fact, development infuses all aspects of the EPA. This is given clear expression in (1) an overarching chapter on development, which provides a holistic approach for (2) the subject-specific measure in all subsequent chapters. The objectives of the EPA go beyond the expansion of trade as a stimulus of sustainable economic development to encompass the progressive integration of the CARIFORUM countries into the world economy, the elimination of poverty, and the strengthening of regional integration.

Increasing economic growth and export diversification to put growth on a sustainable basis are important goals for the CARIFORUM countries, given their economic performance in recent years and the circumstances they must confront. The rate of growth of GDP during the period 1990–2005 was 2.8 replace percent lower than that of developing countries and small states. In addition, "average growth has slowed in each decade since the 1970s, the gap between rich and poor states in the region continues to widen, and total factor productivity appears to have stagnated."[58] Many governments are confronting difficult fiscal situations while encumbered by high levels of public debt.[59]

Expansion and Diversification of Exports

The EPA represents a major opportunity to export to the EU market and to attract foreign investment, which together with local investment can produce goods and services for the EU market. The capacity of the EPA to stimulate economic development among the CARIFORUM countries derives primarily from the expanded and unprecedented access to the EU market for goods and services. This increased market access creates opportunities for increased exports from existing and new products and services, and for the diversification of exports.

Increased Market Access for Goods

The gravamen of the market access provisions of the EPA is duty-free, quota-free access for all products except sugar and rice from the January 1, 2008, when there is provisional application of the EPA. Duty-free, quota-free treatment for these two products will be phased over a transition period not exceeding two years. This represents expanded and improved market access compared to that available under previous agreements, that is, the Lomé Convention and the Cotonou Agreement. The EPA includes the elimination of all tariffs and tariff rate quotas on products not fully liberalized under the Cotonou trade regime such as bananas, beef, other meat, dairy products, wheat, and all other cereals, as well as a range of fruits and vegetables.

The market access available in the EPA is similar to that provided to the LDCs by the "EBA" initiative granted by the EU. It will also be available to other ACP countries that have signed either an EPA or an Interim Agreement. However, the market access is superior to that of all non-ACP countries both developed and developing. This access to a high-income market of 450 million consumers and producers can (1) stimulate an increase in existing exports of goods, (2) prompt new exports, and (3) attract inflows of FDI seeking to use the CARIFORUM as a platform for exporting to the EU. In 2005, the value of merchandise imports into the EU accounted for approximately US$414 billion.[60] In like manner, the expansion of production for export to the EU market will generate increased foreign exchange earnings, employment, investment both domestic and foreign, and tax revenue.

The extent to which there is market access depends not only on the reduction/elimination of tariffs and nontariff barriers but also on rules of origin. Rules of origin govern which goods qualify for the benefits of preferential treatment in a trade agreement. The rules of origin in the EPA maintain the structure of the rules of origin in the Cotonou Agreement while providing for changes in the conditions pertaining to production and manufacture of some goods. (1) Arrangements for handling production or manufacture provide for relaxed qualifying conditions on a range of exports of interest to the CARIFORUM states, including biscuits and other baked products, jams and jellies, fruit juices and other beverages, garments (knitted and nonknitted), and air conditioning units. (2) The arrangements for certification of origin in the Cotonou Agreement were felt to be adequate and have been retained. (3) The provisions for administrative cooperation and verification are largely unchanged.

Increased Market Access for Services

Services constitute a very significant proportion of the GDP of the countries of the CARIFORUM region. Services accounted for 66 percent of the GDP of CARICOM member states and in the less developed countries the figure was 86 percent.[61]

Tourism accounts for 70 percent of total services exports of CARICOM.[62] The services exports of CARICOM (excluding government services) grew by an average of 4.6 percent per annum during 1993–2003, approximately 2 percent below the rates of growth exhibited by the world economy and LDCs. The region's share of the global services market dropped from 0.51 percent in 1993 to 0.42 in 2003.[63]

The EU will liberalize 94 percent of its service sectors, while liberalization in CARIFORUM is limited to 75 percent in the more developed countries and 65 percent in the less developed countries. Haiti and the Bahamas have six months to submit their liberalization schedules. The EU has opened sectors ranging from business services, communications, construction, distribution, environmental, financial, transport, tourism, and recreation services. The commitments started when the EPA enters into force for all EU states except the new members (Eastern and Central European states) whose commitments started in 2011 and for Bulgaria and Romania it will start in 2014.

The competitiveness of the tourism sector will be lifted by the lower costs resulting from the liberalization of trade in transport, communications, and products. In addition, the Tourism Annex introduces disciplines on anticompetitive practices of tourism operators, which will safeguard the interests of the mainly small firms in the Caribbean. This measure was necessary because the global tourism industry is a vertically integrated market and a consolidated distribution channel controlled by a limited number of large international entities. The EPA attempts to improve the prospects for CARIFORUM operators that do not currently have the capabilities to fully exploit increased market access to Europe because of the high cost of marketing in Europe, and their limited access to market information. There are provisions on cooperation between CARIFORUM and European industry associations, and enhanced mechanisms for facilitating Caribbean access to information and training. It also provides for mutual recognition of qualifications and environmental standards.

The EPA was the first time that the EU specifically included the cultural sector into a trade agreement. The cultural provisions were aimed at increasing trade in cultural products and services between the EU and the CARIFORUM countries. There are two types of cultural provisions in the CARIFORUM-EU EPA: (1) Market access provisions for entertainment services, enabling artists and cultural professionals from CARIFORUM countries to provide services to the EU market. (2) The Protocol on Cultural Cooperation, which establishes the framework for co-operating to facilitate and promote cultural activities, goods, and services. Particularly noteworthy was that the EU for the first time conceded significant market access commitments for entertainment services,[64] a sector that CARIFORUM regarded as having enormous potential.[65] The Mode 4 provision was a significant breakthrough for CARIFORUM, given the traditional strong reluctance to allow the temporary entry of natural "persons" into their territories because of immigration concerns. Indeed, entry into and the temporary stay in the EU can be for a period up to 90 days in any 12-month period for artists carrying out noncommercial activities. The EU has agreed to unprecedented access in entertainment services in which CARIFORUM sees substantial opportunities. The market access commitments for entertainment services accomplished (1) enhanced legal certainty to CARIFORUM companies entering European markets, (2) reduction of the previous complexity by making the requirements more transparent and (3) prevention of additional future limitations to market access, and (4) open some new market access.

The EPA does not introduce any new requirements for entry by CARIFORUM entertainers. Article 83(2) of the EPA specifically excludes entertainment, fashion, and chefs de cuisines from the requirement of a university degree. The EPA contains a legally binding market access commitment and therefore provides predictability by removing the discretionary element in the entry of registered entertainers. The eligible duration of working is provided not for the EU as a whole but for each country of the EU. Properly managed, an entertainer could work in the EU for an entire year but not exceed the country-specific limits. Access to the entertainment market is complemented by a Protocol on Cultural Cooperation that includes special provisions on audiovisual activities. Coproduced audiovisual products involving European and Caribbean collaboration will qualify as European works, thereby satisfying EU cultural content rules. The Caribbean partner only needs to fund at least 20 percent of the total film budget.

There has been substantial liberalization of temporary movement of natural persons (Mode 4) as reflected in easier access for Caribbean professionals in 29 sectors including entertainment. The EPA provides market access for Caribbean professionals in 29 sectors for employees of Caribbean firms (Contractual Service Suppliers) to be able to enter the EU to supply services. Suppliers must have a contract and stays are for up to 90 days in a calendar year. In addition, the EU has liberalized 11 sectors for temporary entry by independent professionals (IPs) or self-employed persons. Although there are some conditions in some states, for example, economic needs tests, there are no quotas on the number of service suppliers that can enter the EU market. This is an unprecedented and very important concession by the EU to CARIFORUM, since in the WTO and in other bilateral FTAs, the EU does not have market access commitments of this kind for temporary entry.

Easement of Nontariff Barriers

The EPA provides for an easement in the impact of nontariff barriers:

1. Rules of origin (RoOs) can be used as a protectionist trade barrier[66]; in particular, the complexity[67] and restrictiveness of RoO can stifle trade.[68] Conformity can generate substantial costs such as that of (1) actually meeting the RoO and (2) the expense in time and money to furnish proof that the RoO has been complied with. These compliance costs can have a distorting effect on resource use and resource allocation. RoOs can result in prohibitive compliance costs for exporters, especially small firms and customs authorities in both the exporting and importing country, and this can be particularly onerous for small developing countries. For more on RoOs, see appendix I.

The EPA incorporates a relaxation of the qualifying conditions for a number of products, making it easier for CARIFORUM exports to enter the EU market. Among the products that benefit from this easement are biscuits and other bakery products, jams and jellies, fruit juices and other beverages, garments, and air conditioning units. Inputs from any CARIFORUM country, the EU, ACP countries (with some exceptions), and, under certain conditions, neighboring developing countries will qualify as "originating goods" and so can be used in the production of final goods that will qualify for preferential treatment.

2. The application of the principle of national treatment in the EPA is intended to prevent discrimination that could impede exports from CARIFORUM countries. First, internal taxes and charges may not be applied to imports from CARIFORUM if they are not similarly applied to products of domestic origin. Second, there must be no discrimination between imports and domestic products in the application of laws and regulations affecting internal sales, offers for sale, purchase, transportation, distribution, or use of a product. Third, the EU is obliged to eliminate export subsidies on products that the CARIFORUM countries have agreed to liberalize, but the CARIFORUM countries are permitted to maintain this type of subsidy on their products for the duration of the transition periods afforded to developing countries by both the WTO.

Simplification of Customs[69]

Both parties are committed to compliance with relevant international standards and regulations, including WTO rules, the World Customs Organization (WCO), and the Kyoto Convention. The EU and CARIFORUM have agreed to work toward a simplification of their respective customs operations by (1) the reduction, simplification, and standardization of documentation; (2) simplification procedures for goods clearance; and (3) public disclosure and explanation of laws and regulations related to customs. In recognition of the financial and administrative expense involved for CARIFORUM governments to meet this obligation, the EU will provide financial support and technical assistance to CARIFORUM to help in the development of modern customs techniques and automation of customs procedures.

Transitional Arrangements for Key Agricultural Commodities

Traditionally, most of the value of exports from CARIFORUM to the EU has consisted of three agricultural products: sugar, bananas, and rice. There were specially designed and managed preferential arrangements for each of these commodities. The arrangements for bananas had to be changed by the EU to comply with rulings from the Dispute Settlement Mechanism of the WTO. In the case of sugar, the EU's internal policy reforms have been the primary driver of changes in the access arrangements for the ACP. Some developing countries were engaged in challenging the arrangements for sugar in the WTO.

The Protocols governing sugar and banana were replaced by new arrangements that were WTO compatible. The EPA commits the EU to engage in consultations with CARIFORUM prior to any policy developments that may affect the competitive position of the region's traditional exports in the EU market. This is particularly important in the context of possible developments in the WTO and bilateral free trade agreements, which the EU may negotiate. The commitment extends to the EU's internal regulatory framework.

CARIFORUM gained an additional 60,000 tons of access for sugar exports to the EU market over and above the 160,000 tons available to Sugar Protocol

(SP) signatories during the period up to the end of September 2009. Of the additional amount, 30,000 tons will be reserved for the SP countries, namely, those of CARICOM and the remainder is allotted to the Dominican Republic. While the SP remains in effect (until September 2009), the EU has given assurances that it will seek to ensure that any shortfalls on the SP quotas are reallocated among those CARIFORUM countries, which are party to the protocol. In respect of a number of manufactured products that contain sugar, the EU has committed to reviewing that list of products, with a view to reducing it, at the end of three years following signature of the agreement.

Bananas will gain full duty-free and quota-free access to the EU market from the inception of the EPA. In effect, the ruling of the WTO dispute settlement panel against the EU's preferences granted to ACP banana exporters will become null and void insofar as CARIFORUM banana exports are concerned since the duty-free preferences will now be protected under WTO rules governing free trade areas. The EC maintains a tariff of €176 on imports of bananas from non-ACP suppliers. The beneficiaries of this measure are the CARIFORUM countries that will sign an EPA and Cameroon and Cote d'Ivoire who have signed interim agreements.

The EPA contains a comprehensive Joint Declaration on Bananas, which acknowledges the importance of the industry to several CARIFORUM countries and which recognizes the need for the EU to maintain significant preferences for the product. The Declaration also commits the EU to provide funding to assist the industry in making the necessary adjustments, including diversification and international competitiveness and addressing the social impacts that may arise from the new trading arrangements.

CARIFORUM rice exporting countries will have quotas of 187,000 tons for 2008 and 250,000 tons for 2009. The new quotas for 2008 and 2009 represent increases of 29 and 72 percent, respectively, over the present quota available to Guyana and Suriname. After 2009 CARIFORUM exports will have duty-free and quota-free access. The EPA contains a joint declaration committing the EU for keeping the licensing and other arrangements relating to the quota under review with aim of ensuring that CARIFORUM exporters obtain the maximum benefit from the trade.

Rules of Origin

The RoO in the EPA were important for the CARIFORUM countries because they wanted to be sure that the RoO did not become a barrier to exports. CARIFORUM's position was that the provisions of Article 37 of the Cotonou Agreement, which called for a review of the RoO in the negotiation of the EPA, meant that the RoO would be perused and revised where the RoO were restrictive to CARIFORUM's exporters. The EC initial proposal sought far-reaching changes to origin, the gravamen of which was the employment of the value-added method in substitution for the change in tariff heading method utilized by the RoO in the Cotonou Agreement. This means that the systems for operating the RoO are unchanged and familiar as they relate to arrangements for consignment, certification of origin, administrative cooperation, and verification of origin. The EPA makes provision for a technical review of the RoO after three years to allow technical amendments and improvements.

Getting There First

The CARIFORUM negotiators set out to get the best agreement for the region within the agreed-upon schedule. Being the only region to achieve this unexpectedly put the region in the position of being the first to have the new expanded access to the EU market. This was an advantage that the CARIFORUM countries had the chance to capitalize on. Being the first to establish a market presence is a time-sensitive advantage to an exporter, but it is one that diminishes as other firms enter the EU market. The comparative value of the duty-free, quota-free market access to the EU depreciates each day because the EU is negotiating FTAs with other countries, including developing countries. In the course of concluding new FTAs and EPAs, the EU is extending duty-free, quota-free market access for goods and, possibly, similar access for services to an ever-increasing number of countries; consequently, the exclusivity of the market access provided through the EPA is being progressively reduced. The region will face increasing competition in the EU market as more countries negotiate similar access. Central America and the EU completed negotiations for an FTA in May 2010.[70] The EU has also signed trade agreements with Peru and Colombia, resumed talks with MERCOSUR,[71] which had been on hold since 2004, and is engaged in discussions about an EU-US trade agreement with the objective of completing the negotiations by the end of 2014. It is therefore incumbent on the CARIFORUM countries that they make the best use of their market access as quickly as possible.

Investment Stimulation

FDI has traditionally accounted for a significant share of gross investment and capital formation in the CARIFORUM countries. The impact of FDI in small developing countries will depend on the local economic environment and policies of the host country[72] such as the quality of human capital.[73] The duty-free/quota-free access to a market of 450 million high income consumers and producers constitutes an enormous export opportunity, which will interest firms looking to export to the EU. Foreign investors seeking this production possibility will not be confined to Europe but will be global in origin. Whether firms, local and foreign, invest and produce for export will be influenced not only by the stimulus of the export opportunity but also significantly by the local economic conditions that include a raft of factors such as interest rates, fiscal incentives, cost of labor, infrastructure, and taxation. Governments can assist in improving the attractiveness of the local business environment by helping to alleviate bottlenecks such as cumbersome customs systems and poor infrastructure. The investment provisions of the EPA in combination of export opportunities and local business environment is what will determine the extent of investment and in the case of FDI will influence the benefits and costs.[74]

FDI can be an important mechanism for the international transfer of technology that can enhance international competitiveness through improved productivity and knowledge spillovers. Trans-border transmission of technology is a complex phenomenon influenced by a myriad of factors of which FDI is only one. Anything that makes it more difficult or expensive for firms, local or foreign, to access and adopt the latest technology will impede economic growth.[75] Impediments can take a variety of forms including the regime governing foreign investment. An important consideration is the state of IPRs and the efficacy of enforcement because it influences the willingness of foreign investors to engage in international technology transfer. Saggi summarizes the gravamen of the pertinent literature: "liberalization of trade and FDI policies needs to be complemented by appropriate policy measures with respect to education, R&D and human capital accumulation if developing countries are to take full advantage of increased trade and FDI."[76] The CARIFORUM can utilize the EPA to attract investments in research and development utilizing the access it now receives to the Framework program 7 (FP7, an EU program to fund research and development among academic institutions, government agencies, and private sector investors).

Investment Rules

The EPA includes the conventional rules on establishing, namely, national treatment and MFN treatment. Both parties can subject national treatment to qualifications, for example, restrictions on foreign ownership of land. It encompasses investment provisions that provide transparency and predictability across an array of sectors, thereby enhancing the CARIFORUM region as a destination for foreign investment. The coverage includes the industrial, agricultural, and services sectors. The investment provisions of the EPA are not exhaustive and can coexist with current bilateral investment treaties(BITs) and do not preclude the negotiation of new BITs.[77] While encouraging foreign investment, the rules governing investment in CARIFORUM countries have excluded public services and utilities and maintained reservations to shelter small- and medium-sized enterprises in specified sectors. The EPA also embodies obligations that are aimed at ensuring that investors adhere to international standards of labor, occupational health, safety, and environmental standards. There is also a provision in Article 72 that seeks to prevent corruption in the form of bribery of government officials.

Investment Visibility

An important factor is that the EPA also serves to give greater international visibility to investment possibilities in CARIFORUM countries and to highlight the quality of the investment regime in these countries. This is important because as Friedman points out: "Foreign investors managing internationally diversified portfolios may find it difficult to keep abreast of conditions in a myriad of countries. The smaller the emerging market, the less the incentive for large investors to do so."[78] The increased visibility and investment provisions of the EPA should contribute to fostering strategic corporate alliances and other forms of collaboration. Partnerships with companies in developed countries can be instrumental to building export capacity in firms in developing countries.[79] This possibility is of considerable importance to the small firms in the services sector of the CARICOM countries.[80] The positive impact of foreign investment on growth[81] is derived from the technology transfers and knowledge diffusion. The presence of foreign companies creates pressure on local firms to improve productivity; they are pushed to meet international standards in quality and reliability of goods and services.

Export Production-induced Investment

Access to the EU market of almost 500 million on the basis of preferential market access, plus the availability of skilled labor in stable democratic countries, will make CARIFORUM economies more attractive to foreign investors from the EU and elsewhere for export production for global markets.

Market-induced Investment

The CARIFORUM market, though not particularly large, will be of interest to some foreign investors both from Europe and elsewhere. The CARIFORUM countries have committed to open 50–75 percent of their service sectors in order to encourage investment and the transfer of technology. The new sectors for market opening include tourism, business services, computer and computer-related services, entertainment, environmental services, maritime transport, and research and development. With CARIFORUM the only non-EU region to receive market access to the European cultural industries market, the EPA can provide the platform for attracting investments into the region in this sector. Currently, the EPA allows for investors in CARIFORUM's cultural industry to enter into coproduction arrangements with European audiovisual firms to access the market. It also allows for service providers in the industry to travel to the EU to provide services once they are legal persons of a CARIFORUM state.

Improving International Competitiveness

Increased Investment

Increased levels of local and foreign private investment, stimulated by enhanced market access and export opportunities, can play a vital role in improving productivity and international competitiveness. FDI brings with it technology, international management, strategic alliances, and international marketing know-how. The extent to which there are private capital inflows and increased domestic investment depends both on the measures in the EPA to promote investment and the national and regional development policies of governments in the CARIFORUM countries.

Trade Facilitation

Trade facilitation measures can make an important contribution to economic growth by reducing the costs of conducting international trade. The aim of trade facilitation is to reduce the costs of importing and exporting by reducing or eliminating procedural delays, costs of compliance with onerous regulations, sluggish bureaucratic execution, and the cost of trade-related services. Estimates of the cost of trade procedures ranges from 1.5 to 7.5 percent of the value of trade flows.[82] Improved trade facilitation can reduce total trade costs by as much as 15.5 percent in developing countries.[83] Trade facilitation refers to the simplification, standardization, and automation of trade procedures for import, export, and transit requirements and procedures applied by customs and other government agencies. Modernization and reform of customs are the principal concern of trade facilitation. Trade facilitation is also affected by the efficiency of ministries such as agriculture and health, standards regulating bureaus, and private sector entities such as customs brokers.

Costly, inefficient, bureaucratic, and time-consuming customs systems can adversely affect international trade because they add to the cost of goods being traded and impair the international competitiveness. They can cause direct loss or depreciation if goods are perishable, and loss of business opportunities and inventory holding costs. Trade transaction costs incurred in import and export procedures can amount to as much as 15 percent of the value of the goods being traded.[84] Improved trade facilitation can boost exports as was illustrated by the experience of Jamaica. Up to 1993, export consignments required 23 steps, which routinely took two to three days to be completed. With the aid of technical assistance, an action plan was prepared and implemented so that within two years export clearance time was reduced to 10–20 minutes.[85] The cost was negligible because it involved changes to administrative systems and procedures. This episode demonstrates what is possible in a small developing country without large financial outlays. Engman's survey of empirical studies reports that in several developing countries customs reform has increased revenue collection "by a factor of two or sometimes by more over a relatively short period of time."[86] This finding will undoubtedly be of considerable interest to the CARIFORUM governments that depend heavily on revenues collected by their customs administrations.

Without adequate trade facilitation, it would be difficult to realize the full potential of any trade agreement. For this reason, the EPA creates reciprocal obligations in trade facilitation for the EU and CARIFORUM countries. The objective is to ensure improved efficiency, transparency, and nondiscrimination in customs operations and border management procedures. This includes (1) the application of modern customs techniques and automation of customs procedures and (2) the introduction of procedures and practices that meet international and WTO standards. The chapter on Customs and Trade Facilitation in the EPA calls for the legislation, provisions, and procedures of both parties to be informed by international agreements and standards applicable in the field of customs and trade. Among these would be agreements such as the WCO Framework of Standards to Secure and Facilitate Global Trade (SAFE), the revised Kyoto Convention on the Simplification and Harmonization of Customs Procedures (1999), and the WCO Customs Data Model and Harmonized System of Commodity Description and Coding (HS).

There is a strong emphasis on cooperation on customs issues between the parties taking into account the differences in the level of development of institutional capacities of the customs administrations in the EU and CARIFORUM. The provisions of the chapter on trade facilitation do not contain language that imposes on CARIFORUM states specific dates for the completion of these objectives; the commitments are to best endeavors and are conditional on technical and financial support being provided to CARIFORUM countries. There is a link between the attainment of commitments by CARIFORUM and the delivery of EU support.

The state of customs administration varies considerably across the CARIFORUM group in systems, the extent of automation, and the goals and pace of proposed modernization. The extent of the differences is illustrated by the fact that while all countries are applying the WCO's HS, four are using HS2007, three are using HS2002, six are using HS1996, and one is using HS1992.[87] The governments of CARIFORUM need to put in place a range of measures to achieve the goals that the EPA subscribes to and seeks to attain. These include electronic systems for the exchange of data among traders, customs administrations, and related agencies, making publicly available, ideally through electronic means, all legislation, administrative notices, procedural requirements, contact points for information, fees, and charges. Ultimately, there should to the extent possible standardization across the CARIFORUM states and ideally a single administrative document in electronic form for the CARIFORUM region. The creation of a single administrative document is subject to the proviso that "a joint review of the situation shall be carried out three years after entry into force of the Agreement."[88]

Easing the Movement of Service Providers

A critically important avenue to take advantage of the opportunities to supply services to the EU markets is the movement of service suppliers. The EPA makes provisions for the movement of service suppliers on an unprecedented scale and there are provisions that make it much easier than in the pre-EPA era for service suppliers seeking to transit the EU countries. The commitments for services will make it easier for business travel and staff transfers. Short-term entry visas are available for business travel in all the services sectors.

Temporary entry visas issued for up to 90 days in any 12-month period can be obtained for business purposes such as arranging sales or purchases, conducting market research, trade promotion, and attending training trade fairs and exhibitions. Intracompany transfers are facilitated for personnel of CARIFORUM firms that establish a commercial presence in Europe, for example, transferring staff from the Caribbean to work in the business in Europe. Three types of visa are available (with some minor reservations): (1) senior staff responsible for establishing a commercial presence in Europe can have a visa for up to 90 days in any 12-month period, (2) intracompany transfers of managers, specialists, and graduate trainees. Employees that fall within these categories are eligible for posting in the Europe-based business for a period not exceeding three years, and (3) new graduate trainees can obtain a visa for up to one year.

A Caribbean firm that does not have a commercial presence in Europe but has a contract to supply services in an EC country can send employees to Europe to provide the service. To obtain a visa, the contractual service supplier must satisfy certain stipulations. These stipulations are intended to prevent the abuse of visas for purposes of migration and will not frustrate serious business persons. They include the person must be an employee of a firm that has a valid service contract in Europe and must have been employed by the business for one year. The employee is also required to possess a university degree or pertinent professional qualifications where required and have a minimum of three-years professional experience in the relevant field. The temporary entry will be valid for a cumulative period not exceeding six months (or 25 weeks in Luxembourg) during a 12-month period. A self-employed professional who has a contract to supply services but who does not have a commercial presence in Europe can travel to Europe, provided that they meet criteria similar to those for firms. In order to purvey services in EU countries, the qualifications of CARIFORUM individuals will need to be recognized and accepted in EU countries.

IPRs for Innovation and Investment

The intensification of competition and constant upgrading of competitiveness and productivity in response to new technology is inherent in globalization. The imperative for small developing economies is to meet this challenge and avoid the impoverishment that is often the result of marginalization from the dynamic of global trade and investment. An important aspect of international competitiveness is the use of the most efficient technology. This, in turn, requires the generation of new technology and/or its adaption in the production process. Small developing countries are unlikely to have the capacity or the resources, financial and human, to produce new technologies across the gamut of economic activities. Consequently, it (1) must specialize in those activities where it has and can conduct the necessary research and development and (2) should concentrate on developing the environment and facilities to encourage the acquisition, dissemination, adoption, and adaptation of the latest technologies available globally. IPRs are an essential component of any strategy to generate or acquire new technology, foster innovation by safeguarding the rewards of creativity, and encourage technology transfer.

The spread and transfer of new technology can take place through FDI, licensing, and international trade in goods and services. The extent and speed of technology transfer through these channels are affected by the state of a country's IPRs.[89] IPR are a complex amalgam of copyrights, patents, trademarks, and other rights that have separate modalities that vary by subject matter. For IPR to be effective contributories to economic development, they must calibrate in a delicate balance (1) sufficient incentives to galvanize new technology and original artistic expressions and (2) promoting their transformation and diffusion into products and services. IPR do not guarantee FDI and technology transfer but can help.[90] It is, however, one of several interacting factors and it is difficult to isolate the impact that can be attributed solely to IPR. Skeptics point to the inconclusive nature of the empirical studies on the relationship between IPR and foreign investment and technology transfer.[91] It should also be conceded that in some instances stronger IPR if enforced could cause increases in the cost of importing certain goods and services. This is well illustrated by the issue of medicines and the TRIPS Agreement.

IPR can protect local producers, particularly, in the creative industries in realizing the fruits of their labor through royalties that previously were pirated. This has been for a long time an issue of considerable angst in the Caribbean, particularly in the music industry. This concern has coexisted with a limited awareness of how effectively IPR can contribute to economic development. Ideological and institutional factors in developing countries have hindered the recognition of the positive contributions that can flow from IPR.[92] The economics profession was slow to appreciate the possibilities of IPRs.[93]

Small countries such as those of CARIFORUM have in the past generated technological innovations in livestock, bananas, and sugar cane, and there is no reason why they should not continue to pioneer new technologies. It is important to be disabused of the mindset that it is only in the developed countries that new technology invention and innovation are generated and that all that takes place in developing countries is merely diffusion, adaptation, and imitation.

The EPA locates the provisions on IPRs in the framework of a chapter on innovation systems, with the objective of strengthening regional and national systems of innovation[94] in the CARIFORUM region. The main objective of the EPA provisions on IPR is to stimulate innovation through EU cooperation and development support for the promotion and development of IPR in the CARIFORUM region. This approach is aimed at being a catalyst to innovation and thereby to competitiveness. The EU support and technical cooperation are targeted to the development of a number of clusters in science and technology, eco-innovation and renewable energy, and ICTs.

The fundamental determinant of competitiveness and productivity in a modern dynamic economy engaged in the global economy is knowledge. Innovation systems which of necessity encompass IPR are essential for the generation, adoption, and diffusion of economically useful knowledge integral to production and distribution of goods and services. Given the extent and intensity of globalization, an increasing number of aspects of innovation become transnational and therefore innovation systems are likely to be more fecund if they extend beyond the nation state, in the case of the EPA encourages the emergence of regional innovation systems.[95]

The intensive competition inherent in globalization compels companies to continually search worldwide for the most supportive business environment and to locate and/or relocate whenever there are advantages to be garnered. Access to the latest technology and management innovations will encourage foreign firms to establish and operate in developing countries and will reward local companies for creativity and stimulate risk taking. One of the attractions in any business environment is the extent to which it facilitates continual retaining and regaining of competitive edge—that is, the capacity for innovation including research infrastructure, highly trained labor force, institutional arrangements that encourage knowledge generation and learning, and clusters of firms for forward and backward linkages. IPRs that are modern in coverage and up-to-date are a necessary condition, but they need to be enforceable.[96]

The EPA seeks to facilitate (1) the process of innovation in firms in the CARIFORUM region, (2) the transfer of EU innovations to CARIFORUM firms, and (3) the commercialization of innovations by CARIFORUM firms in the EU market. The IPR provisions will encourage the commercialization and application of new technology by the establishment and enforcement of the IPR of CARIFORUM firms and the licensing to EU firms.

Strengthening Regional Integration

The strengthening of regional economic integration among the CARIFORUM countries is one of the objectives of the EPA. This is a complex task because the four coexisting streams of integration constitute a variable geometry, specifically (1) the CSME, (2) the CARICOM-Dominican Republic Free Trade Agreement, (3) the Bahamas, which participates in neither the CSME nor the CARICOM-DR FTA, and (4) the special case of Haiti. Despite these circumstances, regional integration is replete throughout the EPA, reflecting the fact that it has been and remains a central tenet of the development policy of both the EU and CARIFORUM. In some important respects, the ambit of the EPA negotiations was constrained by the limited advancement of CARICOM integration.[97] The CARIFORUM negotiators successfully resisted EC demands for market access in government procurement so as to protect the integrity of the regional integration process as represented by the CSME. Ironically the proposed commitments to be undertaken on government procurement in the CSME go beyond those that CARIFORUM countries will assume under the EPA. The EPA makes provision for cooperation and assistance to establish the CSME regime and improve national regimes so that the regional and national processes can move in tandem.

Even before seeking to strengthen regional integration in and among the existing streams of integration, coexisting within the CARIFORUM economic space was to ensure that the EPA did not disrupt these processes. The most fundamental safeguard was the completion of the EPA. This obviated the need for each CARIFORUM country to separately negotiate an interim agreement or opt to operate under the EU system of GSP. Either of these would have fragmented the already variegated common external tariff of the CSME.

The CARIFORUM negotiators also ensured that the EPA did not breach the integrity of the design and pace of regional economic integration as embodied in the Treaty of Chaguaramas and the CSME. A notable example is resisting the relentless pressure from the EU for market access in government procurement. No right of market access is granted or conferred in the provisions in the EPA, which allows the intra-CARICOM process to proceed on its own volition.

The EPA will not require the acceleration of the implementation of the CARICOM Single Market (CSM). The latest version of the frequently postponed schedule for implementation of the CSM calls for completion by 2015. If the region achieves this target date, the CSM will be fully operational long before the trade liberalization involved in the EPA begins in earnest. By 2015, less than 10 percent of imports from the EU will be subject to tariff liberalization. Given that less than 15 percent of our total imports come from the EU, it means that less than 2 percent of total imports will be affected before the CSM is completed. Figure 6.1 shows the minute share of total imports affected by tariff liberalization resulting from the EPA.

If the implementation of the EPA induces acceleration in the completion of the CSME, this would be to the good of the region. It would be unfortunate if this happened because of a development, external to the integration process. Given the history of the CSME, there is justifiable worry that completion of the CSME will be not be realized on schedule. A continuation of the dismal record of implementation

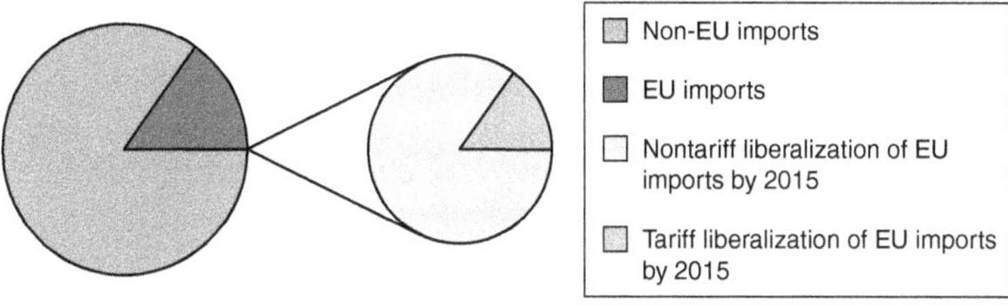

Figure 6.1 CARIFORUM imports.

of the CSM cannot be allowed to delay the EPA schedule. CARIFORUM does not have the luxury of adjusting at its own pace because the global economy waits for no man. The world is not changing; it has changed.

Regional preference as embodied in the EPA is consistent with Article 8 of the Revised Treaty of Chaguaramas. This provision means that any concession granted by one CARIFORUM state to the EU must be conferred on all other CARIFORUM states. The regional preference provision does not prevent CARIFORUM states from granting each other more favorable treatment without conferring such treatment to the EU. Among CARIFORUM states, the Dominican Republic has liberalized the most with the EU and those liberalization commitments must be granted to other CARIFORUM states. An important benefit will be the removal of Law 173 of the Dominican Republic—perhaps the most contentious issue in the negotiations of the built-in agenda of the CARICOM-Dominican Republic Free Trade Agreement.

The EPA contains an MFN clause covering goods and services, which provides for both CARIFORUM and the EU to automatically confer on each other any better treatment granted by one party to a major trading partner. Such entities are defined as countries or regional blocs garnering 1 or 1.5 percent and above of world merchandise exports.

One of the constraints of small developing economies is the small size of the national market, which precludes the realization of economies of scale in a wide range of lines of production. An important part of the rationale for regional economic integration is that the amalgamation of national markets may produce a regional market, which allows the attainment of economies of scale. This may not materialize if the resulting region is still too small, as has been the experience of CARICOM. This is where access to large external markets or to the world market and other benefits. The EPA is valuable to CARICOM because a market of the size of the EU is sufficiently large to allow CARICOM-based firms to achieve economies of scale through exporting.

The concept of the CSME is not cast in tablets of stone because it would then be immutable in an environment of rapid and profound changes in the global economy. Adjustments have to be made to the CSME model to keep it relevant in changing local, regional, and international circumstances. The Treaty of Chaguaramas is couched in sufficiently flexible language that what it is interpreted to permit can be modified without redacting the text—but if warranted the "sacred text" can and should be amended. If the Treaty mandates a static model of regional integration, then it will increasingly represent occlusion rather than a creative foundation for regional development.

Extended, Asymmetrical, and Managed Adjustment and Implementation

Extended Implementation of Import Liberalization

Whenever a trade agreement involves countries, which differ substantially in level of development and size, asymmetric tariff liberalization is appropriate. This well-recognized principle has been given expression in the tariff liberalization process in the WTO, where a distinction is made between developing countries and other countries. The EPA is founded on a clear recognition that the two groups of countries differ in size and level of development. This recognition is embedded throughout the agreement, most explicitly in the schedules of tariff liberalization. The objectives of extended schedules of import liberalization were (1) to allow time for adjustment by economies as a whole and by firms to imports from the EU and (2) to make the loss of revenue from tariff reduction/elimination as gradual as possible over long periods so as to minimize the impact on fiscal revenue. The gradual pace of import liberalization, however, will delay the benefit of lower prices for imports from the EU, with some loss to consumers and producers.

The CARIFORUM (1) will liberalize 86.9 percent of imports from the EU with 82.7 percent within 15 years. (2) The rest of the imports from the EU are on an exclusions list in perpetuity covering some 463 items. (3) There is a three-year moratorium before any tariff reduction commences. (4) There is a moratorium of ten years for revenue-sensitive products such as gasoline, motor vehicles, and parts. (5) Tariffs for a limited number of products will be reduced over periods extending to 25 years. (6) Other duties and charges will remain unchanged for seven years and will be eliminated in years eight, nine, and ten. (7) Tariffs on motor vehicles will decrease after a ten-year moratorium. (8) Items currently on the Revised Treaty of Chaguaramas Article 164 list of products (relating to industrial development in the LDCs) have been exempted from the liberalization process and any items so designated in the future. The CARIFORUM tariff liberalization schedule is listed in table 6.1.

Table 6.1 CARIFORUM tariff liberalization commitments

Phasing period	*Share of imports (replace)*	*Cumulative share (replace)*	*Total trade (replace)*
0 year	52.8	52.8	70.0
5 years	3.2	56.0	72.0
10 years	8.3	61.1	75.3
15 years	21.7	82.7	89.3
20 years	1.9	84.6	90.5
25 years	2.3	86.9	92.0

Source: Caribbean Regional Negotiating Machinery.

The advantages of the arrangements for import liberalization include (1) implementation periods, extending in some cases up to 25 years, will allow firms and governments to adjust gradually in keeping with their capacities. If firms and farms in CARICOM cannot become sufficiently competitive in 10–25 years, they never will and should not be in operation. (2) The moratoria for the elimination of tariff and other duties and charges will allow time to plan and execute fiscal reform. The magnitude of the problem is much less than feared because EU imports account for approximately 15 percent of total imports and 50 percent of imports from the EU were duty-free before the EPA. (3) Lower prices for imported inputs entering export production can enhance their competitiveness and export prospects. (4) Lower prices for consumers and inputs into production for the domestic market.

Less expensive imports from the EU could displace (1) more costly local goods and services, (2) relatively more expensive imports from CARICOM partners, and /or (3) imports from extraregional countries. These consequences are beneficial to consumers and producers for both the domestic and export markets and must be understood in relation to the secure improved access to the EU market.

Import liberalization may cause some local firms to adjust, but this is a normal part of every economy and not peculiarly related to the EPA. The ebbs and flows of enterprises are an inevitable aspect of the fluidity of economic life, particularly in a period of rapid technological change and increasingly pervasive globalization. These phenomena are going to occur in CARICOM countries in which the price elasticity of demand for imports is such that consumers are willing to substitute in response to changes in tariffs.[98] The impact will be very limited because of (1) the exclusions list of 463 products, (2) the fact that EU imports account for only 10 percent of total imports (table 6.2), (3) many imports from the EU were already duty free, and (4) the most sensitive imports will not be liberalized for at least ten years.

CARIFORUM agricultural producers are afforded protection from EU export subsidies. The EU is obligated under the EPA to eliminate export subsidies on all agricultural products for which CARIFORUM has agreed to liberalize. On the other hand, CARIFORUM is not required to eliminate export subsidies that are sanctioned by the WTO under the Agreement on Agriculture and the Agreement on Subsidies and Countervailing Measures.

One of the most important objectives of the exclusion list and the tariff structure was to ensure food security by the continued viability of domestic food production insulating domestic food production from imports. The EU is not a major supplier of food to the region, and where it does, these are products not produced in the region or not traditionally available in adequate supplies.[99] The EPA is consistent with the goal of the maximum feasible self-sufficiency (food sovereignty) in the Caribbean. As net food importers, the CARIFORUM countries wanted to maintain domestic food supply and rural development and were very careful to ensure that the EPA would not adversely affect the small farmers in the region. International trade, trade policy, and food security are enmeshed through a range of linkages[100] because imports are a vital source of nutritional staples in the diet. Food imports affect food availability, access, utilization, and stability, the four dimensions in the conventional definition of food security. The cost and stability of food supply affect consumers and the producers.

Table 6.2 Imports from the EU as a percentage of total imports of CARICOM

OECS	*1991–1995*	*1996–2000*	*2001–2004*	*Average*
	14.18	*10.88*	*10.95*	*11.44*
Antigua and Barbuda	–	7.49	–	7.49
Dominica	16.36	12.22	12.14	13.57
Grenada	13.42	10.71	10.53	11.55
St. Kitts and Nevis	8.54	6.74	6.88	7.39
Saint Lucia	14.88	13.08	12.12	13.36
St. Vincent and the Grenadines	17.72	15.04	13.06	15.27
LDCs	11.15	9.10	8.48	9.69
Belize	8.11	7.31	6.01	7.15
MDCs	13.41	10.47	11.61	11.17
Bahamas	–	1.81	1.17	1.49
Barbados	12.18	11.17	12.38	11.91
Guyana	15.44	10.64	10.97	12.35
Jamaica	7.02	7.00	7.86	7.29
Suriname	17.34	21.19	21.99	20.17
Trinidad and Tobago	15.07	11.00	15.27	13.78
CARICOM	12.28	9.78	10.04	10.43

Source: Inter-American Development Bank and World Bank.

Management by Trade Defense Measures

"Trade defense measure" is unfortunate nomenclature that refers to temporary measures that can be employed to manage the adjustment and implementation process in order to prevent injury from imports. The EPA does not prevent the parties from invoking their rights under the WTO. If increased imports from either party or, indeed, from a third party that is not a part of the EPA but a member of the WTO is causing injury to a domestic industry, the CARIFORUM and EU states can invoke the WTO Safeguard Clause, subject to the terms and conditions of Article XIX of the GATT. Article 240 of the EPA states, "Where any Signatory CARIFORUM States or the EC Party is in serious balance of payments and external financial difficulties, or under threat thereof, it may adopt or maintain restrictive measures with regard to trade in goods, services and establishment." It qualifies this by stating that the restrictive measure adopted or maintained under this Article shall be nondiscriminatory and of limited duration and shall not go beyond what is necessary to remedy the balance of payments and external financial situation. The EPA allows both CARIFORUM and the EU the use of a bilateral safeguard mechanism for a limited period of time in circumstances where the importation of goods from the other party causes or threatens to cause (1) serious injury to domestic industries, (2) sector-related disturbances that cause major social problems, or (3) disturbances to agricultural markets or mechanisms that regulate those markets. The parties are permitted the use of Antidumping Duties to prevent the unfair and/or predatory trade practice of selling goods in overseas markets below their cost of production in accordance with provisions of the WTO. If situations of unfair competition arise from subsidized imports, resort can be made to the WTO Agreement on Subsidies and Countervailing Measures, which permits the injured party to impose duties.

Domestic Policy Space for Adjustment and International Competitiveness

The EPA preserves the development policy space for governments in the CARIFORUM countries and what is important is how this space is used by individual countries and how it is employed regionally in the CARIFORUM economic space. This will lead to a substantial effect and will determine the extent to which the EPA promotes economic development for CARIFORUM. The EPA constitutes an amalgam of actual and prospective opportunities for CARIFORUM to benefit in terms of export opportunities and foreign investment. The extent to which this happens depends on the development strategies employed and the macroeconomic policies applied. The experiences of the countries in the CARICOM region provide ample evidence of the importance of economic policies. Henry and Miller make the telling point that the economic growth rates of Barbados and Jamaica differ significantly despite having similar institutions and attribute the divergence in growth to differences in economic policy.[101] The truism of national economic policy being a major determinant of the extent to which the opportunities of a trade agreement are converted into tangible gains is also valid for the benefits that can be derived from development assistance. On the basis of a comprehensive review of US development assistance, Ruttan draws the conclusion the "effectiveness of economic assistance is strongly conditioned by both the macroeconomic and the sectoral economic policies of the host country."[102] The critical point is for both the EU and CARIFORUM to see development assistance as not merely supplemental funds but as funds that will assist the governments of CARIFORUM to pursue development policies of their own design. As long ago as 1968, Mikesell advised donors and beneficiaries that "the function of concessionary aid is not primarily to supplement the resources of the recipient, but rather to help to help the recipient to mobilize its own resources and perhaps to attract private and public non-concessionary external capital for achieving its development goals."[103]

The economic policy and institutional framework that will boost the sustainable development in a particular economy are unique to that economy. There are commonalities that can be derived from studying successful economies, but the precise blend and application will be unique to each economy. In addition, for maintaining the maximum development policy space so that policies designed for the local economy are as free of constraints as possible, there is the international and competitive dimension of economic policy. This dimension reflects the reality of global competition for capital, technology, finance, and skilled human resources. The implication is that development policy is efficacious to the extent that it is more conducive to international flows and local enterprise than such policy competing jurisdictions. CARIFORUM must assess its policy environment relative to its competitors. The

Table 6.3 Doing business: selected indicators Caribbean and comparable developing countries (2008)

Country	*Doing business rank*	*Time for export (days)*	*Cost of export (US$) per container*	*Time for import (days)*	*Cost of import (US$) per container*
Antigua and Barbuda	55	19	1,107	19	1,174
Belize	116	23	1,800	26	2,130
Dominica	80	16	1,197	18	11,107
Dominican Republic	35	12	815	13	1,015
Grenada	52	19	820	23	1,178
Guyana	101	30	850	35	856
Haiti	153	52	1,650	53	1,860
Jamaica	92	21	1,750	22	1,350
St. Kitts	22	15	750	17	756
St. Lucia	88	18	1,375	21	1,420
St. Vincent	75	15	1,770	16	1,769
Trinidad and Tobago	49	14	693	26	1,100
LAC average	–	22	1,107	26	1,228
East Asian average	–	24	775	25	917

Source: Doing Business Reports, various years.

ease of doing business is a very important factor in international competitiveness and economic growth. CARIFORUM's comparative position is listed in table 6.3.

Preservation of Policy Space

The United Nations Conference on Trade and Development (UNCTAD) defines policy space as "the extent to which national governments have the authority to make decisions concerning economic policy and, correspondingly, the extent to which such authority is constrained by international disciplines and processes."[104] Policy space is progressively redimensioned by two influences. First, as globalization proceeds and countries become more integrated into the world economy, there is a reduction of the degrees of freedom for national economic policy. Second, redimensioning occurs whenever governments enter into international agreements including, but not confined to, trade agreements in which they voluntarily trade some of their sovereignty over economic policy for the gains they expect to realize from these agreements. Striking a balance in the trade-off is a matter of judgment by the parties in entering into a trade agreement. Some authors argue that the reduction of autonomous national economic policy should be accepted since resistance would be harmful to economic growth. Thomas Friedman takes the extreme position that to benefit from globalization a country must accept the "rules of the game" or perish economically. He refers to this set of policies as the "Golden Straitjacket,"[105] and while this is an extreme formulation, it makes the important point that preservation and erosion of policy space are not only about formal agreements. The penalties for not abiding by these rules are extracted by the global market. Others have taken a diametrically opposed position, arguing that the maximum policy space should be allowed to developing countries because if used successfully it can be beneficial to economic development.[106] Realistically the answer is somewhere between these polar opposites; where exactly that is for each country is a matter for judgment.

Trade agreements are of the genre of formally trading reduced policy space for gains such as market access in other countries, for example, a bilateral free trade agreement or for membership in an international community, such as the WTO, whose conduct is bound by mutually agreed rules. Yielding the independent policy space is always only partial and may be permanent or temporary. In the former situation, for example, Member states of the WTO agree to abide by a mixture of common rules and obligations specific to their own country. The WTO enforces the rules by sanctions and disputes over interpretation are adjudicated by the Dispute Settlement Mechanism. An example of the temporary relinquishing of policy space is when a country agrees to a facility with the International Monetary Fund entailing conditionality that requires eschewing certain policies for the term of the programme.

It is a fact of life that developed countries vigorously press for multilateral rules that create an increasingly open global economy because they perceive a comparative advantage that they can exploit, at times depriving developing countries of some infant industry measure that they employed during their formative development period in an earlier era. However, it would oversimplify to categorize this as selfishly "kicking away the ladder"[107] and caricature the multilateral rules codified in the WTO agreements as foreclosing development options for which there is little gain or even loss.[108] Multilateral rules have to strike a balance between what neoclassical economists describe as global welfare and national welfare. Cooper as far back as 1968, prior to the WTO, explains the dilemma as "how to keep the manifold benefits of extensive international economic intercourse free of crippling restrictions while at the same time preserving a maximum degree of freedom for each nation to pursue its legitimate economic interests."[109] Indeed, as pointed out by Mayer, policy sovereignty and policy autonomy can also be beneficial as a defense against protectionism of more powerful trading partners and as a means of protection against beggar-thy-neighbor policy.[110]

The issue of policy space is complicated by the fact that situations differ and therefore the policy space that would be helpful to a country's development differs among countries. The answer to this question will differ across the developing world. The development policies for a small, vulnerable developing economy with midlevel GDP per capita, such as the CARIFORUM economies, would be different for LDCs such as most African countries of the ACP and certainly very different from those of large emerging market economies such as Brazil. The South Center correctly advises that to make effective "use of policy space in achieving development, developing countries need to formulate their country-specific development strategy."[111]

One of the issues on which the EU and CARIFORUM differed was the approach to development. The EU perspective was rooted in the paradigm based on the conviction that the liberalization of market access by itself will automatically produce economic growth and that this can be further enhanced if the countries ensure that their economic policies and institutional arrangements conform to a standard package. In addition to drawing on their own experience, the EU believes that regional economic integration will create an economic space that adds economies of scale and scope. Development assistance can make the implementation of the conventional approach more palatable, ease the burden of adjustment, and accelerate implementation.

The fundamental flaws in the conventional approach that the EU applied to the negotiations of EPAs with the ACP countries are as follows:

1. Market access to the EU is a necessary but not sufficient condition for the promotion of economic development of the developing economies of the ACP group. Improved access to the developed country markets of the EU can stimulate an expansion of exports to these markets. For this to come to fruition, the CARIFORUM economies have to be in a position to take advantage of the export opportunities. The voluminous empirical literature documents that there is no automatic link between openness/trade liberalization and increased economic growth—much less economic development.[112] While some countries have prospered from the openness and trade liberalization, in those cases they pursued development strategies that consisted of a policy mix that was unique to their circumstances and involved an interventionist role for the state. In preparing to take advantage of export opportunities, there is a proactive and strategic role for government. The involvement of the state is appositely explained by Sir Arthur Lewis, Caribbean Nobel Laureate in Economics, when he gave the following advice: "Sensible people do not get involved in arguments about whether economic progress is due to government activity or to individual initiative: they know it is due to both, and they concern themselves with asking what is the proper contribution of each."[113]
2. The "one-size-fits-all" conventional paradigm deprives developing countries of the space for their own development policy. Successful development policy cannot be a standard policy prescription imported wholesale into which each developing country must be made to conform. Even when it is conceded that each country is unique, some like Freidman[114] have mistakenly assumed that the standard policy package is dictated by the very logic of globalization. Those advocating the standard package because of self-interests, fundamentalist neo-liberalism, or myopia would deprive developing countries of the policy space and autonomy, which they themselves had in their period of nascent development and which they no longer need.

Each country has to devise an economic strategy tailored to its own unique local conditions. Rodrik advises that "transitions to high economic growth are rarely sparked by blueprints imported from abroad. Opening up the economy is hardly ever a key factor at the outset. The initiating reforms instead tend to be a combination of unconventional institutional innovations with some of the elements drawn from the orthodox recipe. These combinations tend to be country-specific, requiring local knowledge and experimentation for successful implementation."[115]

CARIFORUM negotiators were fully aware that improved market access to the EU market was an important opportunity albeit only one component in the promotion of economic development. CARIFORUM was cognizant of the benefits of regional integration and that development assistance could play an important role in managing the costs of adjustment and implementation arising from the EPA. All of this was crucially dependent on having the maximum development policy space to allow governments to design their development strategies based on their specific circumstances. The major difference in approach between the EU and CARIFORUM was over the issue of development policy space. CARIFORUM prevailed over the strenuous opposition to enshrine the centrality of development in a separate chapter, providing an overarching framework of goals and principles and infusing specific development measures in each subject area. Preserving development policy space involved the following:

1. Resisting the inclusion of certain issues because they were too intrusive in the regional integration process and in national economic policies. A notable example was the rejection of the repeated EU proposal to address in a substantive manner the so-called governance in taxation. The EC pressed for what it described as the elimination of harmful tax practices and the promotion of transparency and effective exchange of information for tax purposes. CARIFORUM was resolute in the position that this subject lies outside the ambit of a trade agreement, would undermine the sovereignty of CARIFORUM states, and would be detrimental to the viability of the region's offshore financial sector.

2. Refusing to go beyond where the negotiations in the WTO have reached or in treating certain subjects not being negotiated in the WTO. For example, the EPA includes certain broad principles on competition policy, which do not prejudice either the outcome on this issue if it is negotiated in the WTO or preempt development of a competition policy regime in the CSME. This approach has the benefit of a balancing (1) inclusion of principles that will provide support for development and (2) not foreclosing future positions on subjects not yet being negotiated in the WTO. These include the following: (1) transparency in public procurement, which can improve real and perceived management of scarce public resources in the pursuit of value for money objectives; (2) competition policy, where the EPA broadly proscribes the most common forms of anticompetitive behavior; and (3) the inclusion of internationally accepted principles for the protection of personal data, in support of the development and growth of service sectors that involve the receipt, processing, and/or transfer of personal data such as education, health care, tourism, and business services, for example, medical billing and transcription and/or consumer product ordering or technical support calls.

3. Rejecting measures that would breach the integrity of the design and planned pace of implementation of the CSME, for example, market access in public procurement. The treatment of some issues that CARIFORUM states could not immediately commit to are given extended periods for resolution. CARIFORUM has until January 1, 2014, to establish a system for the protection of geographical indications. The treatment of some issues is confined to a signal of their relevance and is framed in nonbinding language. The relationship between trade and the environment was important to both parties; hence, the EPA seeks to facilitate the development of trade in a manner that promotes the protection and preservation of the environment. The

parties will regulate in accordance with their own goals for sustainable development priorities, provided that such regulation does not constitute arbitrary or unjustifiable restrictions on trade. The chapter is couched in "best endeavor" language, leaving the CARIFORUM states free to enact and implement measures in accordance with their own needs.

One of the important respects in which development policy space was preserved was the area of government procurement, where, despite concerted pressure from the EU, there were no Market access commitments by CARIFORUM. This was done to preserve development policy space and to not let the commitments in the EPA get ahead of the pace of the regional integration process. The provisions of the EPA do not confer rights of access to the procurement markets of the Parties. Governments are free to pursue the national or regional policies of their choice.

4. Avoiding commitments that could be invoked after the agreement went into force and that could restrict policy space. One such issue of concern to both sides was the treatment of labor standards. Chapter 5 is a reaffirmation of the existing commitments to the core labor standards as defined by the International Labour Organization (ILO). The chapter prevents the use of labor standards for protectionist purposes and ensures that trade practices do not undermine social and economic objectives. The parties have the expressed right to set and superintend labor standards in accordance with their own social development priorities, provided that these are consistent with the core rights and standards identified by the ILO. Another example is the provisions on investment that make exceptions to the application of the MFN principle. According to Article 9.1, the MFN obligation only requires CARIFORUM states to provide EU investors treatment no less favorable than they provide to investors from a "major trading economy," which is defined as "any industrialized country, or any country accounting for a share of world merchandise exports above one percent." Article 9.2 allows CARIFORUM states to not treat EU investors as favorably as they treat investors from other CARIFORUM states.

5. Many areas of macroeconomic policy are beyond the scope of the EPA, and many of these are of fundamental importance in the management and development of CARIFORUM economies, such as exchange rate policy and economy-wide prices including interest rates. However, even the development policy space beyond multilateral[116] and bilateral trade rules is not necessarily entirely free as it can be impinged on by other considerations such as the conditionality accompanying the use of IMF facilities and World Bank loans.

The completed CARIFORUM-EU EPA preserves the development policy space of the CARIFORUM countries. It is now up to the government of each CARIFORUM country to formulate and implement a strategy that allows the extraction of the maximum yield to strengthen and promote economic development.

One issue related to policy space was the inclusion of a MFN clause. This is discussed in appendix I.

Minimizing the Fiscal Impact

To minimize the loss of tax revenue, the schedule of implementation provides for extended periods of adjustment. CARIFORUM will liberalize over a 25-year period involving (1) liberalizing 82.7 percent of imports within 15 years, (2) other imports from the EU on an exclusions list in perpetuity covering some 463 items, (3) a three-year moratorium before any tariff reduction commences, (4) a moratorium of ten years for revenue-sensitive products such as gasoline, motor vehicles, and parts, (5) tariff reductions for a limited number of products over periods extending to 25 years, (6) other duties and charges remain unchanged for seven years and be eliminated in years eight, nine, and ten, (7) tariffs on motor vehicles decrease after a ten-year moratorium, and (8) items currently on the Revised Treaty of Chaguaramas Article 164 list of products (relating to industrial development in the LDCs) have been exempted from the liberalization process, as are any items so designated in the future.

The gradualism in implementation means that the loss of revenue from lowering tariffs does not happen immediately but over an extended time period.[117] Empirical research on the fiscal impact shows this erosion to be insignificant. King's calculations revealed that the impact on Guyana, Jamaica, St. Lucia, and Trinidad and Tobago was very small. "Ignoring both the likelihood of productivity growth and the redeployment of any productive factors, Jamaica, Trinidad & Tobago, and Guyana suffer production contractions of one-tenth of a percent of GDP and employment. St. Lucia's contraction is as much as one percent."[118] The loss of indirect tax revenue is small in Trinidad and Tobago and Jamaica where it amounted to 1 percent, but it represents nearly 13 percent in St. Lucia. The loss, while negligible in Jamaica and Trinidad and Tobago, would be the equivalent of 1 percent of GDP in Guyana and almost 3 percent in St. Lucia.[119] The EPA anticipated this situation and the process of lowering tariff will take place over 25 years.

Development Assistance

The CARIFORUM-EU EPA is complemented by development assistance from the EU. Development assistance from the EU is aimed at the following:

1. Building the human and institutional capacity of CARIFORUM states to strengthen their capacity to implement the commitments in the EPA.
2. Enhancing the international competitiveness of the private sector.
3. Facilitating the expansion and diversification of exports of goods and services.
4. Strengthening and improving the infrastructure that will enable to seize the trade and investment opportunities available through the EPA.
5. Assisting with legal and administrative measures that have to be put in place to meet the obligations of the EPA.
6. Helping with the reform of tax administration and easing the shift to alternative forms of indirect taxation to offset revenue foregone due to reduced tariffs.

EU development assistance related to the EPA is available through a variety of channels and facilities. First, the 10th European Development Fund (EDF) programme is estimated at €165 million, with approx €143 million (86.6%) allocated to Regional Economic Integration purposes within the CARIFORUM Regional Indicative Programme (CRIP) and €74.8 (45.3%) million allocated directly to support EPA implementation. This amount is divided in two major programs. One is the Regional Private Sector Programme currently under implementation through Caribbean Export Development Agency (€28.3 million), which is aimed at enhancing the capacity of Caribbean private sector operators to exploit the advantages of the EPA. The second one is the Support to CARIFORUM for EPA Implementation (€46.5 million), which is aimed at providing institutional support to governments in areas such as fiscal reforms and adjustment, sanitary and phitosanitary measures, technical barriers to trade, statistics, and facilitation trade in services among others.

This is complemented by an allocation of €27.5 million (16.6%) from the CRIP to the CSME on which several EPA commitments are based. Furthermore, another €8.6 million from the CRIP has been assigned to the Economic Integration and Trade of the OECS Region. Some CARIFORUM states, such as the Dominican Republic and Jamaica, have already decided to target EPA implementation as one of the primary areas to be supported by their National Indicative Programmes.

Second, the region also have access to an all-ACP facility of €2.7 billion in the 10th EDF. In this context, the Caribbean Component of the Intra-ACP Agriculture Programme amounts to €8.6 million to provide support toward the implementation of a regional agricultural policy and strategy based on the Jagdeo Initiative and the Liliendaal Declaration.

Third, as part of the all ACP-Facility, on March 2013 the Caribbean Investment Facility (CIF) was launched, with an initial capital of €40.0 million to support programmes in areas such as energy, transport, water, institutional strengthening, private sector growth including SMEs, and so on.

Fourth, the EU initially announced that it will contribute €2 billion to Aid for Trade. Unfortunately, the level of Aid for Trade cooperation has been disappointing compare to the promises made. Only the United Kingdom and Germany have made contributions to support EPA implementation.

Fifth, the Regional Preparatory Task Force (RPTF) identifies projects related to EPA implementation, which can be funded through the CARIFORUM Technical Cooperation Facility, with €400,000 of unutilized funds and the Caribbean Integration Support Programme that has €150,000 allocated for studies and another €75,000 for secure the participation of NSAs in the Consultative Committee.

The governments of CARIFORUM and the regional organizations charged with the implementation of the EPA must design a programme of projects to be funded by EU development assistance. A matrix of development that needs to be financed by EU development assistance has been compiled. A matrix prepared by the CRNM is listed in table 6.4. Undoubtedly, additional needs will emerge as the implementation proceeds because it is impossible to anticipate with complete accuracy all the demands that will emerge. Those items not funded under the 10th EDF will be included under the 11th EDF. The task of mobilization of additional resources will require both technical and political work. At the technical level, a plan and schedule of the EPA on a CARIFORUM-wide basis should be prepared, which puts precise financial costs to each target. At the political level, a strategy has to be designed and operationalized. The pitch must be tangible evidence that the region is making a serious effort to implement the EPA and that governments are endeavoring to rely on their own resources. The plausible case can then be made that the local efforts could be complemented and boosted by additional resources. The campaign cannot be confined to London and Brussels as it was during the negotiations for the EPA. The demarche must be extended to as many European countries as possible. This is feasible because it does not necessitate travel to the capitals of Europe, although this would be ideal. A more cost-effective approach is attending fora where several or all EU states are represented at the appropriate political level and working the plenary and in particular engaging in meetings with individual country delegations.

The governments of CARIFORUM have expressed concern about the adequacy of the amount of development assistance, which the EU has indicated it will provide and how funds will be allocated between between bilateral and regional and among countries This concern derives in part from the fact that the EPA is permanent and the resource allocation by the EU at the inception of the EPA is not intended to be the total that will be required for its implementation. This means that some of the funding to cover EPA implementation is not quantified, earmarked, or approved. The EU has stated a commitment for future funding, but this is not a money figure. The Europeans point to their record and intimate that their word is bankable. The CARIFORUM governments wanted to know from the date of signing the exact the amount of aid to be delivered. The implications of the EU sequential process are both positive and negative. To CARIFORUM it means that planning cannot be more than indicative, but it could result in more aid because needs assessment would have to be conducted every couple of years, and this is safer than trying to anticipate all the needs throughout the entire life of the EPA. A realistic figure for the entire course of the EPA would certainly encounter severe difficulty in the EU political process.

A major and justifiable concern is the underdelivery of EDF funds over the last 30 years. The percentage of funds disbursed was as low as 20 percent in the seventh EDF during the period 1995–2000 (table 6.4). This has not change. One of the problems of EPA implementation is precisely the fact that the cooperation only started to be disbursed four and five years after the signing of the Agreement. This record of underperformance is a consequence of the bureaucratic nature of the EU system of project evaluation and disbursement as well as weaknesses in the project design and execution in CARIFORUM at the state and regional levels. The EU has repeatedly expressed the intention to improve the operation of their process for disbursement of EDF funds.

If the CARIFORUM states want more development assistance, they will have to launch a diplomatic demarche to garner additional resources. As middle-income developing countries, their case is not perceived by donors as approaching the urgency or need of the LDCs—and there are many of these in the ACP group who are claimants on the same pool of money. The approach to the EU must take full cognizance of the growing donor fatigue in the EU and other developed countries.

Table 6.4 Allocation and expenditure of EDF funds 1975–2013 (million euro)

EDF assistance package	*Funds allocated during the 5-year envelope (nominal value)*	*Real value of envelope (1975 base year)*	*Disbursements in the 5 years in which the envelope was allocated*	*Percent of total allocation disbursed in the 5 years in which it was allocated (nearest replace)*
4th EDF (1975–80)	3,390	2,696	1,454.5	43
5th EDF (1980–85)	5,227	2,586	2,041	39
6th EDF (1985–90)	8,400	3,264	3,341.6	40
7th EDF (1990–95)	12,000	3,514	4,417.9	37
8th EDF (1995–2000)	14,625	3,463	2,921.6	20
9th EDF (2000–07)	15,200	3,131	4,239.0	28
10th EDF (2008–2013)	165 Million		Approx €10 million up to 2012	Approx. 9–12%

Source: Roger Hosein, "CARIFORUM-EU Economic Partnership Agreement: The Welfare Impact and Implications for Trinidad and Tobago," *Business, Finance & Economics in Emerging Markets* 3, no. 1 (2008): 2 and CARICOM Secretariat.

There must also be recognition that the EPA is neither a panacea nor an aid agreement; it is a trade agreement. EU development assistance that supports the EPA cannot be taken to encompass every social and development need but must have some direct connection to adjustment caused by the EPA or some expense, which emanates from EPA implementation.

The platform for more aid will not succeed if it relies entirely on being small and vulnerable, but must build it by a posture based on actual application to adjustment. The pitch must be that the region is adjusting and assistance could strengthen this effort. Too often in the past, the region has been in the invidious position of asking for money for adjustment, while at the same time displaying a convincing unwillingness to even contemplate adjustment. The more propitious stance is one of "we know where we are going, we are on the way, we could accomplish more and faster if we had additional resources." The traditional approaches derided by some in and out of the region as mendicancy would reinforce the view that the region consists of aid-seeking governments.

The programming and implementation of the 11th EDF will be a challenging process due to the current financial situation of many EU Members, the implementation of the differentiation approach, and the possibility of new requirements for disbursement in order to show more transparency on the use of funds to comply with the requirements of the European Court of Auditors. It is clear that after 5 years of implementation, development cooperation for EPA implementation has not had the impact originally expected. Table 6.5 provides a list of needs identified by CARIFORUM.

Table 6.5 Development assistance needs identified by CARIFORUM

EPA chapters	*Identified CARIFORUM developmental needs*
Customs and trade facilitation	1. The application of modern customs techniques, including risk assessment, simplified procedures for entry and release of goods, postrelease controls, and company audit methods; 2. international instruments and standards applicable in the field of customs and trade, including WTO rules and WCO instruments and standards, inter alia, the revised Kyoto Convention on the simplification and harmonization of customs procedures and the WCO Framework of Standard to Secure and Facilitate Global Trade; and 3. the automation of customs and other trade procedures.
Agriculture	The establishment of a Joint Cooperative Mechanism on the promotion of agriculture, food, and rural development in the Caribbean States. The Mechanism shall have the following objectives and mandates: 1. to provide an on-going forum within which representatives of governments, the private sector, and NSAs can engage regularly in the formulation of forward-looking strategies; 2. identify the policy and institutional changes needed to underpin the transformation of the sector; 3. determine ways of encouraging additional investment in the Caribbean agricultural and food sectors; 4. provide the necessary inputs for the formulation of a Caribbean-wide Agricultural, Food, and Rural Development Strategy; 5. identify the of cost the various components of the development strategy and promote their implementation; and 6. provide an interface with EU-based and other development funding agencies.
Fisheries	1. Technical assistance for the further mapping, valuation, and assessment of fisheries resources and the development of regional and national policies and control authorities; 2. strengthening of systems for monitoring, control, and surveillance (MCS) and the elimination of illegal, unreported, and unregulated (IUU) fishing in the region; 3. improving the socioeconomic conditions of small-scale fishing operations and facilitating their participation in regional and international trade; 4. the encouragement of joint ventures in fisheries, including processing, between Caribbean and European interests; 5. updating and strengthening harmonized food quality assurance legislation and policy including systems for use on fishing vessels; 6. improving the ability of Caribbean operators to comply with national, regional, and international technical, health, and quality standards for fish and fish products; 7. building and/or strengthening the scientific and technical human and regional institutional capability dedicated to sustainable use, management, and conservation of fisheries;

continued

Table 6.5 Continued

EPA chapters	*Identified CARIFORUM developmental needs*
	8. regional efforts for the development and implementation of a common fisheries policies and regimes aimed at promoting sustainable development, management, and conservation of the region's fisheries and aquatic resources including aquaculture through closer regional cooperation ; and 9. development of human resources in all aspects of fisheries and aquaculture.
Technical barriers to trade	1. Establishment of the appropriate arrangements for the sharing of expertise, including appropriate training intended to ensure adequate and enduring technical competence of the relevant CARIFORUM standard setting and conformity assessment bodies; 2. development of centers of expertise within CARIFORUM for the certification of goods as meeting the requirements for access into the EU market; 3. development of CARIFORUM private sector capacity to meet standards set by relevant market conditions, particularly where these standards exceed regulatory requirements; and 4. developing and adopting harmonized technical regulations, standards, and conformity assessment procedures based on relevant international standards.
Sanitary and phyto-sanitary measures	1. Establishment of the appropriate arrangements for the sharing of expertise, to address issues of plant, animal, and public health, such collaboration shall include the development of ways in which such issues can be addressed by CARIFORUM in both the short term and in a sustainable manner; 2. development of CARIFORUM private sector capacity to meet requirements established by the private sector; and 3. cooperation in international standard setting bodies, including the facilitation by the EU of participation of representatives of CARIFORUM states in the meeting of these bodies.
Services	1. Assistance to CARIFORUM Professional Associations to achieve international accreditation; 2. support for the establishment of CARIFORUM-EC Forum for professional associations; 3. designing business development programme for CARIFORUM service suppliers; 4. training and implementation trade development projects in selected services subsectors, with special focus on SMEs in the export value chain; 5. programmes aimed at enhancing SME's use of e-commerce; 6. developing matchmaking services for EU and CARIFORUM firms; and 7. support the establishment of a Caribbean School of Design and Promotion of creative industries.

EPA chapters	*Identified CARIFORUM developmental needs*
Competition policy	1. Joint initiative to raise the awareness about the science and technology capacity building programmes of the European Community including the international dimension of the seventh European and Technological Development and Demonstration Programme (FP7); 2. joint research networks in areas of common interest; 3. exchanges of researchers and experts to promote project preparation and participation to FP7 and to the other research programmes of the European community; 4. joint scientific meetings to foster exchanges of information and interaction and to identify areas for joint research; 5. the promotion of activities linked to scientific and technological forward studies that contribute to the long-term sustainable development of both parties; 6. the development of links between the public and private sectors; 7. the evaluation of joint work and the dissemination of results; 8. policy dialogue and exchanges of scientific and technological information and experience at regional level; and 9. exchange of information at regional level on regional science and technology programmes, and dissemination of information on the international dimension of the FP7 of the European Commission and its eventual successors, and about the science and technology capacity building programmes of the European community.
Competitiveness and innovation	1. Dialogue on the various issues of the information society, including promotion and monitoring of the emergence of the information society; 2. cooperation on regulatory and policy aspects of telecommunications; 3. exchange of information on standards, conformity assessment, and type approval; 4. dissemination of new ICTs; 5. joint research projects on information and communication technologies and pilot projects in the field of information society applications; 6. promotion of exchange and training of specialists, in particular, for young professionals; and 7. exchange and dissemination of experiences from government initiatives that apply information technologies in their relationship with society.
Science and technology	1. Exchanges of information, know-how, and experts; 2. raising awareness and training activities; 3. preparation of studies and provision of technical assistance; 4. collaboration in research and development; 5. pilot and demonstration projects; and 6. promotion of eco-innovation networks and clusters, including through public–private partnership.

continued

Table 6.5 Continued

EPA chapters	*Identified CARIFORUM developmental needs*
Information and communication technologies	1. Reinforcement of regional initiatives, organizations, and offices in the field of IPRs, including the training of personnel, with a view for improving regional regulatory capacity, regional laws and regulations, as well as regional implementation, with respect to intellectual property commitments undertaken in this sector, including on enforcement. This shall, in particular, involve support to countries not party but wishing to adhere to regional initiatives, as well as regional management of copyright and related rights; 2. identification of products that could benefit from protection as geographical indications and any other action aimed at achieving protection as geographical indications for these products. In so doing, the European Community and the Signatory CARIFORUM States shall pay particular attention to promoting and preserving local traditional knowledge and biodiversity through the establishment of geographical indications; and 3. where appropriate, support in the preparation of national laws and regulations for the protection and enforcement of IPRs, and in the establishment and reinforcement, including the training of personnel, of domestic offices and other agencies in the field of IPRs including on enforcement.
Environment, eco-innovation and renewable energy	1. Exchanging experience and information about best practices and regulatory frameworks; and 2. establishment and maintenance of appropriate systems and mechanisms to facilitate compliance with the obligations in this chapter.
Intellectual property	1. Reinforcement of regional initiatives, organizations, and offices in the field of IPRs, including the training of personnel, with a view to improving regional regulatory capacity, regional laws and regulations, as well as regional implementation, with respect to intellectual property commitments undertaken under this title, including that on enforcement. This shall, in particular, involve support to countries not party, but wishing to adhere to regional initiatives, as well as regional management of copyright and related rights; 2. identification of products that could benefit from protection as geographical indications and any other action aimed at achieving protection as geographical indications for these products. In so doing, the European community and the Signatory CARIFORUM states shall pay particular attention to promoting and preserving local traditional knowledge and biodiversity through the establishment of geographical indications; and 3. where appropriate, support in the preparation of national laws and regulations for the protection and enforcement of IPRs, and in the establishment and reinforcement, including the training of personnel, of domestic offices and other agencies in the field of IPRs including on enforcement.

EPA chapters	*Identified CARIFORUM developmental needs*
Investment	1. Develop appropriate means of identifying investment opportunities and improving information channels regarding investment regulations; 2. provide information on European investment regimes (such as technical assistance, direct financial support, fiscal incentives, and investment insurance) related to outward investments and enhancing the possibility for CARIFORUM to benefit from them; 3. support the creation of a legal environment conducive to investment among the Parties, and where appropriate through the conclusion by the Parties of agreements to prevent double taxation; 4. promote the creation of joint ventures between European and CARIFORUM firms especially for small and medium enterprises (SMEs); 5. establish mechanisms for encouraging and promoting investments and enhancing investment promotion agencies in CARIFORUM states; and 6. develop mechanisms favorable to the development of private enterprise, in order to stimulate the growth and the diversification of industrial production in particular through the (1) the establishment of a corporate finance brokerage facility; and (2) improvement of access to investment finance by the establishment of a mutual guarantee company to enhance SMEs negotiation power to obtain better terms and conditions for credit facilities and insurance.
Government procurement	1. Exchange of experience and information about best practices and regulatory frameworks; and 2. establishment and maintenance of appropriate systems and mechanisms to facilitate compliance with the obligations of the chapter.

Conclusion

In the previous chapter, the overarching goal of sustainable development was elaborated into seven principal goals that CARIFORUM wanted to achieve in the negotiations of the EPA. This chapter explains that these goals were attained by the incorporation of provisions: these are grouped under the related goals. It is most important to note that this classification of measures should not obscure the interconnectedness of the provisions and measures. For example, increased investment is treated as a separate goal, but its procreative impact can be felt in increased productive capacity, increased productivity, and enhanced international competitiveness. Similarly, improved IPRs can encourage investment, technology transfer, and local innovation, all of which contribute to improved international competitiveness. Development assistance was not included in the EPA, but the commitment to support adjustment and implementation was included: actual amounts would not be in the EPA itself as it is strictly speaking a trade agreement. The case for development assistance depended on the cost of adjustment, the estimated expense of implementation, traditional levels of aid, and assistance to sectors that had lost preferential arrangements. Obviously, development assistance, in the form of financial resources and technical assistance, will have an impact on many aspects of the EPA.

Appendix I

Concern has been expressed that the MFN clause in the EPA undermines the Enabling Clause,[120] which is intended to promote trade by and among developing countries. Within CARIFORUM countries, the opinion has been voiced that it will discourage trade among developing countries because it creates a disincentive for the Caribbean to negotiate agreements with other developing countries[121] that might include more favorable market access conditions than those enjoyed by the EU under the EPA.

Brazil[122] has expressed concern about the MFN clause in the EPA and its implications for the Enabling Clause. Brazil has suggested that the MFN clause in EPAs undermines the Enabling Clause and South–South trade because the MFN clause provides disincentive for ACPs to negotiate agreements with other developing countries that may contain more favorable market access conditions than those enjoyed by the EC under the EPAs with ACP countries. The MFN clause will "prevent" third countries from negotiating FTAs with EPA parties and constrain South–South trade. At Brazil's request, the matter was discussed in the General Council of the WTO in February 2008, albeit without any conclusion—and will undoubtedly be discussed when the notified EPAs are reviewed in the Committee on Regional Trade Agreements (CRTA). Legal opinions differ on the question but legal opinion commissioned by the ACP finds that the MFN Clause of EPAs is not a breach to the Enabling Clause. What lies behind the juridical question and is the gravamen of Brazil's complaint is that the MFN provision in the EPA would be the ceiling above which the CARIFORUM would not be willing to go in any FTA with a developing country because they would have to extend the same to the EU, a group of developed countries.

The assertion that the MFN Clause restricts CARIFORUM's ability to negotiate trade agreements with developing countries arises from a misunderstanding of the MFN clause in the EPA. The EPA does not constitute a formal legal barrier to what CARIFORUM can do in future trade agreements. It is the prerogative of CARIFORUM to decide if wants to go beyond the terms of the EPA and, if this involved countries on the agreed list, to consult on extending that more favorable treatment to the EU.

The MFN principle is Article 1 of the GATT[123] and is a reciprocal right granted between countries in international trade, which guarantees that other country will be given more favorable treatment in subsequent trade agreements. As applied in multilateral trade arrangements, it is given expression in Article 1 of the GATT 1994, which states "any advantage, favour, privilege or immunity granted by any contracting party to any product originating in or destined for any other country shall be accorded immediately and unconditionally to the like product originating in or destined for the territories of all other contracting parties." The importance of the MFN principle in the WTO is that it ensures nondiscrimination among all members of the WTO, except where derogation is explicitly permitted. The Enabling Clause[124] provides derogation from the MFN.

The Enabling Clause is common parlance for the Decision on Differential and More Favourable Treatment, Reciprocity, and Fuller Participation of Developing Countries. Paragraph 2(c) of the Enabling Clause allows developing countries to apply the provisions of GATT Article XXIV in FTAs and customs unions among themselves with greater flexibility to promote South–South trade. The provisions of GATT Article XXIV to be applied with greater flexibility under the Enabling Clause include (1) lower thresholds to determine "substantially all trade," that is, the percentage of tariff lines or goods trade to be liberalized by the parties, (2) elimination of duties and other restrictive regulations of commerce, and (3) the length of the transition period. The intention of the Enabling Clause is to (1) permit preferential treatment for developing countries and (2) to allow developing countries to give each other special and differential treatment (SDT) in trade arrangements among developing countries.

Article XXIV of the GATT provides an exception from the MFN principle for customs unions and FTAs provided that they meet two criteria, namely, (1) trade restrictions are removed from "substantially all the trade" and (2) customs duties shall not be higher thereafter than the duties prevailing on average prior to the formation of the customs union or FTA. An FTA is a preferential agreement among a limited number of countries or customs territories, which takes liberalization beyond the level existing in the WTO. Such arrangements notified under Article XXIV of GATT 1994 or the Enabling Clause are exemptions from the MFN principle of GATT Article I. FTAs notified under Article XXIV of the GATT can be among developed countries, developed, and developing countries (e.g., the CARIFORUM-EC EPA) or among developing countries.

The WTO database shows that as of July 31, 2010, 474 RTAs, counting goods, and services notifications separately have been notified to the GATT/WTO. Of that number, 351 RTAs were notified under Article XXIV of the GATT 1947 or WTO 1994, 31 were notified under the Enabling Clause, and 92 were notified under Article V of the GATS. On the same date, there are 283 agreements in force.[125]

An FTA that embodies an MFN provision (with unconditional or conditional obligations) is intended to ensure that if one of the parties subsequently concludes a trade agreement with a third country in which it provides to that country more generous terms than to the parties to its existing agreement, then the MFN provision obligates the terms of the new agreement to be extended to the parties of the previous agreement.

An MFN provision is not new to trade arrangements between the EU and the ACP since it was embodied in the Lomé Conventions. The Lomé Convention in Article 174[2(a)] stipulates that the ACP countries provide no-less-favorable treatment to the EEC than provided to any developed country.[126] The ACP/EU Cotonou Agreement, concluded in 2000, included a limited MFN Declaration carried over from previous Lomé Conventions. This MFN provision only kicked in if the ACP countries granted more favorable treatment to other developed states. Declaration XXXI of the Cotonou Agreement continues this provision when it states that "the ACP States shall grant the Community treatment no less favourable than that which they grant to developed states under trade agreements where those States do not grant the ACP States greater preferences than those granted by the Community." Article 19[127] states, "More favourable treatment resulting from free trade agreements:

1. With respect to matters covered by this Chapter, the EC Party shall accord to the CARIFORUM States any more favourable treatment applicable as a result of the EC Party becoming party to a free trade agreement with third parties after the signature of this Agreement.
2. With respect to matters covered by this Chapter, the CARIFORUM States or any Signatory CARIFORUM State shall accord to the EC Party any more favourable treatment applicable as a result of the CARIFORUM States or any Signatory CARIFORUM State becoming party to a free trade agreement with any major trading economy after the signature of this Agreement.
3. The provisions of this chapter shall not be so construed as to oblige the EC Party or any Signatory CARIFORUM State extend reciprocally any preferential treatment applicable as a result of the EC Party or any Signatory CARIFORUM State being party to a free trade agreement with third parties on the date of signature of this Agreement.
4. For the purposes of this article, 'major trading economy' means any developed country, or any country or territory accounting for a share of world merchandise exports above one per cent in the year before the entry into force of the free trade agreement referred to in paragraph 2, or any group of countries acting individually, collectively or through an free trade agreement accounting collectively for a share of world merchandise exports above 1.5 per cent in the year before the entry into force of the free trade agreement referred to in paragraph 2.
5. Where any Signatory CARIFORUM State becomes party to a free trade agreement with a third party referred to in paragraph 2 and such a free trade agreement provides for more favourable treatment to such third party than that granted by the Signatory CARIFORUM State to the EC Party pursuant to this Agreement, the Parties shall enter into consultations. The Parties may decide whether the concerned Signatory CARIFORUM State may deny the more favourable treatment contained in the free trade agreement to the EC Party. The Joint CARIFORUM-EC Council may adopt any necessary measures to adopt the provisions of this Agreement."

Major considerations relating to Article 19 of the EPA, the MFN Clauses were as follows:

1. The MFN provision also protects the CARIFORUM countries because the EU is obliged to extend to CARIFORUM all preferences granted to third parties in future FTAs between the EU and those third parties. If improved terms are granted in future EPAs, those terms have to be extended to CARIFORUM by the EU. This was important because the EU-CARIFORUM EPA was the first to be concluded and insulates the EPA from erosion by subsequent trade agreements.

2. CARIFORUM is not constrained except with regard to the countries on the agreed list. The MFN obligations of CARIFORUM in the EPA are conditional as it

applies only to major trading economies with a share of world merchandise exports above 1 percent per annum. The MFN Clause does not prevent CARIFORUM from giving (1) more favorable treatment to countries whose trade amounts to less than 1 percent of world merchandise exports and (2) it does not prevent CARIFORUM/CARICOM from negotiating FTAs with advanced developing countries/emerging market economies and offering them levels of concessions similar to that accorded to the EC.

The EU provided duty-free, quota-free access to their market in exchange for a specified market access of CARIFORUM. If CARIFORUM offered better access to another country or countries, the EU's access to the CARIFORUM market would no longer be preferential. This situation is only worrisome to the EU if the country or countries so privileged are capable of competing with the EU in the CARIFORUM market. The EU wanted to be sure that their access to the CARIFORUM market would be no worse than that of their trade competitors. The EU regard their trade competitors as no longer confined to the category of developed countries; they include as viable competitors the large developing countries or emerging market economies such as Brazil, China, India, Korea, and South Africa. This position of the EU is eminently reasonable since these are countries that are among the most internationally competitive as is evidenced by a raft of indicators. Their share of world trade has grown significantly and their cost of production is much lower, especially wage levels.

In reality, the issue is why would CARIFORUM want to give better market access to countries that (1) had not given duty-free, quota-free market access and (2) even if they did, whose costs of production are lower because of lower wages or large domestic markets, which facilitate the realization of economies of scale. CARIFORUM countries are small developing economies, most of which are middle-income countries in which producers including exporters find it difficult to attain economies of scale. The CARIFORUM domestic producers would be at a greater disadvantage competing against imports from emerging market countries such as China, India, and Brazil than against imports from developed countries such as those in the EU. These are not countries that CARIFORUM wants to expose their producers to in the short run. Therefore, CARIFORUM is most unlikely to be seeking trade agreement with countries whose costs of production by and large are much lower than in the CARIFORUM economies, most of which are middle-income status. One indication of this disposition is that CARICOM subsequent to the conclusion of the EPA negotiations is only pursuing negotiations for an FTA with Canada.

On the other hand, it is hard to imagine why a developing country interested in promoting the development by facilitating South–South trade would seek to exact more market access and concessions from CARIFORUM/CARICOM than afforded to the EU, a group of developed countries, under the EPA. It is almost inconceivable that either CARIFORUM or another developing country or group of countries would want to go beyond the terms of the CARIFORUM-EU EPA.

3. The extension of MFN treatment is not automatic or inevitable as Article 19, Paragraph 5 (and Article 70 and Article 79) provides for the parties to enter into consultations to decide if the more favorable treatment is extended or denied to the EU. The decision on an extension to the EU of more favorable preferences granted

to third parties by any CARIFORUM state in an FTA is to be made on a case-by-case basis after consultations between CARIFORUM and the EU. Any decision to deny the extension of more favorable treatment to the EU is open to interpretation as the text does not indicate under what conditions the CARIFORUM is entitled to deny said conditions to the EU. In such a case, the EU would have the option to argue the case that it will suffer damage and substantiate the claim of damages.

4. Nothing prevents CARIFORUM from entering into agreements with terms more favorable than the EPA if these agreements are partial or sectoral and do not meet the definition of an FTA or customs union. The MFN clause is applicable only to FTAs and is governed by GATT Article XXIV and not the Enabling Clause that does not cover FTAs. The rights of developing countries to facilitate South–South trade by extending preferential arrangements among each other than by FTAs is allowed under the Enabling Clause are therefore not compromised by the EPA MFN. Under Article XXIV of GATT sector, agreements between developing countries are not subject to automatic extension to the EU because of Section 2 (c) of the Enabling Clause.

CHAPTER 7

Governance, Recalibration, and Implementation

This chapter deals with two issues: first, it explains the arrangements that are provided by the EPA for the governance and recalibration of the agreement and, second, provides a short overview of the implementation of the agreement.

Governance

The EPA is a permanent agreement and cannot possibly anticipate the needs of both parties; the trade relationship evolves over time, and therefore, there must be some arrangements for making amendments to the agreement. Every trade agreement creates some institutional machinery to oversee implementation, to permit the redaction of the text where and when necessary, and to provide for dispute settlement. The EPA establishes an institutional apparatus to monitor the implementation and consider possible amendments to the agreement. The EPA establishes a number of institutions vested with specific responsibilities. These include (1) Joint CARIFORUM-EU Council, (2) CARIFORUM-EU Trade and Development Committee, (3) CARIFORUM-EU Parliamentary Committee, and (4) CARIFORUM-EU Consultative Committee. None of these institutions in any way impinges on the sovereignty of CARIFORUM, CARICOM, or its member states because their membership is composed of representatives of CARIFORUM member states and decisions have to be by mutual agreement of all sides.

The Joint CARIFORUM-EU Council will meet at Ministerial level at intervals not exceeding two years. This institution has responsibility for superintending the implementation of the EPA. The CARIFORUM-EU Trade and Development Committee is charged with assisting the Joint CARIFORUM-EU Council in supervising the implementation of the Agreement, ensuring disputes are resolved in an expeditious manner and that the development goals are attained. It will oversee specific trade-related and development-related matters, for example, (1) to review the cooperation priorities and make recommendations on the inclusion of new priorities; (2) to implement the cooperation provisions and coordinate such action with third-party donors; (3) to undertake action to avoid disputes and to resolve disputes; and (4) to make recommendations on trade-related cooperation between the parties. The CARIFORUM-EU Parliamentary Committee is to comprise representatives of the European Parliament and of the legislatures of the CARIFORUM states. The CARIFORUM-EU Consultative Committee is a forum for civil society to have a say in the EPA implementation process.

The EPA institutions do not in any way conflict with the powers and autonomy of the organs created by the Revised Treaty of Chaguaramas to govern the Caribbean Community. The Organs of the Community are (1) the Conference of Heads of Governments, (2) the Community Council of Ministers, (3) the Council for Finance and Planning, (4) the Council for Trade and Economic Development, (5) the Council for Foreign and Community Relations, and (6) the Council for Human and Social Development. They have functions specific only to the internal administration of the Community, with respect to the conclusion of agreements on behalf of the Community and with respect to determining the internal and external policies of the Community. Institutions created by the EPA have functions and responsibilities for the implementation of the EPA and have no role or authority in determining the internal or external policies of the Community or of any CARIFORUM state. Without prejudice to the functions of the Council of Ministers as defined in Article 15 of the Cotonou Agreement, the Joint CARIFORUM-EC Council shall generally be responsible for the operation and implementation of the EPA and for monitoring the fulfillment of its objectives.

The institutional arrangements for monitoring the implementation of the EPA in no way pose any threat to the sovereignty of CARIFORUM states. Every trade agreement has some institutional arrangements for overseeing implementation and examining any disputes that may arise. The EPA is therefore not unusual in this respect. In fact, it is good to have a mechanism to ensure that the EU fulfills its commitments. First, the purview of these institutional arrangements is the EPA and does not extend to overall external trade policy, nor do they have any authority over internal policy of either CARICOM or its member states. Second, all decisions are to be made by consensus; therefore, the EU cannot unilaterally make a decision and impose it on CARIFORUM. It is reasonable to assume that the officials deployed to represent the region in these joint committees will be acting on the instructions of their governments and will act in accordance with the best interests of the people of the Caribbean.

Recalibration

No agreement that is permanent can anticipate everything that can occur in implementation; therefore, provisions were included in the text of the EPA that establish institutional machinery for review and calibration of the operation of the EPA. Article 246 (1) recognizes that the parties may "agree to consider extending this Agreement with the aim of broadening and supplementing its scope... by amending it or concluding agreements on specific sectors or activities in the light of the experience gained during its implementation." Either of the parties to the agreement can raise any issue at any time and if they so agree can adjust how the EPA operates. According to Article 5, "The Parties undertake to monitor continuously the operation of the Agreement through their respective participative processes and institutions, as well as those set up under this Agreement, in order to ensure that the objectives of the Agreement are realized, the Agreement is properly implemented and the benefits for the men, women, young people and children deriving from their partnership are maximized. The parties also undertake to consult each other promptly over any problem that may arise."

The importance of reviewing the implementation of the EPA is clearly recognized in the EPA text. Article 246 (2)states, "As regards the implementation of this Agreement, either Party may make suggestions oriented towards adjusting trade-related cooperation, taking into account the experience acquired during the implementation thereof." In addition, the EPA is replete with language committing the parties to review a wide range of aspects of the EPA at any time that both parties agree. For example, Article 7 on states that Development Cooperation "Shall be kept under ongoing review and shall be revised as necessary." On Rules of Origin, Article 10 states, "Within the first five years of the entry into force of this Agreement the Parties shall review the provisions of Protocol I." Article 246 states, "The Parties agree that this Agreement may need to be reviewed." Article 246 lists provides for:

1. The Parties agree to consider extending this Agreement with the aim of broadening and supplementing its scope in accordance with their respective legislation, by amending it or concluding agreements on specific sectors or activities in the light of the experience gained during its implementation. The Parties may also consider revising this Agreement to bring Overseas Countries and Territories associated with the European Community within the scope of this Agreement.
2. As regard to the implementation of this Agreement, either Party may make suggestions oriented toward adjusting trade-related cooperation, taking into account the experience acquired during the implementation thereof.
3. The Parties agree that this Agreement may need to be reviewed in the light of the expiration of the Cotonou Agreement.

Subparagraph 1 is designed to ensure that the agreement keeps pace with the institutional practice that it generates and continues to meet WTO requirements and multilateral developments. Subparagraph 2 provides a mechanism through which the parties can ensure that the agreement remains responsive to the development needs of the CARIFORUM states. It is therefore supportive of the following powers of the Trade and Development Committee articulated in Article 230 (3) (b):

(i) to monitor the implementation of the cooperation provisions laid down in this Agreement and to coordinate such action with third party donors;
(ii) to make recommendations on trade-related cooperation between the Parties;

(iii) to keep under periodic review the cooperation priorities set out in this Agreement and to make recommendations on the inclusion of new priorities, as appropriate; and
(iv) to review and discuss cooperation issues pertaining to regional integration and implementation of this Agreement and rationally connected with Article 5, which provides for general monitoring of the Agreement in the following terms.

The Parties undertake to monitor continuously the operation of the Agreement through their respective participative processes and institutions, as well as those set up under this Agreement, in order to ensure that the objectives of the Agreement are realized, the Agreement is properly implemented, and the benefits for men, women, young people, and children deriving from their Partnership are maximized. The Parties also undertake to consult each other promptly over any problem that may arise. Subparagraph 3 of course was necessary because of the expiry of the Cotonou Agreement in 2020, given that this Agreement contains the development finance related to the EPA.

A review of any aspect of the EPA or the EPA in its entirety does have to await the passage of five years. In some instances, however, reviews are stipulated earlier than five years, for example, with regard to implementation, Article 181 Review states that the parties "will review the operation of this Chapter every three years, shall also examine proposals and recommendations from the Parties for the review of this Agreement." The EPA anticipates the need for quick corrective action, and therefore, Article 16, dealing with customs duties on imports of products originating in the EC Party, states, "In the event of serious difficulties in respect of imports of a given product, If CARIFORUM-EC Trade and Development Committee has not taken a decision within thirty days of an application to review the timetable, CARIFORUM States may suspend the timetable provisionally for a period that may not exceed one year."

The EPA establishes various institutional mechanisms at the technical and ministerial levels for dialogue and review if necessary. The EPA anticipates the need for quick corrective action and, therefore in Article 16 dealing with customs duties on imports of products originating in the EU, allows the CARIFORUM states to suspend the timetable provisionally for a period that may not exceed one year in the event of serious difficulties in respect of imports of a given product.

The possibility of revision or recalibration of the EPA or parts thereof is recognized and provided for by Article 246 (1). To date, CARIFORUM as a group has not invoked this article, nor has any government indicated a desire to review the EPA. Article 5 of the Joint Declaration in the EPA allows for a "comprehensive review, not later than 5 years after the date of signature," which would be by October 2013.

Implementation

The EPA can promote the economic development of the individual countries of CARIFORUM, but they must move expeditiously with a comprehensive programme of implementation. The execution of the programme is so important that it requires (1) disaggregation, with specific tasks being allocated to the appropriate specialized institutions and (2) the establishment of a CARIFORUM organ at the political level to provide oversight and superintend implementation. Development will not automatically happen, nor should the extent of the effort to seize opportunities be entirely dependent on EU development assistance. The CARICOM Secretariat needs to concentrate on the long-delayed completion of CSME. The CARICOM Secretariat needs to coordinate and synchronize its work programme with the implementation units in the various member states and with the Dominican Republic. There is no reason why the CARIFORUM group of states should doubt its capacity to successfully implement the EPA and thereby promote the sustainable economic development of the region.

The EU-CARIFORUM EPA was initialed in December 2007 and provisionally applied from December 29, 2008. To date, there has been limited implementation of the Agreement by both the CARIFORUM and the EU.[1] This is reflected by the fact that only seven CARIFORUM countries have ratified the EPA as listed in table 7.1. A few persons have called for the implementation of the EPA to be delayed or postponed pending a renegotiation of the agreement. Their arguments were not found to be compelling, and no government has acceded to this demand; hence, it has not been one of the factors delaying implementation. These are discussed in appendix III. Indeed, on the contrary, as argued earlier in the text, every effort should be made to achieve the implementation of the EPA as expeditiously as possible, given the prevailing and prospective circumstances that derive from being the first region to conclude an EPA.

Table 7.1 Table EPA ratification

Number	*CARIFORUM country*	*Date of ratification*
1	Dominican Republic	October 29, 2008
2	Antigua and Barbuda	December 19, 2008
3	Dominica	November 30, 2009
4	Belize	May 31, 2011
5	Guyana	June 14, 2012
6	St. Lucia	September 25, 2012
7	St. Vincent & Grenadines	November 22, 2012
Number	*EU country*	*Date of ratification*
1	United Kingdom	January 25, 2010
2	Sweden	January 29, 2010
3	Spain	March 11, 2010
4	Slovakia	April 13, 2010
5	Malta	May 7, 2010
6	Denmark	September 21, 2011
7	Finland	November 25, 2011
8	Greece	November 29, 2011
9	Italy	January 25, 2012
10	Lithuania	January 26, 2012
11	Bulgaria	August 2, 2012
12	France	March 4, 2013

Status of Implementation

Following the signing of the EPA in June 2008, the process of implementation and ratification should have commenced in earnest. The CARIFORUM governments have not moved on the implementation of the EPA as quickly as anticipated, for example, in establishing the relevant mechanisms at the national level to coordinate and oversee the implementation of the Agreement. Two years after the signing Owen Arthur, former prime minister of Barbados bemoaned the pace of implementation, pointing out that "The sooner the region, and Jamaica, gear themselves to make the most of the EPA by perfecting their strategies for implementation, the more benefits will be realised."[2] Nearly five years after the signing in June 2008, only nine countries have made the tariff cuts according to the schedule committed to in the EPA.

Joint EU-CARIFORUM Actions

Except for the Consultative Committee, all other joint consultative committees for governance and implementation have been constituted and have held at least two meetings by the end of the first quarter of 2013. It is expected that the Consultative Committee comprising representatives from the private sector and civil society will meet before the end of 2013.

Actions by CARIFORUM Regional Institutions

The CARICOM Secretariat established an EPA Implementation Unit on February 16, 2009. This was just in time, as there were obligations that required action on January 1, 2009. In May 2011, the Unit was placed under the CARIFORUM Directorate of the CARICOM Secretariat to better reflect the regional scope of its work. The mandate of the unit is "The EPA Implementation Unit is mandated to assist CARIFORUM States in the implementation of the provisions of the CARIFORUM-EU EPA. In this regard, the Unit is tasked with providing CARIFORUM States direct 'hands-on' (sometimes in-country) technical guidance and assistance in meeting the commitments and enjoying the benefits outlined in the Agreement. To focus the implementation effort of CARIFORUM States and to effectively schedule the activities of the EPA Implementation Unit, an EPA Implementation Roadmap has been drawn up, in chronological order, of the obligations in the Agreement." Its activities include national meetings to brief member states. For example, the three-day National EPA Implementation Plan meeting in St. Vincent and the Grenadines in March 2013 was attended by persons from the public and private sectors. The meeting was the launch of the consultative process for the formulation of a National EPA Implementation Plan. Similar implementation plans are being developed or already exist for Antigua and Barbuda, Belize, the Bahamas, Dominica, Grenada, and Saint Lucia. The Implementation Plans are the result of an initiative funded under the Caribbean Aid for Trade and Regional Integration Trust Fund (CARTFund). In addition, the EPA Implementing Unit has carried out in-country consultations with potential service suppliers, and conducted reviews of pertinent legislation of the respective CARIFORUM states, in order to identify the areas requiring amendment and bring national legislation into conformity with the provisions of the EPA.

The work and capacity of the Unit can be supplemented by the technical expertise of the Office of Trade Negotiations and of specialized regional organizations such as the CARICOM Regional Organization for Standards and Quality (CROSQ) and the Caribbean Export Development Agency (CEDA). There will be an important role for CEDA, which is a regional trade and investment development promotion organization of the 15 CARIFORUM member states and the Dominican Republic. A variety of implementation exercises have been undertaken with assistance provided by CEDA within the framework of the 10th EDF private Sector Programme to support efforts of CARIFORUM goods exporters and service suppliers to access the EU, for instance, through study tours and promotional events.

The CARIFORUM EPA Implementation Network has been established in the form of a public interactive intranet platform for the implementation of the EPA in the Caribbean and for assistance to implementing authorities in CARIFORUM. It is an important mechanism to facilitate information sharing and networking among all stakeholders.

CEDA is a regional organization whose mandate is to promote exports, diversify exports, and promote investment related to exports. It has been active in familiarizing the private sector with the opportunities of the EPA through seminars and workshops.

Actions by CARIFORUM Governments

The implementation of the EPA has to be carried out by national governments that have the responsibility of executing the obligations contained in the agreement and by regional institutions that are engaged in dispensing information, preparing implementation strategies, advising governments, and servicing meetings between the EU and CARIFORUM. The CARIFORUM countries have established arrangements to implement the EPA, including outreach to private-sector stakeholders,[3] within the ministries responsible for international trade. Despite the hosting of seminars, briefings, and the publication of material explaining the EPA and pointing out the opportunities, the private sector continues to complain about the "need for adequate, timely and relevant information."[4]

The CARIFORUM governments have put in place arrangements to implement the EPA. Seven governments have established EPE Implementation Units: Antigua and Barbuda, Barbados, Belize, Dominican Republic, Grenada, St. Kitts and Nevis, and St. Vincent and the Grenadines. The Bahamas is in the process of establishing an implementation unit. Some are serving the EPA from generic units such as the Trade Agreement Implementation coordination unit in the ministry of Foreign Affairs and Foreign Trade or the Trade Implementation Unit in the ministry of Trade and Industry in Trinidad and Tobago. Others are implementing through the mainstream of the ministries responsible for foreign trade. This is not a sign of neglect; these ministries are sometimes extremely small, for example, St. Kitts and Nevis. The implementation effort usually involves a threefold process of (1) a public information programme that includes specially prepared booklets and briefing papers available in print and from websites. This is reinforced by workshops and training seminars for the private sector particularly exporters and officials involved in execution of various aspects of the Agreement. The governments have formulated action plans to improve awareness about the EPA, the opportunities it presents, and the actions required to take advantage of those opportunities. (2) Driving implementation actions across the various agencies, departments, and ministries of government such as support for drafting legislation, administrative adjustments, and monitoring implementation, for example, in customs administration. (3) Interfacing with the numerous regional institutions charged with implementation of the EPA. As part of the collaboration with CARIFORUM states, in August 2012, the EPA Implementation Unit of the CARIFORUM Directorate organized a meeting of National EPA Coordinators and heads of national EPA implementation units and like entities. The meeting provided a forum for sharing experiences and best practices and for the clarification of the provisions and requirements of the EPA.

Actions by the EU

The implementation of the EPA has to be carried out by the EU commission and by the individual member states of the EU. The EU has fulfilled on schedule the obligations that it has control over, but the pace of implementation has varied among the member states.

Factors Affecting Implementation by CARIFORUM

Several factors have affecting the implementation of the agreement. These include the following.

Scope of the Agreement

The Agreement is the most comprehensive trade agreement in which CARICOM has been involved, and the first such agreement in which CARIFORUM, that is, CARICOM and the Dominican Republic, has been a single entity. The economic subject matter encompassed in the scope of the EPA is wide and, therefore, has implications for numerous aspects of the CARICOM integration process. In particular, a rapid implementation of the EPA would involve the acceleration of implementation of parts of the CSME. In addition, it raises long-postponed issues between the Dominican Republic and CARICOM. These have implications for the revision and updating of the CARICOM-Dominican Republic Free-Trade Agreement, and for aspects of the CARICOM integration process. The resolution of the issues of coverage and the issues arising from the built-in agenda of the CARICOM-DR FTA have languished for far too long and the EPA obligations could be a fortuitous impetus for progress. The solution can be found in a multispeed implementation within limits that do not establish an unevenness that undermines the value of common regimes. The Dominican Republic within limits could proceed at a somewhat faster pace than CARICOM or the Dominican Republic, and the so-called more developed countries could allow a more extended phasing of obligations by the so-called less developed countries of CARICOM. Dual-speed assumptions of obligations and differentiated implementation schedules have been an integral practice within CARICOM for decades. It is not beyond the capacity of CARIFORUM to employ this practice.

Cost

The issue of cost is always a constraint for the small, fiscally challenged member states of CARICOM. Indeed, over the last 30 years, contributions from member states have fallen far short of what is required for self-financing the integration process, at both the regional and national levels. Consequently, financial contributions and technical assistance from bilateral donor agencies and multilateral development institutions have been critical in sustaining the CARICOM Secretariat and its operations. The critics of the EPA have argued that the implementation of a trade agreement that has such an expansive scope will overburden the already financially strapped regional institutions and national governments. Furthermore, they have suggested that the cost should be compensated by development aid from the EU especially since the EPA is not unilateral nonreciprocity.

It has been said that the fiscal adjustment required by the EPA is already onerous for the governments of the region. Fortuitously, (1) many actions require time, rather than money, and governments could concentrate on these activities; and (2) the first couple of years involve minimal displacement of tariff revenue.

Aid for Trade

The history of EU aid to the ACP countries is replete with bureaucratic delays; however, the aid for trade (AfT) to be provided by the EU will be vital to the small states of CARIFORUM. The capacity to implement the EPA in these states is constrained by limited institutional capacity and limited financial resources. CARIFORUM states anticipated EU resources to fund some of the costs of implementation, but the dispensation of funds from the EU AfT facility has not proceeded as anticipated. Humphrey reports that "the prevailing view across the Caribbean is that EU Member States, with the exception of the United Kingdom and Germany, have not fulfilled promises made during and after the EPA negotiations."[5]

Benefits of Prompt Implementation

The EPA should be implemented immediately and as quickly and comprehensively as possible because this will accelerate the realization of the opportunities provided by the EPA. The benefits of a rapid implementation include the following:

Faster Synchronization of Internal and External Aspects of Development

The ambit of its coverage and its comprehensiveness means that the EPA has implications for a wide range of aspects of economic development at both the national and regional levels. National development strategies in the region and regional economic integration, in its various forms and in its most recent vision as the CSME, have never adequately tackled the issue of how international economic relations can be made to contribute to the economic development process in a comprehensive and coherent overall economic and institutional framework. The partial implementation of the CSME has been a major problem for the realization of a single, seamless, regional economic space. What Girvan has described as "the frequency of missed targets and the unevenness of compliance among countries in completing the CSME"[6] has deprived the integration process of the synergies, which could have resulted from a synchronized implementation of the components and measures of the CSME. The EPA will prompt the region to press ahead with the CSME because much of what has to be done to implement the EPA is consistent with fulfillment of the CSME.

The EPA was designed not to pressure the CSME to address issues it was not close to resolving. The provisions on government procurement are a clear example of the EPA sensitivity to CSME. The provisions deal with improving transparency and do not address the subject of market access. This approach was deliberate because at the time of the negotiations the CARICOM governments had no clear position on how this subject would be handled in the CSME. There is the intention to eventually include government procurement in the CSME and at the time of the negotiations technical work was in progress on a CARICOM government procurement regime. In these circumstances, it was too early to make any commitments in market access. A recent independent evaluation of the government procurement provisions in the EPA by Dawar and Evenett concluded that "Promoting value-for-money and choice in public purchasing and deterring and punishing anti-competitive corporate acts both have important societal payoffs, in developing and richer countries alike. This paper reviews the evidence and arguments concerning the efficacy of public procurement reform and promoting competition in developing countries and argues that both are worthy objectives of state policymaking. No provisions in the CARIFORUM EPA were found to undermine these pro-developmental objectives. If anything, our concern is that the relevant CARIFORUM EPA provisions do not go far enough and, by implication, that the level of ambition sought by developing countries and the EC in future EPA negotiations should be higher."[7]

Accelerating the Completion of the CSME

The CSME is a small part of the economic life of the CARIFORUM countries. (1) The Dominican Republic that is the largest economy CARIFORUM is not a participant. (2) It encompasses a small part of the economic life of CARICOM because intraregional trade and investment are small. This is evident the small share of intraregional trade in the total trade of CARICOM countries. While there has been growth in total trade of CARICOM over the period 1998–2004, intraregional exports have declined as a share of total exports from 21.5 percent to 13.4 percent. During the same time period, intraregional imports increased from 8.9 percent to 12.3 percent of total imports. Total intraregional trade has in recent years hovered around 10–12 percent of total trade,[8] which clearly indicates that it is not the driving force in the economic growth of the region with the exception of the regional market to the consumer goods manufacturing sector of Trinidad and Tobago.

Another feature of intraregional trade is very limited and concentrated essentially on one economy, namely, Trinidad and Tobago, which accounts for 85 percent of total exports; the rest of the countries account for 15 percent of total exports.[9] Jamaica is the largest market for the region's imports accounting for nearly 40 percent,[10] and this means that intra-CARICOM trade is largely Trinidadian exports to Jamaica; hence, intraregional trade is of marginal significance to the majority of member states. Intra-CARICOM investment flows are of even less significance as a share of total investment in the region. A functioning regional capital market does not yet exist and much remains to bring this into meaningful operation.

There is no language in the Revised Treaty of Chaguaramas explicitly forbidding CARICOM from negotiating and signing trade agreements, which entail obligations in areas that have not been completed in the CSME process. The Revised Treaty does explicitly link the CSME to the external trade negotiations, by constraining member states in bilateral agreements to not prejudice their obligations under the Treaty.[11] This reference could reasonably be interpreted to mean that the same restriction applies to agreements entered into by CARICOM as a collective one.

A perusal of the goals and objectives of the CSME and the EPA reveals an overall similarity of vision. Be that as it may, the test of how economic development is promoted is in the design of the agreement, not merely the stated goals. To the extent that the implementation of the EPA requires CARICOM to commence or accelerate the implementation of the CSME, this is actually a good thing for the integration process. The original date envisioned for the completion of the CSME was 1993, but nearly 20 years later this has not been accomplished. By all accounts, there has been a very significant "implementation deficit"[12] in the CSME process. Girvan estimated that as of 2007 (just before the completion of the EPA negotiations) "just 55 percent of the measures required for full CSME implementation had actually been carried out."[13] The implementation of the EPA may contribute an external element pushing governments to take actions that the discretionary natures of the CARICOM governance system and process have allowed member states to postpone. Brewster has repeatedly pointed to this weakness in the CARICOM governance arrangements.[14]

The CSME was in a state of virtual atrophy before the EPA was negotiated and implemented. If the EPA accelerates the establishment of the CSME, it will have helped to accomplish something that should have preceded the implementation of the EPA. In fact, the state of the CSME and a prognosis for continued slow implementation were taken fully into account in the negotiations and is reflected throughout the EPA. In many subject areas of considerable interest to the EU, negotiations were capped at a level calculated not to disrupt the CSME, nor to force decisions that would interfere with the integrity of the integration process, and the regional and national capacities for bringing the CSME into reality. This is a pity, because in a rapidly globalizing world economy, it is not possible to disengage, nor is it possible to avoid increasing interaction with and integration into the global marketplace. The CSME was the template that CARICOM designed to prepare itself to participate in the global economy in a manner that would enhance its economic development. Owen Arthur, while prime minister of Barbados with responsibility within CARICOM for overseeing the implementation of the CSME, explained the importance of the CSME as "the only realistic and viable option by which to achieve sustainable development" and "the most effective means by which the individual economies of the region can be successfully integrated into the proposed new hemispheric economy and the evolving global economic system."[15]

While the CSME is supposed to be a platform for enhancing the capability of the region to engage the global economy, the region's exports and imports of goods and services as a share of world trade has declined from 0.5 percent in 1980 to 0.15 percent in 2006 according to the World Bank.[16] To the extent that the EPA pushes progress in completing the CSME process, it will serve to help the region enhance its international competitiveness through gradual exposure to a group of developed economies. This will act as a preparatory step to the inevitable exposure to other developed and highly competitive countries, for example, China, Brazil, and India, which is inevitable in a globalizing world economy. The completion of the CSME and the implementation of the EPA involve actions that help the CARIFORUM economies to prepare for the international competition, which is inherent in and inevitable in the global economy.

Delays May Complicate Implementation

Delays in commencing the steps necessary for the execution of the implementation process can complicate implementation, compromise agreed-on schedules, postpone the realization of benefits, and cause distrust among the partners. There are several issues that the sooner they are addressed the more efficacious implementation will be. The most important is building or enhancing the institutional capacity to implement complex trade agreements. The region, while having the CARICOM Secretariat, has not had the experience of implementing this type of trade agreement either at the regional or national level. Governments have implemented the requirements of the WTO and CARICOM member states have some experience in implementing region-wide regimes but their execution never adhered to binding schedules as is amply demonstrated by the Common External Tariff of CARICOM. Experience or lack thereof was a hindering factor in Costa Rica's experience, with implementation of US-Central America Free Trade Agreement (CAFTA).[17]

There are two kinds of costs related to the implementation of the EPA: first, the cost of implementation of new measures and obligations and, second, the tax revenue lost as tariffs are lowered. Certainly in the case of the former cost, there could be an escalation if implementation is postponed or spread over an extended period. There are administrative, institutional, and legislative actions involved in the complete implementation of the EPA. It is not contemplated anywhere in the text of the EPA that these actions would be done immediately, or even in the short run. They would be implemented over the course of the Agreement, which is permanent: (1) moreover, implementation periods extend up to 25 years; (2) many obligations are conditional on the provision by the EU of financial resources and technical assistance. If this is not forthcoming, the region is not obliged to implement the applicable sections, even if this would be beneficial to the region's economic development, and (3) the EPA will be accompanied by EU development assistance as well as the availability of aid for trade funds and technical assistance from a variety of bilateral and multilateral sources.

Faster Development Gains

The EPA is designed to deliver benefits immediately as improved market access became effective immediately upon provisional application. This was part of the rationale for asymmetrically phased implementation and for special and differential treatment. The EU immediately provided duty-free, quota-free access for goods from CARIFORUM countries and, in return, will receive less than full reciprocity implemented over periods as long as 25 years for the most sensitive products. The negotiators were firmly of the view that trade liberalization for the small developing economies must be based on a template of special and differential treatment,[18] although this should not be conflated with permanent unilateral preferential treatment. These were fundamental tenets of the region's trade negotiations, which preceded the EPA such as the FTAA.[19]

Those benefits and opportunities that did not start with the EPA can be realized by implementation of the agreement. The more quickly the EPA is implemented, the faster the CARIFORUM economies will derive economic benefits from it. Implementing the EPA will bring into operation other aspects of the Agreement that will enhance its development impact. To the extent that implementation requires the acceleration and deepening of the CSME process, this is a major advantage. The globalization process, even with the setback of the global financial crisis, is moving at a pace, and in a profound manner that requires that the CARIFORUM region moves as expeditiously as possible to be ready and not to be marginalized from the process. The adjustment required by the EPA is similar but on a smaller scale to that which is required to proactively mediate with globalization.

Revisions Can Be Made While Implementation Proceeds

The implementation of the EPA should not be delayed because CARIFORUM may desire to review or revise some aspects because both processes can proceed simultaneously. The EPA makes provisions for review and, if necessary, revision of the EPA. The review clause in the EPA is designed to ensure that the agreement continues to meet its objectives despite changing circumstances. The Agreement was entered into voluntarily by all member states of the EU and CARIFORUM. Changing circumstances will, obviously, require modification of some of the schedules and that is taken account of in the joint institutional mechanisms, whose decisions are taken by consensus. These institutions also exist so that the text of the Agreement can be redacted to include additional elements and to advance the liberalization process.

The importance of reviewing the implementation of the EPA is clearly recognized in the EPA text and does not require any additional declaratory statements. The EPA already made provision for in Article 5: "The Parties undertake to monitor continuously the operation of the Agreement through their respective participative processes and institutions, as well as those set up under this Agreement, in order to ensure that the objectives of the Agreement are realized, the Agreement is properly implemented and the benefits for the men, women, young people and children deriving from their partnership are maximized. The parties also undertake to consult each other promptly over any problem that may arise." In addition, the EPA is replete with language committing the parties to review a wide range of aspects the EPA at any time that both parties agree. For example, Article 7 states that Development Cooperation "shall be kept under ongoing review and shall be revised as necessary." Article 10 states Rules of Origin "Within the first five years of the entry into force of this Agreement the Parties shall review the provisions of Protocol I."

Retaining Credibility in International Relations

If the governments of CARIFORUM states were to renege on the commitments made in the EPA, it would seriously damage their international credibility individually and collectively. Any suggestion of resiling from the voluntarily entered into and solemn commitments of the governments of the region would irreparably harm the international credibility of the region. The credibility of the Governments of CARIFORUM requires that they honor the obligations of an international treaty: (1) If there are disputes arising from different interpretations of the text of the EPA as it relates to implementation the joint institutional arrangements can be convened with a view to resolving the issues; and (2) many of the commitments on implementation are conditional on the availability of funding and technical assistance from the EU. If these are not forthcoming or are inadequate, there is no breach if the implementation of the items concerned is not executed. Implementation will be constrained by the availability of resources and may mean that implementation will not proceed as quickly as originally anticipated. Delays of this kind are an entirely different matter from a decision to delay the entire process of implementation. The credibility that comes from genuine efforts to accomplish the commitments involved in implementation of the EPA is important as the basis for establishing the need for development assistance. CARIFORUM governments would be in an invidious position of calling for aid while not implementing the EPA from which the need for aid derives.

Conclusion

No agreement that is permanent can anticipate everything that can occur during implementation, nor can the need for amendments or additions be ruled out, because circumstances can change. The EPA text establishes institutional machinery for governance, review, and recalibration of the EPA. These institutional arrangements are in operation and are working well.

The contribution of the EPA to the sustainable economic development of the CARIFORUM countries can best be realized by the full implementation of the Agreement. Delay will only reduce its development value and dissipate the advantages of being the first group of countries to bring into effect an EPA with the EU. The advantages of implementing the EPA far outweigh the arguments for delay. For the implementation process to proceed expeditiously and comprehensively, it must be placed and maintained on a sustainable path.

The disappointments of the CSME and the CARICOM-Dominican Republic Free Trade Agreement should be ever-present reminders to CARIFORUM countries that delayed implementation of sound development frameworks with considerable potential benefits can fail to come to fruition. Delayed implementation has caused these development mechanisms to discredited and increasingly disparaged as useless. It would be a great pity if delayed or not sustained implementation were to cause the same experience to befall the CARIFORUM-EU EPA. The postponement of the implementation of the EPA would be ill-advised and is synonymous with postponing the mediation of the encounter with the global economy. The same actions required to prepare for being internationally competitive in the world economy are those envisioned by both the CSME and the EPA. Therefore, in implementing the EPA, the region is accelerating its preparation for, and capacity to engage in, the global economy in a manner propitious for its economic development.

CHAPTER 8

Strategic Global Repositioning

> The difficulty lies not so much in developing new ideas as in escaping from the old ones.
>
> —J. M. Keynes

The EPA is not a panacea for the economic development of CARIFORUM, but it is a definite and potentially fecund opportunity that if properly and fully utilized can contribute to the development of the region. The EPA is not some "deus ex machina" but can complement national and regional strategies of economic development. The EPA is not going to foist an external development strategy on CARIFORUM, although this may well have been the objective of the EU when it began the negotiations. In the negotiations, CARIFORUM was able to ensure that the EPA does not preempt the economic development strategies of the region, its member states, or the CSME. This objective is reflected in the development space provided in the EPA, but because there is no agreed definition of the concept of development space, beauty is in the eye of the beholder; the extent of development space is a matter of judgment and therefore open to different interpretations.[1] The necessity to preserve maximum development space was constantly in the minds of the negotiators and government officials throughout the negotiators.

The CARIFORUM-EU EPA is an instrument that can be used by the CARIFORUM countries to strengthen and accelerate their development. The EPA provides an opportunity to export to the vast EU market for goods and service on a preferential basis. This market access will make the region a platform for exporting to the EU and should attract foreign and domestic investment. The agreement allows for a very manageable pace of import liberalization and is complemented by development assistance to support the adjustment process and the strengthening of institutional capacity. The potential benefits of the EPA will not automatically come to fruition. The extent to which this materializes will depend on national and regional efforts, that is, the CSME and the completion of the built-in agenda of the CARICOM-Dominican Republic Free Trade Agreement. Efforts at the national level need to be conceptualized and those at the regional level need to be accelerated—in particular the long-ossified CSME. All efforts must be directed at improving, on a continuous basis, the production of internationally competitive goods and services. The EPA constitutes a new way to mediate the engagement with the global economy and the success of this endeavor will involve new approaches, which in turn require new ideas. New ideas and new policies that can achieve transformation and economic development begin with a change of mind.

Structural Characteristics, Negotiation Goals, and the Provisions of the EPA

To ensure that the EPA promotes and facilitates economic development, the agreement incorporates specific measures to address structural characteristics of the CARIFORUM economies that have to be changed to allow and facilitate economic development. This is explained in matrix format in table 8.1. The specific goals that comprise the overall goal of economic development and how they are linked directly to specific measures in the EPA are listed in table 8.2.

The EPA as Part of Strategic Global Repositioning

Individually and collectively the governments of the CARIFORUM countries must create national and regional economic environments, which are conducive to economic development. To gain the maximum benefit from the EPA, the CARIFORUM countries will have to formulate and implement a programme of strategic global repositioning.[2] Strategic global repositioning is a proactive approach to effective participation and beneficial integration with the global economy. The ambit and ambition of this approach are, therefore, not confined to adjustments to enable these economies to seize the opportunities available through the EPA. In adjusting to the EPA, the CARIFORUM countries will in fact be adjusting to the global economy. Indeed, there is no need to separate the responses because the EPA at a genteel pace introduces CARIFORUM to what developments in the global economy portend and the responses required. The components in the EPA are in varying degrees about the subject matter and issues that have been and are being mooted in bilateral and RTAs as well as in the Doha Development Agenda of the WTO. The EPA is an amalgam of subjects and measures to address and give effect to these subjects and is not a complete response to the agenda that emanates from and is driven by globalization. Several issues that continue to be a part of the international economic agenda were not addressed or only partially dealt with. It is also to be recognized that new issues and subjects will emerge, which are not encompassed in the EPA and not even anticipated. The conclusion to be derived is that adjustment to the EPA is not the be all and end all of economic adjustment. Adjustment occasioned by the EPA is the commencement of an ongoing process. The only permanence is change, and in the context of globalization, this is likely to be rapid and profound; hence, reacting to change is unlikely to be more advantageous when postponed.

Seizing the opportunities created by the EPA will require active government collaboration with the private sector in the CARIFORUM countries in pursuit of

Table 8.1 Relationship between characteristics of small developing economies and components of the EPA

Measures features	*Asymmetric obligations*	*Extended and phased import liberalization*	*Increased market access*	*Strengthening Regional Integration*	*Safeguards*	*Investment promotion*	*IPRs*	*Technical assistance*	*Development Assistance*
Acute vulnerability	X	X	X	X	X	X			X
Volatile growth			X	X	X	X			X
Imperfect market	X	X	X	X		X		X	X
Small size of firms	X	X	X	X		X			X
Dependence on trade taxes	X	X	X		X				X
Low international competitiveness				X			X	X	X
Constrained adjustment capacity	X	X		X	X	X		X	X
Limited institutional capacity	X	X	X	X			X	X	X

Table 8.2 Relationship between CARIFORUM economic goals and components of the economic partnership agreement

Goals/EPA	*Asymmetric obligation*	*Asymmetrically phased import liberalization*	*Increased market access*	*Investment promotion*	*Safeguards*	*Technical assistance*	*IPRs*	*Development assistance*	*Trade facilitation*
Export expansion			X	X		X		X	X
Export diversification			X	X		X		X	X
Increased investment				X	X	X	X		X
Strengthening regional integration					X	X		X	
Improving international competitiveness				X		X	X	X	
Retain policy space	X	X			X	X			
Extended adjustment and implementation	X	X			X	X	X	X	X

proactive, strategic development policy. The market alone will not automatically produce sustainable economic development. Functioning markets are a necessary but not sufficient condition for international competitiveness and export expansion. The state needs to play a complementary role to facilitate new exports and revamp existing ones. Export diversification does always necessitate creating new industries because in some situations the growth of an existing export industry may stimulate the expansion of other sectors via backward intersectoral linkages. Tourism has substantial potential to stimulate other sectors, for example, by tourist purchasing handicrafts.[3]

Seizing the Opportunities of the EPA

Trade agreements create opportunities for exports and trade creation. Export opportunities if utilized can result in increased volumes of existing exports and the emergence of new exports, resulting in increased foreign exchange earnings and a diversification of exports, thereby reducing acute vulnerability of CARIFORUM economies. The latter process is known "trade creation,"[4] that is, the shifting of domestic consumption away from relatively high-cost domestic production to relatively low-cost imports. The implementation of the EPA involves tariff liberalization of imports of goods from the EU. This is a partial liberalization, which will reduce the bias against tradables and will shift incentives toward tradables, in particular, exportables. Import liberalization will also reduce or eliminate some inefficient unproductive rent-seeking activities[5] and small developing economies that insult producers from exposure to international competition maintain production, which is in many cases inefficient by global standards.

The beneficial effects of a trade agreement such as the EPA do not automatically accrue because trade liberalization is a necessary but not sufficient condition for the expansion of trade, which can promote economic growth and economic development. The sufficient condition is that national and, where appropriate, regional integration policies create an economic environment that allows/encourages producers to seize export opportunities. Exports must be the priority goal because as Dadush and Shaw remind us "no country has sustained growth without increasing exports."[6]

Trade promoted economic development involves three interrelated processes, which have three objectives and three requirements. The objectives are (1) export expansion, (2) export diversification, and (3) efficient mix of imports and domestic production. The three requirements are (1) efficient resource allocation, (2) increased resource mobilization, and (3) increased resource creation.

The package of economic policies that can achieve the resource allocation, mobilization, and creation necessary for the promotion of exports must be specifically designed for and suited to the unique circumstances, which exist in each individual country.[7] The accepted wisdom among economic development practitioners is that "growth-promoting policies tend to be context specific."[8] In addition, the factors that drive economic growth are constantly changing[9] because of changing local and more so external factors, given the restless nature of globalization.

On the basis of the experience of developing countries, there are some broad commonalities to the type of economic policy measures, which are conducive to increased exports both in volume and diversity. What follows is an overview of these broad commonalities that constitute the economic policy framework, which could allow CARIFORUM countries in the EPA to seize and create export opportunities. These policies form a part of a wider process of strategic global repositioning, which is not an economic policy reform agenda but an approach to economic transformation and a framework for development promoting policies that emanate from and are designed specifically for a combination of (1) national circumstances and very importantly in small developing economies (2) global economic conditions.

Strategic Global Repositioning

Strategic global repositioning is a process of repositioning a country in the global economy by implementing a strategic plan. Such a plan is designed to consolidate and improve existing production while reorienting the economy by creating new types of economic activities. In most small developing countries, this means structural transformation, not structural adjustment, to achieve economic diversification, in particular, export diversification. The need for strategic global repositioning is derived from trends in the global economy, and the composition of exports of small, developing economies, which is skewed to primary products. Strategic global repositioning must be accompanied by policies, which improve the competitiveness and efficiency of companies, by creating a stimulating entrepreneurial environment. Selective trade, fiscal and credit policies supported by medium term education, and technology policies focused on "strategic sectors," and close cooperation between government and the business sector contribute to the targeted development of internationally competitive industries. Market-orientated and strategic state management, combined with the cooperation of companies, government agencies, research institutions, and funding institutions, can create dynamic competitive advantages. These kinds of policies must be directed to long-term strategies to mobilize market forces, build up world-market-standard firms, and systematically develop efficient economic locations.

Predictable Institutional Arrangements for Governance

It is important that small, developing countries mobilize capital, technology, and the human skills necessary for effective competition in the world economy. These inputs, which are necessary to development, can be garnered in the global marketplace, provided the national economic environment is attractive. One of the most important foundations of a predictable national economic environment is a stable and working system of institutions. The importance of such institutions has justifiably been emphasized as a basis for a private-sector-led, market-driven economy. Political stability emanating from transparent governance is an important part of maintaining a modern business environment that is consistent with current global standards and best practices and open to foreign talent and investment. Stiglitz opines, "A major factor determining how well a country will do is the 'quality' of the public and private institutions, which in turn is related to how decisions get made and in whose interest, a subject broadly referred to as governance."[10]

Secure property rights, the rule of law, and sound institutions encourage enterprise and efficiency because they lower the cost of transactions.[11] Predictable institutions lead to symbiotic relations with economic organizations and to a society characterized by a high level of trust. Firms and households in an atmosphere of trust[12] are more willing to enter in to long-term contracts and economic agreements.

The critical importance for developing countries is the shift of the business environment from one dominated by uncertainty to the one where risk can be identified and managed. Risk is a probability that can be calculated and quantified in monetary terms and can be managed by firms and individuals by means such as insurance. Uncertainty exists where information/knowledge about events is imprecise and, therefore, cannot be calculated and countervailing action cannot be planned.[13] In small developing economies, uncertainty arises from vulnerability to external shocks and imperfect markets, and therefore, good governance and efficient government services is vital to attenuate uncertainty or convert it to manageable risk. The development of institutions and mechanisms for coping with risk increases the propensity of households and firms for saving, investment, and reduces hedging. The less risky the business environment is perceived to be the longer the time horizon of economic decisions making.

Stable Macroeconomics Policy Framework

It is essential that stability in macroeconomic policy be sustained in the medium term, providing an economic environment conducive to investment and minimizing dislocating expectations. The macroeconomic policy instruments such as fiscal policy, monetary policy, and exchange rate policy must be applied in a consistent manner and complemented by an institutional framework, which facilitates private-sector-led, market-driven growth. Stable macroeconomic economic policies also contribute to economic growth by reducing uncertainty and risk in the business environment and can reduce vulnerability to external contagion. Rodrik's study of developing economies concludes that "the ability to maintain macro-economic stability in the face of often-turbulent external conditions is the single most important factor accounting for the diversity of post-1975 economic performance in the developing world."[14]

A stable macroeconomic policy in a developing country must be a combination of stabilization and structural transformation because stabilization is a necessary not sufficient condition for economic development. The approach to macroeconomic policy in the short run must be consistent with a medium to long term development approach. The approach must go beyond the components of the "Washington Consensus"[15] to a wider ambit, which incorporates structural elements.[16] Macroeconomic and development have to be integrated into a fundamental complementary best described as "development macroeconomic."[17]

A stable macroeconomic policy does not imply an immutable policy such as a fixed exchange rate but is a regime where change is orderly because economic actors, be they consumers or producers, understand the market forces and underlying rationale for the policy changes. A market-determined exchange is an example of an economy-wide price, which is never exactly the same over time but where economic actors understand how demand and supply interact and the basis on which the central bank may choose to intervene in the foreign exchange market. Care must be exercised to avoid what C. Y. Thomas in describing the experience of Barbados in confronting economic stress as "a bias by the authorities toward unsustainable compensatory increases in public expenditure."[18] Several CARIFORUM governments[19] have lost fiscal space to support efforts to seize the opportunities of the EPA because of the encumbrance of unsustainable levels of public debt. There is scope to improve the budget formulation and execution process[20] and to move fiscal policy away from an accounting approach to one in which fiscal policy is an instrument of development policy.

Global Best Practice Business Environment

The CARIFORUM governments must strive to create in their economies and at the regional level a globally best practice business environment. This is made necessary by the extreme globalization of the world economy, which means that there is really only one market and that is the global market and national economies, regardless of size and level of development, are subject to the dominance of capital accumulation on a world scale. Countries have to engineer a business environment that can extract the maximum benefits from the global economy while minimizing effects harmful to their national economy. The catenation with and growth producing engagement in the global economic process can be accomplished by having a national business environment that is open to and facilitates international interaction through a blend of best practices facilitating internationally competitive business. For example, a government will endeavor as much as possible to facilitate investment but not at the expense of labor standards, the quality of the natural environment, inter alia.

It is not likely that an efficient private sector can exist and function without a facilitating and supportive public sector. The state has a development role to perform without impinging on the scope and creativity of the private sector. This requires the provision of security, infrastructure, efficient administrative services, and social investment particularly in health and education. The role of the state must involve appropriate regulation of business practices while liberating entrepreneurial initiative and encouraging innovation both at the enterprise level and the national level. It is important that in performing its regulatory role, the state most not become an impediment through bureaucratic procedures. Growth promoting policies should start growth diagnostics[21] by identifying constraints to growth, devising policies to eliminate or reduce these, and crucially important institutionalize this capacity because the constraints to economic growth change over time.[22]

A crucial aspect of growth-enhancing policy is the promotion of international competitiveness and export growth, and diversification is the removal at best and at least the reduction of the barriers and bureaucratic impediments to business and proactive strategic collaboration to support exporters.[23] The reduction in bureaucracy can also release entrepreneurship[24] particularly at the microenterprise level.[25] The removal of impediments such as government bureaucracy is an important factor in encouraging innovation and adoption of technology. The economic environment must "foster and exploit continuous technological innovation."[26]

Envisioning New Development Perspectives

The only constant and the only certainty in economic life is change and firms have to compete and survive Schumpeterian "creative destruction,"[27] which is inherent in a private sector, market-driven society. Many long-standing firms and brands perish, for example, PanAm and Kodak, and new firms emerge or existing ones reorganize. In today's world digital "networked society,"[28] the pace of change is very rapid[29] and increasingly unpredictable. Indeed, creative destruction is not only about collapse and elimination of enterprises but it is also paralleled by the birth, emergence, and hypergrowth of new firms, which is evident in the rapid rise of firms from emerging market economies to global prominence.[30] The firms that succeed are characterized by what the CEO of Exxon called "the relentless pursuit of efficiency."[31] Government policy must seek to release and stimulate innovative entrepreneurs rather than replicative entrepreneurs,[32] and this can be do through devising national and Caribbean-wide innovation systems. Each government must encourage innovators[33] by devising an interactive nexus of institution, incentives, and organizational structure that create and sustain a productive dialectic of ideas and innovation.[34]

The implications of change are profound, and therefore, the societies that succeed in economic development are those that foster a culture of openness to timely and managed change and a proactive quest for the new and innovative. This culture has to pervade all aspects of economic life and imbue the conduct and outlook of all classes and interests. This change of mindset must encompass participation in the global economy through exports,[35] knowledge acquisition, and investment. The change of mindset has to occur simultaneously in both the private and the public sector. If this does not happen, then the society fails to understand the imperative for strategic global repositioning[36] and governments persist with development strategies long after they are redundant. Industrialization in the parts of the Caribbean is a clear example.

Small, developing countries of CARIFORUM over the last 50 years have attempted a transition from agriculturally based economies, which exported primary products to an industrialized economy exporting manufactured goods. The motivations were obvious, given that in the 1950s and 1960s industrialization was regarded as synonymous with development and high per capita incomes. The conventional wisdom in the early years of the discipline of development economics was that "the" strategy for transforming developing economies into developed ones was industrialization. The CARIFORUM countries attempted industrialization, in the vast majority of cases, by an initial phase of import-substitution industrialization. Having nurtured infant industries by protectionist measures and incentives to foreign investment, economies were supposed to become exporters of manufactured goods, capitalizing on wage differentials between developed and developing countries, as well as taking advantage of raw material availability and energy, where available. However, very few countries succeeded in achieving this scenario because of their small market, narrow range of indigenous raw materials, imported energy, and labor relatively high compared to Asia. A few developing countries with more propitious circumstances have become known as the newly industrialized economies, the most notable examples being the "Asian Tigers." Changes in the world economy and technological innovations have made labor-intensive, low-wage manufacturing less viable. In addition, to a large extent, the very success of the newly industrialized countries filled this niche in the international division of labor and the attendant industrialization and export opportunities.

Therefore, the option of industrialization has been largely preempted and is no longer feasible for the vast majority of developing countries. This, however, is not the disaster that it appears to be, because, for some countries, with the necessary attributes, it is both possible and desirable to relinquish the unquestioning faith in the procreative power of industrialization, and switch immediately to service-oriented economies. The export of services can provide the so-far elusive development, given that services are the fastest growing component of the world economy. Like industrialization, this is not an option, which every developing country can pursue. Those with the potential must move immediately to seize this opportunity.

There must be both recognition of the need to change and a willingness to innovate. Every process of adjustment begins with a change of mind, outlook, and attitude. This process of adjustment will only commence in earnest when there is a change of mind in both the public and private sector and entrepreneurs dare to think the new and adventurous. There has to be a paradigm shift, which should now be possible since reality so clearly contradicts the viability of the entrenched, dominant "industrialization" paradigm. The "industrialization paradigm" based on import stabilization industrialization behind protectionist barriers rationalized by "infant industry" arguments has exhausted the national market. This regional integration proffered the solution, as the amalgamation of economies into a regional market, which would permit economies of scale and improve efficiency through competition.

Continuous Enhancing of International Competitiveness

International competition is inescapable to point where it is increasingly meaningless to make the distinction between the local market and the external market. There is in reality only one market and that is the global market. Producers cannot insulate themselves even with formal barriers such as tariffs because borders are porous and consumers are aware of the globally available alternatives. International competition is relentless in the sourcing of inputs such as labor, technology, finance, and management. Sirkin, Hemerling, and Bhattacharya describe these circumstances as "globality" by which they mean "competing with everyone from everywhere for everything."[37] This is because the world economy has been moving toward a situation that for want of a more apposite term Friedman calls a "Flat World."[38]

The outlook for the demand and prices for raw materials and primary products is not encouraging. Given the history of fluctuating commodity prices and declining terms of trade against manufactured goods, it is important that the products that are exported are determined by demand considerations and not supply first considerations. Exports cannot be decided only on the basis of what the country can supply; instead, production of exports must start from what the world market demands. Exports of goods and service have to be continuously improved and refreshed to meet and induce changing tastes and to meet international competitors. Prices have to stay ahead or at least abreast of the competition. To stay internationally competitive, firms must continuously build technical and organizational capabilities for innovation within the connectivity between firms and their customers. This connectivity drives the cocreation of value through global networks.[39]

International competitiveness must be a strategic priority for governments and must be the fundamental tenet of economic policy that undergirds economic policy decisions and leitmotif for development planning. A critically important aspect of a business environment, which is conducive to international competitiveness, is a taxation system that provides incentives to foreign and local investment and encourages innovation and easy corporate restructuring. This fiscal thrust will best be accomplished as part of a comprehensive, coherent tax reform, which is long overdue[40] in the majority of CARIFORUM countries. While there is an ongoing debate about the efficacy of industrial policy and the use of fiscal incentives to entice FDI,[41] such incentives if properly utilized[42] can make a tangible contribution.[43] Tax and other incentives can encourage foreign investment, which can be an important source technology. Developing countries such as those of CARIFORUM must create the capacity to attract, assimilate, diffuse, and adapt new technology on a continuous basis. Capacity building must enable firms, in particular exporters[44] as well as the society in general.

It is firms, not countries, that carry out international trade and investment; therefore, international competitiveness is that of firms not countries, though the two are interrelated. Krugman declares, "competitiveness is a meaningless word when applied to national economies."[45] Kogut emphasizes the fact that "globalization is less and less about national competition around sectoral dominance but about the location of the value-added activities that compose the global community chains. From this perspective, firm strategies matter more, since comparative advantage and firm advantage are more de-linked today than they have been before."[46] Poor competitiveness at the macroeconomic level can even retard firm-level competitiveness and contribute to a divergence between national and firm competitiveness. Whatever the circumstances the operations of firms are competitive, if "an interest in innovation needs to infuse the whole business."[47]

Fluidity in Resource Allocation/Mobilization

If there is to be export diversification and increased exports, then international competitiveness has to be continually upgraded and reinvented to keep pace with or ahead of trends and changes in the global marketplace in this case the EU. An essential aspect of the business environment must be the fluidity of resource allocation and mobilization so that production can be adjusted to meet changing demand and survive competitors. The process of corporate reinvention and continuous upgrading of international competitiveness must not be inhibited by rigidities or institutional barriers to resource creation and reallocation. Essential to the dynamic fluidity of resource allocation and reallocation is the operation of competitive markets. As noted earlier, markets in small developing economies are not as competitive as they should be and therefore government intervention is necessary to control or minimize tendencies that can overwhelm or divert the competitive nature of the markets. Government intervention and regulatory has to balance controlling these tendencies that undermine competition without allowing controls to have the same deleterious effect.

Fluidity is an essential quality of a dynamic business environment because firms have to continually reorganize and reposition to survive and to operate profitable. The hallmark of international competitiveness in firms is the capacity to adapt and innovate by continually reevaluated and recalibrated their business strategies, for example, Starbucks.[48] The best of these firms do more than adapt to market changes and new technologies they create demand by creating new products, new services, and new technologies, for example, Google.[49] Starbucks and Google are apposite examples because they started as small enterprises.

Improving Productivity

Productivity is a process of identifying and executing ways to more efficiently use the existing land, labor, and capital. Globalization necessitates continual improvements in productivity, in particular, attention will have to be given to increasing labor productivity, improving managerial capacity, and upgrading infrastructure. Essential to achieving productivity enhancement is that the government must make improving productivity a priority, which infuses all its economic policies. Productivity also crucially depends on a business environment that encourages innovation and transformational entrepreneurship.

Management

Management will have to become more sophisticated, be constantly in touch with developments in international markets, and constantly update itself on new technological innovations. Managerial capacity has improved considerably, and professionalism has increased in recent years. However, there is still room for improvement, particularly in the public sector. In the short run, the private sector's managerial capacity can be upgraded by importing skilled managers and other professionals. This need not mean that foreigners, unaware of the country's culture and traditions, take over top managerial posts. There are more than enough skilled "Caribbean professionals" overseas, who under the right circumstances would be willing to return to home. Countries must no longer be viewed as physical places but as a "nations without borders." In the long run, this requires a reorientation of postsecondary education away from an emphasis on the arts, and toward management, accounting, computer programming, and all aspects of modem technology.

In a business environment, characterized by frequent changes requiring rapid responses, management and workers must evolve a new relationship in which traditional roles and attitudes must be replaced by a collaborative interaction. The relationship between management and workers and between different levels within the production process will have to change in a way that ensures incentives that maximize productivity. The interaction within the work place will have to be more cooperative and the divisions less rigid, permitting more dialogue between trade unions and management. If productivity is to be increased and innovations encouraged, it is imperative that the atmosphere become less adversarial and more genuinely interactive. The traditional notion of worker will have to be abandoned and a new concept that recognizes worker participation in managerial decisions and employee stock ownership programs. These developments will require trade unions to expand their traditional role beyond wages and working conditions to include employment creation/preservation, education/training, and ownership participation.

Labor

The productivity of labor (workers and managers) needs to be upgraded, and this means improvement in the quantity and quality of education. The importance of this is illustrated by the experience of the East Asian countries. The expansion and transformation of education and training during the last three decades has been a key factor in the "economic miracle" of East Asian economies.[50] This has to be tackled both within the individual enterprise and in the society as a whole. Firms need to put more emphasis on vocational training and on the job education. The new technology of learning can help. For example, multimedia training enables workers to learn faster and in more detail, particularly those workers who are functionally illiterate.

Increasingly, the world economy will be dominated by knowledge-based industries, especially services, making the quality of human capital a critical factor. In the case of many developing countries, much of their human capital resides outside of their borders. Every effort must be made to repatriate it. Just as incentives and special programs exist for foreign investment, similar schemes must be established to induce overseas nationals with professional skills to return home or establish enterprises that utilize national products. It might even be necessary to mount special campaigns to attract skilled foreign professionals and entrepreneurs. Overseas communities and returning professionals and businessmen have spearheaded several of the new growth sectors in India, for example, computer hardware and software. In Jamaica the owner/manager of small firms that became exporters had lived, studied, and/or worked in foreign countries.[51] The quest for talent and skill involves retaining local human resources and attracting nationals and foreigners to come to live and work in the Caribbean.

Human resources are the critical determinant of international competitiveness in this phase of globalization, and there is a very competitive global labor market.[52] Developing countries such as those of CARIFORUM must participate in the global labor market because they will lose some skilled and unskilled labor, but they can also benefit from inflows of labor. The movement of labor is not confined to what is described as the "brain drain" because skilled human resources flow in all directions and can contribute to growth in developing countries. Global mobility of labor is beneficial to both developed and developing countries[53] and should be embraced. Those lost to the Caribbean economies contribute in many ways including remittances[54] and as vital "diaspora entrepreneurial networks."[55]

Infrastructure

There is an urgent need to improve the extent and quality of physical infrastructure such as roads, irrigation, electricity, and telecommunications in order to reduce the operating costs of firms in all sectors. Road transportation and telecommunications now require a quantitative leap in anticipation of increased demand and must be state-of-the-art technology. Under the right conditions, much of the required expansion in physical infrastructure could be financed by private capital, including foreign capital. This has already begun to happen in electricity generation and airport expansion. The improvement in infrastructure must focus not only on modernization but also must take cognizance of the need to close the gap with developed countries. The quality of infrastructure is an important factor in attracting foreign investment into the CARIFORUM countries. A World Bank survey of 159 international companies with operations in the Caribbean found that they "attach more importance to the quality of infrastructure than any other aspect of the investment climate."[56]

Access to information is the very core of the operation of global economic activity and is crucially dependent on ICT capability. Rapid and continuous innovation in ICT has transformed international economic transactions as well as most aspects of everyday life.[57] The new technologies have been influential in shaping the current phase of globalization, which has encompassed and transformed the world economy by creating unprecedented levels of economic connectivity.[58] International economic interaction established a new level of inclusiveness that has confirmed the global market as the dominant economic environment for both tradable and nontradable goods and services. The challenge for the CARIFORUM countries will be to extricate themselves from being "digital diasporas" and leapfrog the "digital divide" of missed, outdated, or redundant aspects of development.

Knowledge, Education, and Training

The quality of human resources is an important factor in economic growth but is even more so in small developing economies.[59] Small developing economies suffer from a narrow range of indigenous raw materials, lack of indigenous technological innovation, and small land area; hence, the importance of human capital, a critical determinant of total factor productivity, and the basis of much comparative advantage. The value of human capital will become increasingly important to small developing economies as globalization continues. The amount and quality of education are critical to the quality of human resources and the capacity of the workforce to access and utilize information and knowledge. In today's knowledge-based societies, the continuous reskilling and enhancement of skills is an ongoing accumulative process pervading all aspects of economic life. Workplace training of the workforce after graduation from school or university is essential. International competitiveness is increasingly dependent on the knowledge and skills that are made available through a combination of the public and private sectors. Developing countries need to plug into international knowledge exchange networks as knowledge is now a global public good.[60] In this regard, tertiary education especially universities have a critical role both to train and an export of education services.[61] Wildavsky points out that "another form of globalization involves a nation's concerted effort to compete internationally by creating world-class universities."[62] The more developed is the education system, the greater the capacity of societies to use technology and to make technical change and growth of knowledge a symbiotic endogenous process.[63]

Connectivity

Connectivity is crucial to small developing economies especially those that are small islands where size, location, and remoteness severely hamper air travel and cargo shipping. Services-oriented economic activity can flourish in small developing countries if there is modern and efficient internet capacity at competitive prices. Access to information is crucially dependent on the ICT capabilities of individuals, households, firms, and countries. In a world of differences in size (corporate and national), level of economic development, and national power, access to ICTs varies considerably, giving rise to a complex dialectic in which ICTs are simultaneously a means of narrowing or closing the development gap and the mechanism for perpetuating and widening the differentiation. The fundamental development dilemma of the modern era is how small developing countries can extricate themselves from being "digital diasporas" and how they can leapfrog the missed, outdated, or redundant aspects of their development. The complexities of the impact of ICTs and the possibilities for crossing the "digital divide" are compounded by the fact that the confining and liberating dimensions of ICTs operate simultaneously. This is the development enigma that policy makers and development planners have to tackle by the formulation and implementation of policies, which are efficacious in the promotion and facilitation of economic development.[64]

Corporate Redimensioning and Renewal

Firms in the CARIFORUM countries are small by global comparison;[65] indeed, they are nanofirms. They will be exposed to international competition to export to the EU markets even with the preferential arrangements built into the EPA. To survive imports and to export, these firms will have to become more robust and reliant to competition from much larger firms, including MNCs. Small size puts exporting firms at a severe disadvantage and, therefore, there is a need for collaborative corporate alliances or mergers to provide a larger capital base, pool resources, and expertise and access the latest technology. Scaling up of the scope and operations of local firms has many benefits, including attaining economies of scale and scope.

Corporate integration, consolidation, and restructuring through cross-border mergers and acquisitions have been limited in the CARICOM countries.[66] Some firms and financial institutions from small, developing countries including the CARIFORUM countries have become MNCs. A merger movement would make firms more viable and more likely joint-venture partners with foreign investors. Enlargement of local firms should be encouraged and facilitated to enable CARIFORM firms to be more robust competitors and cope with more intensive competition from larger foreign and European firms in the EU markets. Mergers and strategic alliances with foreign corporations can be beneficial and a distinct possibility in today's global economy where capital has no nationality. Indeed, even bitter political differences and economic rivalry have been swept aside by strategic corporate alliances between firms in China and Taiwan. Strategic alliances or networks of small firms can mitigate some of the expenses that might be too much for a single firm.[67] Friedman advises that "one way small companies flourish in the flat world is by learning to act really big. And the key to being small and acting big is being quick to take advantage of all the new tools of collaboration to reach farther, faster, wider and deeper."[68]

Enlargement of CARIFORUM firms will be necessary in many circumstances, but there are still viable opportunities for small firms that specialize especially in services and in products where economies of scale are not decisive. While the world economy is well on the way to being flat, there are still enduring and significant national differences, and firms must there corporate and export strategies accordingly.[69]The development of clusters of firms has many advantages and is an alternative to the enlargement of individual firms.[70] The development of firms and their preparedness for exposure to and participation in global competition need not be left to market-driven impulses. The state can perform an important role in nurturing privately nationally owned firms[71] through establishment, evolution through adaptive learning to the development of efficient operations.

There is no single and precise mix of factors that account for why economic growth takes place. There is no one-size-fits-all formula because the factors driving growth in any given country at any particular time are in constant interaction.[72] In fact, the small countries that have achieved rapid growth have not followed any particular model but devised their unique strategies.[73] However, some insights can be gleaned from studying the experience of countries that have achieved high rates of economic growth over a sustained period. These insights can be useful as long as it is borne in mind that they cannot be transplanted but have to be modified to suit local conditions.

Modernization of International Marketing

There are problems with production in small developing economies, for example, inconsistent quality, irregularities in supply, and poor labeling. Inadequate marketing has also been a severe constraint on exports. However, there are some sectors, which have achieved sophisticated levels of marketing, for example, in some services, notably tourism. In some instances, this weakness has been obviated by strategic corporate alliances, commodity agreements, and subcontracting. However, much can be done to catch up with new marketing techniques and technologies, in particular, interactive electronic marketing. Interactive retailing, which is growing rapidly in developed countries, can take many forms, including personal computer users linked to online services and internet-based retailers, multimedia kiosks, interactive home shopping programs over cable and satellite TV networks, and CD-ROM-based shopping catalogues. All of these formats allow the consumer to purchase by telephone or computer and pay credit card, while allowing the retailer reduced costs of storage and display areas for products. The necessity to develop electronic marketing is suggested by the worldwide growth of internet users.

Poor or unsophisticated international marketing has prevented many firms from exporting even when they are capable of producing goods and services that are internationally competitive in price and quality. There is a supportive role for governments in the form of export promotion agencies[74] and programmes to assist firms with international marketing with market information, training, trade missions, and advertising. Government's export promotion efforts of governments can extend for establishing the country as a brand, for example, the Caribbean is a regional brand in tourism. While government's can assist, there is inevitable firm-level learning[75] that is involved in exporting.

Recalibrated Strategic Planning

It is important that small, developing countries mobilize capital, technology, and the human skills necessary for effective competition in the world economy. These inputs, which are necessary to development, can be garnered in the global marketplace, provided the national economic environment is attractive. Strategic planning namely a process of continuous dialogue and interaction between the leadership of the private sector, the public sector, the trade unions, and social sectors is essential. This can be augmented by inputs from individuals and organizations abroad. Close and continuous cooperation between the leadership of these sectors is essential in order to effectively formulate strategic planning and targeted implementation. What is needed is a marriage that harnesses the vision and expertise of all sectors. This cooperation has been a critical factor in the economic success of Japan and the newly industrialized countries of Asia, particularly, private–public sector synergy and the allocation of decisions between the market and public administration.[76] Strategic planning and the resultant development strategy must be kept under continuous review and be subjected to regular recalibration to meet changing national and international circumstances. Institutionalized arrangements that facilitate a continuous dialogue between the private sector, unions, and the government is essential to synchronize business strategies with the government's economic development strategy.[77]

Seamless Regional Economic Space

The EPA strengthens the formation/completion of a seamless regional economic space. This can contribute to seizing the opportunities opened up by the EPA by the production and delivery of regional public goods and by an arena in which firms can redimension and enhance their international competitiveness. To date, the CARICOM integration has concentrated on the liberalization of trade, while there has been insufficient attention devoted to the free movement of labor and capital. The persistence of barriers to intraregional investment such as national restrictions on the sectors in which foreign investment is permitted, national ownership requirements, prohibitions on land ownership, and differences in company law. All of these restrictions are prevalent in one form or another in the member states of CARICOM. Symptomatic of this malaise was the failure to even approve the CARICOM Enterprise Regime (CER) whose objective is to provide "national treatment" to any CARICOM Enterprise. A CARICOM enterprise was a company owned and controlled by nationals of at least two member states. Originally mooted in 1974 and revived in 1985, the CER was established in1988 but never came into effect. The official history of CARICOM explains the member states "did not put in place the national legislation to give effect to the CER in a timely manner and by the early 1990's when a sufficient number had done so, our Community has already taken the decision to establish a Single Market and Economy."[78]

Liberalization of capital would facilitate the emergence of a regional capital market. A CARIFORUM-wide capital market can help to improve the international competitiveness of the nanofirms of CARICOM by (1) improving access to capital and lowering the cost of funds for investment, it can reduce the costs of operation both absolutely and relatively to extra-regional sources of funding. The ability of CARICOM firms to compete effectively in external markets requires them to modernize and restructure their operations, technology, and management systems to continuously improve their productivity. The ability to raise financing on competitive terms has been a major problem for most nanofirms, especially microenterprises and individual service providers in entertainment and consultants and other professional services. (2) Facilitating the consolidation of nanofirms by strengthening their capital base, thereby adding to their resilience and making them more attractive as partners in strategic alliances [79] with larger firms and even MNCs. Size is often a particularly severe impediment in exporting, and in many instances, an appropriate strategic alliance can provide additional resources, access to marketing networks, management expertise, and new technology. Strategic alliances or networks of small firms can mitigate some of the expenses that might be too much for a single firm. (3) Expands the options and prospects for raising funds to meet the costs of penetrating foreign markets, learning the new market environment, for example, customs procedures, phyto-sanitary regulations, and negotiating with foreign government agencies. Larger firms dominate export activity whether their national economies are developed or developing. Competing internationally either by exporting or by establishment in overseas markets is invariably linked to foreign investment.[80] The size factor is particularly important in industrial activity,[81] and small firms will seek to attain scale through alliances unless they occupy a niche in which they are large relative to their competitors.[82]

The measures required to achieve capital market integration among CARICOM countries are required at both the national and regional levels. Measures to strengthen and deepen the capital markets by the number and sophistication of instruments, institutions, and resort to capital markets in preference to commercial banks for corporate financing. The Caribbean Trade & Investment Report of 2005 summarizes the state of the regional capital market: "Despite the advances made in recent years, there are some critical conditions that need to be implemented in order to sustained growth and development of the regional bond market. Some measures will require a high-level of co-operation and co-ordination by regional governments, central banks, regulatory bodies, securities exchanges and market actors. The necessary actions are not straightforward nor are they necessarily in keeping with nationalistic interests that continue to paralyze a number of regional initiatives, including a regional stock exchange mechanism."[83]

Conclusion

The beneficial effects of a trade agreement such as the EPA do not automatically accrue: trade liberalization is a necessary but not sufficient condition for the expansion of trade that can promote economic growth and economic development. The sufficient condition is that national and, where appropriate, regional integration policies create an economic environment that allows and encourages producers to seize export opportunities. Seizing the opportunities created by the EPA will require active government collaboration with the private sector in the CARIFORUM countries in pursuit of proactive, strategic development policy. The market alone will not automatically produce sustainable economic development. Individually and collectively the governments of the CARIFORUM countries must create national and regional economic environments that are conducive to economic development. To gain the maximum benefit from the EPA, the CARIFORUM countries will have to formulate and implement a programme of strategic global repositioning.[84] Strategic global repositioning is a proactive approach to effective participation and beneficial integration with the global economy.

CHAPTER 9

Summary

Autarky is not a viable option especially for small developing economies; hence, exposure and involvement with globalization is unavoidable and therefore the issue for ever country is how to mediate the encounter with globalization in a manner that can benefit their economic growth and promote their economic development. Globalization poses both challenges and opportunities for all countries, large and small, developed and developing. To seize the opportunities in the global economy, countries have to be proactive and strategic in their international economic policy and pursue domestic economic policy, which continuously improves their international competitiveness of the goods and services they produce for export and national consumption. Specifically countries can use international trade agreements at the multilateral level through the WTO or at the regional or bilateral level to influence the terms of their integration into the global economy and the opportunities that are available to them. The degree to which countries are successful in concluding the type of trade agreements that can accomplish these goals depends on a raft of economic, political, and institutional factors.

The context in which the CARIFORUM-EU EPA was mooted and negotiated was one of the rapid and profound globalization. The goal of having an EPA and the objectives pursued by both the EU and the CARIFORUM in the negotiations were strongly influenced the state of globalization and the actual and anticipated trends of globalization. Globalization involves the progressive reduction or elimination of national barriers to the international movement of goods, services, capital, and technology. Globalization is a multidimensional process that is not a unilinear in its evolution, instead is an uneven one different aspects proceeding at varying speeds. There is not a complete standardization of the rules governing international transactions and flows; however, a basic set of principles guiding trade rules has been enshrine in the agreements that constitute the WTO. Coverage is not universal in either subject matter or membership of countries, and hence, countries seek to create arrangements that give them benefits beyond those available under the WTO. Regional and bilateral trade agreements have been given momentum because of the difficulty of negotiating the extension of the coverage and depth of WTO rules. In these circumstances, here has been a pronounced proliferation of bilateral, regional, and plurilateral trade agreements. In a world where developed countries and gigantic MNCs can exercise disproportionate power to avoid, circumvent, ignore, and override multilateral rules and overwhelm the sovereignty of small, poor, and developing countries, trade agreements assume considerable importance to the weaker partners. In this milieu, small developing countries seek gains in regional and bilateral preferential trade agreement where their influence in negotiations is greater than in the multilateral arena.

Entering the first decade of this century, the EU like many other developed countries found that they were facing increased international competition as globalization exposed them to more intensive international competition and, therefore, sought to use their international trade policy to address this issue. In the EU, there was a growing concern over the ability to cope with competition from several developing countries variously described as the Asian Tigers, the newly industrialized countries, and emerging markets and in particular China. Part of the shift in EU thinking was to change the terms of their engagement with developing countries including the ACP countries. The EU decided to convert extant preferential trade arrangements into WTO-compatible reciprocity. The EU also had an interest in preserving access to export markets developing countries and conveniently to maintain access to those markets in the ACP with which it had a long association. The enlargement of the EU coincided with the pronounced decline in empathy for developing countries in the developed countries and consequently a shift in thinking away from preferential trade and aid to every country for itself in the global marketplace. The conventional wisdom on international trade had by the 1990s come to gravitate around the notion of free trade, and there was a hardening of attitudes against special and differential treatment for developing countries. In this political atmosphere, it would have been increasingly difficult for the EU to get the membership of the WTO to grant waivers of the kind that would have been required by the continuation of the Lomé Conventions. The EU was not willing to expend further political capital to secure a WTO waiver for its trade agreements with ACP. This was indicative that trade with the ACP was no longer a priority. More specifically, the CARIFORUM markets, with the exception of the Dominican Republic, are so small that increasing their market share was not a major motivator for the EU. At the commencement of the negotiations, the total CARIFORUM market was 25 million and total GDP was approximately $70 billion less than a third of Ireland's GDP. The waning of interest in the EU was accompanied by a shift in development philosophy from aid in the forms of preferential trade and financial aid to trade supported by aid. The overall objective of the EU was to replace preferential trade arrangements with an agreement that had sufficient reciprocity to be WTO compatible.

The CARIFORUM countries were influenced by two profound factors: first, the characteristics of their small developing economies and, second, developments emanating from globalization. The structural and institutional characteristics of CARIFORUM economies are small developing economies. The dominant feature is their small size relative to the majority of countries in the world. Small developing economies have certain characteristics, such as a high degree of openness, limited diversity in economic activity, export concentration on one to three products, significant dependency on trade taxes, and small size of firms. Some developing countries and LDCs, in general, may exhibit some of the characteristics listed as defining small developing economies. This has led some to argue that many of the problems attributed to small developing economies are not unique to them or can be addressed by appropriate policy measures; therefore, smallness does not differentiate economies. However, careful analysis reveals that the characteristics, which small developing economies share with other types of developing countries, differ by degree between the different types of developing countries. What sets small developing economies apart and defines them as a distinct genre of developing country is the combination of characteristics and the degree or extent to which these characteristics predominate.

Trends at the global level included globalization with all that it entailed and the policies of developed countries, in particular, the erosion of preferential trade arrangements and declining empathy for developing countries, reducing the prospects for development assistance. CARICOM countries more so than the larger Dominican Republic were aware that the reduction or loss of preferences would have an adverse impact, particularly in the smallest countries and along with the ACP of agreeing in the Cotonou Agreement to EPAs based on reciprocity, which was compatible to the standard set by the WTO. The ACP may have felt safe in signing believing that the key commodity protocols for sugar and bananas were sacrosanct. If pressure from the United States and some developing comes in, the WTO that compelled the EU eventually relinquished to protocols. While officially the EU resisted the dismantling of the protocols, there were also those in the EU who wanted to dismantle the protocols. The ACP may also have feared that not signing the Cotonou Agreement may have put development assistance in jeopardy. The CARIFORUM countries wanted an EPA that would promote sustainable economic development by incorporating as much special and differential treatment as possible.

In order to conduct negotiations as a single unit with joint positions, the CARIFORUM utilized the CRNM. The CRNM pooled the technical expertise of the region and deployed a team of negotiators drawn from the member states. The negotiations for the EPA were successfully completed on the agreed schedule. The EU-CARIFORUM EPA was the first to be concluded, and the only EPA to be completed on schedule. The structure and operation of the CRNM provides valuable lessons for developing countries to conduct international trade negotiations as a group.

CARIFORUM's overarching goal of sustainable economic development was elaborated as seven principal goals, namely, (1) increasing the amount and range of exports, (2) promoting investment, (3) improving international competitiveness, (4) strengthening regional economic integration, (5) extending adjustment and implementation and (6) retaining maximum policy space, and (7) minimizing the impact of fiscal revenue, which CARIFORUM wanted to achieve in the negotiations of the EPA. These goals were attained by the incorporation of provisions based on differential treatment in favor of the CARIFORUM and asymmetrically phased implementation, allowing CARIFORUM extended periods for implementation while the EU provided immediate duty-free, quota-free market access. The provisions of the EPA were designed to promote economic development in the CARIFORUM countries both in specific areas, for example, market access and as a collective of interconnectedness of the provisions. For example, increased investment is treated as a separate goal, but its procreative impact can be felt in increased productive capacity, increased productivity, and enhanced international competitiveness. Similarly, improved intellectual property rights can encourage investment, technology transfer, and local innovation, all of which contribute to improved international competitiveness.

Development assistance was not included in the EPA text but is complementary to the EPA. While the provisions of the EPA indicate the areas in which EU aid is intended to support adjustment and implementation, the EPA does not contain the actual amounts. Naturally the case aid and technical assistance depend not only on the cost of adjustment and the estimated expense of implementation but also on traditional levels of aid and assistance to sectors that had lost preferential arrangements. Obviously, development assistance both in the form of financial resources and technical assistance will have an impact on many aspects of the EPA and the pace of implementation. Work on implementation is being facilitated by an implementation unit at the regional level and similar units in individual countries.

No agreement that is permanent can anticipate everything that can occur during implementation nor can the need for amendments or additions be ruled since circumstances can change. The EPA text made provision for the establishment a group of related institutional fora for governance and to facilitate the review and recalibration of the EPA. These institutional arrangements are in operation after a slow start.

The contribution of the EPA to the sustainable economic development of the CARIFORUM countries can best be realized by the full implementation of the Agreement. Delaying the implementation of the CARIFORUM-EU EPA will only reduce its development value and dissipate the advantages of being the first group of countries to bring into effect an EPA with the EU. For the implementation process to proceed expeditiously and comprehensively, it must be placed and maintained on a sustainable path. The postponement of the implementation of the EPA would be ill-advised is synonymous with postponing the mediation of the encounter with the global economy. The same actions required to prepare for being internationally competitive in the world economy are those envisioned by both the CSME and the EPA. Therefore, in implementing the EPA, the region is accelerating its preparation for, and capacity to engage in, the global economy in a manner propitious for its economic development.

The beneficial effects of a trade agreement such as the EPA do not automatically accrue because trade liberalization is a necessary but not sufficient condition for the expansion of trade that can promote economic growth and economic development. The sufficient condition is that national and, where appropriate, regional integration policies create an economic environment, which allows/encourages producers to seize export opportunities. Seizing the opportunities created by the EPA will require active government collaboration with the private sector in the CARIFORUM countries in pursuit of proactive, strategic development policy. The market alone will not automatically produce sustainable economic development. Individually and collectively, the governments of the CARIFORUM countries must create national and regional economic environments that are conducive to economic development. To gain the maximum benefit from the EPA, the CARIFORUM countries will have to formulate and implement a programme of strategic global repositioning. Strategic global repositioning is a proactive approach to effective participation and beneficial integration with the global economy.

Notes

Introduction

1. CARIFORUM consists of Antigua and Barbuda, the Bahamas, Barbados, Belize, Dominica, the Dominican Republic, Grenada, Guyana, Haiti, Jamaica, St. Kitts and Nevis, St. Lucia, St. Vincent and the Grenadines, Suriname, and Trinidad and Tobago.

1 Globalization and the Economic Partnership Agreement

1. Trade negotiations are proceeding simultaneously on both tracks. There are different views on whether regional trade agreements are a stumbling block or a building block for multilateral trade negotiations.
2. Louise Curran, Lars Nilsson, and Douglas Brew, "The Economic Partnership Agreements: Rationale, Misperceptions and Non-trade Aspects," *Development Policy Review* 26, no. 5 (2008): 529–553. See p. 533.
3. The Results of the Uruguay Round of Multilateral Trade Negotiations. *The Legal Texts* (Geneva: World Trade Organization, 1995), 32.
4. *World Trade Report 2010* (Geneva: World Trade Organization, 2011).
5. *International Trade Statistics 2012* (Geneva: World Trade Organization, 2013), 21.
6. *Overview of Developments in the International Trading Environment* (Geneva: World Trade Organization, 2001), 1.
7. *Liberalizing International Transactions in Services: A Handbook* (New York and Geneva: United Nations, 1994), 14.
8. Thomas L. Friedman, *The World Is Flat: A Brief History of the Twenty-first Century* (New York: Farrar Straus & Giroux; Revised Edition, 2006).
9. Regional Trade Agreements Information Systems, wto.org (February 2013).
10. Peter F. Drucker, "Beyond the Information Revolution," *The Atlantic Monthly* October 1999, 51.
11. Steven Cohen, "Geo-economics and America's Mistakes," in *The New Global Economy in the Information Age*, ed. Martin Carnoy (London: McMillian, 1993), 98.
12. Frances Cairncross, *The Death of Distance: How the Communications Revolution Will Change Our Lives* (Boston: Harvard Business School Press, 1997).
13. Don Tapscott, *The Digital Economy: Promise and Peril in the Age of Networked Intelligence* (New York: McGraw-Hill, 1996).
14. Karl Marx, Friedrich Engels, and Eric Hobsbawm, *The Communist Manifesto: A Modern Edition* (London: Verso, 1998), 38.

15. Joseph A. Schumpeter, *Capitalism, Socialism and Democracy* (London: Routledge, originally 1942, this edition 1994), 82–83.
16. Richard L. Bernal, "Nano-firms, Integration and International Competitiveness: The Experience and Dilemma of the CSME," in *The CARICOM Single Market and Economy: Genesis and Prognosis*, ed. Kenneth Hall and Myrtle Chung-A-Sang (Kingston: Ian Randle Publishers, 2007), 127–151.
17. Chuck Martin, *Net Future: The 7 Cyber Trends that Will Drive Your Business, Create New Wealth and Define Your Future* (New York: McGraw-Hill, 1999), 30.
18. *Electronic Commerce and the Role of the WTO* (Geneva: World Trade Organization, 1998), 10.
19. Stan Davis and Christopher Meyer, *Blur: The Speed of Change in the Connected Economy* (New York: Time Warner Books, 1999).
20. *International Trade Statistics 2012* (Geneva: World Trade Organization, 2013), 146.
21. Ibid.
22. *World Trade Report 2003* (Geneva: World Trade Organization, 2003), 10. For a review of the trends, see A. Maurer and P. Chauvet, "The Magnitude of Flows of Global Trade in Services," in *Development, Trade and the WTO. A Handbook*, ed. Bernard Hoekman, Aaditya Mattoo, and Philip English (Washington, DC: World Bank, 2002), 235.
23. *Global Economic Prospects and the Developing Countries* (Washington, DC: World Bank, 1995), 47–48 and *World Investment Report 2001: Promoting Linkages* (New York and Geneva: United Nations, 2001).
24. *World Development Indicators 2000* (Washington, DC: World Bank, 2000).
25. Hamish McRae, *The World in 20–20. Power, Culture and Prosperity: A Vision of the Future* (London: Harper Collins Publishers, 1994), 27.
26. *Global Economic Prospects and the Developing Countries* (Washington, DC: World Bank, 1995), 48.
27. Aaditya Mattoo, Robert M. Stern, and Gianni Zanini, eds., *A Handbook of International Trade in Services* (Oxford: Oxford University Press, 2008), 10.
28. There is an extensive literature on the internationalization of finance; see, for example, Walter B. Wriston, *The Twilight of Sovereignty* (New York: Charles Scribner's Sons, 1992).
29. Susan Strange, *Casino Capitalism* (Manchester: Manchester University Press, 1997).
30. Dani Rodrik, *The Globalization Paradox: Democracy and the Future of the World Economy* (New York: W. W. Norton & Sons, 2011), 95.
31. Avinash D. Persaud, "International Finance," in *Global Economics in Extraordinary Times: Essays in Honor of John Williamson*, ed. C. Fred Bergsten and C. Randal Henning (Washington, DC: Institute for International Economics, 2012), 107–122. See pp. 107–108.
32. Nouriel Roubini and Stephen Mihm, *Crisis Economics: A Crash Course in the Future of Finance* (New York: Penguin, 2012).
33. Richard L. Bernal, *Trade Blocks: A Regionally Specific Phenomenon, or Global Trend?*, Walter Sterling Surrey Memorial Series (Washington, DC: National Planning Association, September 1997).
34. *Regionalism and the World Trading System* (Geneva: World Trade Organization, 1995), 25; *Reflections on Regionalism. Report of the Study Group on International Trade* (Washington: Carnegie Endowment for International Peace, 1997).
35. Raymond Vernon, *In the Hurricane's Eye: The Troubled Prospects of Multinational Enterprises* (Cambridge: Harvard University Press, 1998), 10.
36. John Stopford and Susan Strange, *Rival States, Rival Firms* (Cambridge: Cambridge University Press, 1991), 15.

37. *World Investment Report, 1998: Trends and Determinants* (Geneva: United Nations, 1998), 39.
38. Cesar Calderon, Norman Loayza, and Luis Serven, "Greenfield Foreign Direct Investment and Mergers and Acquisitions: Feedback and Macroeconomic Effects," *World Bank Policy Research Working Paper No. 3192* (Washington DC: World Bank, January 2004).
39. Giorgio Barba Navaretti and Anthony J. Venables, *Multinational Firms in the World Economy* (Princeton: Princeton University Press, 2004), 9.
40. *World Investment Report 2000* (New York: United Nations, 2003), 14.
41. Grazia Ietto-Gilles, Meloria Meschi, and Roberto Simonetti, "Cross-border mergers and acquisitions," in *European Integration and Global Corporate Strategies*, ed. Francis Chesnais, Grazia Ietto-Giles, and Roberto Simonetti (London: Routledge, 2000), 52–71.
42. *World Investment Report 2012* (Geneva: UNCTAD, 2012), 6.
43. J. Stopford and Susan Strange, *Rival States, Rival Firms* (Cambridge: Cambridge University Press, 1991), 40–41.
44. Susan Strange, *The Retreat of the State: The Diffusion of Power in the World Economy* (Cambridge: Cambridge University Press, 1996); David C. Korten, *When Corporations Rule the World* (Hartford: Kumarian Press and San Francisco: Barrett-Kochler, 1995).
45. Carlo Pietrobelli and Roberta Rabellotti, eds., *Upgrading to compete: Global Value Chains, Clusters, and SMEs in Latin America* (Washington, DC: David Rockefeller Center for Latin American Studies/Inter-American Development Bank, 2007).
46. *World Investment Report* 1994 (Geneva: UNCTAD, 1994).
47. James Gleick, *Faster: The Acceleration of Just About Everything* (New York: Pantheon Books, 1999).
48. Manuel Castells, *The Rise of the Network Society* (New York: Blackwell, 2000).
49. Letter from Prime Minister P. J. Patterson of Jamaica to the President of the European Commission, April 6, 1998.
50. Constantine Michalopoulos, *Developing Countries in the WTO* (London: Palgrave, 2001), 30.
51 Ha-Joon Chang, *Kicking Away the Ladder: Development Strategy in Historical Perspective* (London: Anthem Press, 2002).
52. V. Topp, *Trade Preferences: Are They Helpful in Advancing Economic Development in Poor Countries?* (Canberra: Australian Bureau of Agricultural and Resource Economics, 2001).
53. Caribbean sugar producers that export under preferential trade arrangements with the United States and the EU have production costs that in some cases are twice and triple that of the world's leading free market exporters. See *A Time to Choose: Caribbean Development in the 21st Century* (Washington, DC: World Bank, April 2005), 83; D. Larson and B. Borrell, "Sugar Policy and Reform," *World Bank Policy Research Paper No. 2602* (Washington, DC: World Bank, 2002).
54. Sheila Page and A. Hewitt, "The New European Trade Preferences: Does 'Everything But Arms' (EBA) Help the Poor," *Development Policy Review* 20, no. 1 (2002), 91–102.
55. Anna Krueger, *Trade Policies for Developing Countries* (Washington, DC: Brookings Institution, 1995); Caglar Ozden and Eric Reinhardt, "The Perversity of Preferences: Generalized System of Preferences and Developing Country Policies, 1976–2000," *World Bank Policy Research Working Paper No. 2955* (Washington, DC: World Bank, January 2003); and Arvind Panagariya, "EU Preferential Trade Arrangements and Developing Countries," *World Economy* 25, no. 10 (2002), 1415–1432.

56. Caglar Ozden and Eric Reinhardt, "The Perversity of Preferences: Generalized System of Preferences and Developing Country Policies, 1976–2000," *World Bank Policy Research Working Paper No. 2955* (Washington, DC: World Bank, January 2003).
57. Hollis Chenery and Alan Stout, "Foreign Assistance and Economic Development," *American Economic Review* 56, no. 3 (September 1966), 679–728.
58. Milton Freidman, "Foreign Aid: Means and Objectives," *Yale Review* no. 47 (Summer 1958): 500–516.
59. Joan M. Nelson, *Aid, Influence, and Foreign Policy* (New York: MacMillan, 1968).
60. Rubin Patterson, *Foreign Aid after the Cold War: The Dynamics of Multipolar Economic Competition* (Trenton: Africa World Press, 1997), xxii.
61. Herbert Feis, *Foreign Aid and Foreign Policy* (New York: St. Martin's Press, 1964).
62. I. M. D. Little and J. M. Clifford, *International Aid* (Chicago: Aldine Publishing Company, 1966), 86.
63. Teresa Hayter, *Aid as Imperialism* (Harmondsworth: Penguin, 1971).
64. The interaction and coexistence of multiple motives is well illustrated by the Marshall Plan. See Greg Berhman, *The Most Noble Adventure: The Marshall Plan and the Time When America Helped Save Europe* (New York: Free Press, 2008); Nicolaus Mills, *Winning the Peace: The Marshall Plan and Americas Coming of Age as a Superpower* (New York: Wiley, 2008).
65. Michael J. Hogan, *The Marshall Plan: America, Britain and the Reconstruction of Western Europe, 1947–1952* (Cambridge: Cambridge University Press, 1989).
66. *Human Development Report 2005* (New York: United Nations Development Programme, 2006), 84.
67. Allison Berg and Olga Jonas, eds., *The World Bank in Action in Small States* (Washington, DC: World Bank, 2005).
68. Robert Cassen & Associates, *Does Aid Work? Report to an Intergovernmental Task Force* (Oxford: Oxford University Press, 1986).
69. Peter T. Bauer, *Dissent on Development* (Cambridge: Harvard University Press, 1972) and *Equality: The Third World and Economic Delusion* (Cambridge: Harvard University Press, 1982), 66–155.
70. William Easterly, "Can Aid Buy Growth," *Journal of Economic Perspectives* 17, (2003): 23–48 and *The White Man's Burden. Why the West's Efforts to Aid the Rest Have Done So Much Ill and So Little Good* (New York: Penguin Press, 2006)
71. Dambisa Moyo, *Dead Aid: Why Aid Is Not Working and How There Is a Better Way* (New York: Farrar, Strauss and Giroux, 2009), 28.
72. Tsidi M. Tsikata, "Aid Effectiveness: A Survey of the Recent Empirical Literature," *IMF Paper on Policy Analysis and Assessment, PPAA/98/1* (Washington, DC: International Monetary Fund, March 1998).
73. Camelia Minoiu and Sanjay G. Reddy, "Development Aid and Economic Growth: A Positive Long-Relation," *IMF Working Paper WP/09/118* (Washington, DC: International Monetary Fund, May 2009).
74. D. D. Headey, "Geopolitics and the Effectiveness of Aid on Economic Growth: 1970–2001," *Journal of International Development* vol. 20, no. 2 (March 2008): 161–180.
75. Craig Burnside and David Dollar, "Aid, Policies and Growth," *Policy Research Working Paper No. 1777* (Washington, DC: World Bank, June 1997).
76. Paul Mosley, John Hudson, and Sara Horrell, "Aid, The Public Sector and the Market in Less Developed Countries: A Return to the Scene," *Journal of International Development* 4, no. 2 (1992): 139–150.

77. Michael Clements, Steven Radelet, and Rikhil Bhavnani, "Counting Chickens When They Hatch: The Short Term Effect of Aid on Growth," *Working Paper 44* (Washington, DC: Center for Global Development, 2004).
78. Stephen Knack, "Aid, Dependence and the Quality of Governance: A Cross-country Empirical Analysis," *World Bank Policy Research Paper* (Washington, DC: World Bank, 2000).
79. Raghuram Rajan and Arvind Subramanian, "Aid and Growth: What Does the Cross-country Evidence Really Show," *IMF Working Paper 05/127* (Washington, DC: International Monetary Fund, 2005).
80. Craig Burnside and David Dollar, "Aid, Policies and Growth," *American Economic Review* 90, no. 4 (December 1997): 847.
81. "Development Assistance and Economic Development in the Caribbean Region: Is There a Correlation," *World Bank Report No. 24164-LAC* (Washington, DC: World Bank, June 2002).
82. William Easterly, *The Elusive Quest for Growth: Economists' Adventures in the Tropics* (Cambridge, Massachusetts: MIT Press, 2001).
83. I. William Zartman, "Introduction," in *Europe and Africa: The New Phase*, ed. I. William Zartman (Boulder: Lynne Rienner Publishers, 1993), 6.
84. Sir Shridath Ramphal. *Caribbean Challenges: Sir Shridath Ramphal's Collected Counsel* (Hertford: Hansib Publications, 2012), 25.
85. Roman Grynberg and Sacha Silva, *Preference-dependent Economies and Multilateral Liberalization: Impacts and Options* (London: Commonwealth Secretariat, October 2004).
86. Donald Mitchell, "Sugar in the Caribbean. Adjusting to Eroding Preferences," *World Bank Working Paper 3802* (Washington, DC: World Bank, December 2005), 4.
87. *Towards a New Agenda for Growth: Organization of Eastern Caribbean States* (Washington, DC: World Bank, April 2005), 25–26.
88. Katerina Alexandraki and Hans Peter Lankes, "The Impact of Preference Erosion on Middle-income Developing Countries," *IMF Working Paper WP/04/169* (Washington, DC: International Monetary Fund, September 2004).
89. *A Time to Choose: Caribbean Development in the 21st Century* (Washington, DC: World Bank, April 2005), 78.
90. Christopher Stevens, Matthew McQueen, and Jane Kennan, *After Lome IV: A Strategy for ACP- EU Relations in 21st Century* (London: Commonwealth Secretariat, 1999), 14.
91. US policy was instigated and driven by the Chiquita (previously the United Fruit Company). See Gordon Myers, *Banana Wars: The Price of Free Trade* (London: Zed Books, 2004).
92. Paul Goodison, "EU Assistance to the ACP Countries Since 1975," in *Navigating New Waters. A Reader on ACP-EU Trade Relations*, ed. Sinoussi Bilal and Roman Grynberg (London: Commonwealth Secretariat, 2007), vol. 1, 183–208. See p. 184.
93. Alice Clarke, "An Analysis of EU-ACPAid Flows through the EDF from Lome to the Contonou Agreement and Proposals for the 10th and 11th EDFs," in *Navigating New Waters: A Reader on ACP-EU Trade Relations,* eds Sinoussi Bilal and Roman Grynberg (London: Commonwealth Secretariat, 2007), vol. 1, 209–232. See p. 210.
94. Sir Roland Sanders, "Last Chance for a Better Agreement between Europe and the Caribbean," November 1, 2007.
95. John Mayers, "Golding Slams Critics—Says They Suffer from Mendicancy," *Daily Gleaner* February 1, 2008.

96. Some argue that increased openness is associated with increased economic growth; see Jeffrey A. Frankel and David H. Romer, "Does Trade Cause Growth," *American Economic Review* 83, no. 3 (1999): 379–399. For a critical view, see Francisco Rodriquez and Dani Rodrik, "Trade Policy and Economic Growth: A Skeptic's Guide," in *NBER Macroeconomic Annual 2000*, ed. Ben S Bernake and Kenneth S. Rogoff (Cambridge: MIT Press, 2000).
97. Vivek Arora and Athanasios Vamvakidis, "How Much Do Trading Partners Matter for Economic Growth," *IMF Staff Papers* 52, no. 1 (April 2005): 24–40.
98. *World Economic Output* (Washington, DC: International Monetary Fund, October 2007), p. 33.
99. John Ravenhill, "Back to the Nest? Europe's Relations with the African, Pacific and Caribbean Group of Countries," in *EU Trade Strategies: Between Regionalism and Globalism*, ed. Vinod K. Aggarwal and Edward A. Fogarty (London: Palgrave Macmillan, 2004), 122.
100. Richard L. Bernal, "The Caribbean's Future Is Not What It Was," *Social and Economic Studies* 52, no. 1 (March 2000): 185–217.
101. Havelock Brewster and Clive Y. Thomas, *The Dynamics of West Indian Economic Integration* (Mona: Institute of Social and Economic Research, University of the West Indies, 1967), 333.
102. John Ravenhill, "Back to the Nest? Europe's Relations with the African, Caribbean and Pacific Group," in *EU Trade Strategies: Between Regionalism and Globalism*, ed. Vinod Aggarwal and Edward A. Fogarty (New York: Palgrave Macmillan, 2004), 118–147. See p. 129.
103. *Accelerating Trade and Integration in the Caribbean. Policy Options for Sustained Growth, Job Creation and Poverty Reduction* (Washington, DC: World Bank, 2009), 15.

2 Structure and Process of Negotiations

1. Statement by the president of the Council of ACP Ministers at the Opening of the Negotiations to Successor Agreement to the Lome Convention, Brussels, July 24, 1978.
2. Joanna Moss and John Ravenhill, "Trade between the ACP and EEC during Lome I," in *EEC and the Third World: A Survey, Vol. 3, The Atlantic Rift*, ed. Christopher Stevens (London: Hodder and Stoughton, 1983), 133–151.
3. Adrian Hewitt and Christopher Stevens, "The Second Lome Convention," in *EEC and the Third World: A Survey*, ed. Christopher Stevens (London: Hodder and Stoughton, 1981), 30–59.
4. Hewitt and Stevens, op. cit., 30–59.
5. Paul Sutton, "From Neo-colonialism to Neo-colonialism: Britain and the EEC in the Commonwealth Caribbean," in *Dependency under challenge. The political economy of the Commonwealth Caribbean*, ed. Anthony Payne and Paul Sutton (Manchester: Manchester University Press, 1984), 231.
6. John Ravenhill, "Asymmetrical Interdependence: Renegotiating the Lome Convention," in *The Political Economy of EEC Relations with African, Caribbean and Pacific States*, ed. Frank Long (Oxford: Pergamon Press, 1980), 33–50.
7. John Ravenhill, *Collective Clientelism: The Lome Conventions and North-South Relations* (New York: Columbia University Press, 1985).
8. Hewitt and Stevens, op., cit., 33.
9. R. B. Manderson-Jones, *Jamaican Foreign Policy in the Caribbean 1962–1988* (Kingston: Caricom Publishers, 1990), 85.

10. Paul Sutton, "From Neo-colonialism to Neo-colonialism: Britain and the EEC in the Commonwealth Caribbean," in *Dependency under Challenge: The Political Economy of the Commonwealth Caribbean*, ed. Anthony Payne and Paul Sutton (Manchester: Manchester University Press, 1984), 206.
11. Sutton, op. cit., 207.
12. Carol Cosgrove Twitchett, *A Framework for Development: The EEC and the ACP* (London: Allen & Unwin, 1981).
13. David Dabydeen and John Gilmore, eds., "No Island is an island," *Selected Speeches of Sir Shridath Ramphal* (London: Macmillan Education, 2000), 110.
14. Enzo R. Grilli, *The European Community and the Developing Countries* (Cambridge: Cambridge University Press, 1993), 92.
15. Colin A. Palmer, Eric Williams and the Making of the Modern Caribbean (Kingston: Ian Randle Publishers, 2006), 63.
16. On the Relationship between the European Union and the ACP Countries on the Eve of the 21st Century, European Commission, 1996.
17. Remco Vahl, "From Cotonou to Bridgetown: The Birth of the Caribbean EPA," in *The CARIFORUM-EU Economic PartnershipAgreement: A Practioners' Analysis*, ed. Americo Biviglia Zampetti and Junior Lodge (The Netherlands: Kluwer Law International, 2011), 1–10. See p. 3
18. Edwin Laurent, "Small States in the Banana Dispute," in *WTO at the Margins: Small States and the Multilateral Trading System*, ed. Roman Grynberg (Cambridge: Cambridge University Press, 2006), 444.
19. Kusha Harasingh, "On the Front Line: The Lome Experience Dissected," in *Caribbean Survival and the Global Challenge*, ed. Ramesh Ramsaran (Kingston: Ian Randle Publishers, 2002), 366–383. See p. 368.
20. Thomas Peckenham, The Scramble for Africa: White Man's Conquest of the Dark Continent from 1876–1912 9Avon Books, 1992).
21. The legacy of the European partition of Africa goes beyond the incongruous regions to the problems that have bedeviled the nation state in Africa. See Basil Davidson, *Black Man's Burden: Africa and the Curse of the Nation State* (London: James Currey, 1992).
22. The desire to interact with the Caribbean states as a regional group is not confined to the EU nor is it a recent template. The British government from the 1920s encouraged the then West Indies states to form a political federation, which eventually happened in 1957 and in December, 1945, the United States, Britain, France, and the Netherlands established the Caribbean Commission to jointly deal with the Caribbean as a region. See Bernard L. Poole, *The Caribbean Commission: Background of Cooperation in the West Indies* (Columbia: University of South Carolina, 1951).
23. For a recent overview of African countries, see Richard Dowden, *Africa: Altered States. Ordinary Miracles* (New York: Public Affairs, 2009).
24. John Ravenhill, *Collective Clientelism: The Lome Conventions and North-South Relations* (New York: Columbia University Press, 1985), passim and chapter 9.
25. John Ravenhill, "Back to the Nest? Relations with the African, Caribbean and the Pacific Group of Countries," in *EU Trade Strategies: Between Regionalism and Globalism*, ed. Vinod Aggawal and Edward A. Fogarty (London: Palgrave Macmillan, 2004), 143.
26. John Ravenhill, *Collective Clientelism: The Lome Conventions and North-South Relations* (New York: Columbia University Press, 1985), 316.
27. Francoise Moreau, "The Cotonu Agreement: Building on the Experience of 30 years of ACP-EC Partnership," in *Partnership Agreement ACP-EC* (Brussels: European Commission, 2006), 14.

28 Jessica Byron, "Singing From the Same Hymn sheet: Caribbean Diplomacy and the Cotonou Agreement," *Revista Europea de Estudios Latinoamericos y del Caribe* 79 (Octubre de 2005): 3–24.
29. Ambassador Lingston Cumberbatch, Chairman of the ECDPM Board, "Can Cotonou stand the test of time?," in *The Cotonu Partnership Agreement: What Role in a Changing World, ECDPM Policy Management Report No. 13*, ed. Geert Laporte (Brussels: European Centre for Development Policy Management, November 2007), x.
30. Ibid., xiv.
31. Peter Clegg, "Banana Splits and Policy Challenges: The ACP Caribbean and the Fragmentation of Interest Coalitions," *Revista Europea de Estudios Latinoamericanos y del Caribe*, no. 79 (Octubre 2005): 27–45.
32. Anthony J. Payne, *The Political History of CARICOM* (Kingston: Ian Randle, 2008), 176.
33. *Revised Treaty Establishing the Caribbean Community Including the Caricom Single Market and Economy*, Article 6, 8 (Georgetown: CARICOM Secretariat).
34. CARICOM, *Our Caribbean Community: An Introduction* (Kingston: Ian Randle Publishers, 2005), 289.
35. Achille Bassilekin, Possibility of obtaining a new ACP-EC waiver at the WTO, ECDPM Discussion Paper No. 71 Maastricht: European Centre for Development Policy Management, March, 2007) page 7.
36. Principal Negotiator for CARIFORUM and Director General of the Regional Negotiating Machinery.
37. Dame Billy Miller, deputy prime minister and minister of Foreign Affairs and Foreign Trade of Barbados.
38. Owen Arthur, "Making the Most of the EPA," presentation at the *Private Sector Organization of Jamaica Chairman's Club Forum*, Kingston, Jamaica, February 3, 2009, 3.
39. Ibid., 8–9.
40. Bruce Golding, Statement at the CARICOM Heads of Government 19th Intersessional, March 2008.
41. Ibid.
42. Regardless of how information is provided, some persons distrust their governments. This kind of behavior is not confined to the Caribbean. See, for example, the following statement about trade negotiations in general. "This difficulty in obtaining and understanding the actual agreements is not an accident; it reflects a purposeful effort by the government negotiators to conceal the terms and effect of the agreements from the public, the news media, and even Congress. They would rather have citizens read a sanitized summary suitably interpreted by the agreements boosters." Ralph Nader et al., *The Case Against Free Trade: GATT, NAFTA, and the Globalization of Corporate Power* (San Francisco: Earth Island Press, 1993), 5.
43. Caribbean Regional Negotiating Machinery.
44. Caribbean Regional Negotiating Machinery.

3 Negotiation by CARIFORUM Regional Cooperation

1. The CARICOM Secretariat estimates the figure to be 95 percent of intraregional trade. Cited by Havelock R. Brewster, "The CARICOM Single Market and Economy: Is It Realistic Without Commitment to Political Unity?," *Journal of Eastern Caribbean Studies* 28, no. 3 (September 2003), 4.

2. Havelock Brewster, Luis Abugattas, Tom Dolan, Taimoon Stewart, and Noel Watson, "CARICOM Single Market and Economy: Assessment of the Region's Support Needs," *Report prepared for the CARICOM Secretariat* (Georgetown, June 2003), v.
3. Norman Girvan, "Whither CSME," *Journal of Caribbean International Relations* no. 1 (April 2005): 13–32.
4. *Revised Treaty of Chaguaramas*, Article 6 (g) (Georgetown: CARICOM Secretariat).
5. Lori Wallach and Patrick Woodall, *Whose Trade Organisation?* (New York: The New Press, 2004); Fatoumata Jawara and Aillen Kwa, *Behind the Scences at the WTO: The Real World of International Trade Negotiations* (London: Zed Books, 2003).
6. Bernard Hoekman and Michael Koslecki, *The Political Economy of the World Trading System: From GATT to WTO* (Oxford: Oxford University Press, 1995), 40.
7. Anneke Jessen, "Regional Public Goods and Small Economies: The Caribbean Regional Negotiating Machinery," in *Regional Public Goods: From Theory to Practice* (Washington, DC: Inter-American Development Bank, 2004), 301–323. See p. 303.
8. Richard L. Bernal, "Participation of Small Developing Countries in the Governance of the Multilateral Trading System," *Working Paper No. 44*, Centre for International Governance Innovation, Waterloo, Canada (December 2009).
9. The Pacific Island Forum includes Fiji, Papua New Guinea, Solomon Islands, Samoa, Vanuatu, and Tonga.
10. Chakriya Bowman, *The Pacific Island Nations: Towards Shared Representation*, WTO Managing the Challenges of WTO Participation: Case Study No. 33 (nd), 2005.
11. "Constantine Michalopoulos, Developing Countries' Participation in the World Trade Organization," *Policy Research Working Paper No. 1906* (Washington, DC: World Bank, March 1998).
12. Bernard Hoekman and B. Kostecki, *The Political Economy of the World Trading System: The WTO and Beyond* (Oxford: Oxford University Press, 2001).

4 Characteristics of CARIFORUM Economies

1. There is a view that small countries are so heterogeneous that they do not exhibit uniform characteristics and do not behave in the same way similar circumstances. See Peter J. Lloyd, *International Trade Problems of Small Nations* (Durham, NC: Duke University Press, 1968).
2. T. N. Srinivasan, "The Costs and Benefits of Being a Small, Island Landlocked, or Ministate Economy," *World Bank Research Observer* 1, no. 2 (July 1986): 205–218.
3. Anthony Gonzales, Policy Implications of Smallness as a Factor in the Lome, FTAA and WTO Negotiations, *Caribbean RNM/IDB Regional Technical Cooperation Project*, September 2000.
4. *Small and Relatively Less Developed Economies and Western Hemisphere Integration OAS/ Ser. W/XIII.7* (Washington, DC: Organization of American States, September 1996).
5. Caribbean. *Accelerating Trade Integration: Policy Options for Sustained Growth, Job Creation, and Poverty Reduction* (Washington, DC: World Bank, 2009), 35.
6. Edgardo M. Favaro and David Peretz, "Introduction," in *Small States, Smart Solutions: Improving Connectivity and Increasing the Effectiveness of Public Services*, ed. Edgardo M. Favaro (Washington, DC: World Bank, 2008), 4.
7. J. Love, "Commodity Concentration and Export Earnings Instability: A Shift from Cross-section to Time Series Analysis," *Journal of Development Economics* 24 no. 2 (1986): 239–248.
8. Marion Jansen, "Income Volatility in Small and Developing Countries," *WTO Discussion Paper* (Geneva: WTO, December 2004), 5.

9. M. Ayhan Kose and Eswar S. Prasad, "Thinking Big," *Finance and Development* 39, no. 4 (December2002): 38–41.
10. Irving W. Andre and Gabriel J. Christian, *In Search of Eden: The Travails of a Caribbean Mini State* (Roseau: Pond Casse Press, 1992), 209.
11. Barbara Welsh, "Banana Dependency: Albatross or Lifeline for the Windwards," *Social and Economic Studies* 43, no. 1 (March 1994), 123–149. See p. 136.
12. Sugar Industry Authority of Jamaica.
13. http://www.onecaribbean.org/statistics/2009stats/default.aspx (accessed December 9, 2010).
14. George Beckford, *Persistent Poverty: Underdevelopment in Plantation Economies of the Third World* (Oxford: Oxford University Press, 1972).
15. Peter N. Davies, *Fyffes and the Banana: Musa Sapientum. A Centenary History 1888–1988* (London: Athlone Press, 1990).
16. Gerald K. Helleiner, *Intra-firm Trade and the Developing Countries* (London: Macmillan, 1981).
17. Norman Girvan, *Corporate Imperialism: Conflict and Expropriation: Transnational Corporations and Economic Nationalism in the Third World* (New York: Monthly Review Press, 1976).
18. Anne Simpson and Chris Lee, *Whose Gold? Geest and the Banana Trade* (London: Latin American Bureau, 1990).
19. Peter Glegg, *The Caribbean Banana Trade: From Colonialism to Globalization* (New York: Palgrave, 2002), 79.
20. Lino Briguglio, "Small Island Developing States and Their Economic Vulnerabilities," *World Development* 23, no. 9 (1995): 1615–1632; Jonathan P. Atkins, Sonia Mazzi, and Christopher D. Easter, "Small States: A Composite Vulnerability Index," in *Small States in the Global Economy*, ed. David Peretz, Rumman Faruqi and Eliawony J. Kisanga (London: Commonwealth Secretariat, 2001), 53–92.
21. Anthony Gonzales, "Policy Implications of Smallness as a Factor in the Lome, FTAA and WTO Negotiations," *Caribbean RNM/IDB Regional Technical Cooperation Project No. ATN/JF/SF-6158-RG* (September 2000).
22. Chris Becker, "Small Island Sates in the Pacific: the Tyranny of Distance," *IMF Working Paper, WP/12/223* (Washington DC: International Monetary Fund, September, 2012).
23. Jonathan P. Atkins, Sonia Mazzi, and Christopher D. Easter, "Small States: A Composite Vulnerability Index," in *Small States in the Global Economy*, ed. David Peretz, Rumman Faruqi, and Eliawony J. Kisanga (London: Commonwealth Secretariat, 2001), 63.
24. "Small States: Meeting Challenges in the Global Economy," *Interim Report of the Commonwealth Secretariat/World Bank Joint Taskforce on Small States* (London: Commonwealth Secretariat/Washington, DC: World Bank, October 1999), 13.
25. Lino Briguglio, "Small Island Developing States and Their Economic Vulnerabilities," *World Development* 23, no. 9 (1995): 1615–1632.
26. Chris Milner and T. Westaway, "Country Size and the Medium-Term Growth Process: Some Cross-country Evidence," *World Development* 21, no. 2 (1993): 203–211; H. W. Armstrong and R. Read, "Trade and Growth in Small States: The Impact of Global Trade Liberalization," *World Economy* 21, no. 4 (June 1998): 563–585.
27. Nita Thacker, Sebastian Acevedo, and Roberto Perrelli, "Caribbean Growth in an International Perspective: The Role of Tourism and Size," *IMF Working Paper WP/12/235* (Washington, DC: International Monetary Fund, September 2012), 16.
28. *Overcoming Volatility: Economic and Social Progress in Latin America, 1995 Report* (Washington, DC: Inter-American Development Bank, 1995), 194–195; Holger

Wolf, "Volatility: Definitions and Consequences," in *Managing Economic Volatility and Crises: A Practitioner's Guide*, ed. Joshua Aizenman and Brian Pinto (Cambridge: Cambridge University Press, 2005), 45–64.

29. William Easterly and Aart Kraay, "Small States, Small Problems? Income, Growth and Volatility in Small States," *World Development* 28, no. 11 (2000): 2013–2027; Viktoria Hnatkovska and Norman Loayza, "Volatility and Growth," in *Managing Economic Volatility and Crises. A Practitioner's Guide*, ed. Joshua Aizenman and Brian Pinto (Cambridge: Cambridge University Press, 2005), 65–100; Garey Remy and Valerie A. Remy, "Cross-country Evidence on the Link between Volatility and Growth," *American Economic Review* 85, no. 5 (December 1995): 1138–1151.
30. Joshua Aizenmann and Nancy Marion, "Volatility and Investment: Interpreting Evidence from Developing Countries," *Economica* 66, no. 2 (1999): 157–181.
31. Dani Rodrik, "Why Do More Open Economies Have Bigger Governments?," *Journal of Political Economy* 106, no. 5 (1998): 997–1032; William R. Easterly, R. Islam, and Joseph Stiglitz, "Shaken and Stirred: Explaining Growth Volatility," in *Annual World Bank Conference on Development*, ed. B. Plesokovic and Nicholas Stern (Washington, DC: World Bank, 2001).
32. Eduardo A. Cavallo, "Output Volatility and Openness to Trade: A Reassessment," *Research Department Working Paper Series No. 604* (Washington, DC: Inter-American Development Bank, 2007).
33. Mona E. Haddad, Jamus Jerome Lim, and Christian Saborowski, "Trade Openness Reduces Growth Volatility When Countries Are Well Diversified," *World Bank Policy Research Working Paper No. 5222* (Washington, DC: World Bank, February 2010).
34. William Easterly and Aart Kraay, "Small States, Small Problems? Income, Growth, and Volatility in Small States," *World Development* 28, no. 11 (2000): 2013–2027.
35. Garey Ramey and Valery A. Ramey, "Cross-country Evidence on the Link between Volatility and Growth," *American Economic Review* 86 (1995): 1138–1151.
36. William Easterly and Aart Kraay, "Small States, Small Problems? Income, Growth and Volatility in Small States," *World Development* 28, no. 11 (2000): 2013–2027.
37. Marion Jansen, "Income volatility in Small Developing Economies: Export Concentration Matters," *WTO Discussion Paper* (Geneva: WTO, December 2004).
38. "Small States, Meeting Challenges in the Global Economy," *Interim Report of the Commonwealth Secretariat/World Bank Joint Taskforce on Small States* (London: Commonwealth Secretariat/Washington, DC: World Bank, October 1999), 13.
39. Robert E. Looney, "Economic Characteristics Associated with Size: Development Problems Confronting Smaller Third World States," *Singapore Economic Review* 37, no. 2 (October 1992): 1–19.
40. *Human Development Report 2003* (New York: United Nations Development Programme, 2003), 72.
41. Chris Becker, "Small Island Sates in the Pacific: The Tyranny of Distance," *IMF Working Paper, WP/12/223* (Washington, DC: International Monetary Fund, September 2012), 10.
42. M. Ayhan Kose and Eswar S. Prasad, "Thinking Big," *Finance and Development* 39, no. 4(December 2002): 38–41; Edgardo Favaro, Dorte Dömeland, William O'Boyle, andTihomir Stucka, "Small States, the Financial Crisis, and the Aftermath," in*Sovereign Debt and the Financial Crisis: Will ThisTime Be Different?*, ed. Carlos A.Prima Braga and Gallina Vincelette (Washington, DC: The World Bank, 2010).
43. Marion Jansen, "Income Volatility in Small Developing Economies: Export Concentration Matters," *WTO Discussion Paper* (Geneva: WTO, December 2004).

44. Claudio E. Raddatz, "Are External Shocks Responsible for the Instability of Output in Low-income Countries?," *Journal of Development Economics* 84, no. 1 (September 2007): 155–187.
45. On the instability of primary product export earnings, see *Global Economic Prospects and the Developing Countries 1994* (Washington, DC: World Bank, 1994), chapter 2.
46. Ransford Palmer, "Export Earnings, Instability, and Economic Growth, 1957 to 1986," in *External Linkages in Small Economies*, ed. David L. Mckee (Westport: Praeger, 1994), 31–34.
47. Sebastian Sosa and Paul Cashin, "Macroeconomic Fluctuations in the Caribbean: The Role of Climatic and External Shocks," *IMF Working Paper WP/09/159* (Washington, DC: International Monetary Fund, July 2009).
48. Tobias N. Rasmussen, "Macroeconomic Implications of Natural Disasters in the Caribbean," *IMF Working Paper WP/04/224* (Washington, DC: International Monetary Fund, December, 2004), 7.
49. Martin Heger, Alex Julca, and Oliver Paddison, "Analysing the Impact of Natural Disasters in Small Economies: The Caribbean Case," *UNU-WIDER Research Paper No. 2008/25* (March 2008).
50. Charlotte Benson and Edward Clay with Franklyn V. Michael and Alistair W. Robertson, "Dominica: Natural Disasters and Economic Development in a Small Island State," *Disaster Risk Management Working Paper Series No. 2* (Washington, DC: World Bank, October 2001).
51. Stephen G. Hannaford, *Market Domination! The Impact of Industry Consolidation on Competition, Innovation and Consumer Choice* (Westport: Praeger Publishers, 2007), 23.
52. Mark Stone and Seiichi Shimizu, "Small Steps," *Finance and Development* 46, no. 1 (March 2009).
53. Hervé Ferhani, Mark Stone, Anna Nordstrom, and Seiichi Shimizu, "Developing Essential Financial Markets in Smaller Economies: Stylized Facts and Policy," *IMF Occaisional Paper No. 265* (Washington, DC: International Monetary Fund, 2009), ix.
54. Hervé Ferhani, Mark Stone, Anna Nordstrom, and Seiichi Shimizu, "Developing Essential Financial Markets in Smaller Economies: Stylized Facts and Policy," *IMF Occaisional Paper No. 265* (Washington, DC: International Monetary Fund, 2009), 6.
55. Jean-Christophe Dumont and Georges Lemaitre, *Counting Immigrants and Expatriates in OECD Countries: A New Perspective* (Paris: OECD, 2005), 14.
56. Richard L. Bernal, "Nano-firms, Integration and International Competitiveness: The Experience and Dilemma of the CSME," in *Production Integration in Caribbean: From Theory to Action*, ed. Denis Benn and Kenneth Hall (Kingston: Ian Randle Publishers, 2006), 90–115.
57. William E. Northdurft, *Going Global: How Europe Helps Small Firms Export* (Washington, DC: Brookings Institution, 1992).
58. Lawrence Nicholson, "Jamaican Family-owned Businesses: Homogenous or Non-homogenous," *Social and Economic Studies* 59, no. 3 (September 2010): pages 7–30.
59. Richard L. Bernal, "Nano-firms, Integration and International Competitiveness: The Experience and Dilemma of the CSME," in *Production Integration in Caribbean: From Theory to Action*, ed. Denis Benn and Kenneth Hall (Kingston: Ian Randle Publishers, 2006), 90–115.
60. Small firms experience delays in undertaking R&D and product enhancement because of financial constraints; Giuseppe Scellato, "Patents, Firm Size and Financial

Constraints: An Empirical Analysis for a Panel of Italian Manufacturing Firms," *Cambridge Journal of Economics* 31, no. 1 (January 2007): 55–76.

61. Zoltan J. Acs, Randall Morck, J. Myles Shaver, and Bernard Yeoug, "The Internationalization of Small and Medium-sized Enterprises," in *Small and Medium-sized Enterprises in the Global Economy*, ed. Zoltan J. Acs and Bernard Yeong (Ann Arbor: University of Michigan Press, 1999), 52.
62. Ganesh Wignarja, Marlon Lezama, and David Joiner, *Small States in Transition: From Vulnerability to Competitiveness* (London: Commonwealth Secretariat, 2004).
63. Ramesh Chaitoo, "Aid for Trade for Services in Small Economies: Some Considerations from the Caribbean," in *Aid for Trade and Development*, ed. Dominique Njinkeu and Hugo Cameron (New York: Cambridge University Press, 2008), 300–313. See p. 304.
64. Donald B. Keesing, "Population and Industrial Development: Some Evidence from Trade Patterns," *American Economic Review* 58, no. 3 (1968): 448–455.
65. *Doing Business in Small Island Developing States 2009* (Washington, DC: World Bank, 2008), 21.
66. Firms in small developing economies are discussed in Alvin G. Wint, *Managing Towards International Competitiveness: Cases and Lessons from the Caribbean* (Kingston: Ian Randle Publishers, 1997); Alvin G. Wint, *Competitiveness in Small Developing Economies: Insights from the Caribbean* (Kingston: University of the West Indies Press, 2003).
67. The cost disadvantages suffered by small firms result from the lack of economies of scale, higher costs of inputs, and higher transportation cost. See L. Alan Winters and Pedro M.G. Martins, "Beautiful but Costly: Business Costs in Small Remote Economies," (London: Commonwealth Secretariat, 2004). For the opposing view, see Boris Blazic-Metzner and Helen Hughes, "Growth Experience of Small Countries," in *Problems and Policies in Small Economies*, ed. B. Jalan (New York: St. Martin's Press, 1982), 85–102.
68. Michael E. Porter, *The Competitive Advantage of Nations* (New York: Free Press, 1990), 71–73.
69. Christopher A. Bartlett and Sumantra Ghoshal, *Managing across Borders* (Boston: Harvard Business School Press, 1989).
70. Alan L. Winters and Pedro M. G. Martins, "Beautiful but Costly: Business Costs in Small Remote Economies," (New York: St. Martin's Press, 2004).
71. Barbara Graham, *Profile of the Small Scale Farming in the Caribbean* (Rome: Food and Argiculture Organization, 2012).
72. Dennis Pantin, *The Economics of Sustainable Development in Small Caribbean Islands* (Mona, Jamaica: Centre for Environment and Development, University of the West Indies, 1994), 16.
73. *A Future for Small States: Overcoming Vulnerability* (London: Commonwealth Secretariat, 1997), 29; M. Ayhan Kose and Eswar S. Prasad, "Thinking Big," *Finance and Development* 39, no. 4 (December 2002).
74. *UNCTAD Review of Maritime Transport* (Geneva: UNCTAD, 1997).
75. Alberto Alesina and Enrico Spolaore, *The Size of Nations* (Cambridge: MIT Press, 2003).
76. *Asia and Pacific Small States: Raising Potential Growth and Enhancing Resilience to Shocks* (Washington DC: International Monetary Fund, February 20, 2013), 5.
77. Stephanie Medina Cas and Rui Ota, "Big Government, High Debt, and Fiscal Adjustment in Small States," *IMF Working Paper WP/08/39* (Washington, DC: International Monetary Fund, February 2008).

78. Robert E. Looney, "Profiles of Small Lesser Developed Economies," *Canadian Journal of Development Studies* 10, no. 1 (1989): 21–37; Michael Howard, *Public Finance in Small Open Economies: The Caribbean Experience* (Westport: Praeger, 1992); Alberto Alesin and Enrico Spolaore, *The Size of Nations* (Cambridge: MIT Press, 2003), chapter 10; M. Ayhan Kose and Eswar S. Prasad, "Thinking Big," *Finance and Development* 39, no. 4 (December 2002): 38–41.
79. Deryck R. Brown, "Institutional Development in Small Sates: Evidence from the Commonwealth Caribbean," *Halduskultuur-Administrative Culture* 11, no. 1 (2010): 44–65. See also R. Baler, "Scale and Administrative Performance: The Governannce of Small States and Microstates," in *Public Administration in Small and Island States*, ed. R. Baker (Hartford: Kumarian Press, 1992), 5–25.
80. *Doing Business in Small Island Developing States 2009* (Washington, DC: World Bank, 2008), 13.
81. Giuseppe Scellato, "Patents, Firm Size and Financial Constraints: An Empirical Analysis for a Panel of Italian Manufacturing Firms," *Cambridge Journal of Economics* 31, no. 1 (January 2007): 55–76.
82. O. Andersen and L. S. Kheam, "Resource-based Theory and International Growth Strategies: An Exploratory Study," *International Business Review* 7, no. 2 (1998): 163–184.
83. "Food Safety and Agricultural Health Standards. Challenges and Opportunities for Developing Country Exports," *World Bank Report No. 31207* (Washington DC: World Bank, January 10, 2005), 62.
84. Denzil A. Williams, *Understanding Exporting in the Small and Micro Enterprise* (New York: New Science Publishers, 2009).
85. Rebecca Torres and Janet Henshall Momsen, "Challenges and Potential for Linking Tourism and Agriculture to Achieve Pro-poor Tourism Objectives," *Progress in Development Studies* 4, no. 4 (October 2004): 294–318.
86. This is particularly the case in the smallest economies of CARIFORUM. See Ruby Randall, "Eastern Caribbean Tourism: Recent Development s and Outlook," in *The Caribbean: From Vulnerability to Sustainable Growth*, ed. Ratna Sahay, David O. Robinson and Paul Cashin (Washington, DC: International Monetary Fund, 2006), 285–306.
87. M. Ayhan Kose and Eswar Prasad, "Thinking Big," *Finance and Development* 39, no. 4 (December 2002).
88. Lino Briguglio, Bishnodat Persaud, and Richard Stern, *Toward an Outward-oriented Development Strategy for Small States: Issues, Opportunities, and Resilience Building* (August 2006), 5.
89. Paul Collier and David Dollar, *Aid, Risk and the Special Concerns of Small States* (Washington, DC: Development Research Group, World Bank, February 1999).
90. Paul Collier and David Dollar, "Aid, Risk and the Special Concerns of the Small states," in *Small States in the Global Economy*, ed. David Peretz, Rumman Faruqi and Eliawony J. Kisanga (London: Commonwealth Secretariat/World Bank, 2001), 11–38.
91. *World Investment Report 2012* (Geneva: UNCTAD, 2012), 71.
92. Amos Peters, *The Fiscal Effects of Tariff Reduction in the Caribbean Community* (Georgetown: CARICOM Secretariat, 2002).
93. Gerald K. Helleiner, "Why Small countries Worry: Neglected Issues in Current Analyses of the Benefits and Costs of Small Countries of Integrating with Large Ones," *World Economy* 19, no. 6 (November 1996): 759–763.

5 CARIFORUM's Development Objectives

1. Marion Jansen, "Income Volatility in Small and Developing Economies: Export Concentration Matters," *WTO Discussion Paper No. 3* (Geneva: WTO, 2004).
2. Mona E. Haddad, Jamus Jerome Lim, and Christi an Saborowski, "Trade Openness Reduces Growth Volatility When Countries Are Well Diversified," *Policy Research Working Paper No. 5222* (Washington, DC: World Bank, February 2010).
3. Lino Briguglio, Bishnodat Persaud, and Richard Stern, "Toward an Outward-oriented Development Strategy for Small States: Issues, Opportunities, and Resilience Building," (August 2006), 3.
4. Pablo Fajnzylber and Humbert J. Lopez, eds., *Remittances and Development: Lessons from Latin America* (Washington, DC: World Bank, 2008), 27.
5. Gordon Myers, *The Price of Free Trade: A Caribbean Perspective* (London: Zed Books, 2004).
6. *Time to Choose: Caribbean Development in the 21st Century* (Washington, DC: World Bank, 2005), Table 1.2.
7. Ibid., 65.
8. *Caribbean: Accelerating Trade Integration. Policy Options for Sustained Growth, Job Creation, and Poverty Reduction* (Washington, DC: World Bank, 2009), v.
9. Anthony Payne and Paul Sutton, *Repositioning the Caribbean within Globalization Centre for International Governance Innovation*, Waterloo, Canada, 16.
10. Richard L. Bernal, "The Globalization of Health-care: Opportunities for the Caribbean," *CEPAL Review* no. 92 (August 2007): 83–100.
11. Anthony Clayton, "Developing a Biodiversity Cluster in Jamaica: A Step Towards Building a Skills-based Economy," *Social and Economic Studies* 50, no. 2 (June 2001): 1–38.
12. Heiko Hesse, "Export Diversification and Economic Growth," in *Breaking into Markets. Emerging Lessons for Export Diversification*, ed. Richard Newfarmer, William Shaw, and Peter Walkenhorst (Washington, DC: World Bank, 2009), 55–80.
13. Atish R. Ghosh and Jonathan D. Ostry, "Export Instability and the External Balance in Developing Countries," *IMF Staff Papers* 41, no. 2 (1994): 214–235.
14. Hollis Chenery, *Structural Change and Development Policy* (New York: Oxford University Press, 1979).
15. Improving Competitiveness for Caribbean Development, *Report of the Caribbean Trade and Adjustment*, prepared for the Caribbean Regional Negotiating Machinery, Bridgetown, Barbados (2001).
16. *A Time to Choose: Caribbean Development in the 21st Century* (Washington, DC: World Bank, 2006), 67.
17. Fiscal Trends and Policy Issues and Implications for the Caribbean, *Report No. LC/CAR/G.771* (Port of Spain: Economic Commission for Latin America and the Caribbean, 2003).
18. CARICOM, *Our Caribbean Community: An Introduction* (Kingston: Ian Randle Publishers, 2005), 394.
19. *Revised Treaty of Chaguaramas Establishing the Caribbean Community including the CARICOM Single Market & Economy* (Georgetown: CARICOM Secretariat, 2001), 53.
20. Norman Girvan, "Implications of the EPA for the CSME," *Social and Economic Studies* 58, no. 2 (June 2009): 124.
21. Richard L. Bernal, "The CARICOM Single Market and Economy and External Trade Negotiations," *Caribbean Journal of International Relations* 1, no. 1 (April 2005):

33–48; "CARICOM's External Trade Negotiations without the Completion of the CSME," in *The CSME: Status, Issues and Priorities* (Washington, DC: Institute for the Integration of Latin America and the Caribbean, Inter-American Development Bank, 2006).

22. Richard L. Bernal, "The CARICOM Single Market and Economy and External Trade Negotiations," *Caribbean Journal of International Relations* 1, no. 1 (April 2005): 33–48.
23. "Improving Competitiveness for Caribbean Development," *Report of the Caribbean Trade and Adjustment Group* (Kingston: Ian Randle Publishers, 2003), 1.
24. Yair Aharoni, "How Small Firms Can Achieve Competitive Advantage in an Interdependent World," in *Small Firms in Global Competition*, ed. Agmon Tamir and Richard L. Drobnick (New York: Oxford University Press, 1994), 14.
25. The absence of an export-oriented mindset has been a constraint on export growth in Jamaica; see Maxine Garvey, *Jamaica's International Business Performance: Managerial Mindsets and Export Outcomes* (Kingston: Arawak Publications, 2002).

6 How the EPA Promotes Economic Development

1. The main tenets of this doctrine are set out in Joseph Schumpeter, *History of Economic Analysis* (London: George Allen & Unwin, 1952), 335–376.
2. Eli F. Heckscher, "The Effects of Foreign Trade on the Distribution of Income," in *Readings in International Trade*, ed. H. Ellis and L. Metzler (Homewood: Richard D. Irwin, 1950).
3. Samuel Hollander, *The Economics of Adam Smith* (Toronto: University of Toronto Press, 1973).
4. David Ricardo, "On the Principles of Political Economy and Taxation" (1817) and "Essay on the Influence of a Low Price of Corn on the Profits of Stock" (1815) in Volumes I and IV, *Works and Correspondence of David Ricardo*, ed. Piero Sraffa (Cambridge: Cambridge University Press, 1951).
5. Jacob Viner, *International Trade and Economic Development* (Glencoe: Free Press, 1952).
6. Gottfried Harberler, *International Trade and Economic Development* (Cairo: National Bank, 1959).
7 A. K. Craincross, "International Trade and Economic Development," *Kyklos* 13, no. 4 (November, 1960); pages 545–558."International Trade and Economic Development," *Economica* 28, no. 3 (August 1961): 235–251.
8. Phyllis Deane and W. A. Cole, *British Economic Growth* (Cambridge: Cambridge University Press, 1969).
9. Robert M. Stern, *Foreign Trade and Economic Growth in Italy* (New York: Praeger, 1967).
10. Douglas V. North, *The Economic Growth of the United States, 1790–1860* (New York: Prentice- Hall, 1961).
11. Ragnar Nurske, "Patterns of Trade and Development" in *Problems of Capital Formation in Underdeveloped Countries and Patterns of Trade and Development* (Oxford: Oxford University Press, 1967).
12. Jonathon V. Levin, *The Export Economies* (Cambridge: Harvard University Press, 1960).
13. Raul Prebisch, *The Economic Development of Latin America and Its Principal Problems* (New York: United Nations Economic Commission for Latin America, 1950);

"Commercial Policy in the Underdeveloped Countries," *American Economic Review* 49, no. 2 (May 1959): 251–273.

14. H. W. Singer, "The Distribution of Gains Between Investing and Borrowing Countries," *American Economic Review* 40, no. 2 (May 1950): 473–485.
15. W. Arthur Lewis, "Economic Development with Unlimited Supplies of Labour," *Manchester School of Economics and Social Studies* 24, no. 2 (May 1954): 139–191.
16. Gunnar Myrdal, *An International Economy, Problems and Prospects* (New York: Harper & Row, 1956); *Economic Theory and Under-developed Regions* (London: Methuen, 1965).
17. Matthias Lutz, "The Effects of Volatility in the Terms of Trade on Output Growth," *World Development* 22, no. 12 (1994): 1959–1975.
18. Paul a. Samuelson, "The Gains from International Trade," *Canadian Journal of Economics and Political Science* 5, no. 2 (May 1939): 195–205.
19. Eli Hecksher, "The Effects of Foreign Trade on the Distribution of Income" (1919) in *Readings in International Trade*, ed. H. Ellis and L. Metzler (Homewood: Richard D. Irwin, 1950); Bertil Ohlin, *International and Inter-regional Trade* (Cambridge: Harvard University Press, 1933).
20. Murray C. Kemp, *The Pure Theory of International Trade and Investment* (Englewoods Cliffs: Prentice-Hall, 1969).
21. Carlos F. Diaz-Alejandro, "Trade Policies and Economic Development," in *International Trade and Finance*, ed. Peter Kenan (Cambridge: Cambridge University Press, 1976), 96.
22. Paul Krugman, "Increasing Returns, Imperfect Competition and the Positive Theory of International Trade," in *Handbook of International Economics*, vol. 3 (New York: Elsevier-North-Holland), 1243–1277.
23. Jose Antonio Ocampo, "New Theories of International Trade and Trade Policy in Developing Countries," in *Trade and Growth: New Dilemmas in Trade Policy*, ed. Manuel R. Agosin and Diana Tussie (New York: St. Martin's Press, 1993), 121–141.
24. *Open Markets Matter: The Benefits of Trade and Investment Liberalization* (Paris: Organization for Economic Cooperation and Development, 1998), 10.
25. Bela Belassa, "Economic Development in Small Countries," *Acta Oeconomica* 37, no. 3–4 (1986): 325–340; David Dollar, "Outward Oriented Development Economies Really Do Grow More Rapidly: Evidence from 95 LDCs, 1976–1985," *Economic and Cultural Change* 40, no. 3 (April 1992): 523–544; Jeffrey Sachs and A. Warner, "Economic Reform and the Process of Global Integration," *Brookings Papers on Economic Activity* no. 1 (1995): 1–95; Sabastian Edwards, "Openness, Productivity and Growth: What Do We Really Know," *Economic Journal* vol.108, no. 447 (March 1998): 383–398; Jacob A. Frankel and D. Romer, "Does Trade Cause Growth?, *American Economic Review* 89 no. 3 (June 1999): 379–399; David Dollar and Aart Kraay, *Growth Is Good for the Poor* (Washington, DC: World Bank, Development Research Group, 2000).
26. Andreas Billmeier and Tommaso Nannicini, "Trade Openness and Growth: Pursuing Empirical Glasnost," *IMF Staff Papers* 56, no. 3 (March 2009), 447–475. See pp. 447–448.
27. Francisco Rodriquez and Dani Rodrik, "Trade Policy and Economic Growth: A Skeptic's Guide to the Cross-national Evidence," *NBER Working Paper 7081* (Cambridge: National Bureau of Economic Research, April 1999). For similar findings, see A. Harrison and G. Hanson, "Who Gains from Trade Reform? Some Remaining Puzzles," *Journal of Development Economics* 59 issue 1(1999): 125–154.

28. Armeane M. Choksi, Demetrius Papageorgiou, and Michael Michaely, *Liberalizing Trade*, Vol. 7, Lessons of Experience in the Developing World (Oxford: Blackwell, 1991).
29. Jagdish N. Bhagwati, *Anatomy and Consequences of Exchange Control Regimes and Economic Development*, vol. 11 (Cambridge: Ballinger, 1978); Anne O. Krueger, *Liberalization Attempts and Consequences*, Vol. 10, Foreign Trade Regimes and Economic Development (Cambridge: Ballinger, 1978).
30. Dani Rodrik, *The New Global Economy and Developing Countries: Making Openness Work* (Washington, DC: Overseas Development Council, 1999).
31. The Asian Tigers are frequently cited as examples of the stimulating effect of openness on growth. This much heralded "success" has been questioned; for example, Paul Krugman, "The Myth of the Asia Miracle," *Foreign Affairs* 73, no. 6 (1994): 62–78.
32. Alice H. Amsden, "Trade Policy and Economic Performance in South Korea," in *Trade and Growth: New Dilemmas in Trade Policy*, ed. Manuel R. Agosin and Diana Tussie (New York: St. Martin's Press, 1993), 187–214; Robert Wade, *Governing the Market: Economic Theory and the Role of Government in East Asian Industrialization* (Princeton: Princeton University Press, 1990), 113–158.
33. Roberto Chang, Linda Kaltani, and Norman V. Loayza, "Openness Can Be Good for Growth: The Role of Policy Complementarities," *Journal of Development Economics* 90, no. 1 (September 2009): 33–49.
34. Ha-Joon Chang, *Kicking Away the Ladder: Development Strategy in Historical Perspectives* (London: Anthem Press, 2002).
35. Paul Krugman, "Increasing Returns, Imperfect Competition and the Positive Theory of International Trade," in *Handbook of International Economics*, vol. 3 (New York: Elsevier-North-Holland, 1995), 1243–1277.
36. Jose Antonio Ocampo, "New Theories of International Trade and Trade Policy in Developing Countries," in *Trade and Growth: New Dilemmas in Trade Policy*, ed. Manuel R. Agosin and Diana Tussie (New York: St. Martin's Press, 1993), 121–141.
37. Raul Prebisch, *The Economic Development of Latin America and Its Principal Problems* (New York: United Nations Economic Commission for Latin America, 1950); "Commercial Policy in the Underdeveloped Countries," *American Economic Review* 49, no. 2 (May 1959): 251–273.
38. H. W. Singer, "The Distribution of Gains Between Investing and Borrowing Countries," *American Economic Review* 41, no. 2 (May 1950): 473–485.
39. Celso Furtado, *Development and Underdevelopment* (Berkeley: University of California, 1974).
40. Fernando Henrique Cardoso and Enzo Faletto, *Dependence and Develoment in Latin America* (Berkeley: University of California, 1979).
41. Osvaldo Sunkel, "The Centre-periphery Model," *Social and Economic Studies* 22, no. 1 (March 1973): 132–176.
42. Samir Amin, *Accumulation on a World Scale* (New York: Monthly Review Press, 1973); *Imperialism and Unequal Development* (New York: Monthly Review Press, 1996).
43. Arghiri Emmanuel, *Unequal Exchange: A Study of the Imperialism of Trade* (New York: Monthly Review Press, 1972).
44. George Beckford, *Persistent Poverty: Underdevelopment in Plantation Economies of the Third World* (Oxford: Oxford University Press, 1972).
45. Norman Girvan, *Corporate Imperialism. Conflict and Expropriation: Transnational Corporations and Economic Nationalism in the Third World* (New York: Monthly Review Press, 1978).
46. Manuel Mejido Costoya, Peter Utting, and Gloria Carrión, *The Changing Coordinates of Trade and Power in Latin America: Implications for Policy Space and Policy Coherence*

Markets, Business and Regulation Programme Paper Number 7 (Geneva: United Nations Research Institute for Social Development May 2010).

47. Jagdish Bhagwati, *Free Trade Today* (Princeton: Princeton University Press, 2002), 12.
48. Robert E. Hudec, *Developing Countries in the GATT Legal System* (London: Gower, 1987).
49. Caglar Ozden and Eric Reinhardt, "The Perversity of Preferences: The Generalized System of Preferences and Developing Country Trade Policies, 1976 – 2000," *Policy Research Working Paper No. 2955* (Washington, DC: World Bank, 2003).
50. J. Michael Finger and L. Alan Winters, "What Can the WTO do for Developing Countries," in *The WTO as an International Organization*, ed. Anne Krueger (Chicago: University of Chicago, 1998), 390.
51. *Human Development Report 2003* (New York: United Nations Development Programme, 2003), 155.
52. Ibid., 156.
53. Cotonou Agreement, Article 35.3.
54. The package of S&DT consist of a variety of components; see Richard L. Bernal, "Special and Differential Treatment for Small Developing Economies," in *WTO at the Margins: Small States and the Multilateral Trading System*, ed. Roman Grynberg (Cambridge: Cambridge University Press, 2006), 309–355.
55. Dani Rodrik, *The New Global Economy and Developing Countries: Making Openness Work* (Washington, DC: Overseas Development Council, 1999). Ocampo's survey of the literature on new theories of trade indicates that trade liberalization should be coupled with an active industrial policy, particularly in sectors subject to significant economies of scale. See José Antonio Ocampo, "New Theories of International Trade and Trade Policy in Developing Countries," in *Trade and Growth: New Dilemmas Trade Policy*, ed. Manuel R. Agosin and Diana Tussie (New York: St. Martin's Press, 1993), 121–141.
56. Dani Rodrik, "Trade Policy Reform as Institutional Reform," in *Development Trade and the WTO*, ed. Bernard Hoekman, Aaditya Mattoo, and Philip English (Washington, DC: World Bank, 2002), 3–10.
57. Stuart Crainer, *The Real Power of Brands: Making Brands Work for Competitive Advantage* (London: Pitman Publishing, 1995); Scott Bedbury, *A Brand New World* (New York: Viking, 2002).
58. Lino Briguglio, Bishnodat Persaud, and Richard Stern, *Toward an Outward-oriented Development Strategy for Small States: Issues, Opportunities, and Resilience Building* (August 2006), 3.
59. Sahay Ratna, "Stabilization, Debt and Fiscal Policy in the Caribbean," *IMF Working Paper WP 05/26* (Washington, DC: International Monetary Fund, 2005).
60. *World Trade Report 2007* (Geneva: WTO, 2007), 200.
61. *CARICOM Report No. 2* (Washington, DC: Inter-American Development Bank, August 2005).
62. Ramesh Chaitoo, "Aid for Trade for Services in Small Economies: Some Considerations from the Caribbean," in *Aid for Trade and Development*, ed. Hugo Cameron and Dominique Nijenkeu (Cambridge: Cambridge University Press, 2008), 303.
63. *CARICOM Report No. 2* (Washington, DC: Inter-American Development Bank, August 2005), 60.
64. The entertainment services (other than audiovisual services) cover the services provided by actors, singers, musicians, bands, orchestras, authors, composers, sculptors, entertainers, discotheques, and dance instructors.
65. Keith Nurse, "The Economic Partnership Agreement and the Creative Sector: Implications and Prospects for CARIFORUM," in *The CARIFORUM-EU Economic Partnership Agreement: A Practitioner's Analysis*, ed. Americo Beviglia Zampetti and Junior Lodge (The Netherlands: Kluwer Law International, 2011), 149–164.

66. Anne O. Krueger, "Free Trade Agreements as Protectionist Devices: Rules of Origin," *NBER Working Paper no. 4352* (Cambridge: National Bureau of Economic Research, 1993).
67. There are than 200 product specific RoO in PTAs throughout the world with some agreements having as many as 80 different RoO. See Antoni Estevadeordal, Jeremy Harris, and Kai Suominen "Structure, Restrictiveness, and Trends in Rules of Origin Around the World," in *Gatekeepers of Global Commerce: Rules of Origin and International Economic Integration*, ed. Antoni Estevadeordal and Kai Suominen (Washington, DC: Inter-American Development Bank, 2008), 11–81.
68. Antoni Estevadeordal and Kai Suominen, "What Are the Trade Effects of Rules of Origin," in *Gatekeepers of Global Commerce: Rules of Origin and International Economic Integration*, ed. Antoni Estevadeordal and Kai Suominen (Washington, DC: Inter-American Development Bank, 2008), 161–219.
69. Simplification of trade procedures can boost trade in lower-middle and upper-middle income countries. See Evdokia Moise and Silvia Sorescu, "Trade Facilitation Indicators: The Potential Impact of Trade Facilitation on Developing Countries," *OECD Trade Policy Paper No. 144* (Paris, 2013).
70. John W. Miller, "EU, Central America Reach Trade Agreement," *Wall Street Journal* May 18, 2010, 4.
71. "EU Resumes Trade Talks with Mercosur, Concludes Talks with Central America," *Bridges Weekly Trade News Digest* 14, no. 18 (May 19, 2010).
72. For a discussion of the benefits and costs of foreign investment in developing countries, see Richard L. Bernal, "Foreign Investment and Development in Jamaica," *Inter-American Economic Affairs* 38, no. 2 (Autumn 1984): 3–21.
73. E. Borenzstein, J. W. Lee, and J. De Gregorio, "How Does Foreign Investment Affect Growth," *Working Paper No. 5057* (Cambridge, MA: National Bureau of Economic Research, 1995).
74. Whether direct foreign investment has a net positive or negative impact depends on the policies of host countries, see Theodore H. Moran, *Foreign Direct Investment and Development: The New Agenda for Developing Countries and Economies of Transition* (Washington, DC: Institute for International Economic, 1999).
75. Stephen L. Parente and Edward C. Prescott, "Barriers to Technology Adoption and Development," *Journal of Political Economy* 102, no. 2 (1994): 298–321.
76. Kamal Saggi, "International Technology Transfers to Developing Countries," *Economic Paper No. 64* (London: Commonwealth Secretariat, 2004), 74.
77. The investment section of the EPA was not as ambitious as CARIFORUM had set out to achieve because of limitations on the EU arising from the fact that foreign direct foreign investment was not then within the scope of the European Commission's jurisdiction. This inability of the EU to negotiate certain topics is reflected in the absence from the EPA of provisions on investment protection and dispute settlement.
78. Thomas L. Friedman, the Lexus, and the Olive, *Understanding Globalization* (New York: Farrar, Straus and Giroux, 1999), 107.
79. J. Nelson and D. Taglioni, "Services Trade Liberalization: Identifying Opportunities and Gains," *OECD Trade Policy Paper No. 1* (Paris: Organization for Economic Cooperation and Development, 2004).
80. Dorothy Riddle, "Issues Regarding Small Services Suppliers in the Context of the FTAA," Prepared for the Caribbean Regional Negotiating Machinery, 2002.
81. Ewe-Ghee Lim, "Determinants of, and the Relation Between Direct Investment and Growth: A Summary of the Recent Literature," *IMF Working Paper WP/01/175* (Washington, DC: International Monetary Fund, November 2001).

82. Joseph E. Stiglitz and Andrew Charlton, *Fair Trade for All: How Trade Can Promote Development* (Oxford: Oxford University Press, 2005), 277.
83. Evdokia Moise and Silvia Sorescu, "Trade Facilitation Indicators. The Potential Impact of Trade Facilitation on Developing Countries," *OECD Trade Policy Paper No. 144* (Paris: OECD, 2013).
84. Michael Engman, "The Economic Impact of Trade Facilitation," *OECD Trade Policy Papers, No. 21* (Paris: OECD, 2005), 8.
85. Brian Rankin Staples, "Trade Facilitation: The Improvement of Invisible Infrastructure," in *Development, Trade and the WTO: A Handbook*, ed. Bernard Hoekman, Aaditya Mattoo and Philip English (Washington, DC: World Bank, 2002), 145–146.
86. Michael Engman, "The Economic Impact of Trade Facilitation," *OECD Trade Policy Papers No. 21* (Paris: OECD, 2005), 19.
87. Study to support CARIFORUM in the Implementation of commitments undertaken under the *Customs and Trade Facilitation Chapter of the CARIFORUM-EC Economic Partnership Agreement*, Prepared by I2K Inc. (November 2008), 28.
88. CARIFORUM-EU Economic Partnership Agreement, Article 3, para 2(c).
89. Keith E. Maskus, "Benefiting from Intellectual Property Rights," in *Development, Trade and the WTO: A Handbook*, ed. Bernard Hoekman, Aaditya Mattoo, and Philip English (Washington, DC: World Bank, 2002), 369–381.
90. Keith E. Maskus, "The Role of Intellectual Property Rights in Encouraging Foreign Direct Investment and Technology Transfer," *Duke Journal of Comparative and International Law* 9, no. 1 (1998): 109–161.
91. Carlos M. Correa, *Intellectual Property Rights, the WTO and Developing Countries. The TRIPS Agreement and Policy Options* (London: Zed Books/Penang: Third World Network, 2000), 23–36.
92. Carlos Primo Braga, "Intellectual Property Rights and the GATT: A View from the South," *Vanderbilt Journal of Transnational Law* 22, no. 2 (1989), XX.
93. Robert M. Sherwood, *Intellectual Property and Economic Development* (Boulder: Westview Press, 1990), 67–100.
94. Bengt-Ake Lundvall, ed., *National Systems of Innovation* (London: Pinter, 1992); Steven Casper and Frans van Waarden, eds., *Innovation and Institutions: A Multidisciplinary Review of the Study of Innovation Systems* (Cheltenham: Edward Elgar, 2005).
95. Regional is used here to refer the CARIFORUM region and not in the conventional sense of a region within a country as, for example, in Philip Cooke, ed., *Regional Innovation Systems* (London: Routledge, 2nd ed., 2004).
96. IPR must be enforceable to be an effective stimulant. See Keith E. Maskus, *Intellectual Property Rights in the Global Economy* (Washington, DC: Institute for International Economics, 200), 147–150.
97. The incomplete state of the CARICOM Single Market and Economy was a concern in the EPA negotiations; see Richard L. Bernal, "CARICOM's External Trade Negotiations without the completion of the CSME," in *The CSME: Status, Issues and Priorities* (Washington, DC: Institute for the Integration of Latin America and the Caribbean, Inter-American Development Bank, 2006); Richard L. Bernal, "The CARICOM Single Market And Economy and External Trade Negotiations," *Caribbean Journal of International Relations* 1, no. 1 (April 2006): 33–48.
98. Azim Sadikov, "External Tariff Liberalization in CARICOM: A Commodity-Level Analysis," *IMF Working Paper WP/08/33* (Washington, DC: International Monetary Fund, February 2008).
99. There have been criticisms of EPAs with African countries; see Aileen Kwa, *African Countries and EPAs: Do Agriculture Safeguards Afford Adequate Protection?*

(Geneva: South Centre, 2008). These have been shown to be overblown; see Alan Matthews, "Economic Partnership Agreements and Food Security," *IIIS Discussion Paper No. 319* (Dublin: Institute for International Integration Studies, Trinity College, March 2010).

100. J. R. Deep Ford and Greg Rollins, "Trade Policy, trade and food security in the Caribbean," in *Agricultural Food Policy and Food Security in the Caribbean*, ed. J. R. Deep Ford, Crescenso dell'Aquila, and Piero Conforti (Rome: Food and Agricultural Organization of the United Nations, 2007), 7–40.
101. Peter Blair Henry and Conrad Miller, "Institutions Versus Policies: A Tale of Two Islands," *American Economic Review* 99, no. 2 (May 2009): 261–267.
102. Vernon W. Ruttan, *United States Development Assistance Policy: The Domestic Politics of Foreign Aid* (Baltimore: Johns Hopkins University Press, 1996), 476.
103. Raymond F. Mikesell, *The Economic of Foreign Aid* (Chicago: Aldine Publishing Company, 1968), 156–157.
104. UNCTAD, Notes on the Concept of Economic Policy Space, UNCTAD, March 4, 2004, para. 1. Cited in Policy Space for the Development of the South, TR.A.D.E. Policy Brief, No. 1/2005 (November, 2005), 7.
105. Thomas L. Friedman, *The Lexus and the Olive: Understanding Globalization* (New York: Farrar, Straus and Giroux, 1999), 86–87.
106. Kevin P. Gallagher, *Putting Development First: The Importance of Policy Space in the WTO and IFIs* (London: Zed Books, 2005); Nagesh Kumar and Kevin P. Gallagher, "Relevance of 'Policy Space' for Development: Implications for Multilateral Trade Negotiations," *RIS-DP No. 120* (New Delhi: Research and Information System for Developing Countries, March, 2007).
107. Ha-Joon Chang, *Kicking Away the Ladder: Development Policy in Historical Perspective* (London: Anthem Press, 2002).
108. Alisa Dicaprio and Kevin P. Kallagher, "The Shrinking Development Space: How Big is the Bite?," *Journal of World Investment and Trade* 7, no. 5 (2006): 781–803.
109. Richard N. Cooper, *The Economics of Interdependence: Economic Policy in the Atlantic Community* (New York: McGraw Hill for the Council on Foreign Relations, 1968), 5.
110. Jorg Mayer, "Policy Space: What, For What, and Where?," *UNCTAD Discussion Paper No. 191* (Geneva: UNCTAD, October 2008), 4.
111. Policy Space for the Development of the South, *T.R.A.D.E. Policy Brief, No. 1/2005* (November 2005), 7.
112. Francisco Rodriquez and Dani Rodrik, "Trade Policy and Economic Growth. A Skeptic's Guide to the Cross-National Evidence," in *NBER Economics Annual 2000*, ed. Ben Bernanke and Kenneth S. Rogoff (Cambridge: MIT Press, 2001).
113. W. Arthur Lewis, *The Theory of Economic Growth* (London: Unwin, 1955), 376.
114. Thomas L. Friedman, *The Lexus and the Olive Tree: Understanding Globalization* (New York: Farrar, Straus and Giroux, 1999).
115. Dani Rodrick, *One Economics. Many Recipes. Globalization, Institutions and Economic Growth* (Princeton: Princeton University Press, 2007), 214–215.
116. Yilmaz Akyuz, *Multilateral Disciplines and the Question of Policy Space, Trade & Development Series, No. 38* (Penang: Third World Network, 2009).
117. Havelock Brewster, Norman Girvan, and Vaughn Lewis, "Problem Areas in the EPA and the Case for Content Review," submitted for the consideration of the Reflections Group on EPA Negotiations.
118. Damian King and Collette Campbell, *The Impact of the EPA on Caribbean Economies. A Structural Analysis of Four Caribbean Countries* (Kingston: Caribbean Policy research Institute, April, November 2010), 47.

119. Damian King and Collette Campbell, *The Impact of the EPA on Caribbean Economies: A Structural Analysis of Four Caribbean Countries* (Kingston: Caribbean Policy Research Institute, April, November 2010).
120. Cheikh Tidiane Dieye and Victoria Hanson, "MFN Provisions in EPAs: A Threat to South-South Trade?," *Trade Negotiations Insights* 7, no. 2 (March 2008): 1–3.
121. "EPA: The Opposition's View Point," *Jamaica Gleaner* March 30, 2008.
122. *Brazil's Declaration to the General Council of the WTO*, February 5, 2008.
123. The Most Favoured Nation (MFN) principle has been an accepted practice long before it was made a tenet of the 1947 General Agreement on Tariffs and Trade (GATT).
124. In 1979 at the conclusion of the Tokyo Round of multilateral trade negotiations, the GATT Contracting Parties adopted the Decision on Differential and More Favourable Treatment (S&DT), Reciprocity and Fuller Participation of Developing Countries, which subsequently became known as the Enabling Clause.
125. From wto.org (accessed November 27, 2012).
126. This was common knowledge; see Richard L. Bernal, "The Compatibility of Caribbean Membership in Lomé, NAFTA and GATT," *Social and Economic Studies* 43, no. 2 (June 1994): 139–147.
127. CARIFORUM-EC Economic Partnership Agreement, Article 19.

7 Governance, Recalibration, and Implementation

1. For example, the implementation of the cultural provisions of EPA got off to a slow start. See "Implementing Cultural Provisions of CARIFORUM-EU EPA. How Do They Benefit the Caribbean Cultural Sector?" *Discussion Paper No 118* (European Centre for Development Policy Management (ECDPM), June 2011).
2. Owen Arthur, "Making the Most of the EPA," Presentation at the *Private Sector Organization of Jamaica*, Kingston, Jamaica, February 3, 2010.
3. DTZ, "Economic Partnership Agreement Implementation: Stakeholders Analysis," *The CARIFORUM Context* (Bonn: German Technical Cooperation, March 2009).
4. Errol Humphrey, "Implementing the Economic Partnership Agreement: Challenges and Bottlenecks in the CARIFORUM Region," *Discussion Paper No. 117* (Brussels: European Centre for Development Policy Management, June 2011), 33.
5. Ibid., viii.
6 Norman Girvan, "Implications of the EPA for the CSME," *Social and Economic Studies* 58, no. 2 (June 2009): 95.
7. Kamala Dawar and Simon J. Evenett, "The Cariforum-EC EPA: An Analysis of Its Government Procurement and Competition Law-related Provisions, *Working Paper*, Commissioned by Deutsche Gesellschaft fur Technische Zusammenarbeit (GTZ) for the Federal Ministry for Economic Cooperation and Development, Bonn (June 18, 2008), 47.
8. CARICOM, *Caribbean Trade and Investment Report 2005* (Georgetown: Caribbean Community Secretariat, 2006), 12, 14.
9 "Accelerating Trade and Integration in the Caribbean: Policy options for Sustained Growth, Job Creation and Poverty Reduction" (Washington, DC: World Bank, 2009), 31.
10. Ibid., 32.
11. "Revised Treaty Establishing the Caribbean Community including the Caricom Single Market and Economy," *Article 80*, 54.
12. Norman Girvan, "Reflections on the CSME," *Trinidad and Tobago Review* 26, no. 4 (April 5, 2004): pages 16–19.

13. Norman Girvan, "Implications of the EPA for the CSME," *Social and Economic Studies* 58, no. 2 (June 2009): 95.
14. Havelock Brewster, "From Community to Single Market and Economy," in *Governance in the Age of Globalization: Caribbean Perspectives*, ed. Kenneth O. Hall and Denis Benn (Kingston: Ian Randle Publishers, 2003), 499–508.
15. Rt. Hon. Owen Arthur, "Implementation of the Caricom Single Market and Economy, and Its Implications for US-Caricom Economic Relations," Address to the *Special Symposium by the American Business and Consulting Group*, Brooklyn, New York, April 2, 2004, 2–3.
16. "Accelerating Trade and Integration in the Caribbean: Policy Options for Sustained Growth, Job Creation and Poverty Reduction" (Washington, DC: World Bank, 2009), xx.
17. Anabel Gonzales, "The Experience of Costa Rica in Implementing CAFTA-DR," Paper presented at the *Conference on Implementing Free Trade Agreements in Latin America at the Inter-American Development Bank*, Washington, DC, April 7, 2010.
18. This is certainly the case for the Principal Negotiator of the EPA and DG of the CRNM. See Richard L. Bernal, "Special and Differential Treatment for Small Developing Economies," in *WTO at the Margins: Small States and the Multilateral Trading System*, ed. Roman Grynberg (Cambridge: Cambridge University Press, 2006), 309–355; "Small Developing Economies in the World Trade Organization," in *Agriculture, Trade, and the WTO*, ed. Merlinda D. Ingco (Washington, DC: World Bank, 2003), 108–122.
19. Richard L. Bernal, "The Integration of Small Economies in the Free Trade Area of the Americas," *CSIS, Policy Paper on the Americas*, vol. IX, Study No. 1 (Washington, DC: Center for Strategic and International Studies, February 2, 1998).

8 Strategic Global Repositioning

1. For different perspectives on the impact of the EPA on economic development of CARIFORUM, see Richard L. Bernal, *Globalization. Everything But Alms: The EPA and Economic Development* (Kingston: Grace Kennedy Foundation, April 2008); Norman Girvan, "Implications of the EPA for the CSME," *Social and Economic Studies* 58, no. 2 (June 2009): 95.
2. Richard L. Bernal, "Strategic Global Repositioning and the Future Economic Development of Jamaica," *North South Agenda Paper No. 18* (Miami: North South Center, University of Miami, May 1996); "Globalization and Small Developing Countries: The Imperative for Repositioning," in *Globalization: A Calculus of Inequality*, ed. Denis Benn and Kenneth Hall (Kingston: Ian Randle Publishers, 2000), 88–128.
3. Iza Lejarraga and Peter Walkenhorst, "Fostering Productive Diversification Through Tourism," in *Breaking into New Markets: Emerging Markets for Export Diversification*, ed. Richard Newfarmer, William Shaw, and Peter Walkenhorst (Washington, DC: World Bank, 2009), 197–210.
4. Jacob Viner, *The Customs Union Issue* (New York: Carnegie Endowment for International Peace, 1950), chapter 4; Harry G. Johnson, *Money, Trade and Economic Growth* (London: Allen and Unwin, 1962), chapter 3.
5. A. O. Krueger, "The Political Economy of the Rent-seeking Society," *American Economic Review* 64, no. 2 (June 1974): 291–303.
6. Uri Dadush and William Shaw, *Juggernaut: How Emerging Markets Are Shaping Globalization* (Washington, DC: Carnegie Endowment for Peace, 2011), 6.
7. Vinod Thomas, John Nash, and Associates, *Best Practices in Trade Policy Reform* (New York: Oxford University Press, 1991).

8. Dani Rodrik, *Open Economics, Many Recipes: Globalization, Institutions and Economic Growth* (Princeton: Princeton University Press, 2007), 15.
9. Ruchir Sharma, *Breakout Nations: In Pursuit of the Next Economic Miracles* (New York: W. W. Norton & Company, 2012), 11.
10. Joseph E. Stiglitz, *Making Globalization Work* (New York: W.W. Norton & Company, 2006), 55.
11. Douglass C. North, *Institutions, Institutional Change and Economic Performance* (Cambridge: Cambridge University Press, 1990).
12. Francis Fukuyama, *Trust: The Social Virtues and the Creation of Prosperity* (New York: Free Press, 1996).
13. The relationship between risk, uncertainty, and economic development is explored in Hilton J. Root, *Capital and Collusion: The Political Logic of Economic Development* (Princeton: Princeton University Press, 2006).
14. Dani Rodrik, *The New Global Economy and Developing Countries: Making Openness Work* (Washington, DC: Overseas Development Council, 1999), 17.
15. The Washington Consensus is not at one end of a continuum policy packages because some of its policy measures are shared by other approaches to macroeconomic policy. Iglesias noted that "economic thinking had evolved in a parallel fashion in both Washington and Latin America, as part of a global intellectual movement." Enrique V. Prebisch, ed., *The Legacy of Raul Prebisch* (Washington, DC: Inter-American Development Bank, 1994), 5.
16. Lance Taylor, *Structuralist Macroeconomics* (New York: Basic Books, 1983); Justin Yifu Lin, ed., *New Structural Economics: A Framework for Thinking Development and Policy* (Washington, DC: World Bank, 2012).
17. Pierre-Richard Agenor and Peter J. Montiel, *Development Macroeconomics* (Princeton: Princeton University Press, 2008).
18. Clive Y. Thomas, "Productivity and Competitiveness," in *Barbados: Meeting the Challenges of Competitiveness in the 21st Century*, ed. Lianna Rojas-Suarez and Desmond Thomas (Washington, DC: Inter-American Development Bank, 2006), 35.
19. Ratna Sahay, "Stabilization, Debt and Fiscal Policy in the Caribbean," *IMF Working Paper WP/05/26* (Washington DC: IMF, February 2005).
20. Roberto Garcia Lopez and Mauricio Garcia Moreno, *Managing for Development Results. Progress and Challenges in Latin America and the Caribbean* (Washington, DC: Inter-American Development Bank, 2011). They comment on page 46 that these countries have not even begun to make the transition toward constructing the necessary capacity for the development of results-based budgeting.
21. Ricardo Houseman, Dani Rodrik, and Andres Velasco, "Growth Diagnostics," in *The Washington Consensus Reconsidered: Towards a New Global Governance*, ed. Narcis Serra and Joseph E. Stiglitz (Oxford: Oxford University Press, 2008), 324–355; Justin Yifu Lin and Celestin Monga, "Growth Identification and Facilitation: The Role of the State in the Dynamics of Structural Change," in *New Structural Economics: A Framework for Thinking Development and Policy*, ed. Justin Yifu Lin (Washington, DC: World Bank. 2012), 143–180
22. Dani Rodrik, "A Practical Approach to Formulating Growth Strategies," in *The Washington Consensus Reconsidered: Towards a New Global Governance*, ed. Narcis Serra And Joseph E. Stiglitz (Oxford: Oxford University Press, 2008), 356–366.
23. Richard Newfarmer, William Shaw, and Peter Walkenhorst, "Breaking into New Markets: An Overview," in *Breaking into New Markets*, ed. Richard Newfarmer, William Shaw and Peter Walkenhorst (Washington, DC: World Bank, 2009), 1–35.
24. Benjamin Powell, *Making Poor Nations Rich: Entrepreneurship and the Process of Economic Development* (Stanford: Stanford Economics and Finance, 2007).

25. Hernando De Soto, *The Mystery of Capital: Why Capitalism Triumphs in the West and Fails Everywhere Else* (New York: Basic Books, 2000).
26. George Magnus, *Uprising: Will Emerging Markets Shape or Shake the World Economy* (New York: John Wiley, 2011), 41.
27. Joseph A. Schumpeter, *Capitalism, Socialism and Democracy* (London; Routledge, 1994, originally published 1942), 137. See also David Harvey, *The Limits of Capital* (London: Verso, 2nd ed., 2007), 200–203.
28. Manuel Castells, *The Rise of the Network Society* (Oxford: Blackwell Publishers, 2nd ed., 2000).
29. James Glick, *Faster: The Acceleration of Just About Everything* (New York: Pantheon Books, 1999); Stan Davis and Christopher Meyer, *Blur: The Speed of Change in the Connected Economy* (New York: Grand Central Publishing, 1999).
30. Antoine W. van Agtmael, *The Emerging Markets Century: How a New Breed of World-class Company Is Overtaking the World* (New York: Free Press, 2007).
31. Steve Coll, *Private Empire: ExxonMobil and American Power* (New York: Penguin Press, 2012), 41.
32. This important distinction is explained in William J. Baumol, *The Microtheory of Innovative Entrepreneurship* (Princeton: Princeton University Press, 2010).
33. *Innovation Policy: A Guide to Developing Countries* (Washington, DC: World Bank, 2010), chapter 3.
34. Steven Casper and Frances van Waarden, eds., *Innovation and Institutions: A Multidisciplinary Review of the Study of Innovation Systems* (Chelthenham: Edward Elgar, 2005).
35. Mind set was one of the factors inhibiting exports in Jamaica. Maxine L. Garvey, *Jamaica's International Business Performance: Managerial Mindsets and Export Outcomes* (Kingston: Arawak Publishers, 2002).
36. The imperative for strategic global repositioning derives from the objective circumstances but is often not perceived. Richard L. Bernal, "Globalization and Small Developing Countries. The Imperative for Repositioning," in *Globalization: A Calculus of Inequality. Perspectives from the South*, ed. Denis Benn and Kenneth Hall (Kingston: Ian Randle Publishers, 2000), 88–127.
37. Harold L. Sirkin, James W. Hemerling, and Arindom K. Bhattacharya, *Globality: Competing with Everyone from Everywhere for Everything* (New York: Business Plus, 2008).
38. Thomas L. Friedman, *The World Is Flat 3.0: A Brief History of the Twenty-first Century* (New York: Pacador, 2007).
39. C. K. Prahaland and M. S. Krishanan, *The New Age of Innovation: Driving Co-created Value Through Global Networks* (New York: McGraw-Hill, 2008).
40. The need for tax reform is established is explained in Roy Bahl and Sally Wallace, *Tax Reform and Economic Development: The Jamaican Case* (Kingston: Planning Institute of Jamaica, 2007).
41. OECD, *Corporate Tax Incentives for Foreign Direct Investment, OECD Tax Policy Study 4* (Paris: OECD, 2001).
42. The effect on encouraging foreign investment has to weighed against the tax revenue foregone; see Jingqing Chai and Rishi Gozal, "Tax Concessions and Foreign Investment Direct in the Eastern Caribbean Currency Union," in *The Caribbean: From Vulnerability to Sustained Growth* (Washington, DC: International Monetary Fund, 2006), 258–282; Sebastian R. Sosa, "Tax Incentives and Investment in the Eastern Caribbean," *Working Paper No. 06/23* (Washington, DC: International Monetary Fund, January 2006).

43. Stefan Van Parys and Sebastian James, "The Effectiveness of Tax Incentives in Attracting FDI: Evidence from the Tourism Sector in the Caribbean," *Working Paper 675* (Ghent: Universiteit Gent, September 2010).
44. Vandana Chandra, ed., *Technology, Adaption, and Exports—How Some Developing Countries Got It Right* (Washington, DC: World Bank, 2006), 1–47.
45. Paul Krugman, "Competitiveness—A Dangerous Obsession," *Foreign Affairs* 73, no. 2 (March–April 1994), 44.
46. Bruce Kogut, "Conclusions: From Regions and Firms to Multinational Highways: Knowledge and Its Diffusion as a Factor in the Globalization of Industries," in *Locating Global Advantage: Industry Dynamics in the International Economy*, ed. Martin Kenney with Richard Florida (Stanford: Stanford University Press, 2004), 280.
47. Frances Cairncross, *The Company of the Future* (London: Profile Books, 2002), 39.
48. Joseph A. Michelli, *The Starbucks Experience: 5 Principles for Turning Ordinary into Extraordinary* (New York: McGraw-Hill, 2007).
49. Randall Stross, *Planet Google: One Company's Audacious Plan to Organize Everything We Know* (New York: Free Press, 2009).
50. The East Asian Miracle. World Bank Policy Research Report (Oxford: Oxford University Press, 1993), 43–46.
51. Densil A.Williams, *Understanding Exporting in the Small and Micro Enterprise* (New York: Nova Science Publishers, 2009).
52. Richard Florida, *The Flight of the Creative Class: The New Global Competition for Talent* (New York: Harper Business, 2005).
53. Lant Pritchett, *Let Their People Come: Breaking the Gridlock of Global Labour Mobility* (Washington, DC: Center for Global Development, 2006).
54. Remittances are a vital source of investment. Albert Bollard, David McKenzie, Melanie Morten, and Hillel Rapoport, "Remittances and the Brain Drain Revisited: The Microdata Show that More Educated Migrants Remit More," *The World Bank Economic Review* 25, no. 1 (2011): 132–156.
55. Ina Baghdiantz McCade, Gelina Harlaftis, and Joanna Pepelasis Minoglou, eds, *Diaspora Entrepreneurial Networks: Four Centuries of History* (Oxford: Berg, 2005).
56. *A Time to Choose: Caribbean Development in the 21st Century* (Washington, DC: World Bank, 2005), 50.
57. Don Tapscott and Anthony D. Williams, *Wikinomics: How Mass Collaboration Changes Everything* (New York: Portfolio, 2007); James E. Katz and Ronald E. Rice, *Social Consequences of Internet Use: Access, Involvement and Interaction* (Cambridge: MIT Press, 2002).
58. Alberto Chong, ed., *Development Connections: Unveiling the Impact of the New Information Technologies* (New York: Palgrave Macmillan, 2011).
59. Robert Read, "The Implications of Increasing Globalization and Regionalism for the Economic Growth of Small Island States," *World Development* 32, no. 2 (2004): 365–378. See p. 370.
60. Joseph E. Stiglitz, "Knowledge as a Global Public Goods," in *Global Public Goods: International Cooperation in the 21st Century*, I. Kaul, I. Grunberg, and M. A. Stern, ed. (New York: Oxford University Press, 1999), 308–325.
61. Mahvash Qureshi and Dirk Willem te Velde, *Working Smart and Small: The Role of Knowledge-based and Service Industries in Growth Strategies for Small States* (London: Commonwealth Secretariat, 2008).
62. Ben Wildavsky, *The Great Brain Race: How Global Universities Are Reshaping the World* (Princeton: Princeton University Press, 2010), 70.

63. David Warsh, *Knowledge and the Wealth of Nations: A Story of Economic Discovery* (New York: W. W. Norton & Company, 2006).
64. Hopeton Dunn, ed., *Ringtones of Opportunity: Policy, Technology and Access in Caribbean Communications* (Kingston: Ian Randle Publishers, 2012).
65. Richard L. Bernal, "Nano-firms, Integration and International Competitiveness: The Experience and Dilemma of the CSME," in *The CARICOM Single Market and Economy: Genesis and Prognosis*, ed. Kenneth Hall and Myrtle Chuck-A-Sang (Kingston: Ian Randle Publishers, 2007), 127–151.
66. *Caribbean Trade & Investment Report: Corporate Integration & Cross-border Development 2005* (Georgetown: Caribbean Community Secretariat, 2006).
67. Yair Aharoni, "How Small Firms Can Achieve Competitive Advantage in an Interdependent World," in *Small Firms in Global Competition*, Agmon Tamir and Richard L. Drobnick, ed. (New York: Oxford University Press, 1994), 14.
68. Thomas L. Friedman, *The World is Flat: A Brief History of the Twenty-first Century* (New York: Farrar, Straus and Giroux, 2005), 345.
69. This line of argument is fully developed in Pankaj Ghemawat, *Redefining Global Strategy. Crossing Borders in a World Where Differences Still Matter* (Boston: Harvard Business School Press, 2007).
70. Michael E. Porter, *The Competitive Advantages of Nations* (New York: Free Press, 1998), 101–102.
71. Alice H. Amsden, "The Wild Ones: Industrial Policies in the Developing World," in *The Washington Consensus Reconsidered: Towards A New Global Governance*, Narcis Serra And Joseph E. Stiglitz, ed. (Oxford: Oxford University Press, 2008), 95–118.
72. Ruchir Sharma, *Breakout Nations: In Pursuit of the Next Economic Miracles* (New York: W. W. Norton, 2012), x, 11.
73. Shahid Yusuf and Kaoru Nabeshima, *Some Small Countries Do It Better: Rapid Growth and Its Causes in Singapore, Finland and Ireland* (Washington, DC: World Bank, 2012).
74. Recent empirical evidence shows that export promotion agencies have had a positive effect on exports. See Daniel Lederman, Marcelo Olarreaga, and Lucy Payton, "Export Promotion Agencies: Strategies and Impacts," in *Breaking into New Markets*, ed. Richard Newfarmer, William Shaw, and Peter Walkenhorst (Washington, DC: World Bank, 2009), 211–221.
75. Michael Fairbanks and Stace Lindsay, *Plowing the Sea: Nuturing the Hidden Sources of Growth in the Developing World* (Boston: Harvard Business School Press, 1997), 134–170.
76. Robert Wade, *Governing the Market: Economic Theory and the Role of Government in East Asian Industrialization* (Princeton: Princeton University Press, 1990).
77. Philip Kotler, Somkid Jatusripitak, and Suvit Maesincee, *The Marketing of Nations: A Strategic Approach to Building National Wealth* (New York: Free Press, 1997), chapter 15.
78. CARICOM, *Our Caribbean Community: An Introduction* (Kingston: Ian Randle Publishers, 2005), 67.
79. The importance of strategic alliances is extensively documented. See Joseph L. Badaraco Jr., *The Knowledge Link: How Firms Compete through Strategic Alliances* (Boston: Harvard Business School Press, 1991); Martin K. Starr, *Global Corporate Alliances and the Competitive Edge* (New York: Quorum Books, 1991); Benjamin Gomes-Casseres, *The Alliance Revolution: The New Shape of Business Rivalry* (Cambridge: Harvard University Press, 1996); and Michael Y. Yashino and U. Srinivasa Rangan, *Strategic*

Alliance: An Entrepreneurial Approach to Globalization (Cambridge: Harvard Business School Press, 1995).

80. Richard E. Caves, *Multinational Enterprise and Economic Analysis* (Cambridge: Cambridge University Press, 1982).
81. Alfred D. Chandler Jr., "The Enduring Logic of Industrial Success," *Harvard Business Review* 71, no. 2 (March–April 1990), 130–140.
82. Benjamin Gomes-Casseres, "Alliance Strategies of Small Firms," in *Small and Medium-sized Enterprises in the Global Economy*, ed. Zoltan J. Acs and Bernard Yeung (Ann Arbor: University of Michigan Press, 1999), 67–87.
83. *Caribbean Trade & Investment Report 2005* (Georgetown: Caribbean Community Secretariat, 2006), 248.
84. Richard L. Bernal, "Strategic Global Repositioning and the Future Economic Development of Jamaica," *North South Agenda Paper No. 18* (Miami: North South Center, University of Miami, May 1996); "Globalization and Small Developing Countries: The Imperative for Repositioning," in *Globalization: A Calculus of Inequality*, ed. Denis Benn and Kenneth Hall (Kingston: Ian Randle Publishers, 2000), 88–128.

Bibliography

Books

Agenor, Pierre-Richard, and Peter J. Montiel. *Development Macroeconomics.* Princeton: Princeton University Press, 2008.

Akyuz, Yilmaz. *Multilateral Disciplines and the Question of Policy Space, Trade & Development Series, No. 38.* Penang: Third World Network, 2009.

Alesina, Alberto, and Enrico Spolaore. *The Size of Nations.* Cambridge: MIT Press, 2003.

Amin, Samir. *Accumulation on a World Scale.* New York: Monthly Review Press, 1973.

———. *Imperialism and Unequal Development.* New York: Monthly Review Press, 1996.

Andre, Irving W., and Gabriel J. Christian. *In Search of Eden: The Travails of a Caribbean Mini State.* Roseau: Pond Casse Press, 1992, 209.

Anthony, Kenny D. *At the Rainbow's Edge: Selected Speeches of Kenny D. Anthony 1996–2002.* Kingston: Ian Randle Publishers, 2004, 240.

Badaraco, Joseph L., Jr. *The Knowledge Link: How Firms Compete Through Strategic Alliances.* Boston: Harvard Business School Press, 1991.

Baghdiantz McCade, Ina, Gelina Harlaftis, and Joanna Pepelasis Minoglou, eds. *Diaspora Entrepreneurial Networks. Four Centuries of History.* Oxford: Berg, 2005.

Bahl, Roy, and Sally Wallace. *Tax Reform and Economic Development: The Jamaican Case.* Kingston: Planning Institute of Jamaica, 2007.

Bartlett, Christopher A., and Sumantra Ghoshal. *Managing Across Borders.* Boston: Harvard Business School Press, 1989.

Bauer, Peter T. *Dissent on Development.* Cambridge: Harvard University Press, 1972.

———. *Equality, the Third World and Economic Delusion.* Cambridge: Harvard University Press, 1982, 66–155.

Baumol, William J. *The Microtheory of Innovative Entrepreneurship.* Princeton: Princeton University Press, 2010.

Beckford, George. *Persistent Poverty: Underdevelopment in Plantation Economies of the Third World.* Oxford: Oxford University Press, 1972.

Bedbury, Scott. *A Brand New World.* New York: Viking, 2002.

Berg, Allison, and Olga Jonas, eds. *The World Bank in Action in Small States.* Washington, DC: World Bank, 2005.

Berhman, Greg. *The Most Noble Adventure: The Marshall Plan and the Time When America Helped Save Europe.* New York: Free Press, 2008.

Bhagwati, Jagdish N. *Free Trade Today.* Princeton: Princeton University Press, 2002, 12.

———. *Anatomy and Consequences of Exchange Control Regimes and Economic Development.* Cambridge: Ballinger, 1978.

Brewster, Havelock, and Clive Y. Thomas. *The Dynamics of West Indian Economic Integration.* Mona: Institute of Social and Economic Research, University of the West Indies, 1967.

Cairncross, Frances. *The Company of the Future.* London: Profile Books, 2002.

———. *The Death of Distance: How the Communications Revolution Will Change Our Lives.* Boston: Harvard Business School Press, 1997.

Cardoso, Fernando Henrique, and Enzo Faletto. *Dependence and Development in Latin America.* Berkeley: University of California, 1979.

CARICOM. *Our Caribbean Community: An Introduction.* Kingston: Ian Randle Publishers, 2005: 67–289.

Casper, Steven, and Frances van Waarden, eds. *Innovation and Institutions: A Multidisciplinary Review of the Study of Innovation Systems.* Chelthenham: Edward Elgar, 2005.

Cassen, Robert & Associates. *Does Aid Work? Report to an Intergovernmental Task Force.* Oxford: Oxford University Press, 1986.

Castells, Manuel. *The Rise of the Network Society*, 2nd ed. Oxford: Blackwell Publishers, 2000.

Caves, Richard E. *Multinational Enterprise and Economic Analysis.* Cambridge: Cambridge University Press, 1982.

Chandra, Vandana, ed. *Technology, Adaption, and Exports—How Some Developing Countries Got It Right.* Washington, DC: World Bank, 2006.

Chang, Ha-Joon. *Kicking Away the Ladder: Development Strategy in Historical Perspective.* London: Anthem Press, 2002.

Chenery, Hollis. *Structural Change and Development Policy.* New York: Oxford University Press, 1979.

Choksi, Armeane M., Demetrius Papageorgiou, and Michael Michaely, *Liberalizing Trade, Vol. 7, Lessons of Experience in the Developing World.* Oxford: Blackwell, 1991.

Chong, Alberto, ed. *Development Connections: Unveiling the Impact of the New Information Technologies.* New York: Palgrave Macmillan, 2011.

Coll, Steve. *Private Empire: ExxonMobil and American Power.* New York: Penguin Press, 2012.

Cooke, Philip, ed. *Regional Innovation Systems*, 2nd ed. London: Routledge, 2004.

Cooper, Richard N. *The Economics of Interdependence: Economic Policy in the Atlantic Community.* New York: McGraw Hill for the Council on Foreign Relations, 1968.

Correa, Carlos M. *Intellectual Property Rights, the WTO and Developing Countries: The TRIPS Agreement and Policy Options.* London: Zed Books/Penang, Third World Network, 2000.

Cosgrove Twitchett, Carol. *A Framework for Development: The EEC and the ACP.* London: Allen & Unwin, 1981.

Crainer, Stuart. *The Real Power of Brands: Making Brands Work for Competitive Advantage.* London: Pitman Publishing, 1995.

Dabydeen, David, and John Gilmore, eds. *No Island Is an Island: Selected Speeches of Sir Shridath Ramphal.* London: Macmillan Education, 2000.

Dadush, Uri, and William Shaw. *Juggernaut: How Emerging Markets are Shaping Globalization.* Washington, DC: Carnegie Endowment for Peace, 2011.

Davidson, Basil. *Black Man's Burden: Africa and the Curse of the Nation State.* London: James Currey, 1992.

Davies, Peter N. *Fyffes and the Banana: Musa Sapientum. A Centenary History, 1888–1988.* London: Athlone Press, 1990.

Davis, Stan, and Christopher Meyer. *Blur: The Speed of Change in the Connected Economy.* New York: Time Warner Books, 1999.

De Soto, Hernando. *The Mystery of Capital: Why Capitalism Triumphs in the West and Fails Everywhere Else.* New York: Basic Books, 2000.

Deane, Phyllis, and W. A. Cole. *British Economic Growth*. Cambridge: Cambridge University Press, 1969.

Dollar, David, and Aart Kraay. *Growth Is Good for the Poor*. Washington, DC: World Bank, Development Research Group, 2000.

Dowden, Richard. *Africa: Altered States, Ordinary Miracles*. New York: Public Affairs, 2009.

Dumont, Jean-Christophe, and Georges Lemaitre. *Counting Immigrants and Expatriates in OECD Countries: A New Perspective*. Paris: OECD, 2005.

Dunn, Hopeton, ed. *Ringtones of Opportunity: Policy, Technology and Access in Caribbean Communications*. Kingston: Ian Randle Publishers, 2012.

Easterly, William. *The Elusive Quest for Growth: Economists' Adventures in the Tropics*. Cambridge: MIT Press, 2001.

———. *The White Man's Burden: Why the West's Efforts to Aid the Rest Have Done So Much and So Little Good*. New York: Penguin Press, 2006.

Emmanuel, Arghiri. *Unequal Exchange: A Study of the Imperialism of Trade*. New York: Monthly Review Press, 1972.

Fairbanks, Michael, and Stace Lindsay. *Plowing the Sea: Nurturing the Hidden Sources of Growth in the Developing World*. Boston: Harvard Business School Press, 1997: 134–70.

Feis, Herbert. *Foreign Aid and Foreign Policy*. New York: St. Martin's Press, 1964.

Florida, Richard. *The Flight of the Creative Class: The New Global Competition for Talent*. New York: Harper Business, 2005.

Friedman, Thomas L. *The Lexus and the Olive Tree: Understanding Globalization*. New York: Farrar, Straus and Giroux, 1999.

———. *The World Is Flat: A Brief History of the Twenty-First Century*, Revised ed. New York: Farrar Straus & Giroux, 2006.

———. *The World Is Flat 3.0.: A Brief History of the Twenty-first Century*. New York: Pacador, 2007.

Fukuyama, Francis. *Trust: The Social Virtues and the Creation of Prosperity*. New York: Free Press, 1996.

Furtado, Celso. *Development and Underdevelopment*. Berkeley: University of California, 1974.

Gallagher, Kevin P. *Putting Development First: The Importance of Policy Space in the WTO and IFIs*. London: Zed Books, 2005.

Garcia Lopez, Roberto, and Mauricio Garcia Moreno. *Managing for Development Results: Progress and Challenges in Latin America and the Caribbean*. Washington, DC: Inter-American Development Bank, 2011.

Garvey, Maxine. *Jamaica's International Business Performance. Managerial Mindsets and Export Outcomes*. Kingston: Arawak Publications, 2002.

Ghemawat, Pankaj. *Redefining Global Strategy: Crossing Borders in a World Where Differences Still Matter*. Boston: Harvard Business School Press, 2007.

Girvan, Norman. *Corporate Imperialism: Conflict and Expropriation: Essays on Transnational Corporations and Economic Nationalism in the Third World*. New York: Monthly Review Press, 1978.

Glegg, Peter. *The Caribbean Banana Trade: From Colonialism to Globalization*. New York: Palgrave, 2002, 79.

Glick, James. *Faster: The Acceleration of Just About Everything*. New York: Pantheon Books, 1999.

Gomes-Casseres, Benjamin. *The Alliance Revolution: The New Shape of Business Rivalry*. Cambridge: Harvard University Press, 1996.

Grilli, Enzo R. *The European Community and the Developing Countries*. Cambridge: Cambridge University Press, 1993.

Hannaford, Stephen G. *Market Domination! The Impact of Industry Consolidation on Competition, Innovation and Consumer Choice*. Westport: Praeger Publishers, 2007, 23.

Harberler, Gottfried. *International Trade and Economic Development*. Cairo: National Bank, 1959.

Harvey, David. *The Limits of Capital*, 2nd ed. London: Verso, 2007, 200–3.

Hayter, Teresa. *Aid as Imperialism*. Harmondsworth: Penguin, 1971.

Heger Martin, Alex Julca, and Oliver Paddison, "Analysing the Impact of Natural Hazards in Small Economies: The Caribbean Case." Research Paper No. 2008/25. United Nations University/ World Institute Development Economics Research, March 2008, 7.

Helleiner, Gerald K. *Intra-firm Trade and the Developing Countries*. London: Macmillan, 1981.

Hoekman, Bernard, and Michael Koslecki. *The Political Economy of the World Trading System: From GATT to WTO*. Oxford: Oxford University Press, 1995, 40.

Hogan, Michael J. *The Marshall Plan: America, Britain and the Reconstruction of Western Europe, 1947–1952*. Cambridge: Cambridge University Press, 1989.

Hollander, Samuel. *The Economics of Adam Smith*. Toronto: University of Toronto Press, 1973.

Howard, Michael. *Public Finance in Small Open Economies: The Caribbean Experience*. Westport: Praeger, 1992.

Hudec, Robert E. *Developing Countries in the GATT Legal System*. London: Gower, 1987.

Independent Evaluation Group. *Small States: Making the Most of Development Assistance: A Synthesis of Evaluation Findings*. Washington, DC: World Bank, 2006.

Jawara, Fatoumata, and Aillen Kwa. *Behind the Scenes at the WTO: The Real World of International Trade Negotiations*. London: Zed Books, 2003.

Johnson, Harry G. *Money, Trade and Economic Growth*. London: Allen and Unwin, 1962.

Katz, James E., and Ronald E. Rice. *Social Consequences of Internet Use: Access, Involvement and Interaction*. Cambridge: MIT Press, 2002.

Kemp, Murray C. *The Pure Theory of International Trade and Investment*. Englewoods Cliffs: Prentice-Hall, 1969.

King, Damian, and Collette Campbell. *The Impact of the EPA on Caribbean Economies: A Structural Analysis of Four Caribbean Countries*. Kingston: Caribbean Policy research Institute, Apr., Nov. 2010.

Korten, David C. *When Corporations Rule the World Hartford*. Hartford: Kumarian Press and San Francisco: Barrett-Kochler, 1995.

Kotler, Philip, Somkid Jatusripitak, and Suvit Maesincee. *The Marketing of Nations: A Strategic Approach to Building National Wealth*. New York: Free Press, 1997.

Krueger, Anna. *Trade Policies for Developing Countries*. Washington, DC: Brookings Institution, 1995.

———. *Foreign Trade Regimes and Economic Development: Liberalization Attempts and Consequences*. Cambridge: Ballinger, 1978.

Kwa, Aileen. *African Countries and EPAs: Do Agriculture Safeguards Afford Adequate Protection?* Geneva: South Centre, 2008.

Levin, Jonathon V. *The Export Economies*. Cambridge: Harvard University Press, 1960.

Lewis, W. Arthur. *The Theory of Economic Growth*. London: Unwin, 1955.

Lin, Justin Yifu, ed. *New Structural Economics: A Framework for Thinking Development and Policy*. Washington, DC: World Bank, 2012.

Little, I. M. D., and J. M. Clifford. *International Aid*. Chicago: Aldine Publishing Company, 1966.

Lloyd, Peter J. *International Trade Problems of Small Nations.* Durham, NC: Duke University Press, 1968.

Lundvall, Bengt-Ake, ed. *National Systems of Innovation.* London: Pinter, 1992.

Magnus, George. *Uprising: Will Emerging Markets Shape or Shake the World Economy.* New York: John Wiley, 2011.

Manderson-Jones, R.B. *Jamaican Foreign Policy in the Caribbean 1962–1988.* Kingston: CARICOM Publishers, 1990.

Mattoo, Aaditya, Robert M. Stern, and Gianni Zanini, eds. *A Handbook of International Trade in Services.* Oxford: Oxford University Press, 2008.

Martin, Chuck. *Net Future: The 7 Cyber Trends That Will Drive Your Business, Create New Wealth And Define Your Future.* New York: McGraw-Hill, 1999.

Marx, Karl, and Friedrich Engels. *The Communist Manifesto: A Modern Edition.* London: Verso, 1998.

Maskus, Keith E. *Intellectual Property Rights in the Global Economy.* Washington, DC: Institute for International Economics, 2000.

McRae, Hamish. *The World in 20–20: Power, Culture and Prosperity. A Vision of the Future.* London: Harper Collins Publishers, 1994.

Michalopoulos, Constantine. *Developing Countries in the WTO.* London: Palgrave, 2001.

Michelli, Joseph A. *The Starbucks Experience. 5 Principles for Turning Ordinary into Extraordinary.* New York: McGraw-Hill, 2007.

Mikesell, Raymond F. *The Economic of Foreign Aid.* Chicago: Aldine Publishing Company, 1968, 156–7.

Mills, Nicolaus. *Winning the Peace: The Marshall Plan and Americas Coming of Age as a Superpower.* New York: Wiley, 2008.

Moran, Theodore H. *Foreign Direct Investment and Development: The New Agenda for Developing Countries and Economies of Transition.* Washington, DC: Institute for International Economic, 1999.

Moyo, Dambisa. *Dead Aid: Why Aid Is Not Working and How There Is a Better Way.* New York: Farrar, Strauss and Giroux, 2009.

Myers, Gordon. *Banana Wars—The Price of Free Trade: A Caribbean Perspective.* London: Zed Books, 2004.

Myrdal, Gunnar. *An International Economy, Problems and Prospects.* New York: Harper & Row, 1956.

———. *Economic Theory and Under-Developed Regions.* London: Methuen, 1965.

Nader, Ralph, ed. *The Case Against Free Trade: GATT, NAFTA, and the Globalization of Corporate Power.* San Francisco: Earth Island Press, 1993.

Navaretti, Giorgio Barba, and Anthony J. Venables, *Multinational Firms in the World Economy.* Princeton: Princeton University Press, 2004.

Nelson, Joan M. *Aid, Influence, and Foreign Policy.* New York: MacMillan, 1968.

Northdurft, William E. *Going Global: How Europe Helps Small Firms Export.* Washington, DC: Brookings Institution, 1992.

North, Douglas V. *The Economic Growth of the United States, 1790–1860.* New York: Prentice- Hall, 1961.

North, Douglass C. *Institutions, Institutional Change and Economic Performance.* Cambridge: Cambridge University Press, 1990.

Ohlin, Bertil. *International and Inter-regional Trade.* Cambridge: Harvard University Press, 1933.

Palmer, Colin A. *Eric Williams and the Making of the Modern Caribbean.* Kingston: Ian Randle Publishers, 2006.

Pantin, Dennis. *The Economics of Sustainable Development in Small Caribbean Islands*. Mona: Centre for Environment and Development, University of the West Indies, 1994, 16.

Patterson, Rubin. *Foreign Aid after the Cold War: The Dynamics of Multipolar Economic Competition*. Trenton: Africa World Press, 1997.

Payne, Anthony J. *The Political History of CARICOM*. Kingston: Ian Randle, 2008.

Peckenham, Thomas. *The Scramble for Africa: White Man's Conquest of the Dark Continent from 1876–1912*. New York: Avon Books, 1992.

Poole, Bernard L. *The Caribbean Commission: Background of Cooperation in the West Indies*. Columbia: University of South Carolina, 1951.

Porter, Michael E. *The Competitive Advantage of Nations*. New York: Free Press, 1990.

Powell, Benjamin. *Making Poor Nations Rich: Entrepreneurship and the Process of Economic Development*. Stanford: Stanford Economics and Finance, 2007.

Prahaland, C. K., and M. S. Krishanan. *The New Age of Innovation. Driving Co-created Value Through Global Networks*. New York: McGraw-Hill, 2008.

Prebisch, Enrique V., ed. *The Legacy of Raul Prebisch*. Washington, DC: Inter-American Development Bank, 1994.

Prebisch, Raul. *The Economic Development of Latin America and Its Principal Problems*. New York: United Nations Economic Commission for Latin America, 1950.

Pritchett, Lant. *Let Their People Come: Breaking the Gridlock of Global Labour Mobility*. Washington, DC: Center for Global Development, 2006.

Ravenhill, John. *Collective Clientelism: The Lomé Conventions and North-South Relations*. New York: Columbia University Press, 1985.

Ricardo, David. *On the Principles of Political Economy and Taxation. Vol. I, Works and Correspondence of David Ricardo*. Edited by Piero Sraffa. Cambridge: Cambridge University Press, 1951

Rodrick, Dani. *The Globalization Paradox. Democracy and the Future of the World Economy*. New York: W. W. Norton & Sons, 2011.

Rodrik, Dani. *One Economics, Many Recipes: Globalization, Institutions and Economic Growth*. Princeton: Princeton University Press, 2007.

———. *The New Global Economy and Developing Countries: Making Openness Work*. Washington, DC: Overseas Development Council, 1999.

Root, Hilton J. *Capital and Collusion. The Political Logic of Economic Development*. Princeton: Princeton University Press, 2006.

Roubini, Nouriel, and Stephen Mihm, *Crisis Economics: A Crash Course in the Future of Finance*. New York: Penguin, 2012.

Ruttan, Vernon W. *United States Development Assistance Policy: The Domestic Politics of Foreign Aid*. Baltimore: Johns Hopkins University Press, 1996.

Schumpeter, Joseph A. *Capitalism, Socialism and Democracy*. London; Routledge, 1994, originally published 1942.

———. *History of Economic Analysis*. London: George Allen & Unwin, 1952.

Sharma, Ruchir. *Breakout Nations: In Pursuit of the Next Economic Miracles*. New York: W. W. Norton & Company, 2012.

Sherwood, Robert M. *Intellectual Property and Economic Development*. Boulder: Westview Press, 1990.

Simpson, Anne, and Chris Lee. *Whose Gold? Geest and the Banana Trade*. London: Latin American Bureau, 1990.

Sirkin, Harold L., James W. Hemerling, and Arindom K. Bhattacharya. *Globality: Competing with Everyone from Everywhere for Everything*. New York: Business Plus, 2008.

Starr, Martin K. *Global Corporate Alliances and the Competitive Edge*. New York: Quorum Books, 1991.

Stern, Robert M. *Foreign Trade and Economic Growth in Italy*. New York: Praeger, 1967.

Stevens, Christopher, Matthew McQueen, and Jane Kennan. *After Lomé IV: A Strategy for ACP-EU Relations in 21st Century*. London: Commonwealth Secretariat, 1999.

Stiglitz, Joseph E. *Making Globalization Work*. New York: W. W. Norton & Company, 2006.

Stiglitz, Joseph E., and Andrew Charlton. *Fair Trade for All: How Trade Can Promote Development*. Oxford: Oxford University Press, 2005.

Stopford, John and Susan Strange. *Rival States, Rival Firms*. Cambridge: Cambridge University Press, 1991.

Strange, Susan. *Casino Capitalism*. Manchester: Manchester University Press, 1997.

Strange, Susan. *The Retreat of the State: The Diffusion of Power in the World Economy*. Cambridge: Cambridge University Press, 1996.

Stross, Randall. *Planet Google: One Company's Audacious Plan to Organize Everything We Know*. New York: Free Press, 2009.

Tapscott, Don. *The Digital Economy. Promise and Peril in the Age of Networked Intelligence*. New York: McGraw-Hill, 1996.

Tapscott, Don, and Anthony D. Williams. *Wikinomics: How Mass Collaboration Changes Everything*. New York: Portfolio, 2007.

Taylor, Lance. *Structuralist Macroeconomics*. New York: Basic Books, 1983.

Thomas, Vinod, John Nash, and Associates. *Best Practices in Trade Policy Reform*. New York: Oxford University Press, 1991.

Topp, Vernon. *Trade Preferences: Are They Helpful in Advancing Economic Development in Poor Countries?* Canberra: Australian Bureau of Agricultural and Resource Economics, 2001.

Vernon, Raymond. *In the Hurricane's Eye: The Troubled Prospects of Multinational Enterprises*. Cambridge: Harvard University Press, 1998.

van Agtmael, Antoine W. *The Emerging Markets Century: How a New Breed of World-Class Company Is Overtaking the World*. New York: Free Press, 2007.

Viner, Jacob. *The Customs Union Issue*. New York: Carnegie Endowment for International Peace, 1950.

———. *International Trade and Economic Development*. Glencoe: Free Press, 1952.

Wade, Robert. *Governing the Market: Economic Theory and the Role of Government in East Asian Industrialization*. Princeton: Princeton University Press, 1990.

Wallach, Lori, and Patrick Woodall. *Whose Trade Organization?* New York: The New Press, 2004.

Warsh, David. *Knowledge and the Wealth of Nations: A Story of Economic Discovery*. New York: W. W. Norton & Company, 2006.

Wignarja, Ganesh, Marlon Lezama, and David Joiner. *Small States in Transition: From Vulnerability to Competitiveness*. London: Commonwealth Secretariat, 2004.

Wildavsky, Ben. *The Great Brain Race: How Global Universities Are Reshaping the World*. Princeton: Princeton University Press, 2010.

Williams, Densil A. *Understanding Exporting in the Small and Micro Enterprise*. New York: Nova Science Publishers, 2009.

Wint, Alvin G. *Competitiveness in Small Developing Economies: Insights from the Caribbean*. Kingston: University of the West Indies Press, 2003.

———. *Managing Towards International Competitiveness: Cases and Lessons from the Caribbean*. Kingston: Ian Randle Publishers, 1997.

World Bank. *The East Asian Miracle*. Oxford: Oxford University Press, 1993.

World Bank. *Innovation Policy: A Guide to Developing Countries*. Washington, DC: World Bank, 2010.

Yashino, Michael Y., and U. Srinivasa Rangan. *Strategic Alliance: An Entrepreneurial Approach to Globalization.* Cambridge: Harvard Business School Press, 1995.

Yusuf, Shahid, and Kaoru Nabeshima, *Some Small Countries Do It Better: Rapid Growth and Its Causes in Singapore, Finland and Ireland.* Washington, DC: World Bank, 2012.

Articles in Books

Acs, Zoltan J., Randall Morck, J. Myles Shaver, and Bernard Yeoug. "The Internationalization of Small and Medium-Sized Enterprises." In *Small and Medium-sized Enterprises in the Global Economy*, edited by Zoltan J. Acs and Bernard Yeong. Ann Arbor: University of Michigan Press, 1999.

Aharoni, Yair. "How Small Firms Can Achieve Competitive Advantage in an Interdependent World." In *Small Firms in Global Competition*, edited by Agmon Tamir and Richard L. Drobnick. New York: Oxford University Press, 1994.

Amsden, Alice H. "The Wild Ones: Industrial Policies in the Developing World." In *The Washington Consensus Reconsidered: Towards A New Global Governance*, edited by Narcis Serra and Joseph E. Stiglitz, 95–118. Oxford: Oxford University Press, 2008.

———. "Trade Policy and Economic Performance in South Korea." In *Trade and Growth: New Dilemmas in Trade Policy*, edited by Manuel R. Agosin and Diana Tussie, 187–214. New York: St. Martin's Press, 1993.

Atkins, Jonathan P., Sonia Mazzi, and Christopher D. Easter. "Small States: A Composite Vulnerability Index." In *Small States in the Global Economy*, edited by David Peretz, Rumman Faruqi, and Eliawony J. Kisanga, 53–92. London: Commonwealth Secretariat, 2001.

R. Baler. "Scale and Administrative Performance: The Governance of Small States and Microstates." In *Public Administration in Small and Island States,* edited by R. Baker, 5–25. Hartford: Kumarian Press, 1992.

Bernal, Richard L. "Caribbean States and the FTAA: Adequacy of Preparation, Participation and Negotiating Structures." In *Small Caribbean States and the Challenge of International Trade Negotiations*, edited by Anthony Gonzales, 76–103. Port of Spain: Institute of International Relations, University of the West Indies, 1998.

———. "CARICOM's External Trade Negotiations without the completion of the CSME." In *The CSME: Status, Issues and Priorities*. Washington, DC: Institute for the Integration of Latin America and the Caribbean, Inter-American Development Bank, 2006.

———. "Globalization and Small Developing Countries: The Imperative for Repositioning." In *Globalization: A Calculus of Inequality,* edited by Denis Benn and Kenneth Hall, 88–128. Kingston: Ian Randle Publishers, 2000.

———. "Nano-firms, Integration and International Competitiveness: The Experience and Dilemma of the CSME." In *Production Integration in Caribbean: From Theory to Action,* edited by Denis Benn and Kenneth Hall, 90–115. Kingston: Ian Randle Publishers, 2006.

———. "Small Developing Economies in the World Trade Organization." In *Agriculture, Trade, and the WTO*, edited by Merlinda D. Ingco, 108–22. Washington, DC: World Bank, 2003.

———. "Special and Differential Treatment for Small Developing Economies." In *WTO at the Margins: Small States and the Multilateral Trading System,* edited by Roman Grynberg, 309–55. Cambridge: Cambridge University Press, 2006.

Blazic-Metzner, Boris, and Helen Hughes. "Growth Experience of Small Countries." In *Problems and Policies in Small Economies,* edited by B. Jalan, 85–102. New York: St. Martin's Press, 1982.

Brewster, Havelock. "From Community to Single Market and Economy." In *Governance in the Age of Globalisation: Caribbean Perspectives,* edited by Kenneth O. Hall and Denis Benn, 499–508. Kingston: Ian Randle Publishers, 2003.

Chai, Jingqing, and Rishi Gozal. "Tax Concessions and Foreign Investment Direct in the Eastern Caribbean Currency Union." In *The Caribbean: From Vulnerability to Sustained Growth,* edited by Ratna Sahay, David O. Robinson, and Paul Cashin, 258–82. Washington, DC: International Monetary Fund, 2006.

Chaitoo, Ramesh. "Aid for Trade for Services in Small Economies: Some Considerations from the Caribbean." In *Aid for Trade and Development,* edited Hugo Cameron and Dominique Nijenkeu, 303. Cambridge: Cambridge University Press, 2008.

Clarke, Alice. "An Analysis of EU-ACPAid Flows through the EDF from Lome to the Contonou Agreement and Proposals for the 10th and 11th EDFs." In *Navigating New Waters: A Reader on ACP-EU Trade Relations,* edited by Sinoussi Bilal and Roman Grynberg, vol. 1, 209–32. London: Commonwealth Secretariat, 2007.

Cohen, Steven. "Geo-economics and America's Mistakes." In *The New Global Economy in the Information Age,* edited by Martin Carnoy. London: McMillian, 1993.

Paul, Collier, and David Dollar. "Aid, Risk and the Special Concerns of the Small States." In *Small States in the Global Economy,* edited by David Peretz, Rumman Faruqi, and Eliawony J. Kisanga. London: Commonwealth Secretariat/World Bank, 2001, 11–38.

Deep Ford, J. R., and Greg Rollins. "Trade Policy, Trade and Food Security in the Caribbean." In *Agricultural Food Policy and Food Security in the Caribbean,* edited by J. R. Deep Ford, Crescenso dell'Aquila, and Piero Conforti, 7–40. Rome: Food and Agricultural Organization of the United Nations, 2007.

Diaz-Alejandro, Carlos F. "Trade Policies and Economic Development." In *International Trade and Finance,* edited by Peter Kenan, 96. Cambridge: Cambridge University Press, 1976.

Estevadeordal, Antoni, and Kai Suominen. "What Are the Trade Effects of Rules of Origin." In *Gatekeepers of Global Commerce: Rules of Origin and International Economic Integration,* edited by Antoni Estevadeordal and Kai Suominen, 161–219. Washington, DC: Inter-American Development Bank, 2008.

Estevadeordal, Antoni, Jeremy Harris, and Kai Suominen. "Structure, Restrictiveness, and Trends in Rules of Origin Around the World." In *Gatekeepers of Global Commerce. Rules of Origin and International Economic Integration,* edited by Antoni Estevadeordal and Kai Suominen, 11–81. Washington, DC: Inter-American Development Bank, 2008.

Farrell, Trevor M. A. "Caribbean Economic Integration: What Is Happening Now; What Needs to be Done." In *Caribbean Imperatives,* edited by Kenneth Hall and Denis Benn, 178. Oct. 2003.

Favaro, Edgardo M., and David Peretz. "Introduction." In *Small States, Smart Solutions: Improving Connectivity and Increasing the Effectiveness of Public Services,* edited by Edgardo M. Favaro, 4. Washington, DC: World Bank, 2008.

Finger, J. Michael, and L. Alan Winters. "What Can the WTO do for Developing Countries." In *The WTO as an International Organization,* edited by Anne Krueger, 390. Chicago: University of Chicago, 1998.

James Gleick, James. Faster. *The Acceleration of Just About Everything.* New York: Pantheon Books, 1999.

Goodison, Paul."EU Assistance to the ACP Countries Since 1975." In *Navigating New Waters: A Reader on ACP-EU Trade Relations,* edited by Sinoussi Bilal and Roman Grynberg, vol. I, 183– 208. London: Commonwealth Secretariat, 2007.

Gomes-Casseres, Benjamin. "Alliance Strategies of Small Firms." In *Small and Medium-sized Enterprises in the Global Economy,* edited by Zoltan J. Acs and Bernard Yeung, 67–87. Ann Arbor: University of Michigan Press, 1999.

Harasingh, Kusha. "On the Front Line: The Lomé Experience Dissected." In *Caribbean Survival and the Global Challenge,* edited by Ramesh Ramsaran, 366–83. Kingston: Ian Randle Publishers, 2002.

Heckscher, Eli F. "The Effects of Foreign Trade on the Distribution of Income." In *Readings in International Trade*, edited by H. Ellis and L. Metzler. Homewood: Richard D. Irwin, 1950.

Hesse, Heiko. "Export Diversification and Economic Growth." In *Breaking into Markets: Emerging Lessons for Export Diversification,* edited by Richard Newfarmer, William Shaw, and Peter Walkenhorst, 55–80. Washington, DC: World Bank, 2009.

Hewitt, Adrian, and Christopher Stevens. "The Second Lomé Convention." In *EEC and the Third World: A Survey*, edited by Christopher Stevens. London: Hodder and Stoughton, 1981.

Hnatkovska, Viktoria, and Norman Loayza. "Volatility and Growth." In *Managing Economic Volatility and Crises: A Practitioner's Guide*, edited by Joshua Aizenman and Brian Pinto, 65–100. Cambridge: Cambridge University Press, 2005.

Houseman, Ricardo, Dani Rodrik, and Andres Velasco. "Growth Diagnostics." In *The Washington Consensus Reconsidered: Towards A New Global Governance*, edited by Narcis Serra and Joseph E. Stiglitz, 324–55. Oxford: Oxford University Press, 2008.

Ietto-Gilles, Grazia, Meloria Meschi, and Roberto Simonetti, "Cross-border Mergers and Acquisitions." In *European Integration and Global Corporate Strategies*, edited by Francis Chesnais, Grazia Ietto-Giles and Roberto Simonetti, 52–71. London: Routledge, 2000.

Jessen, Anneke. "Regional Public Goods and Small Economies: The Caribbean Regional Negotiating Machinery." In *Regional Public Goods: From Theory to Practice*, edited by Brian Frantz, Antoni Estevadeordal, and Tam Robert Nguyen, 301–23. Washington, DC: Inter-American Development Bank, 2004.

Kogut, Bruce. "Conclusions: From Regions and Firms to Multinational Highways: Knowledge and Its Diffusion as a Factor in the Globalization of Industries." In *Locating Global Advantage: Industry Dynamics in the International Economy*, edited by Martin Kenney with Richard Florida, 280. Stanford: Stanford University Press, 2004.

Krugman, Paul. "Increasing Returns, Imperfect Competition and the Positive Theory of International Trade." In *Handbook of International Economics, Vol. 3.*, 1243–77. New York: Elsevier-North-Holland, 1995.

Laurent, Edwin. "Small States in the Banana Dispute." In *WTO at the Margins: Small States and the Multilateral Trading System,* edited by Roman Grynberg. Cambridge: Cambridge University Press, 2006.

Lederman, Daniel, Marcelo Olarreaga, and Lucy Payton. "Export Promotion Agencies: Strategies and Impacts." In *Breaking into New Markets,* edited by Richard Newfarmer, William Shaw, and Peter Walkenhorst, 211–21. Washington, DC: World Bank, 2009.

Lejarraga, Iza, and Peter Walkenhorst. "Fostering Productive Diversification Through Tourism." In *Breaking into New Markets: Emerging Markets for Export Diversification*, edited by Richard Newfarmer, William Shaw, and Peter Walkenhorst. Washington, DC: World Bank, 2009.

Lin, Justin Yifu, and Celestin Monga. "Growth Identification and Facilitation: The Role of the State in the Dynamics of Structural Change." In *New Structural Economics: A Framework for Thinking Development and Policy*, edited by Justin Yifu Lin, 143–80. Washington, DC: World Bank, 2012.

Maskus, Keith E. "Benefiting from Intellectual Property Rights." In *Development, Trade and the WTO: A Handbook,* edited by Bernard Hoekman, Aaditya Mattoo, and Philip English, 369–81. Washington, DC: World Bank, 2002.

Maurer, A., and P. Chauvet, "The Magnitude of Flows of Global Trade in Services." In *Development, Trade and the WTO: A Handbook,* edited by Bernard Hoekman, Aaditya Mattoo, and Philip English, 235. Washington, DC: World Bank, 2002.

Moreau, Francoise. "The Cotonu Agreement: Building on the Experience of 30 Years of ACP-EC Partnership." In *Partnership Agreement ACP-EC,* 14. Brussels: European Commission, 2006.

Moss, Joanna, and John Ravenhill. "Trade between the ACP and EEC during Lomé I." In *EEC and the Third World: A Survey, Vol. 3, The Atlantic Rift,* edited by Christopher Stevens, 133–51. London: Hodder and Stoughton, 1983.

Nauman, Eckart. "Rules of Origin under EPAs: Key Issues and New Directions." In *Navigating New Waters: A Reader on ACP-EU Trade Relations, Vol. I,* edited by Sanoussi Bilal and Roman Grynberg, 305–16. London: Commonwealth Secretariat, 2007.

Newfarmer, Richard, William Shaw, and Peter Walkenhorst. "Breaking into New Markets: An Overview." In *Breaking into New Markets,* edited by Richard Newfarmer, William Shaw, and Peter Walkenhorst, 1–35. Washington, DC: World Bank, 2009.

Nurske, Ragnar. "Patterns of Trade and Development." In *Problems of Capital Formation in Underdeveloped Countries and Patterns of Trade and Development.* Oxford: Oxford University Press, 1967.

Ocampo, Jose Antonio. "New Theories of International Trade and Trade Policy in Developing Countries." In *Trade and Growth: New Dilemmas in Trade Policy,* edited by Manuel R. Agosin and Diana Tussie, 121–41. New York: St. Martin's Press, 1993.

Palmer, Ransford. "Export Earnings, Instability, and Economic Growth, 1957 to 1986." In *External Linkages in Small Economies,* edited by David L. Mckee, 31–4. Westport: Praeger, 1994.

Persaud, Avinash D. "International Finance." In *Global Economics in Extraordinary Times. Essays in Honor of John Williamson,* edited by C. Fred Bergsten and C. Randal Henning, 107–22. Washington, DC: Institute for International Economics, 2012.

Pietrobelli, Carlo, and Roberta Rabellotti, eds. *Upgrading to Compete: Global Value Chains, Clusters, and SMEs in Latin America.* Washington, DC: Inter-American Development Bank, 2007.

Randall, Ruby. "Eastern Caribbean Tourism: Recent Developments and Outlook." In *The Caribbean: From Vulnerability to Sustainable Growth,* edited by Ratna Sahay, David O. Robinson, and Paul Cashin, 285–306. Washington, DC: International Monetary Fund, 2006.

Rankin Staples, Brian. "Trade Facilitation: The Improvement of Invisible Infrastructure." In *Development, Trade and the WTO: A Handbook,* edited by Bernard Hoekman, Aaditya Mattoo, and Philip English, 145–6. Washington, DC: World Bank, 2002.

Ravenhill, John. "Asymmetrical Interdependence: Renegotiating the Lomé Convention." In *The Political Economy of EEC Relations with African, Caribbean and Pacific States,* edited by Frank Long, 33–50. Oxford: Pergamon Press, 1980.

———. "Back to the Nest? Europe's Relations with the African, Pacific and Caribbean Group of Countries." In *EU Trade Strategies: Between Regionalism and Globalism,* edited by Vinod K. Aggarwal and Edward A. Fogarty, 118–43. London: Palgrave Macmillan, 2004.

Ricardo, David. "Essay on the Influence of a Low Price of Corn on the Profits of Stock 1815." In *The Works and Correspondence of David Ricardo. Volumes I and IV,* edited by Piero Sraffa. Cambridge: Cambridge University Press, 1951.

Rodrik, Dani. "A Practical Approach to Formulating Growth Strategies." In *The Washington Consensus Reconsidered: Towards A New Global Governance,* edited by Narcis Serra and Joseph E. Stiglitz, 356–66. Oxford: Oxford University Press, 2008.

Rodrik, Dani. "Trade Policy Reform as Institutional Reform." In *Development Trade and the WTO,* edited by Bernard Hoekman, Aaditya Mattoo, and Philip English, 3–10. Washington, DC: World Bank, 2002.

Rodriquez, Francisco, and Dani Rodrik. "Trade Policy and Economic Growth: A Skeptic's Guide to the Cross-National Evidence." In *NBER Economics Annual 2000,* edited by Ben Bernanke and Kenneth S. Rogoff. Cambridge: MIT Press, 2001.

Stiglitz, Joseph E. "Knowledge as a Global Public Goods." In *Global Public Goods: International Cooperation in the 21st Century,* edited by I. Kaul, I. Grunberg, and M. A. Stern, 308–25. New York: Oxford University Press, 1999.

Sutton, Paul. "From Neo-colonialism to Neo-colonialism: Britain and the EEC in the Commonwealth Caribbean." In *Dependency Under Challenge: The Political Economy of the Commonwealth Caribbean,* edited by Anthony Payne and Paul Sutton. Manchester: Manchester University Press, 1984.

Thomas, Clive Y. "Productivity and Competitiveness." In *Barbados: Meeting the Challenges of Competitiveness in the 21st Century,* edited by Lianna Rojas-Suarez and Desmond Thomas, 35. Washington, DC: Inter-American Development Bank, 2006.

Vahl, Remco. "From Cotonou to Bridgetown: The Birth of the Caribbean EPA." In *The CARIFORUM-EU Economic Partnership Agreement: A Practioners' Analysis,* edited by Americo Biviglia Zampetti and Junior Lodge, 1–10. The Netherlands: Kluwer Law International, 2011.

Wolf, Holger. "Volatility: Definitions and Consequences." In *Managing Economic Volatility and Crises: A Practitioner's Guide,* edited by Joshua Aizenman and Brian Pinto, 45–64. Cambridge: Cambridge University Press, 2005.

Zartman, I. William. "Introduction." In *Europe and Africa: The New Phase I,* edited by William Zartman. Boulder: Lynne Rienner Publishers, 1993.

Articles in Journals

Aizenmann, Joshua, and Nancy Marion. "Volatility and Investment: Interpreting Evidence from Developing Countries." *Economica* 66, no. 2 (1999): 157–81.

Andersen, O., and L. S. Kheam. "Resource-based Theory and International Growth Strategies: An Exploratory Study." *International Business Review* 7, no. 2 (1998): 163–84.

Armstrong, H. W., and R. Read. "Trade and Growth in Small States: The Impact of Global Trade Liberalization." *World Economy* 21, no. 4 (June 1998): 563–85.

Arora, Vivek, and Athanasios Vamvakidis. "How Much Do Trading Partners Matter for Economic Growth." *IMF Staff Papers* 52, no. 1 (Apr. 2005): 24–40.

Belassa, Bela. "Economic Development in Small Countries." *Acta Oeconomica* 37, no. 3–4 (1986): 325–40.

Bernal, Richard L. "The Caribbean's Future Is Not What It Was." *Social and Economic Studies* 52, no. 1 (Mar. 2000): 185–217.

———. "The CARICOM Single Market and Economy and External Trade Negotiations." *Caribbean Journal of International Relations* 1, no. 1 (Apr. 2005): 33–48.

———. "CARIFORUM-EU Economic Partnership Agreement Negotiations: Why and How." *Journal of Eastern Caribbean Studies* 33, no. 2 (June 2008): 1–23.

———. "The Compatibility of Caribbean Membership in Lomé, NAFTA and GATT." *Social and Economic Studies* 43, no. 2 (June 1994): 139–47.

———. "The Globalization of Health-care: Opportunities for the Caribbean." *CEPAL Review* no. 92 (Aug. 2007): 83–100.

———"Foreign Investment and Development in Jamaica." *Inter-American Economic Affairs* 38, no. 2 (Autumn 1984): 3–21.

Billmeier, Andreas, and Tommaso Nannicini. "Trade Openness and Growth: Pursuing Empirical Glasnost." *IMF Staff Papers* 56, no. 3 (Mar. 2009): 447–75.

Bollard, Albert, David McKenzie, Melanie Morten, and Hillel Rapoport. "Remittances and the Brain Drain Revisited: The Microdata Show that More Educated Migrants Remit More." *The World Bank Economic Review* 25, no. 1 (2011): 132–56.

Brewster, Havelock R. "The CARICOM Single Market and Economy: Is It Realistic Without Commitment to Political Unity?" *Journal of Eastern Caribbean Studies* 28, no. 3 (Sept. 2003): 4.

).Briguglio, Lino. "Small Island Developing States and Their Economic Vulnerabilities." *World Development* 23, no. 9 (1995): 1615–32.

Brown, Deryck R. "Institutional Development in Small States: Evidence From the Commonwealth Caribbean." *Halduskultuur-Administrative Culture* 11, no. 1 (2010): 44–65.

Brown, William. "Restructuring North-South Relations: ACP-EU Development Cooperation in a Liberal International Order." *Review of African Political Economy* 27, no. 85 (Sept. 2000): 367–83.

Burnside, Craig, and David Dollar. "Aid, Policies and Growth." *American Economic Review* 90, no. 4 (Dec. 1997): 847–68.

Byron, Jessica. "Singing from the Same Hymn Sheet: Caribbean Diplomacy and the Cotonou Agreement." *Revista Europea de Estudios Latinoamericos y del Caribe* 79 (Oct. 2005): 3–24.

Cairncross, A. K. "International Trade and Economic Development," *Kyklos* 13, no. 4 (1960): 545–58.

Cairncross, Alex K."International Trade and Economic Development." *Economica* 28, no. 3 (Aug. 1961): 235–51.

Chandler, Alfred D. Jr. "The Enduring Logic of Industrial Success." *Harvard Business Review* 71, no. 2 (Mar.–Apr. 1990): 130–40.

Chang, Roberto, Linda Kaltani, and Norman V. Loayza. "Openness Can Be Good for Growth: The Role of Policy Complementarities." *Journal of Development Economics* 90, no. 1 (Sept. 2009): 33–49.

Chenery, Hollis, and Alan Stout. "Foreign Assistance and Economic Development." *American Economic Review* 56, no. 3 (Sept. 1966): 679–728.

Clayton, Anthony. "Developing a Biodiversity Cluster in Jamaica: A Step Towards Building a Skills-based Economy." *Social and Economic Studies* 50, no. 2 (June 2001): 1–38.

Clegg, Peter. "Banana Splits and Policy Challenges: The ACP Caribbean and the Fragmentation of Interest Coalitions." *Revista Europea de Estudios Latinoamericanos y del Caribe* 79 (Oct. 2005): 27–45.

Curran, Louise, Lars Nilsson, and Douglas Brew. "The Economic Partnership Agreements: Rationale, Misperceptions and Non-trade Aspects." *Development Policy Review* 26, no. 5 (Sept. 2008): 529–53.

Dicaprio, Alisa, and Kevin P. Kallagher. "The Shrinking Development Space: How Big is the Bite?" *Journal of World Investment and Trade* 7, no. 5 (2006): 781–803.

Dollar, David. "Outward Oriented Development Economies Really Do Grow More Rapidly: Evidence from 95 LDCs, 1976–1985." *Economic and Cultural Change* 40, no. 3 (Apr. 1992): 523–44.

Drucker, Peter F. "Beyond the Information Revolution." *The Atlantic Monthly* (Oct. 1999).

Easterly, William. "Can Aid Buy Growth." *Journal of Economic Perspectives* 17 (2003): 23–48.

Easterly, William, and Aart Kraay. "Small States, Small Problems? Income, Growth and Volatility in Small States." *World Development* 28, no. 11 (2000): 2013–27.

Edwards, Sabastian. "Openness, Productivity and Growth: What Do We Really Know." *Economic Journal* 108 (1998): 383–98.

Ferhani, Hervé, Mark Stone, Anna Nordstrom, and Seiichi Shimizu, "Developing Essential Financial Markets in Smaller Economies: Stylized Facts and Policy," *IMF Occaisional Paper No. 265*. Washington, DC: International Monetary Fund, 2009.

Frankel, Jacob A., and D. Romer. "Does Trade Cause Growth." *American Economic Review* 83, no. 3 (1999): 379–99.

Freidman, Milton. "Foreign Aid: Means and Objectives." *Yale Review* 47 (Summer 1958): 500–16.

Ghosh, Atish R., and Jonathan D. Ostry. "Export Instability and the External Balance in Developing Countries." *IMF Staff Papers* 41, no. 2 (1994): 214–35.

Girvan, Norman. "Implications of the EPA for the CSME." *Social and Economic Studies* 58, no. 2 (June 2009): 91–127.

———. "Reflections on the CSME." *Trinidad and Tobago Review* 26, no. 4 (Apr. 5, 2004): 16–9.

———. "Whither CSME." *Journal of Caribbean International Relations* 1 (Apr. 2005): 13–32.

Harrison, A., and G. Hanson. "Who Gains from Trade Reform? Some Remaining Puzzles." *Journal of Development Economics* 59 (1999): 125–54.

Headey, D.D. "Geopolitics and the Effectiveness of Aid on Economic Growth: 1970–2001." *Journal of International Development* 20, no. 2: 161–80.

Helleiner, Gerald K. "Why Small Countries Worry: Neglected Issues in Current Analyses of the Benefits and Costs of Small Countries of Integrating with Large Ones." *World Economy* 19, no. 6 (Nov. 1996): 759–63.

Henry, Peter Blair, and Conrad Miller. "Institutions Versus Policies: A Tale of Two Islands." *American Economic Review* 99, no. 2 (May 2009): 261–7.

Keesing, Donald B. "Population and Industrial Development: Some Evidence from Trade Patterns." *American Economic Review* 58, no. 3 (1968): 448–55.

Kose, M. Ayhan, and Eswar S. Prasad. "Thinking Big." *Finance and Development* 39, no. 4 (Dec. 2002).

Krueger, A.O. "The Political Economy of the Rent-seeking Society." *American Economic Review* 64, no. 2 (June 1974): 291–303.

Krugman, Paul. "Competitiveness—A Dangerous Obsession." *Foreign Affairs* 73, no. 2 (Mar.—Apr. 1994): 44.

———. "The Myth of the Asia Miracle." *Foreign Affairs* 73, no. 6 (1994): 62–78.

Lewis, W. Arthur. "Economic Development with Unlimited Supplies of Labour." *Manchester School of Economics and Social Studies* 24, no. 2 (May 1954): 139–91.

Looney, Robert E. "Economic Characteristics Associated with Size: Development Problems Confronting Smaller Third World States." *Singapore Economic Review* 37, no. 2 (Oct. 1992): 1–19.

———. "Profiles of Small Lesser Developed Economies." *Canadian Journal of Development Studies* 10, no. 1 (1989): 21–37.

Love, James. "Commodity Concentration and Export Earnings Instability: A Shift from Cross-section to Time Series Analysis." *Journal of Development Economics* 24, no. 2 (1986): 239–48.

Lutz, Matthias. "The Effects of Volatility in the Terms of Trade on Output Growth." *World Development* 22, no. 12 (1994): 1959–75.

Maskus, Keith E. "The Role of Intellectual Property Rights in Encouraging Foreign Direct Investment and Technology Transfer." *Duke Journal of Comparative and International Law* 9, no. 1 (1998): 109–61.

Mayers, John. "Golding Slams Critics—Says They Suffer from Mendicancy." *Daily Gleaner* Feb. 1, 2008.

Miller, John W. "EU, Central America Reach Trade Agreement." *Wall Street Journal* May 18, 2010.

Milner, Chris, and T. Westaway. "Country Size and the Medium-term Growth Process: Some Cross-Country Evidence." *World Development* 21, no. 2 (1993): 203–11.

Mosley, Paul, John Hudson, and Sara Horrell. "Aid, the Public Sector and the Market in Less Developed Countries. A Return to the Scene." *Journal of International Development* 4, no. 2 (1992): 139–50.

Nicholson, Lawrence. "Jamaican Family-owned Businesses: Homogenous or Non-homogenous." *Social and Economic Studies* 59, no. 3 (Sept. 2010): 7–30.

Page, Sheila, and A. Hewitt, "The New European Trade Preferences: Does 'Everything But Arms' EBA Help the Poor." *Development Policy Review* 20, no. 1 (2002): 91–102.

Panagariya, Arvind. "EU Preferential Trade Arrangements and Developing Countries." *World Economy* 25, no. 10 (2002): 1415–32.

Parente, Stephen L., and Edward C. Prescott. "Barriers to Technology Adoption and Development." *Journal of Political Economy* 102, no. 2 (1994): 298–321.

Prebish, Raul. "Commercial Policy in the Underdeveloped Countries." *American Economic Review* 49, no. 2 (May 1959): 251–73.

Primo Braga, Carlos. "Intellectual Property Rights and the GATT: A View from the South." *Vanderbilt Journal of Transnational Law* 22, no. 2 (1989): 265–84.

Raddatz, Claudio E. "Are External Shocks Responsible for the Instability of Output in Low-income Countries?" *Journal of Development Economics* 84, no. 1 (Sept. 2007): 155–87.

Ramey, Garey, and Valery A. Ramey. "Cross-country Evidence on the Link between Volatility and Growth." *American Economic Review* 86, no. 5 (1995): 1138–51.

Read, Robert "The Implications of Increasing Globalization and Regionalism for the Economic Growth of Small Island States." *World Development* 32, no. 2 (2004): 365–78.

Rodrik, Dani. "Why Do More Open Economies Have Bigger Governments?" *Journal of Political Economy* 106, no. 5 (1998): 997–1032.

Samuelson, Paul A. "The Gains from International Trade." *Canadian Journal of Economics and Political Science* 5, no. 2 (May 1939): 195–205.

Scellato, Giuseppe. "Patents, Firm Size and Financial Constraints: An Empirical Analysis for a Panel of Italian Manufacturing Firms." *Cambridge Journal of Economics* 31, no. 1 (Jan. 2007): 55–76.

Singer, H. W. "The Distribution of Gains Between Investing and Borrowing Countries." *American Economic Review* 40, no. 2 (May 1950):473–85.

Srinivasan, T. N. "The Costs and Benefits of Being a Small, Remote, Island, Landlocked, or Ministate Economy." *World Bank Research Observer* 1, no. 2 (1986): 205–18.

Stone, Mark, and Seiichi Shimizu, "Small Steps." *Finance and Development* 46, no. 1 (Mar. 2009): 50–1.

Sunkel, Osvaldo. "The Centre-periphery Model." *Social and Economic Studies* 22, no. 1(Mar. 1973): 132–76.

Tidiane Dieye, Cheikh, and Victoria Hanson. "MFN provisions in EPAs: A Threat to South-South Trade?" *Trade Negotiations Insights* 7, no. 2 (Mar. 2008): 1–3.

Torres, Rebecca, and Janet Henshall Momsen. "Challenges and Potential for Linking Tourism and Agriculture to Achieve Pro-poor Tourism Objectives." *Progress in Development Studies* 4, no. 4 (Oct. 2004): 294–318.

Welsh, Barbara. "Banana Dependency: Albatross or Lifeline for the Windwards." *Social and Economic Studies* 43, no. 1 (Mar. 1994): 123–49.

Other

*A Time to Choose: Caribbean Development in the 21st Century.*Washington, DC: World Bank, Apr. 2005.

Alexandraki, Katerina, and Hans Peter Lankes. *The Impact of Preference Erosion on Middle- income Developing Countries.* IMF Working Paper WP/04/169. Washington, DC: International Monetary Fund, Sept. 2004.

Arthur, Owen. "Implementation of the CARICOM Single Market and Economy, and its Implications for US-CARICOM Economic Relations." Address to the Special Symposium by the American Business and Consulting Group, Brooklyn, NY, Apr. 2, 2004, 2–3.

——— "Making the Most of the EPA." Presentation at the Private Sector Organization of Jamaica Chairman's Club Forum, Kingston, Jamaica, Feb. 3, 2009.

Asia and Pacific Small States: Raising Potential Growth and Enhancing Resilience to Shocks. Washington, DC: International Monetary Fund, Feb. 20, 2013.

Azim Sadikov. *External Tariff Liberalization in CARICOM: A Commodity-level Analysis.* IMF Working Paper WP/08/33. Washington, DC: International Monetary Fund, Feb. 2008.

Bassilekin, Achille. *Possibility of Obtaining a New ACP-EC Waiver at the WTO.* European Centre for Development Policy Management Discussion Paper 71. Maastricht: European Centre for Development, Mar. 2007, 7.

Becker, Chris. *Small Island Sates in the Pacific: The Tyranny of Distance.* IMF Working Paper WP/12/223. Washington, DC: International Monetary Fund, Sept. 2012.

Benson, Charlotte, and Edward Clay with Franklyn V. Michael, and Alistair W. Robertson. *Dominica: Natural Disasters and Economic Development in a Small Island State.* Disaster Risk Management Working Paper Series 2. Washington, DC: World Bank, Oct. 2001.

Bernal, Richard L. *Participation of Small Developing Countries in the Governance of the Multilateral Trading System.* Centre for International Governance Innovation Working Paper 44. Waterloo: Centre for International Governance Innovation, Dec. 2009.

———. *Strategic Global Repositioning and the Future Economic Development of Jamaica. North South Agenda Paper 18.* Miami: North South Center, University of Miami, May 1996.

———. *The Integration of Small Economies in the Free Trade Area of the Americas.* CSIS, Policy Paper on the Americas, IX. Washington, DC: Center for Strategic and International Studies, Febr. 2, 1998.

———. *Trade Blocks: A Regionally Specific Phenomenon, or Global Trend?* Walter Sterling Surrey Memorial Series. Washington, DC: National Planning Association, Sept. 1997.

Borenzstein, E., J. W. Lee, and J. De Gregorio. *How Does Foreign Investment Affect Growth?* NBER Working Paper No. 5057. Washington, DC: National Bureau of Economic Research, 1995.

Bowman, Chakriya. "The Pacific Island Nations: Towards Shared Representation." Case study 33 in *Managing the Challenges of WTO Participation: 45 Case Studies,* edited by Peter Gallagher, Patrick Low, and Andres Stoler. Cambridge: Cambridge University Press, 2006.

World Trade Organization. *Brazil's Declaration to the General Council of the WTO.* Geneva: WTO, Feb. 5, 2008.

Brenton, Paul. "Rules of Origin in Free Trade Agreements." *Trade Note.* Washington, DC: World Bank, May 29, 2003.

Brewster, Havelock R. "A Declaratory Amendment to the EPA Paves the Way for Guyana to Sign." http://www.normangirvan.info/a-declaratory-amendment-to-the-epa-paves-the-way-for-guyana-to-sign-havelock-brewster. Accessed Feb. 2013.

———. *View from the Rear View Mirror.* Address to the Graduating Class, University of the West Indies, Mona, Nov. 11, 2008.

Brewster, Havelock, Luis Abugattas, Tom Dolan, Taimoon Stewart, and Noel Watson. *CARICOM Single Market and Economy: Assessment of the Region's Support Needs.* Report prepared for the CARICOM Secretariat, Georgetown, June 2003.

Brewster, Havelock, Norman Girvan, and Vaughn Lewis. *Problem Areas in the EPA and the case for Content Review.* Submitted for the consideration of the Reflections Group on EPA Negotiations, [Unpublished] Kingston, Jamaica, February 28–29, 2008.

Briguglio, Lino, Bishnodat Persaud, and Richard Stern. *Toward an Outward-oriented Development Strategy for Small States: Issues, Opportunities, and Resilience Building.* Washijngton, DC: World Bank, Aug. 2006.

Burnside, Craig, and David Dollar. *Aid, Policies and Growth.* Policy Research Working Paper 1777. Washington, DC: World Bank, June 1997.

Accelerating Trade and Integration. Policy Options for Sustained Growth, Job Creation, and Poverty Reduction. Washington, DC: Poverty Reduction and Economic Management Sector Unit, World Bank and Organization of American States, 2009.

Caribbean Trade & Investment Report. Corporate Integration & Cross-Border Development 2005. Georgetown: Caribbean Community Secretariat, 2006.

CARICOM. Our Caribbean Community: An Introduction. Kingston: Ian Randle Publishers, 2005.

CARICOM Report 2. Washington, DC: Inter-American Development Bank, Aug. 2005.

CARICOM, Caribbean Trade and Investment Report 2005. Georgetown: Caribbean Community Secretariat, 2006.

"CARIFORUM Calls on EU to Honour the Cotonou agreement and Economic Partnership Agreements." http://www.caricom.org/jsp/pressreleases/pres215_10.jsp. Retrieved May 18, 2010.

"CARIFORUM Decides to Sign EPA". http://www.caricom.org/jsp/pressreleases/pres283_08.jsp. Accessed Sept. 11, 2008.

Carnegie Endowment for International Peace. *Reflections on Regionalism. Report of the Study Group on International Trade.* Washington, DC: Carnegie Endowment for International Peace, 1997.

CARIFORUM-EC Economic Partnership Agreement. 2008.

Cavallo, Eduardo A. Output Volatility and Openness to Trade: A Reassessment. *Research Department Working Paper Series 604.* Washington, DC: Inter-American Development Bank, 2007.

Calderon, CesarNorman Loayza, and Luis Serven. Greenfield Foreign Direct Investment and Mergers and Acquisitions: Feedback and Macroeconomic Effects. *World Bank Policy Research Working Paper No. 3192.* Washington, DC: World Bank, Jan. 2004.

Commonwealth Secretariat. *A Future for Small States: Overcoming Vulnerability. Report by a Commonwealth Advisory Group.* London: Commonwealth Secretariat, 1997.

Clements, Michael, Steven Radelet, and Rikhil Bhavnani. Counting Chickens When They Hatch: The Short term Effect of Aid on Growth. *Working Paper 44.* Washington, DC: Center for Global Development, 2004.

Collier, Paul, and David Dollar. *Aid, Risk and the Special Concerns of Small States.* Washington, DC: Development Research Group, World Bank, Feb. 1999.

Cotonou Agreement.

Cumberbatch, Lingston. "Can Cotonou Stand the Test of Time?" In *The Cotonu Partnership Agreement: What Role in a Changing World,* edited by Geert Laporte. *ECDPM Policy Management Report 13.* Brussels: European Centre for Development Policy Management, Nov. 2007.

Dawar, Kamala, and Simon J. Evenett. The CARIFORUM-EC EPA: An Analysis of Its Government Procurement and Competition Law-related Provisions. *Working Paper 18.*

Commissioned by Deutsche Gesellschaft fur Technische Zusammenarbeit GTZ for the Federal Ministry for Economic Cooperation and Development, Bonn, June 2008.

Development Assistance and Economic Development in the Caribbean Region: Is There a Correlation. *World Bank Report 24164-LAC.* Washington, DC: World Bank, June 2002.

Doing Business in Small Island Developing States 2009. Washington, DC: World Bank, 2008.

Draft Report on Jamaican Perceptions of Regional Integration, May/June, 2003. Survey. Mona, Jamaica: Sir Arthur Lewis Institute of Social and Economic Research, University of the West Indies, 2003.

Easterly, William R., R. Islam, and Joseph Stiglitz. "Shaken and Stirred: Explaining Growth Volatility." In *Annual World Bank Conference on Development,* edited by B. Plesokovic and Nicholas Stern. Washington, DC: World Bank, 2001, 191–211.

Economic Overview of Caribbean Economies 2002–2003. United Nations Economic Commission for Latin America and the Caribbean, LC/CAR./G.766, Santiago, Dec. 12, 2003.

Electronic Commerce and the Role of the WTO. Geneva: World Trade Organization, 1998.

Engman, Michael. "The Economic Impact of Trade Facilitation." *OECD Trade Policy Papers 21.* Paris: Organization for Economic Cooperation and Development, 2005.

"EPA: the Opposition's view point." *Jamaica Gleaner,* Mar. 30, 2008.

Estevadeordal, Antoni. *Rules of Origin in FTAs: A World Map.* Washington, DC: Pacific Economic Cooperation Council, Apr. 22–23, 2003.

Estevadeordal, Antoni, and Kai Suominen. Rules of Origin in FTAs in Europe and in the Americas: Issues and Implications for the Inter-regional Association Agreement. *INTAL-ITD Working Paper 15,* Washington, DC, Jan. 2004.

"EU Resumes Trade Talks with Mercosur, Concludes Talks with Central America." *Bridges Weekly Trade News Digest,* 14.18, May 19, 2010.

http://ictsd.org/i/news/bridgesweekly/76282/. Retrieved May 19, 2010.

Fajnzylber, Pablo, and Humbert J. Lopez, eds. *Remittances and Development: Lessons from Latin America.* Washington, DC: World Bank, 2008.

Fiscal Trends and Policy Issues and Implications for the Caribbean. *Report No. LC/CAR/G.771.* Economic Commission for Latin America and the Caribbean, Port of Spain, 2003.

Food Safety and Agricultural Health Standards: Challenges and Opportunities for Developing Country Exports. *World Bank Report 31207.* Washington, DC: World Bank, Jan. 10, 2005.

"Get EPA Implementation Going." *Barbados Advocate* Apr. 26, 2010, 5.

Girvan, Norman. *The CARIFORUM-EC EPA. A Critical Evaluation.* Mar. 23, 2008. http://www.normangirvan.info/category/epa-text-and-commentaries/page/5/.

———. "Towards a Single Development Vision and the Role of the Single Economy." *Report Approved by the 28th Conference of CARICOM Heads of Government.* Georgetown: CARICOM Secretariat, July 2007.

Global Economic Prospects and the Developing Countries, 1995. Washington, DC: World Bank, 1995.

Golding, Bruce. *Statement at the CARICOM Heads of Government 19th Intersessional.* Georgetown: CARICOM Secretariat, Mar. 2008.

Gonzales, Anabel. "The Experience of Costa Rica in Implementing CAFTA-DR." Paper presented at the conference on Implementing Free Trade Agreements in Latin America at the Inter-American Development Bank, Washington, DC, Apr. 7, 2010.

Gonzales, Anthony P. "Policy Implications of Smallness as a Factor in the Lomé, FTAA and WTO Negotiations." Caribbean RNM/IDB Regional Technical Cooperation Project, Bridgetown, Sept. 2000.

Global Europe. *Competing in the World: A Contribution to the EU's Growth and Jobs Strategy.* Brussels: European Commission, 2005.

Grynberg, Roman, and Sacha Silva, *Preference-dependent Economies and Multilateral Liberalization: Impacts and Options.* London: Commonwealth Secretariat, Oct. 2004.

Green Paper on the Relationship between the European Union and the ACP Countries on the Eve of the 21st Century. Brussels: European Commission, 1996.

GTZ. *EPA Implementation Stakeholders Analysis: The CARIFORUM Context German Technical Cooperation.* Bonn: GTZ, Mar. 2009.

Haddad, Mona E., Jamus Jerome Lim, and Christian Saborowski. Trade Openness Reduces Growth Volatility When Countries Are Well Diversified. World Bank Policy Research Working Paper 5222. Washington, DC: World Bank, Feb. 2010.

Hamilton, Pamela Coke, Yvonne Tsikata, and Emmanuel Pinto Moreira. "Accelerating Trade and Integration in the Caribbean. Policy options for Sustained Growth, Job Creation and Poverty Reduction." *Study.* Washington, DC: World Bank, 2009.

Heger, Martin, Alex Julca, and Oliver Paddison. Analysing the Impact of Natural Hazards in Small Economies. The Caribbean Case. UNU-WIDER Research Paper 2008/25. Helsinki: United Nations University/ World Institute Development Economics Research, Mar. 2008.

Human Development Report 2003. New York: United Nations Development Programme, 2003.

Human Development Report 2005. New York: United Nations Development Programme, 2006.

Humphrey, Errol. "Implementation of the EPA in the CARIFORUM Countries—Lessons Learned One Year On: The Barbados experience." Paper presented at the Conference on the CARIFORUM-EC Economic Partnership Agreement One Year On: Regional Integration and Sustainable Development, University of West Indies, Barbados, Apr. 22–23, 2010.

IMF World Economic Outlook, April 2010. Washington, DC: International Monetary Fund, Apr. 2010.

"Implementing Cultural Provisions of CARIFORUM-EU EPA: How Do They Benefit the Caribbean Cultural Sector?" ECDPM, Discussion Paper 118. Brussels: European Centre for Development Policy Management, June 2011.

"Improving Competitiveness for Caribbean Development." Report of the Caribbean Trade and Adjustment prepared for the Caribbean Regional Negotiating Machinery, Kingston: Ian Randle Publishers, 2003.

International Trade Statistics 2001. Geneva: World Trade Organization, 2001.

"It's not too late for region to pull out of EPA, says Ramphal." *Jamaica Observer* July 25, 2008.

Jagdeo, Bharrat. "The Caribbean Lost in the Negotiations with Europe." *South Bulletin* Feb. 8, 2008, 6. http://www.southcentre.org/south-bulletin-reflections-and-foresights-issue-8–01-february-2008.

Jansen, Marion. "Income Volatility in Small Developing Economies: Export Concentration Matters." WTO Discussion Paper. Geneva: World Trade Organization, Dec. 2004.

Jessop, David. "That EU Cariforum Economic Partnership Agreement." *CaribWorld News* Aug. 10, 2010.

Knack, Stephen. "Aid, Dependence and the Quality of Governance: A Cross-Country Empirical Analysis." World Bank Policy Research Paper No. 2396. Washington, DC: World Bank, 2000.

Krueger, Anne O. "Free Trade Agreements as Protectionist Devices: Rules of Origin." NBER Working Paper 4352. Cambridge: National Bureau of Economic Research, 1993.

Kumar, Nagesh, and Kevin P. Gallagher. "Relevance of 'Policy Space' for Development: Implications for Multilateral Trade Negotiations." RIS-DP 120. New Delhi: Research and Information System for Developing Countries, Mar. 2007.

Larson, D., and B. Borrell. "Sugar Policy and Reform." World Bank Policy Research Paper 2602. Washington, DC: World Bank, 2002.

Lazaro, Dorothea C., and Erlinda M. Medalla. "Rules of Origin: Evolving Best Practices for RTAs/FTAs." Discussion Paper Series 2006–01. Manila: Philippine Institute for Development Studies, Jan. 2006.

"Letter from Prime Minister P.J. Patterson of Jamaica to the President of the European Commission." Apr. 6, 1998.

Liberalizing International Transactions in Services. A Handbook. New York and Geneva: United Nations, 1994.

Lim, Ewe-Ghee. "Determinants of, and the Relation between Direct Investment and Growth: A Summary of the Recent Literature." IMF Working Paper WP/01/175. Washington, DC: International Monetary Fund, Nov. 2001.

Matthews, Alan. *"Economic Partnership Agreements and Food Security."* IIIS Discussion Paper 319. Dublin: Institute for International Integration Studies, Trinity College, Mar. 2010.

Mayer, Jorg. "Policy Space: What, For What, and Where?" UNCTAD Discussion Paper 191, Geneva: UNCTAD, Oct. 2008, 4.

Medina Cas, Stephanie, and Rui Ota. "Big Government, High Debt, and Fiscal Adjustment in Small States." IMF Working Paper WP/08/39. Washington, DC: International Monetary Fund, Feb. 2008.

Mejido, Costoya, Manuel, Peter Utting, and Gloria Carrión. *The Changing Coordinates of Trade and Power in Latin America. Implications for Policy Space and Policy Coherence Markets.* Business and Regulation Programme Paper 7. United Nations Research Institute for Social Development, May 2010.

Minoiu, Camelia, and Sanjay G. Reddy. *Development Aid and Economic Growth: A Positive Long-Relation.* IMF Working Paper WP/09/118. Washington, DC: International Monetary Fund, May 2009.

Michalopoulos, Constantine. *Developing Countries' Participation in the World Trade Organization.* Policy Research Working Paper No. 1906. Washington, DC: World Bank, Mar. 1998.

Mitchell, Donald. *Sugar in the Caribbean. Adjusting to Eroding Preferences.* World Bank Working Paper 3802. Washington, DC: World Bank, Dec. 2005.

Moise, Evdokia, and Silvia Sorescu, *Trade Facilitation Indicators. The Potential Impact of Trade Facilitation on Developing Countries.* OECD Trade Policy Paper No. 144. Paris: Organization for Economic Cooperation and Development, 2013.

Nelson, J., and D. Taglioni. *Services Trade Liberalization: Identifying Opportunities and Gains.* OECD Trade Policy Paper No. 1. Paris: Organization for Economic Cooperation and Development, 2004.

Corporate Tax Incentives for Foreign Direct Investment. OECD Tax Policy Study 4. Paris: Organization for Economic Cooperation and Development, 2001.

Open Markets Matter: The Benefits of Trade and Investment Liberalization. Paris: Organization for Economic Cooperation and Development, 1998.

Overcoming Volatility: Economic and Social Progress in Latin America, 1995. Report. Washington, DC: Inter-American Development Bank, 1995.

Overview of Developments in the International Trading Environment. Geneva: World Trade Organization, 2001.

Ozden, Caglar, and Eric Reinhardt. *The Perversity of Preferences: Generalized System of Preferences and Developing Country Policies, 1976–2000.* World Bank Policy Research Working Paper No. 2955. Washington, DC: World Bank, Jan. 2003.

Pascal, Phil. "A Critical Reflection on Management of CARICOM." *Jamaica Observer* Feb. 21, 2010. http://www.jamaicaobserver.com/columns/Agenda-column-Feb-21,2010.

Payne, Anthony, and Paul Sutton. *Repositioning the Caribbean within Globalisation.* Caribbean Paper No. 1. Waterloo, Canada: Centre for International Governance Innovation, 2007.

Peters, Amos. *The Fiscal Effects of Tariff Reduction in the Caribbean Community.* CARICOM Secretariat, 2002.

Qureshi, Mahvash, and Dirk Willem te Velde. *Working Smart and Small. The Role of Knowledge-based and Service Industries in Growth Strategies for Small States.* London: Commonwealth Secretariat, 2008.

Policy Space for the Development of the South. TR.A.D.E. Policy Brief, No. 1/2005. Nov. 2005.

Rajan, Raghuram, and Arvind Subramanian. *Aid and Growth: What Does the Cross-country Evidence Really Show.* IMF Working Paper 05/127. Washington, DC: International Monetary Fund, 2005.

Rasmussen, Tobias N. *Macroeconomic Implications of Natural Disasters in the Caribbean.* IMF Working Paper WP/04/224. Washington, DC: International Monetary Fund, Dec. 2004.

Ratna, Sahay. *Stabilization, Debt and Fiscal Policy in the Caribbean.* IMF Working Paper WP/05/26. Washington, DC: International Monetary Fund, 2005.

Revised Treaty of Chaguaramas Establishing the Caribbean Community including the CARICOM Single Market and Economy. Georgetown: CARICOM, 2001.

Riddle, Dorothy. "Issues Regarding Small Services Suppliers in the Context of the FTAA." Prepared for the Caribbean Regional Negotiating Machinery, 2002.

Saggi, Kamal. "International Technology Transfers to Developing Countries." *Economic Paper 64.* London: Commonwealth Secretariat, 2004.

Sahay, Ratna. *Stabilization, Debt and Fiscal Policy in the Caribbean.* IMF Working Paper WP/05/26. Washington, DC: International Monetary Fund, 2005.

Sachs, Jeffrey, and A. Warner. "Economic Reform and the Process of Global Integration." *Brookings Papers on Economic Activity 1.*1995.

Sanders, Roland. "Last Chance for a Better Agreement between Europe and the Caribbean." Nov. 1, 2007.

"Sir Shridath praises President over EPA Stance." *Stabroek News* Oct. 18, 2008. http://www.stabroeknews.com/2008/stories/10/19/sir-shridath-praises-president-over-epa-stance.

Small and Relatively Less Developed Economies and Western Hemisphere Integration. OAS/Ser. W/XIII.7. Washington, DC: Organization of American States, Sept. 1996.

Small States: Meeting Challenges in the Global Economy. *Interim Report of the Commonwealth Secretariat/World Bank Joint Taskforce on Small States.* Oct. 1999, 13.

Sosa, Sebastian, and Paul Cashin. *Macroeconomic Fluctuations in the Caribbean: The Role of Climatic and External Shocks.* IMF Working Paper WP/09/159. Washington, DC: International Monetary Fund, July 2009.

Sosa, Sebastian R. *Tax Incentives and Investment in the Eastern Caribbean.* IMF Working Paper No. 06/23. Washington, DC: International Monetary Fund, Jan. 2006.

Stevens, Christopher, Matthew McQueen, and Jane Kennan. *After Lome IV. A Strategy for ACP- EU Relations in 21st Century.* London: Commonwealth Secretariat, 1999.

"Study to Support CARIFORUM in the Implementation of Commitments Undertaken Under the Customs and Trade Facilitation Chapter of the CARIFORUM-EC Economic Partnership Agreement." Prepared by I2K Inc., Nov. 2008.

The Caribbean Single Market Economy CSME: A Strategy for Globalisation, A Forum for CEOs and Trade Ministers of CARICOM. Jamaica: Montego Bay, Apr. 19–20, 2002.

Thacker, Nita Sebastian Acevedo, and Roberto Perrelli. *Caribbean Growth in an International Perspective: The Role of Tourism and Size.* IMF Working Paper WP/12/235. Washington, DC: International Monetary Fund, Sept. 2012.

Thomas, Clive. "EPA, Sign or Else: Exploding the Myth of a Partnership of Equals." *Stabroek News* Oct. 26, 2008. http://www.stabroeknews.com/2008/features/10/26/guyana-and-the-wider-world.

Tsikata, Tsidi M. *Aid Effectiveness: A Survey of the Recent Empirical Literature.* IMF Paper on Policy Analysis and Assessment, PPAA/98/1. Washington, DC: International Monetary Fund, Mar. 1998.

UNCTAD. *Review of Maritime Transport, 1997.* Geneva: UNCTAD, 1997.

UNCTAD. *Notes on the Concept of Economic Policy Space.* UNCTAD, Mar. 4, 2004, cited in "Policy Space for the Development of the South." TR.A.D.E. Policy Brief, No. 1/2005. Nov. 2005.

United Nations, *World Investment Report, 1998: Trends and Determinants* Geneva: United Nations, 1998.

United Nations, *World Investment Report 2012.* Geneva: UNCTAD, 2012.

Van Parys, Stefan, and Sebastian James. *The Effectiveness of Tax Incentives in Attracting FDI: Evidence from the Tourism Sector in the Caribbean.* Universiteit Gent Working Paper 675. Sept. 2010.

Winters, L. Alan, and Pedro M. G. Martins. "Beautiful but Costly: Business Costs in Small Economies." Study prepared for the Commonwealth Secretariat and the United Nations Conference on Trade and Development, 2004.

World Development Indicators 2000. Washington, DC: World Bank, 2000.

World Bank. *Towards a New Agenda for Growth: Organization of Eastern Caribbean States.* Washington, DC: World Bank, Apr. 2005.

World Trade Organization. *Regionalism and the World Trading System.* Geneva: World Trade Organization, 1995.

———. *International Trade Statistics 2012.* Geneva: World Trade Organization, 2013.

———. *World Economic Output.* Washington, DC: International Monetary Fund, Oct. 2007.

———. *World Investment Report 2001: Promoting Linkages.* New York and Geneva: United Nations, 2001.

———. *The Results of the Uruguay Round of Multilateral Trade Negotiation: The Legal Texts.* Geneva: WTO, 1995.

World Trade Report 2003. Geneva: World Trade Organization, 2003.

World Trade Report 2007. Geneva: World Trade Organization, 2007.

World Trade Report 2010. Geneva: World Trade Organization, 2011.

Index

[Page numbers in *italic* refer to tables or figures.]

www.ingramcontent.com/pod-product-compliance
Lightning Source LLC
Chambersburg PA
CBHW021810270326
41932CB00007B/132

9789766408633